ROUTLEDGE LIBRARY EDITIONS:
IRAN

# THE NASIREAN ETHICS

# THE NASIREAN ETHICS

NAṢĪR AD-DĪN ṬŪSĪ

Translated from the Persian by
G. M. WICKENS

Volume 23

Routledge
Taylor & Francis Group
LONDON AND NEW YORK

First published in 1964

This edition first published in 2011
by Routledge
2 Park Square, Milton Park, Abingdon, Oxon, OX14 4RN

Simultaneously published in the USA and Canada
by Routledge
711 Third Avenue, New York, NY 10017

*Routledge is an imprint of the Taylor & Francis Group, an informa business*



*British Library Cataloguing in Publication Data*
A catalogue record for this book is available from the British Library

ISBN 13: 978-0-415-57033-6 (Set)
eISBN 13: 978-0-203-83010-9 (Set)
ISBN 13: 978-0-415-61047-6 (Volume 23)
eISBN 13: 978-0-203-83221-9 (Volume 23)

# The Nasirean Ethics

*by*

*Naṣīr ad-Dīn Ṭūsī*

TRANSLATED FROM THE PERSIAN

BY

G. M. WICKENS

*Chairman of the Department of Islamic Studies*
*University of Toronto*

*London*

GEORGE ALLEN & UNWIN LTD

RUSKIN HOUSE MUSEUM STREET

FIRST PUBLISHED IN 1964



PRINTED IN GREAT BRITAIN
*in* 10 *point Old Style type*
BY C. TINLING AND CO. LTD
LIVERPOOL, LONDON AND PRESCOT

## CONTENTS

TRANSLATOR'S INTRODUCTION 9–22
A. Work's Significance and Special Quality 9
B. Ṭūsī's Life and Writings 12
C. The Present Rendering 13
D. The Work's Style 15
E. Purpose of Present Version 17
F. Acknowledgements 19
G. Bibliography 19
Notes to Introduction 21

AUTHOR'S PREAMBLE 23–32
Exordium 23
Circumstances of Composition 25
Prolegomena 26
Scheme of Work 29

FIRST DISCOURSE: *On Ethics* 33–149

FIRST DIVISION: *On Principles* 35–73
1. Elementary Principles 35
2. The Human or Rational Soul 36
3. The Faculties of the Human Soul 41
4. Man, the Noblest Being 43
5. The Soul's Perfection and Deficiency 48
6. Wherein lies the Soul's Perfection 51
7. On Good, Felicity and Perfection 59

SECOND DIVISION: *On Ends* 74–149
1. Limit, Nature and Alterability of Disposition 74
2. Noblest of Disciplines is Correction of Dispositions 78
3. Classes of Virtues and Excellences of Dispositions 79
4. Species within Classes of Virtues 82
5. Types of Vices 85
6. Virtues and Pseudo-Virtues 89

7. Justice, Noblest of all Virtues 95
8. Acquisition of Virtues and Degrees of Felicity 108
9. Preserving the Soul's Health 113
10. Treating the Soul's Sicknesses 122

SECOND DISCOURSE: *On Economics* 151–184
1. On Households in General 153
2. Regulation of Property and Provisions 157
3. Regulation of Wives 161
4. Regulation of Children 166
4a. Rights of Parents 178
5. Government of Servants and Slaves 181

THIRD DISCOURSE: *On Politics* 185–260
1. Need for Civilization and Nature of Politics 187
2. On Love, Connecter of Societies 195
3. Divisions of Societies and Conditions of Cities 211
4. Government of Realm and Manners of Kings 226
5. Government of Retainers and Manners of King's Followers 237
6. On Friendship and Friends 242
7. How to Deal with the Different Classes of Mankind 253
8. Testaments Attributed to Plato 258

NOTES 261–333

INDEX 334–352

# INTRODUCTION

## A. THE SIGNIFICANCE AND SPECIAL QUALITY OF THE AKHLĀQ-I NĀṢIRĪ

THE *Nasirean Ethics* of Naṣīr ad-Dīn Ṭūṣī is the best known ethical[a] digest to be composed in mediaeval Persia, if not in all mediaeval Islam. It appeared initially (at least, so its author says in the Supplementary Section *On the Rights of Parents*, allegedly inserted between II:4 and II:5 some thirty years later) in 633/1235, when Ṭūsī was already a celebrated scholar, scientist, politico-religious propagandist, and general man-of-affairs. Ṭūsī gives his own account of the special circumstances of its composition in his preamble, which was itself the object of subsequent reworking (as indeed the whole book may well have been).[b] This preamble, touching as it does the predicament of a powerful and sensitive mind caught up in a process of violent political and spiritual changes, speaks pointedly to men of the second half of the twentieth century; but it has made little appeal to generations content to view the man quite simply as a self-seeking and hypocritical traitor who, with all his gifts, would have been denied membership of any respectable club, regiment or university of their own day.[c]

The work, then, has a special significance as being composed by an outstanding figure at a crucial time in the history he was himself helping to shape: some twenty years later Ṭūsī, at the side of the Mongol prince Hulagu, was to cross the greatest psychological watershed in Islamic civilization, playing a leading part in the capture of Baghdad and the extinction of the generally acknowledged Caliphate there.[d] But even if one knew nothing of all this, it would be difficult not to recognize the cultural zenith indicated by the more or less casual production of so comprehensive and urbane a work of popularization; and the eminence of the elevation is all the more apparent to us now from a careful comparison of the book not only with its extant Arabic forerunners (e.g. the *Tahdhīb al-Akhlāq* of Ibn Miskawaih,[dd] d.421/1030), but also with its progressively inferior Persian successors (such as the *Akhlāq-i Jalālī* of Dawānī, d.908/1502). While greatly indebted to the former (it influenced far more of his book than the First Discourse, to which alone he and others relate it),[e] Ṭūsī himself is wider in scope and more rounded and coherent in arrangement, and his treatment of individual topics is both more developed and more engaging. The later work, on the other hand, can only be regarded (despite the literary pretensions long allowed it, particularly in India and the West)[f] as a barren, disjointed, and at times barely comprehensible fragment by comparison with this its source. The study of Islamic ethical writings has been ill-served by the fact that, probably under Indian influence, it was Dawānī's work that was early (and until recently almost alone) rendered into a Western language,[g] as also by the circumstance that Ṭūsī himself has long been seen in a sort of backward projection through that rendering, and commented on freely into the bargain, by writers (not excluding Persianists) who can hardly have read him extensively or in depth in the original.[h]

There were, to be sure, greater philosophers than Ṭūsī in the annals of Islam who touched on ethical matters with authority, though the overwhelming majority of them—Kindī, Fārābī, Avicenna, Ghazālī, Avempace, Averroes, and the rest—predeceased him and hence may be supposed at his literary service; but none of them produced any one work, of reasonable compass, so admirably offering a conspectus of most of the significant moral and intellectual preoccupations of the mediaeval Islamic world. It is for this reason that the present rendering, the first in any Western language, is directed not only to those Islamists who may not happen to be specialists in Arabic or Persian or philosophy; but also to mediaevalists, and to philosophers and historians of ideas generally. (It is hoped that the consequential ambivalence of this Introduction and of the Notes may be accordingly fruitful in at least as many cases as it proves frustrating, for the ultimate answers to many problems in this book depend on the stimulation of scholars in all these fields).

Ṭūsī is, of course, primarily concerned in this work with the criteria of human behaviour: first, in terms of space and priority allotted, at the individual level (where Man is directly integrated into Creation and immediately responsible to the Creator); secondly, at the economic[a] level (where he operates as a member of the family and of other sub-political units); and thirdly, at the political level (where he becomes, individually and by way of the higher groupings, an organic member of the city community, of a state, and even of an empire). But—in keeping with 'mediaeval' attitudes in general, and repugnantly to the 'modern' mind—he treats nothing in isolation, or relatively, or subjectively, or from a purely pragmatic standpoint. He admits no disparity between the rules laid down or elicited for Man's conduct, the courses of the planets, and the laws of mathematics: all are interdependent, all absolute, real and right. Theory must precede practice: whatever is soundly thought out will be effective, but what may seem at any moment to work must not be adopted as right merely for that reason. Key-words, *leitmotivs* throughout the whole book, are Reason, Wisdom, Justice and Equilibrium—the great and universal abstractions; but there is a truly remarkable Section on Love (III:2); and a polished tact and humanity pervade the whole (not merely the long passage on *Manners* towards the end of II:4), as well as a reiterated awareness that the particularities, the details of application, may vary greatly from individual to individual, and as between different ages or civilizations. Whatever else may be charged against Ṭūsī, he is no inhuman fanatic who would sacrifice all men to a 'system'.

That this is, in the profoundest sense, a 'religious' attitude might seem inevitable in a Muslim writer of the seventh/thirteenth century. Ṭūsī, however, is a heterodox Muslim, an exponent of extreme Shī'ite, not to say Ismā'īlī,[i] doctrines; and as such he belongs in the tradition of Islam's greatest esoterics (many of whom, be it said, were not Ismā'īlīs, while some were not even commonly regarded as heretical). Revelation and legislation he sees as necessary and even valid, but the choicest spirits are able (as all men should strive to be) to approach the Divine direct, through philosophy and ultimately through mystical intuition.[j] The diverse truths do not conflict, being of common origin, but they are hierarchically graded; and all Creation is called to ascend the grades within the limits of capacity. This ascent is the end of all existence, and it is by reference to Man's potentially supreme elevation that his behaviour is to be determined.

These qualities—the work's urbanity and polish, its organic unity of construction (cf. Notes 1845 and 2006), and its deeply philosophical and religious spirit (albeit relieved by shafts of courtesy and tact)—have tended to be largely ignored hitherto, particularly by Western Islamist scholars;[k] for these have been principally concerned to 'place' Ṭūsī (viewed, again, almost entirely through Dawānī) in the line of Islamic political theoreticians and apologists. Contemplating the work as a whole, however, and noting how the three Discourses are interwoven and (so to speak) cross-referenced, it is difficult to see the justification for directing attention so fixedly on comparatively short passages in the Third Discourse. Undoubtedly, in those passages Ṭūsī is touching on the central problems of all religiously based societies: the relationship of time-bound revelation to the continuing and developing need for legislation and authority, the definition of *de jure*, and the practical necessity to harmonize *de jure* and *de facto*. But this is to state only the obvious, and his solutions, it seems to me, are neither so detailed nor so specific that one may regard him as calculatedly preparing briefs to suit the conditions of the time. These problems were assuredly of the greatest practical and personal concern to just such a figure as himself; but I believe that, in the *Nasirean Ethics* at all events, he does little more than offer us a characteristic whiff of what was 'in the air' as he wrote. Ibn Miskawaih[dd] perhaps does rather more than this, and Dawānī can be clearly seen to make deliberate omissions and alterations, the latter albeit of a negative character for the most part. But the particular quality of Ṭūsī's work is that he reviews a whole process of life and thought in an untendentious ledger-book summation.

### B. ṬŪSĪ'S LIFE AND WRITINGS

For present purposes, the main accepted facts of Ṭūsī's life can be catalogued quite briefly.[1] He was born in 597/1201 in Ṭūs (in N.E. Persia, the native area of Ghazālī and of many other Arabo-Persian scholars of mediaeval times, now a ruin); and he died in Baghdad, for five centuries the spiritual and political centre of Islam, in 672/1274. He was the contemporary within Islam of scores of eminent figures (e.g. two of Persia's greatest writers, Rūmī, d.672/1273 and Sa'dī, d.692/1292), with many of whom he was closely acquainted; and, outside Islam, of such unwitting fellow-labourers as Albert the Great, Thomas Aquinas and Roger Bacon, of whom he quite possibly never heard. (Since he allegedly amassed a vast library, containing many foreign books, and as the Mongol period was one of lively foreign contact, it is impossible to be absolutely certain of this).

He early mastered all the various disciplines then constituting learning, but he showed a particular predilection for mathematics, astronomy and philosophy (it is important here that he was especially well-versed in the writings of Avicenna, d.429/1037.) To dramatic notice he comes first in the service of an 'intellectual' Ismā'īlī Governor of Quhistān, for whom (as he explains in his preamble) the present work was written and entitled. Willingly or unwillingly, Ṭūsī remained in Ismā'īlī employ at Quhistān, at the Alamūt headquarters, and elsewhere, until 645/1247, when he finally succeeded in defecting to the all-conquering Mongols under Hulagu. Perhaps the only certain fact about this period of twenty years or more is that it was one of the most productive of his career. For the next seventeen years, however, Ṭūsī is in the very van of momentous affairs, forming one of the remarkable band of Muslims who, so to say, stage-managed the Mongol take-over of many Islamic lands and the extinction of the Caliphate, but made possible thereby the continuance in new and flourishing forms of Islamic learning, law and civilization. During the last eight years of his life he resumed his scholarly publication, working particularly in the field of astronomy, at the great observatory in Marāgha (in Ādharbaijān) which Hulagu had encouraged him to build.

It is not difficult to see why certain aspects of such a life should call forth from luckier men the sort of strictures referred to in the opening paragraph. Be that as it may, to contrast his life in practice with his elaboration of an ethical system of this kind is little more valid an exercise than to contrast a mathematician's overdraft with his writings on harmonic functions!

Of the 100 or more works (most of them in Arabic) traditionally ascribed to Ṭūsī, not many more than fifteen or so are thought to survive in substantial form, and of these only a few are appropriate for mention here.[m]

1. The present work, in Persian of a heavily Arabicized character; belonging to his period of Ismā'īlī service, but reputedly realigned in ideas and terminology later; no good editions, though published in Persia and India many times. At present out of print.

2. *Al-Risālat al-Mu'īnīya*, in Persian, of the same period; on astronomy; facsimile reproduction, Tehran University Press, No. 300, 1335 solar.

3. *Hall Mushkilāt al-Ishārāt*, in Arabic, of the same period; a defence of Avicenna against Fakhr ad-Dīn Rāzī (not the great Rhazes), d.606/1209; a work of prime importance in Avicennan studies; no good edition, though many times published.

4. *Tajrīd al-'Aqā'id*, in Arabic; a leading work on Shī'ite theology; no good edition, though many times published.

5. *Qawā'id al-'Aqā'id*, as for 4.

6. *Zīj-i Īl-Khānī*, in Persian, from his later life; astronomical-astrological calculations of great value, made for Hulagu; no good edition.

7. *Auṣāf al-Ashrāf*, in Persian, from his later life; a Ṣūfī mystical treatise felt by some to conflict with his other writings;[j] no good edition, though many times published.

8. *Rauḍat al-Taslīm* (*Taṣawwurāt*), in Persian, from his earlier life (if, as likely, correctly ascribed to him); a treatise of far-ranging philosophical content, from a markedly Ismā'īlī standpoint, of considerable importance in relation to the present work; well edited by W. Ivanow, Ismaili Society Series A–4 (Brill, Leiden 1950).

## C. THE PRESENT RENDERING

In default of any good edition, or of any superior and accessible MSS, the present rendering has been based for the most part on six texts. The first of these takes priority, supplemented by the second.

1. The Lahore edition of 1952 (no editor's name), loaned to me for a time by the Institute of Oriental Studies, Cambridge University, Unusually well printed, and probably the most generally reliable. Unfortunately, I was obliged to return this text before making my final revision, and could obtain no other.

2. The Lucknow lithograph of 1309/1891, provided in photostat

by the Cambridge University Library. Fairly reliable, but with dangerously misleading annotations betraying ignorance of Ṭūsī's Arabicized style (e.g. to take only one instance, *wāqif* = 'aware' is consistently equated, literally, with Persian *īstāda* = 'standing').

3. A Tehran edition, undated but modern, loaned by the Institute of Islamic Studies, McGill University. The text, belonging to a somewhat different family from 1 and 2, is marred by many grotesque misprints. The paragraphing is helpful.

4. The Lahore edition of 1955. Substantially as 1, but badly printed and with many brief lacunae and repetitions.

5. A slightly defective, well-written MS dated 1055/1645. Probably of a third family, but closer to 3 than to 1 and 2. This was loaned to me by my former pupil, P. W. Avery, now Lecturer in Persian at Cambridge University.

6. Selections (*muntakhab*) from the text, edited for school use by Jalāl ad-Dīn Humā'ī (see Note b to this Introduction) (Tehran 1320 solar). Partially useful, but with several errors and omissions, and many irrelevancies in the annotations. Often tends to agree with 3 or 5.

The lack of any really good, or even readily available, text made it of little or no use to attempt to correlate pagination between my version and the original.

Pending the publication of the 'original', unadapted text of the *Akhlāq* promised by this last scholar,[b] it can be said that the extant families of the generally accepted version show no really serious or significant discrepancies; (yet, if the 'original' version did in fact contain highly controversial material, one might well have expected that a process of drastic revision, after an interval of several years, would have given rise to a whole welter of confusions and variations). Nevertheless, it seemed clearly incumbent upon me to produce a version in English that should, as fully as possible, make up for the continuing lack of a good or even accessible edition, and a great part of my heavy annotation is directed to this end. While it was obviously necessary to provide brief elucidations on Islamic matters for the non-Islamist, or to touch on questions of content interesting to both Islamist and non-Islamist alike, I judged it proper that (in the allotted space I had already considerably exceeded) I should give linguistic concerns a high priority. Any term or turn of phrase considered to be doubtful, unexpected or ambiguous has been reproduced in the original in order that the Islamist may, if he so wishes, arrive at his own evaluation; also given in the original are all but a very few of the most obvious and commonplace technicalities. Such a procedure, even where a good text is readily available, does nothing more than recognize the linguistic disparity of Arabo-Persian on the one hand and English on the other, as also the uncertainty still heavily overhanging the use of the technical terms by the different writers themselves. Thus, while I have in most cases assumed that the Islamist would readily realize that my 'essence' is equivalent to an original *dhāt* (or that *jauhar* normally = 'substance' and '*araḍ* = 'accident'), it seemed more than necessary to make clear that the one word *ṣinā'at* variously renders as 'craft, discipline, art, technique' and so on.

The Notes are used, moreover, to 'bind' the text together by fairly elaborate cross- and back-referencing. Again, this seemed a necessary and logical scheme to follow in view of my thesis, in paragraph A above, that the work has long suffered a grave injustice by being treated as three roughly joined entities, of which only a chapter or so of the third had any real importance. At the same time, and with all these varied considerations, it seemed desirable to leave uncluttered, for more or less rapid reading, a text that was, after all, produced in the first place for just such a purpose. For this reason, the Notes have been relegated to the end in a continuous sequence, the one disadvantage of high numeration being outweighed by many benefits of uniformity and economy of treatment: in the case of technical terms, in particular, the same Note often does duty many times over throughout the book.

## D. THE STYLE OF THE AKHLĀQ-I NĀṢIRĪ

Among the many traditional judgments handed down about this work, one of the most common is that its style is execrable: indeed, I know of only one opinion clearly to the contrary.[n] Difficulty over the style has undoubtedly deterred many scholars from reading the work, much more from venturing to translate it. I hope that my own version will prove that it is possible to turn it into serviceable, if not always very sprightly or attractive, English.

What do the difficulties in fact amount to? First by far, there is the use of an almost exclusively Arabic vocabulary. It is undoubtedly true that the Arabic content is so high that no one not specially trained as an Arabist could handle the text with any ease: the more so, since Ṭūsī often uses his Arabic vocabulary in a way quite foreign to Persian practice at any time (cf. the concentrations of verbal-nouns, with nothing but the genitival relationship to unite them; or Note 1323, drawing attention to the use of *bar-khāstan* as an equivalent for *qāma* when the latter means 'to undertake' rather than 'to rise'). But if this Arabicized style presents no technical problem to one properly equipped, it does constitute an enigma in itself. Why did Ṭūsī insist on using it when it had for some 200 years been more or less possible to write on these matters in fairly normal Persian?[o] If one accepted the theory of simple adaptation from Ibn Miskawaih,[p] one might have supposed that the First Discourse would be a rather literal, pedestrian rendering straight from the Arabic; but even allowing (as I do) that Ibn Miskawaih[dd] influenced far more than the First Discourse, the style is for the most part too uniform to justify this explanation alone.

The other criticism usually directed against the style of the *Akhlāq* touches the length and involvement of the sentences. It can be allowed that Ṭūsī's addiction to conditional and syllogistic arguments may lead him at times to sentences extending over most of a page. But unlike so many other Persian devisers of long sentences, not excluding stylists like Niẓāmī 'Arūḍī,[q] Ṭūsī virtually never loses the logical or the grammatical threads of his discourse. Indeed, at times his mastery is so striking in this respect that I have felt moved, against normal practice in modern English, to reproduce his construction virtually intact (as in the case of the opening paragraphs of the Second Discourse).

The simple fact may well be that both alleged faults were inherent in the man and his subject matter. It may be doubted whether the ingenious attempts of Avicenna and others to Persianize philosophical vocabulary[o] ever established much of a tradition against the weight and universality of Arabic writings in this area. On this type of subject, at any rate, it must have come as naturally to Ṭūsī to lapse into Arabic (or near-Arabic) and formalized sentence-structures as it does to many a modern Muslim scientist or doctor to discuss his specialization in the European language of his own original instruction. Certainly, Ṭūsī could, where no technicalities were involved, write both simple and attractive, as well as lyrical and lofty, passages in his mother tongue: the long passage on *Manners*, at the end of II:4 is an example of the former, the text between Notes 1478 and 1488 provides a fair instance of the latter. It may be remarked that Ṭūsī's very versatility of style, commented on by more than one writer, has often posed problems in the identification of his writings.[r]

My own policy in translating has been to try to follow the changes in pace and style as far as English usage would allow.[s] On the whole, however, I have not parallelled his Arabicisms deliberately with Latinisms, and I have tried in most cases to break up the longer sentences and to vary the constructions as often as permissible. Paragraphing is entirely my own. In one respect, that of transliteration, I have bowed almost wholly to the weight of Arabic (e.g. *bāri'*, 'Creator', not *bārī*): I hope my Persian friends will take no exception to this. I have used parentheses for two purposes: partly to add necessary emphasis or elucidation to the original, partly to mark off long sections of involved arguments; in the former case, only one or two words at a time are normally at issue.

### E. THE PURPOSE OF THE PRESENT VERSION

I have more than once criticized above the frequent assessments of the *Nasirean Ethics* that would appear to be based on no thorough knowledge of the text at first hand. As one who at least now has that knowledge, I have reached the conviction that only years of study, ideally culminating in monographs by several hands, would be adequate to assess the full importance, as well as the derivation and the influence of a work like the present. Basically, the present translation (together with its Notes) represents only a beginning—considerations of space alone would have forbidden its being more. But a beginning was sorely needed: as Sir Hamilton Gibb has suggested in another connection,[t] it is a paralysed reluctance to make a beginning, where there is no sure hope of bringing the enterprise to a definitive conclusion, that is impeding the proper development of Islamic Studies at the present time, particularly in the West.

I do not here propose, then, to offer definitive conclusions on any of the three aspects cited above. Of the work's importance I have tried to give some idea in A. On sources, I am prepared (at least, in a general way) to let Ṭūsī speak for himself: this is in fact what most writers have done, albeit they tend to pounce triumphantly on a precise (or outwardly precise) name rather than to give full weight to Ṭūsī's much more common vaguenesses and generalizations ('The Philosophers say . . .'; 'Plato and others . . .'; 'It has been said . . .'). As regards influences, again, the salient facts are not in dispute: a patient, word-by-word comparison with the *Akhlāq-i Jalālī*, the *Akhlāq-i Muḥsinī* and the rest will certainly turn up some pregnant differences (cf. my Notes 1869, 2006 and 2130 for some typical examples), but it will also produce an overwhelming majority of trivial and arbitrary deviations.

Perhaps the best example of what I have in mind regarding much pretended source-analysis is to be found in the standard comment on the Second Discourse, to the effect that it derives from Bryson through Avicenna (see my Notes 1537 and 1542). One is cheered to see so many having a fuller and easier acquaintance with Bryson than one's own, and one presumes that detailed verification of the facts has been made, at least by the first link in the imposing chain of authority! But it should be obvious to any who read the Second Discourse carefully that a vast amount of identical and similar material can be instanced from earlier Islamic moralistic works and mirrors-for-princes: I would cite, to take only a few cases, the *Shāhnāma*, the *Qābūsnāma*, the *Siyāsatnāma*, and the *Iḥyā'* or the *Kīmiyā* of Ghazālī. (It is perhaps more than a coincidence that all of these works are of Persian origin).[u]

Even where this sort of analysis is conscientiously made, however, and correspondences revealed beyond peradventure, it seems to me to be based on a grotesque misunderstanding of how these mediaeval Islamic scholars commonly went to work. They were not modern Ph.D. candidates, carefully checking their references and going scrupulously to primary sources. (Ṭūsī, for his own purposes or otherwise, often fails—and he is not alone in this—to quote even the Koran exactly, as several instances in the preamble show).[v] By Ṭūsī's own time virtually no Muslim scholar any longer knew, or cared about, the Greek language, and none would be using the translations made by the great interpreters of early Abbasid days. These translations (themselves often hurriedly made, and not always from basic materials) had long since served their purpose in giving a powerful initial release to Islamic thought. Where books were referred to at all, rather than the well-stocked memory of a lifetime of steady absorption, they were for the most part compilations and digests of all kinds, not necessarily devoid of their own originality.

It was not that the late mediaeval Muslims inevitably had a distorted view of the essence of Greek ideas (quite the contrary in many instances), but their perspective was partial, often offhand and careless as to detail, and certainly as to personalities and historical developments (cf. my Note 313 on Porphyry of Tyre, and 435 on Priam of Troy). First and foremost, they were nearly all *Muslim* thinkers: the body of ideas they nurtured and developed were often of Greek origin, sometimes Indian or Persian, occasionally more or less original within Islam itself or of their own individual evolvement; but like most Muslims (and, indeed, most Christians of the same period, if not most men at all times!), they cared little for the exact lineaments of personalities and events outside their own real world. It is this that gives added point to Ghazālī's famous jibe at the Arabicized forms of the great Greek names as *asmā' hā'ila* ('terrifying names'):[w] its sense of revulsion at their uncouth sound in the ears of an Arabic-speaker may be taken for granted, but his charge is that these names are brandished at every turn—often absentmindedly, sometimes to support a weak argument, occasionally disfiguring a good one, but rarely with any close accuracy whatsoever. The classical philosopher, for example, as he reads my version, will be surely struck again and again by the frequency of the name Aristotle in a work that breathes the spirit of Plato!

As with the Greeks, so too (even if in lesser degree) with preceding generations of Muslim thinkers. The words in which Ṭūsī, as an aside almost, derives his Third Discourse are very relevant here: '. . . Fārābī, from whose *dicta* and aphorisms the greater part of the present Discourse is derived, says . . .'.[x] By Ṭūsī's time Fārābī had become the father-figure of Islamic political thought, and Ṭūsī recognized his ritual duty to make an obeisance towards him, even if somewhat belatedly. It would be quite extraordinary, too, if his observations did not in many ways repeat or resemble such of Fārābī's as are known to us, but exact correspondences are few (as the Notes, particularly to III:3, will show). In other words, Ṭūsī cannot reasonably be assumed to have prepared himself here, as a modern scholar might, by collecting Fārābī's writings and re-reading them with a card-index. Even in the case of Ibn Miskawaih,[dd] whose influence is much more direct and central, the closest correspondences often peter out after a few lines, to resume again in the most unexpected places.

Ultimately, what is of real significance here can be expressed (outside the Notes) only in general terms: the work was written by one thoroughly 'at home' in the sciences of his time, deeply immersed in Avicennan ideas and Ismā'īlī doctrines, but with a powerful solvent genius and personality of his own.

### F. ACKNOWLEDGEMENTS

I have to thank:

In the first place, my sometime colleague, Professor A. J. Arberry, of Cambridge University, for proposing my name to UNESCO to do this work; my present colleague, Professor M. E. Marmura, for faithfully reading my material as I produced it in near-final form, and for making many encouraging comments and helpful suggestions; Professor G. F. Hourani, of the University of Michigan, who kindly agreed to read my finished typescript on behalf of UNESCO; Mr Milton Rosenthal, of UNESCO, who displayed only patience and good-humour over an unexpectedly prolonged gestation; three Toronto ladies who, among many other preoccupations, did magnificent work on an unusually difficult manuscript (Miss E. Gladwell, Miss H. N. Borrell and Miss E. M. Burson, my present secretary); the donors and lenders of some of the material listed in C; and not least my wife for enduring the inevitable abstractions and ill-humours to which I have been subject while this work was producing. Its faults are entirely my own.

### G. BIBLIOGRAPHY

One brings to a translation of this kind a professional lifetime of reading and impression, but certain works, more than once referred to in the Notes (often by summary title) or of special value to me, are listed below:

Brockelmann: *Geschichte der Arabischen Litteratur*, by Carl Brockelmann, 2 vols. and 3 suppl vols, Weimar-Leiden 1898–1942 (and reissued).

Dawānī: *Akhlāq-i Jalālī* (also known as *Lawāmi' al-Ishrāq fī Makārim al-Akhlāq*), by Muḥammad b. Asad Dawānī, ed. by W. G. Grey and M. K. Shirazi, Calcutta 1911. See also Note g to this Introduction.

Donaldson: *Studies in Muslim Ethics*, by D. M. Donaldson, London 1953. (Broad in scope and containing much useful detail, but somewhat amateurish).

Dozy: *Supplément aux Dictionnaires Arabes*, by R. Dozy, 2 vols., Leiden-Paris 1927. Invaluable for evidence of some usages.

Dunlop: See Note 1820.

EI: *Encyclopaedia of Islam*: much of the first edition is now outdated, and wherever possible the currently appearing edition has been referred to, or the interim digest *Handwörterbuch des Islam* (Leiden 1941).

Ibn Miskawaih:[dd] *Tahdhīb al-Akhlāq (wa-Taṭhīr al-A'rāq)*, by Aḥmad b. Miskawaih (or Maskūya). Also known, and referred to by Ṭūsī, as the *Kitāb al-Ṭahāra*. Unfortunately, I was not able to make comparisons with this work until quite late, when a Beirut-1961 edition (no editor named) came to hand.

Ivanow: See B 8 above. It may be added that all Ivanow's many writings on Ismā'īlism are valuable.

Lane: *Arabic-English Lexicon*, by E. W. Lane, 8 parts, London 1863–93.

Rosenthal: See Note k to this Introduction.

Walzer: *Greek into Arabic*, by R Walzer, Oxford (Cassirer) 1962. All the articles therein are of great value and most of general reference here, but I, single out one on Ibn Miskawaih, 220–35, which I was able to read at a very late stage in my work.

G. M. WICKENS

Toronto, August 1962

a. 'Ethical' is here used as Ṭūsī himself tends to use *akhlāq*, to cover human behaviour in the widest sense. 'Economic' is similarly used in, and in reference to, this work in the Aristotelian rather than the modern sense.

b. See the article by J. Humā'ī on the original preamble to the work (*Muqaddima-i Qadīm-i Akhlāq-i Nāṣirī*) in the *Majalla-i Dānishkada-i Adabīyāt* of Tehran University, March–April 1956, III/3, 17–25, where a reference is made to four MSS containing the 'original' version of the whole text. My own efforts to be allowed to see these MSS or to compare the hinted diversities have proved unavailing. The published differences in the two preambles are somewhat disappointing to one expecting sensation; at the same time, I believe (cf. Note i below) that the text I have used, even if rewritten, still contains many Ismā'īlī passages.

c. A typical view is that of R. Levy, *Persian Literature* (OUP 1923), 63–65.

d. See my article *Nasir ad-Din Tusi on the Fall of Baghdad, Journal of Semitic Studies*, Spring 1962, VII/1, 23–35.

dd. This name has various permutations and combinations: some authorities omit 'Ibn"; others make the first vowel 'a' instead of 'i'; still others read '. . . awaih' as '. . . ūya'.

e. Ṭūsī in his preamble, other writers by a sort of compulsive reaction wherever the work is discussed (cf. the article by A. K. S. Lambton on *Dawānī* in the new edition of the *Encyclopaedia of Islam*, and also paragraph *E* above).

f. See e.g. J. Rypka, *Iranische Literaturgeschichte* (Leipzig 1959), 301: 'die blumenreichste Ethik von allen'. In fact, Dawānī is not particularly 'flowery' in any sense, often far less so than Ṭūsī himself.

g. W. F. Thompson, *Practical Philosophy of the Muhammadan People* (London 1839).

h. This charge is so generally applicable that it would be invidious to name any one writer, or even two or three together.

i. See *Encyclopaedia of Islam*, articles on *Shī'a* and *Ismā'īlīya*. Whether Ṭusi was a true Ismā'īlī at any time is still a much debated question, and one without good hope of solution (see W. Ivanow, *Taṣauwurāt* (Leiden 1950): xxiv–xxvi). What is certain, at least, is that he wrote in their manner, and I have drawn attention (*pace* A. J. Arberry, *Classical Persian Literature* (London 1958), 257, and other writers also) to places where this seems to show through in the present work.

j. Ṭūsī's pair-in-hand attitude to philosophy and mystical intuition seems to worry more than one writer bound by belief in the traditional analysis of the dilemma facing Ghazālī (cf. Arberry, *op. cit.*, 262). The phenomenon is less rare than these writers suppose, particularly where both terms are given a fairly wide application: to say nothing of the Platonic tradition, an obvious Christian example would seem to be that of St Thomas Aquinas. Esotericism, it may be added, is traced by a recent writer (S. G. Haim, *Arab Nationalism* (University of California 1962), particularly p. 11, on Afghānī) as a powerful quasi-political attitude in the Near East up to quite recent times.

k. Cf. the several writings on the institution of the Caliphate, and on political theory in Islam, by Sir Hamilton A. R. Gibb; the Lambton article referred to in e above; and E. I. J. Rosenthal, *Political Thought in Mediaeval Islam* (Cambridge 1958), particularly Ch. X.

l. Perhaps the most balanced and most easily accessible general account of Ṭūsī's life is to be found in Arberry, *op. cit.*, 253–263. The old *Encyclopaedia of Islam* article is outdated. See also Ivanow, *op. cit.*, xxiii–xxvi. As has been suggested throughout this Introduction, most writers make little allowance for Ṭūsī's position as an Iranian Shī'ite in the long tradition of resistance to the Abbasid Caliphate: cf. the remarkable passage in the text between Notes 2205 and 2210.

m. For a fuller list see article on *Ṭūsī* in the *Encyclopaedia of Islam*, together with the references there assembled. See also recent publications of the University of Tehran,, both by and about Ṭūsī, particularly in connection with the seventh centenary (Islamic lunar reckoning) of Ṭūsī's death, 1956. I would draw particular attention to Nos. 296, 298, 300, 302, 304–9 and 311 in the Tehran University series; as also to many valuable articles throughout 1956–57 in their periodical referred to in b above.

n. Arberry, *op. cit.*, 261, possibly overstates by grouping the merits in one sentence: 'dignified, vigorous and artistic, and well suited to the author's philosophical purpose', but each of these is true in some measure and by turns.

o. See e.g. an article by M. Mu'īn in the periodical named in b above (December 1953, 11/2, 1–38): *Avicenna's Persian terminology and its influence in literature* (in Persian).

p. See Note e above.

q. Flourished early sixth/twelfth century. His celebrated *Four Discourses* was edited by M. M. Qazvīnī and lovingly translated into English by E. G. Browne (Gibb Memorial Series, Old Series XI, 1910 and 1921 respectively).

r. See Arberry, *op. cit.*, 260: my article noted in d, 25–26; Ivanow, *op. cit.*, xxiii and xxxiv.

s. See e.g. remark in last sentence of Note 2 to text.

t. See the Foreword to *Historical Atlas of the Muslim Peoples* (R. Roolvink and others: Amsterdam–London 1957).

u. References to all of these (including the technically Arabic *Iḥyā'*) will be found in any history of Persian literature, for they are all classics of the first rank.

v. See my Note 1.

w. *Tahāfut al-Falāsifa*, ed. M. Bouyges (Beirut 1927), 5.

x. See text between Notes 1820 and 1822.

# PREAMBLE

## EXORDIUM

In the Name of God, the Merciful, the Compassionate:

Praise without limit and lauds unnumbered befit the Majesty of kingdom-possessing might, who, as in the beginning of the primal genesis ('And it is He who originates creation')[1], brings forth the realities of the species from the preludes of generation; and who converted the primary-matter of Man (having the brand of the world of creation) forty times, in ascending degrees towards perfection, from form to form and state to state ('Forty mornings, with my hands I kneaded Adam's clay'); till when it reached utmost order, and there appeared in it the mark of attainment to fitting receptivity, He clothed it, all at once ('Our commandment is but one (word)'), by ' "Be!" and it is' and 'As a twinkling of the eye, or closer', in the garment of human form, which bore the pattern of the world of command ('And He sends down the spirit of His bidding'). Thus its primal existence received the sign of completion and the cycle of formation reached secondary being, and it made ready to bear the divine deposit: 'Then We produced him as another creature', corresponding to the beginning of genesis in the repetition of production ('Then He brings it back again'). Man's spirituality (which is the principle of existence of his form's specificity, and which was brought into being there, i.e. at the beginning of existence, in a twinkling) He causes to pass through the academy of 'Taught man what he knew not' and the workshop of 'Do ye righteously', stripping the essence and refining the attributes, progressing up the ascending degrees of perfection and adorning with righteous deeds, year by year and state by state, step by step and stage by stage; until at length He brings it to the appointed place of 'Return to thy Lord' and all at once asks back its borrowed form, which was the primal dress of human primary-matter, and which in primal being had been distinguished by so much kneading and nurture: 'When their term comes they shall not delay it by a moment nor put it forward'. And so the call 'Whose is the kingdom today?', with the answer 'God's, the One, the Omnipotent', comes down from kingdom-possessing Majesty into the void of the worlds of dominion and power; and the time comes for 'All things perish save His face'; and the promise 'As He originated you, so ye will return' is fulfilled; and the mystery of 'I was a hidden treasure' attains completion. 'That is the ordinance of the Almighty, the All-knowing'.

Blessings unbounded and salutations unnumbered are fitting commendation of the sanctified existence of the leader of guides in religion, the senior exemplar of the people of certainty, His Excellency Muhammad, the Chosen One. The salvation of creatures from the darknesses of perplexity and ignorance is through the light of his direction and guidance; and the safety of the Faithful from the abysses of negligence and error lies in grasping the 'firm halter' of his virtue. God bless him, and his Family, and his Companions, and given them peace, much peace!

To continue: the writer of this discourse and author of this epistle, the meanest of mankind, Muḥammad b. Ḥasan al-Ṭūsī, known as Al-Naṣīr al-Ṭūsī, says thus: the writing of this book, entitled *The Nasirean Ethics*, came about at a time when he had been compelled to leave his native land on account of the turmoil of the age, the hand of destiny having shackled him to residence in the territory of Quhistān. There, for the reason set down and recalled at the outset of the book, this compilation was undertaken; and, to save both himself and his honour, he completed the composition of an exordium in a style appropriate to the custom of that community for the eulogy and adulation of their lords and great ones. This is in accordance with the sense of the verse.

'And humour them while you remain in their house;
'And placate them while you are in their land'

and also the well-attested tradition: 'With whatsoever a man protects himself and his honour, it shall be recorded to him as a favour'. While such a course is contrary to the belief, and divergent from the path, of the People of the Sharī'a and the Sunna, there was nothing else I could do.[2] For this reason, the book was provided with a dedication in the manner aforementioned. Now, inasmuch as the content of this book comprises one of the branches of Philosophy,[6] and bears no relation to the agreement or disagreement of school or sect or denomination, students of profitable matters, despite differences of belief, were eager to peruse it, so that numerous manuscripts thereof were circulated among men. Later, when the favour of our Maker (glorified be His Names!), by the solicitude of the monarch of the age (may his justice become general!), vouchsafed this grateful servant an egress from that discreditable residence, he found that a number of outstanding scholars and virtuous men had honoured this book by deigning to peruse it, the glance of their approval having traced upon it the mark of selection. He resolved accordingly to replace the book's exordium, which was in an unacceptable manner, thus to avoid the disgrace of anyone's hastening to disapprove and revile before being aware of the truth of the situation and the necessity that impelled to such discourse, and in disregard of the sentiment: 'Maybe, while you reproach, he has an excuse.' Thus, in accordance with such an idea, the writer has produced this exordium in place of that preface, so that there may be no sediment at the top of the vat! If copyists will pay heed to these words and open the book in this form, it will be nearer what is right. God it is, who prospers and assists!

## AN ACCOUNT OF THE REASON LEADING TO THE COMPOSITION OF THIS BOOK

(It began) at the time of my residence in Quhistān, in the service of the Governor of that territory, His Highness Nāṣir al-Dīn 'Abd al-Raḥīm b. Abī Manṣūr (God cover him with His mercy!), in the course of a discussion on the *Book of Purity* which the learned doctor and perfect philosopher Abū 'Alī Aḥmad b. Muḥammad b. Ya'qūb Ibn Miskawaih the Treasurer, of Raiy (God water his grave, be pleased with him, and give him pleasure!), devised for the correction of dispositions (*tahdhīb-i akhlāq*)[3], accomplishing its theme by producing the most telling allusion and eloquent expression. (These four lines, once delivered as a fragment, readily describe that book:

'By my soul, a book possessed of every virtue;
  One become a guarantor for the perfection of piety.
'Its author has revealed the truth entire,
  By its composition, after concealment.
'He marked it by the name of 'purity', declaring
  Thus the justice of its purport; nor did he lie.
'He put forth all his powers—with marvellous effect!
  In counselling men he played not false.')

To the writer of these pages the Governor signified that this precious book should be revived by changing its verbal attire and rendering it from Arabic into Persian; for if the people of this age, who are for the most part devoid of the ornament of polish, will deck themselves with the embellishment of virtue by perusing the bejewelled ideas of such a composition, it will be a revival of goodness in the fullest measure. The writer of these pages was minded to accept this intimation obediently, but repeated reflection presented a fresh image to the fancy, and he said: 'To strip such sublime ideas of such subtle words (which are like a tunic fastened upon them), and to transcribe them in the dress of banal expression: this would be perversion itself, and no man of discernment becoming aware thereof could refrain from cavilling and criticism.' Moreover, although that book contains the sublimest of the topics of Practical Philosophy, yet it omits two others, namely Politics and Economics.[4] At the same time, a renewal of the outlines of these two fundamental subjects, which have become obliterated with the process of time, is of importance; indeed, the exigencies of past events render it necessary and essential. Thus, it seemed fitter that my endeavours should not be pledged to the obligation of (merely) translating that book; rather that, while accepting subservience, and within the measure of possibility, a compendium should be drawn up in exposition of *all* the topics of practical philosophy, but one taking an original course and not proceeding by way of copy or imitation. The content of the division comprising Ethics[5] would cover the gist of the work of the learned doctor Abū 'Alī Miskawaih; while, in two other sections, something should be set down, conformable to the primary branch, of the observations and opinions of other philosophers. When this idea expanded in my mind, I presented it to my master, who approved of it. Accordingly, while this servant of no substance did not judge himself apt to a position or footing of such presumption (there seeming no great likelihood, in such an undertaking, of escape from the attack of the critic or the disparagement of the detractor), nevertheless it was insisted that he press on to accomplish the enterprise. In this sense a beginning was made, and by Almighty God's assistance it arrived at completion. As the reason for its composition was my master's extempore observation and behest, I called the book *The Nasirean Ethics*. (Trusting) in the universal generosity and the massive grace of those noble ones to whose notice this compendium may come, we hope that should they observe a slip or a blunder, they will confer upon it the honour of correction and receive with the favour of acceptance the proffer of our excuse—if God Almighty so will!

## A SECTION TO RECOUNT THE PROLEGOMENA THAT MUST PRECEDE ENGAGEMENT WITH THE MATTER IN QUESTION

Since our concern in this book is with one of the parts of Philosophy,[6] it is essential to give first an exposition of the meaning of the term and its division into its components, so to make clear the sense to which our enquiry is limited. Thus, we say that the term 'philosophy', as commonly used by the learned, signifies knowing things as they are and fulfilling functions as one should, within the measure of ability, so that the human soul may arrive at the perfection to which it is directed. This being so, philosophy is divided into two, Theory and Practice.[7] Theory conceives the true natures of existent things, and acknowledges the laws and consequences thereof as they in fact are, within the measure of the human faculty. Practice is the exercise of movements and the perseverance in disciplines, to bring what is in the area of potency out to the limit of the act, so long as it leads from defect to perfection, according to human ability. In whomsoever these two concepts are realized, such is a perfect philosopher[8] and a man of excellence, his rank being the highest among human kind. Thus He says (be He exalted above the mere one who says!): 'He gives Wisdom to whomsoever He will, and whoever is given Wisdom has been given much good.'[9]

Now, since Philosophy is to know all things as they are and to fulfil functions as one should, therefore it is divided with regard to the divisions of existent things, according to those divisions. These are two: that, the existence of which is not determined by the voluntary movements of human persons; and that, the existence of which is dependent upon the control and regulation of this class. Accordingly, knowledge of existent things is also in two divisions: that relating to the first division, called *Speculative Philosophy*; and that of the second division, called *Practical Philosophy*.[10] Speculative Philosophy itself is in two divisions: a knowledge of that, the existence of which is not conditional on involvement with matter; and, secondly, a knowledge of that which cannot exist so long as there be no involvement with matter. This latter division is also twice divided: on the one hand is that, into the intellection and conception of which consideration of involvement with matter does not enter as a condition; on the other, is that which is known only by consideration of involvement with matter. Thus, in this way, there are three divisions of Speculative Philosophy: the first is called *Metaphysics*, the second *Mathematics*, and the third *Natural Science*.[11]

Each of these three sciences contains several parts, some of which are to be considered as fundamentals and others as derivatives.[12] The fundamentals of Metaphysics are in two branches: first, knowledge of God (exalted and almighty be He!) and those brought near His presence, who by His command (mighty and exalted be He!) became the first principles and causes of other existent beings, such as intelligences and souls and their judgments and actions. This is called *Theology*.[13] The second category is knowledge of universal things, the states of existent beings from the standpoint of their being existent, such as unicity and plurality, necessity and potentiality, anteriority and phenomenality, and so on. This is called *Primary Philosophy*,[14] having several sorts of derivatives, such as knowledge of prophecy, the imamate, the circumstances of the life to come, and similar topics.

The fundamentals of Mathematics are of four kinds: first, knowledge of measurements, their laws and consequences, and this is called *Geometry*;[15] second, knowledge of numbers and their properties, and this is called the *Science of Number*;[16] third, knowledge of the different stations of the higher bodies relative to each other and to the lower bodies, and the measurements of their motions and their distances, and this is called *Astronomy*[17] (astrology[18] falls outside this category); fourth comes knowledge of composite relationship and its dispositions, and this is called the *Science of Composition*.[19] (When it is applied to sounds, having regard to their relation to each other, and the amount of time, and the motions and the rests that occur between sounds, it is called the *Science of Music*.[20]) The derivatives of Mathematics are several, e.g. the *Science of Perspective and Optics*, the *Science of Algebra*, the *Science of Mechanics*, and so on.[21]

The fundamentals of Natural Science are of eight kinds: (1) knowledge of the first principles of mutables, such as time and space, motion and rest, finiteness and infinity, and so on, and this is called *Accepted Physics*;[22] (2) knowledge of simple and compound bodies, and the laws of the upper and lower simple elements,[23] and this is called the *Heavens and the World*;[24] (3) knowledge of universal and composite elements,[25] and the interchange of forms upon common matter, and this is called the *Science of Generation and Corruption*;[26] (4) knowledge of the reasons and causes that produce aerial and terrestial phenomena, like thunder and lightning, thunderbolts, rain, snow, earthquakes and the like, and this is called *Meteorology*;[27] (5) knowledge of compounds and the manner of their compounding, and this is called *Mineralogy*;[28] (6) knowledge of organic[29] bodies and of souls and of their faculties, and this is called *Botany*;[30] (7) knowledge of bodies moving by voluntary motion, the principles of motions, and the laws of souls and their faculties, and this is called *Zoology*;[31] (8) knowledge of the states of the rational[32] human soul, and how it regulates and controls the body and what is outside the body, and this is called *Psychology*.[33]

The derivatives of Natural Science are likewise many, e.g. *Medicine*, the *Science of Astrology*, the *Science of Agriculture*,[34] and so on. As for the *Science of Logic*,[35] which the Philosopher[8] Aristotle included (in his scheme), bringing it from potency to act, it is confined to recognizing the modality of things and the method of acquiring the unknown. Thus, in reality, it is a science of instruction and a sort of instrument for the acquisition of other sciences. This completes the divisions of Speculative Philosophy.[36]

Practical Philosophy is the acknowledgement of benefits in voluntary movements and disciplined acts[37] on the part of the human species, in a way that conduces to the ordering of the states of man's life here and hereafter, necessitating arrival at that perfection towards which he is directed. It likewise is divided into two: that which refers to each soul individually, and that which concerns a community in association.[38] The second division is itself subdivided: that which refers to a community associated within a dwelling or home, on the one hand; on the other, that which concerns a community associated within a city, a province, or even a region or a realm. Thus, Practical Philosophy too has three divisions: the first is called *Ethics*, the second *Economics*, and the third *Politics*.[39]

It should be recognized that the principles of beneficial works and virtuous acts on the part of the human species (implying the ordering of their affairs and states) lie, fundamentally, either in nature or in convention.[40] The principle of nature applies in cases whose particulars[46] conform to the understandings of people of insight and the experiences of men of sagacity, unvarying and unchanging with the variations of ages or the revolutions in modes of conduct and traditions. These correspond with the divisions of Practical Philosophy already mentioned. Where the principle lies in convention, if the cause of the convention be the agreed opinion of the community thereon, one speaks of *Manners and Customs*;[41] if the cause of the convention be, however, the exigency of the opinion of a great man, fortified by divine assistance, such as a prophet or an imam, one speaks of *Divine Ordinances*.[42]

The latter are further subdivided into three kinds: that which refers to each soul individually, e.g. devotions and the statutory injunctions;[43] that which refers to the inhabitants of dwellings in association, such as marriages and other transactions; that which refers to the inhabitants of cities and regions, e.g. penal laws and retributions.[44] This type is under the title of the *Science of Jurisprudence*.[45] Now since the principle of this sort of action is that of convention, it is liable to change, with revolutions in circumstances, with the pre-eminence of individual men, the prolongation of time, the disparity between epochs, and the substitution of peoples and dynasties. This category thus falls, as regards the particular,[46] outside the divisions of Philosophy, for the speculation of a philosopher is confined to examining the propositions of intellects and investigating the universalities of things, and these are not touched by decay or transience, nor are they obliterated or replaced according to the obliteration of peoples and the severance of dynasties. From the summary[47] standpoint, however, it does enter into the questions of Practical Philosophy, as will be explained hereafter in the proper place, if God Almighty wills.

## FIRST ENGAGEMENT WITH THE MATTER IN QUESTION: AND A CATALOGUE OF THE SECTIONS OF THE BOOK

In accordance with the foregoing prolegomena on the divisions of the sciences of Philosophy, it is evident that Practical Philosophy has three branches: Ethics, Economics and Politics.[4, 5] It therefore appeared obligatory to set up this treatise, which covers the divisions of Practical Philosophy, on the basis of three Discourses, each Discourse comprising one of these divisions. Each division inevitably contains several Sections, according to the sciences and the questions (involved) in a given Discourse.

## CATALOGUE OF THE BOOK COMPRISING THREE DISCOURSES AND THIRTY SECTIONS

FIRST DISCOURSE: *On Ethics, comprising two Divisions*

*First Division*: On Principles, comprising seven Sections.

First Section: *On knowing the Subject and its Principles.*
Second Section: *On knowing the Human Soul, which is called the Rational*[32] *Soul.*
Third Section: *Enumeration of the Faculties of the Human Soul, and their distinction from other faculties.*
Fourth Section: *How Man is the noblest of the existent beings in this world.*
Fifth Section: *Showing how the human soul has a Perfection and a Defect.*
Sixth Section: *Showing wherein the perfection of the human soul lies, and the refutation of those who have opposed the Truth on this score.*
Seventh Section: *On Good and Felicity, or what is intended by 'arriving at perfection'.*

*Second Division*: On Ends,[48] comprising ten Sections.

First Section: *On the limit and true nature of the Disposition, and showing how alteration thereof is possible.*
Second Section: *Showing how the noblest of disciplines is that of the Correction of Dispositions.*
Third Section: *Showing how the classes of virtues,*[49] *to which Excellences of Disposition refer, are several.*
Fourth Section: *On the species*[50] *subsumed under the classes of virtue.*
Fifth Section: *In enumeration of the opposites of these classes, i.e. the various types of vices.*[51]
Sixth Section: *A distinction between virtues and those states that resemble virtues.*
Seventh Section: *Showing the superiority of Justice*[52] *over other virtues, and an exposition of its states and divisions.*
Eighth Section: *Classification of the acquisition of virtues and the degrees of Felicity.*
Ninth Section: *On preserving the Health of the Soul, which is but the retention of virtues.*
Tenth Section: *On treating the Sicknesses of the Soul, which implies the removal of vices.*

SECOND DISCOURSE: *On Economics,*[39] comprising five Sections.

First Section: *On the reason of the need for Households;*[53] *the bases*[54] *thereof and prefatory matter pertaining thereto.*
Second Section: *Concerning the government and regulation of Property and Provisions.*[55]
Third Section: *Concerning the regulation of Wives.*[56]
Fourth Section: *Concerning the government, regulation and discipline of Children, and the observance of the rights of Parents.*
Fifth Section: *Concerning the government and regulation of Servants and Slaves.*[57]

THIRD DISCOURSE: *On Politics,*[39] *comprising eight Sections.*

First Section: *On the reason of the need for civilized life,*[58] *and an exposition of the nature*[59] *and virtue of this Science.*
Second Section: *On the virtue of Love,*[60] *by which the connection of Societies*[61] *is effected, and the divisions thereof.*
Third Section: *On the divisions of Societies, and an exposition of the various conditions of Cities.*
Fourth Section: *On government of the Realm and the Manners of Kings.*
Fifth Section: *On government of the service of Retainers*[62] *and the Manners of Kings' Followers.*[63]
Sixth Section: *On the virtue of Friendship and the manner of intercourse with Friends.*[64]
Seventh Section: *On the manner of intercourse with the Classes of Mankind.*[65]
Eighth Section: *On the Testaments attributed to Plato, profitable in all matters; on which topic the book is concluded* (*God it is, who prospers and assists!*)

Before embarking on the matter in question, let me say that what is recorded in this book, covering all aspects of Practical Philosophy (whether by way of relation or anecdote, or in the form of chronicles or narrative), is repeated from ancient and modern philosophers; not even a beginning is made to confirm the true or disprove the false, nor—in respect to our own conviction—do we engage to support any opinion or to condemn any particular school of thought. Thus, if the reader encounters an ambiguity on a point, or regards any question as open to objection, he should recognize that the author of this book has no responsibility for rejoinder, and offers no surety for uncovering the face of accuracy. It becomes all to ask for the favour of guidance from the Divine Majesty, who is the spring of mercy's abundance and the source of the light of direction. Likewise, we should hold our aspiration firm upon the attainment of Love and obedience to the Sole Lover, who is Very Truth and Total Good, thus to arrive at everlasting purposes and ends befitting this world and the next. 'God is the guardian of virtue and the inspirer of the understanding: from Him is the beginning and in Him is the conclusion.'

FIRST DISCOURSE

# *On Ethics:*[39] *comprising two Divisions: Principles and Ends*[48]

C

# FIRST DIVISION

# ON PRINCIPLES: COMPRISING SEVEN SECTIONS

## FIRST SECTION

### ON THE SUBJECT-MATTER AND THE ELEMENTARY PRINCIPLES OF THIS SPECIES (OF PHILOSOPHY)[66]

EVERY science has a subject-matter, which is investigated in that science. Thus, in the case of Medicine, it is human bodies from the standpoint of sickness or health, while for Geometry it is measurement. As for elementary principles, if they be not self-evident, they should be demonstrated in another science on a higher level than the science in question, and assumed[67] in the latter. Thus, it is one of the principles of the Science of Medicine that the elements are four and four only, for this question has been demonstrated in Natural Science; the physician must therefore adopt it from the natural scientist, regarding it as assumed in his own science. Similarly, it is one of the principles of Geometry that there are continuous, constant measurements of only three sorts, linear, superficial and solid; for this fact is established in the Divine Science which is called Metaphysics, and it is for the geometrician to adopt it from the master of the latter science and apply it in his own. Metaphysics is that in which all sciences culminate, and it can have no elementary principles that are not self-evident; but there are questions investigated in that science, and in its very entirety it is restricted to those. An exposition of this preamble has been given exhaustively in the Science of Logic.

Now this species (of Philosophy), with which we shall begin, is a science concerned with how the human soul can acquire a disposition such that all its acts, proceeding from it by its will, may be fair and praiseworthy. Thus, the subject-matter of this science is the human soul, inasmuch as from it can proceed, according to its will, acts fair and praiseworthy, or ugly and to be condemned. This being so, it must first be known what the human soul is, and wherein lies the acme of its perfection; what are its faculties, by which (if it uses them properly) it attains what it seeks, namely perfection and felicity; what, again, it is that prevents it from reaching that perfection. In sum, (one must know) in what consists its purification and in what its seduction, themselves inevitably bringing about either its prosperity or its failure. (As God says, mighty be His Name: 'By the soul, and that which shaped it, and inspired it with its wickedness and god-fearing! Prospered has he who purifies it, and failed has he who seduces it.')[68]

Most of the principles of this science are connected with Natural Science, and the place for expounding their proof is in (a treatment of) the questions of that science. However, inasmuch as the present science is of commoner profit and more comprehensive advantage than the latter, the total transference of such preliminaries to that science would necessarily place a large number of students at a loss. Accordingly, they will be set down, in narrative style and summary form, this being sufficient to present the general notions[69] of these matters. A full exposition and a complete proof will be reserved to their proper place, if God Almighty will.

## SECOND SECTION

### CONCERNING THE HUMAN SOUL, ALSO CALLED THE RATIONAL SOUL

The human soul is a simple substance,[70] whose function is to perceive intelligibles by its own essence;[71] and to regulate and control this sensible body, which the majority of mankind call 'Man', by means of faculties and organs. Such a substance is not a body, nor is it corporeal, nor is it sensed by any of the senses. At this point, the need to demonstrate certain points arises, if full treatment is to be given to this matter. (These are) (1) confirmation of the soul's existence; (2) confirmation of its substantiality; (3) confirmation of its simplicity; (4) a demonstration that it is not a body or corporeal; (5) a demonstration that it perceives by essence and controls by organs; (6) that it is not sensed by any of the senses.

In the first case, where it is sought to confirm the soul's existence, there is no need for proof; for the most apparent and evident of things, to a rational being,[72] is his essence and reality: so much so that the sleeper in his sleep, the waking man in wakefulness, the drunkard in his drunkenness, and the sober man in his sobriety—these can be heedless of all things, save of their own selves. How is it conceivable, moreover, to utter a proof for one's own existence? The property of a proof is that it serves as an intermediary to bring the adducer to the thing proven;[73] but if one utters a proof for one's own existence, the proof becomes an intermediary between one thing only, bringing self to self, whereas self is always with self. Therefore, the utterance of a proof for one's own self is absurd and false.

In the second case, where it is sought to confirm the soul's substantiality, I say that every existent being that is, save the Necessarily Existent (be He exalted and sanctified!), is either substance or accident. The demonstration thereof, apt to this occasion, is as follows. (In the case of) every existent being that is (one of two situations arises): either its existence can be consequent on another existent being, other than itself, which existent being is independent in itself, e.g. blackness, which is an indweller[74] in a body, or the shape of a couch, which is a consequence of the existence of wood; for if the body be not, blackness cannot be, and if wood (or some substitute) be not, the form of a couch cannot be. Such an existent being is called an 'accident'. Or it may be otherwise: (the existent being) can in itself have independence, without consequence to another independent, like the body and the wood in the aforementioned example. Such is called a 'substance'. This division having been established, I say it may not be that the essence and reality of Man should be an accident; for the property of an accident is that it should be predicated of, and received by,[75] another thing, which itself has independence, thus to be the sustainer and recipient[76] of that accident. In this manner, the essence of Man is the sustainer and recipient of the forms of intelligibles and the ideas of things perceived,[77] one form and idea constantly appearing therein while another passes away; and such a property is contrary to accidentality. Thus the soul cannot be an accident; but since it is not an accident, it being evident that an existent being is either a substance or an accident, therefore the soul is a substance—QED.

A demonstration of its simplicity is as follows. Every existent thing is, or is not, susceptible of division into parts.[78] That which is not susceptible of division, we here call 'simple', that which is susceptible of division we call 'compound'. Next we say that the soul conceives the idea of 'one', for it judges of things in terms of unity or the privation of unity;[79] indeed, it can conceive no plurality so long as one, being part thereof, be not conceived. If the soul be capable of division,[80] then from division of the receptacle[81] necessarily comes division of the indweller, so that the idea of 'one', indwelling it, would also be susceptible of division;[82] and this is absurd, for that which is susceptible of division is not one. Thus it necessarily follows either that the soul is not divisible, or that it does not conceive the idea of 'one'; and since the invalidity of the latter argument is apparent, that which it was sought to prove, namely the soul's simplicity, is true.

A demonstration that it is neither a body nor corporeal is as follows. Whatever is a body is compound and capable of division, a proof of this being the fact that whenever any hypothetical body becomes an intermediary between two other bodies, so that each is in contact with it on either side, of necessity with that with which it is in contact on one side it cannot be in contact on the other side also. Otherwise, it has offered no obstacle to the contact of the two sides, so that it will have been no intermediary at all, and interpenetration of the bodies necessarily follows. Moreover, as on each side it is in contact with a different thing, it is divisible into parts. Now since a body is a compound, 'corporeal', which is predicated of it and received by it,[75] is also a compound, for division of the receptacle necessitates division of the indweller. Thus, whatever is a body or corporeal is not simple; but we have said that the soul is simple. Therefore the soul is not a body and not corporeal.

Taking another point of view: no body can receive a form until the form which it has previously had has passed away from it. Take, for example, a body having the form of a triangle: until it relinquishes that form, the form of a rectangle cannot indwell it. Or take a piece of wax, which has received the figure of a seal: so long as that figure does not leave it, the figure of another seal will not take form therein; for if anything of the first figure still remain, both figures become confused and neither is fully impressed. This law is constant and general[83] for all bodies. But the state of the soul is contrary to this; for however much the forms of intelligibles and sensibles[84] descend upon it, one after another, it accepts them all without requiring the passing away of the previous form. Indeed, all the forms are fully and perfectly represented[85] in it, and the point is never reached where, from the many forms realized[86] in it, it becomes incapable of receiving another form; rather does the very multiplicity of forms therein assist it the more easily to receive other forms. This is the reason why the more sciences and arts[87] Man brings together, the greater his understanding and sagacity, and the readier he is for instruction and profit. This is a property opposite to the property of bodies; therefore the soul is not a body.

Yet another aspect: in like manner, it is absurd for one body to receive opposites in one state, for one thing cannot be both white and black. For every quality that accrues to a body,[86] an attribute accrues to it also by reason of the descent of that quality; so that it becomes hot from heat, and black from blackness. But the soul's state is contrary to this: not only can forms of opposites come together therein in one state (as when it conceives blackness and whiteness in one state), but it acquires no qualification or attribute[88] from the conception of such qualities and accidents: thus, if it greatly conceive heat, it does not grow hot, and however much it conceives length and breadth, it does not become long or broad; and similarly. Therefore the soul is not a body.

Another aspect: corporeal faculties incline to corporeal perceptions and are bound up with bodily pleasures, as with the inclination of sight to the perception of beautiful forms, and the inclination of hearing to listen to pleasant sounds. Likewise with the concupiscible faculty,[89] whose inclination is to attain the pleasure of appetite; or the irascible faculty,[90] whose longing is to arrive at perfect domination. Moreover, these faculties derive support and grow more perfect from the perception of the things they desire;[91] but the soul, from the dominance of such ideas and the attainment of corporeal perceptions,[92] becomes weaker and more defective. The further away it be from the pursuit of pleasures and association with appetites, the more manifest to it are sound opinions and clearly reasonable notions;[93] at the same time, there is an increase in its eagerness and avidity[94] for knowledge of divine realities, and its inclination and excitement in quest of noble and enduring things, loftier as they are than corporeal concerns. Now this is an evident proof that the soul is neither a body nor corporeal, for everything draws strength from its own kind,[95] but derives weakness from its opposite. But the soul grows weaker from the ascendancy of corporealities, and gains strength from shunning them.

A further aspect: any body can perceive only its own sensible. Thus sight has no knowledge of any thing not perceived visually, and hearing picks up nothing but sounds. Accordingly, no sense perceives its own sensation or the organ of its sensation: so, vision does not see sight or eye. Moreover, no sense is aware[96] of any error to which it is liable: thus the eye sees the sun, which is 160-odd times as great as the earth, as of the size of a span, having no awareness of this enormous discrepancy;[97] and in the case of trees which it sees inverted along the water's edge, it never sees the reason and cause of their inversion by vision (itself). Similarly with its other errors, and with the other senses. But the soul perceives the sensibles of all the senses at once, judging[98] that this sound comes from such and such a thing seen, or that the sound of a particular thing seen is not this sound. Likewise, it perceives what is the faculty of each sense, and which is its organ; and it deduces[99] the reasons and causes for the errors of the senses, and distinguishes between the true and the false in their judgments, acknowledging some but discrediting others.[100] Now it is obvious that such sorts of knowledge[101] have not accrued to its by means of the senses, for what the sense does not have another cannot derive from it;[102] and when its judgment discredits the sense, such judgment has not been acquired[103] from the sense. Thus it is apparent that the human soul is other than corporeal senses; indeed, it is nobler than they and more perfect in perception.

(Next we come to) the proposition that the soul has perception by its essence and control by organs. The reasoning is as follows: it knows itself and knows that it knows itself; and it may not be that its knowing itself should be by an organ, intervening between it and its essence. Once again, the reason is that what perceives by an organ cannot perceive itself or its organ, as we have said; so, an organ cannot intervene between the soul and its essence, or the soul and the organ's essence.[104] This is what philosophers mean when they say that the Intelligent, the Intelligence and the Intelligible are one. Moreover, the soul's control, being by means of organs, is apparent, for it feels by senses, and moves by muscles and nerves; and a detailed treatment of this is set down under Natural Science.

As for the proposition that the soul is not sensed by the senses: the senses can only perceive bodies or corporealities, but the soul is neither a body nor corporeal, therefore it is not sensed. So much was intended in drawing attention to the true nature of the soul,[105] appropriate to this place; thus much suffices for knowledge of the rational soul.

It must be known that the rational soul endures[106] after the dissolution of the compound (we call) the body, death having no way to annihilate it;[107] indeed, non-existence is inadmissible to it in any sense. The proof of this is as follows: every existent being that persists[108] is liable to extinction,[109] persistence being in act within it, and extinction in potency. This being so, the receptacle[81] of persistence in act must be other than the receptacle of extinction in potency; for, in the case of that thing within which persistence is in act, if extinction be also identically[110] within it in potency, it necessarily follows that when extinction passes from potency to act, such a thing unites persistence and extinction in one state. But this is absurd. Thus, that within which persistence is in act must be other than that thing within which extinction is in potency. Furthermore, it must encounter[111] it. If this be not so, the statement that extinction is within it in potency, will not be valid; for it is not valid to qualify a thing by the potentiality of the non-existence of some other thing, there being no encounter between them, like blackness and whiteness, for example. But on the assumption of encounter, such a qualification is valid, as in the qualification of a body by the potentiality of the non-existence of the blackness which indwells it.[74] There can be an ideal encounter, either between indweller and receptacle, or between two indwellers in one receptacle. The encounter between two indwellers in one receptacle is incidental, not necessary,[112] but in the above-mentioned case[113] the encounter is necessary. Thus the encounter of that wherein persistence is in act with that wherein extinction is in potency takes place by way of the inherence[114] of one within another; but the extinction of the receptacle may not occur in the case of an indweller in potency, for the persistence of the indweller after the extinction of the receptacle is impossible.[115] Therefore, in the case of that wherein extinction is in potency, its receptacle is that existent being wherein persistence is in act. Hence it is obvious that every persistent existent being for which extinction is valid indwells a receptacle, the indweller being either a form or an accident: thus extinction is admissible only to form or accident. But we have made clear that the soul is not the indweller of a receptacle, rather a substance subsisting by its own essence,[116] neither a body nor corporeal. Therefore it is not liable to extinction, and does not become non-existent with the dissolution of the compound of the body. Now if, by way of induction,[117] a person considers the states of bodies, first pursuing, with abstruse reflection, things relating to compound and composition and their opposites, and informing himself about the Science of Generation and Corruption: it will become obvious to him that no body becomes totally non-existent. Rather is there a substitution of accidents and situations, compounds and compositions, forms and qualities, in one common object or one persistent matter, the sustainer of these states at all time remaining unmoved.[118] Thus water becomes air, and air fire, but the matter on which these three forms descend in substitution, is existent in all three states. (If this were not so, one could not say that water becomes air, and air fire; similarly, if an existent being becomes non-existent, while another comes into existence, there being nothing common between them, one cannot say that this existent being has become that existent being.) That matter is the sustainer of the potentiality of the extinction of forms. Now as corporeal matters are receptive of extinction, so abstract substances (which are sanctified from material pollution)[119] are the more worthy of non-receptivity to extinction.

Our aim in expounding this matter is that anyone engaging in this science may certainly come to know that the body is a tool and an instrument for the soul, like the tools and the instruments used by artisans and craftsmen. It is not, as some people conceive, the soul's receptacle or locus,[120] for the soul is neither a body nor corporeal that it should take up a connection with receptacle or locus. So the faculty of the body towards the soul is like the faculty of tools relative to the masters of crafts. This idea is to be found in books by men of insight, explicitly and fully treated, and adorned with the citation of veritable proofs. Here so much suffices.

## THIRD SECTION

### ENUMERATION OF THE FACULTIES OF THE HUMAN SOUL, AND THEIR DISTINCTION FROM OTHER FACULTIES

As regards application of the noun itself, the word 'soul' covers several different meanings, three of which are pertinent to this discussion. One is the Vegetative Soul, the manifestation of whose operations[121] includes the types of plant, the species of animal, and individual human beings.[122] Second is the Animal Soul,[123] whose control is restricted to individuals of the animal species. Third comes the Human Soul, by which mankind is distinguished and particularized among other animals.

Each of these souls has several faculties, each of which is the principle of a particular act. The Vegetative Soul has three faculties: one is the Nutritive Faculty,[124] whose function is fulfilled with the aid of four other faculties—the attractive, the retentive, the digestive, and the repulsive;[125] second comes the Augmentative Faculty,[126] whose function is effected with the aid of the Nutritive and one other faculty, called the conversive;[127] third comes the Faculty of Generation of one's like in the species,[128] whose function reaches perfection with the aid of the Nutritive and one other faculty, called the imaginative.[129]

The Animal Soul has two faculties, the Faculty of Organic Perception and the Faculty of Voluntary Motion.[130] The first is of two kinds: that where the organs are external sense-areas,[131] the five of sight, hearing, smell, taste and touch;[132] and, secondly, that where the organs are internal senses,[133] also five, the common sense, fantasy, reflection, estimation and recollection.[134] The Faculty of Voluntary Motion is divided in two: that which is excited to the attraction of a good, called the concupiscible faculty;[89] and another, which is excited to the repulsion of a harm, named the irascible faculty.[90]

The Human Soul is particularized among the souls of animals by a faculty called the Faculty of Rationality:[135] this is endowed with the ability to perceive without organ, and to distinguish between the things perceived. Now, inasmuch as its direction is to knowledge of the realities of existent beings and comprehension of the types of intelligibles, this faculty is called, in this regard, the Speculative Intelligence;[136] and inasmuch as its direction is to control of objects,[137] distinction between good and evil actions, and the discovery of arts for the ordering of life's affairs, so—in this sense—this faculty is called Practical Intelligence.[138] The division of this faculty into these two branches is the reason for the twofold division of the Science of Philosophy, one speculative and the other practical, as has already been explained at the outset of this treatise.

As for a detailed account of the operations of these faculties; proof for the existence of each one, and its distinction from its counterparts;[139] and a discussion as to whether the principle of these faculties, in animal or human individuals, is one abstract soul or various souls and faculties:[140] all this pertains to Natural Science. The purpose of adducing this much in this place is to make apparent the difference between (1) those faculties whose operations issue in accordance with the will and with reason,[141] and whose perfection can be realized by meritorious effort;[142] and (2) those which influence by way of nature, and which are not receptive of any perfection additional to that received in original genesis.[143] The purport of the discipline with which we are about to engage relates to the first category.

Thus we say: of the faculties which we have enumerated, there are three which form the principles of acts and operations in association with opinion, reason, distinction and will.[144] One is the faculty of perceiving intelligibles and distinguishing between good and evil actions, and this is called the faculty of rationality;[135] the second is the concupiscible faculty,[89] which is the principle for the attraction of benefits and the quest of pleasures, by way of foods, drinks, women,[145] and the rest; the third is the irascible faculty,[90] which is the principle for repelling injuries, facing up to perils,[146] and yearning after authority and exaltation. The last two faculties Man shares with other animals, but the first is his alone.

Each of these faculties has an external manifestation[147] in his members, which are like organs to it. In the rational faculty it is the brain, which is the seat of reflection and reason;[148] the irascible faculty has the heart, the mine of innate heat[149] and the source of life; for the concupiscible faculty it is the liver, which is the organ of nutrition and of the distribution of the replacement for solubles[150] to other members. These three faculties—the rational, the irascible and the concupiscible—are sometimes spoken of as three souls. The first is called the Angelic Soul, the second the Savage Soul, and the third is known as the Bestial Soul.[151] As for the other faculties which have been commented upon, such as the nutritive and the augmentative and so on, their control and influence is upon their own objects in accord with nature, will and reason[141] having no access thereto. Indeed, their perfections do not grow beyond what they received in genesis.

## FOURTH SECTION

### SHOWING HOW MAN IS THE NOBLEST OF THE EXISTENT BEINGS IN THIS WORLD

Natural bodies, as bodies, are equal one with another in rank, none having nobility or virtue above the other; for one intelligible definition[152] covers them all, and one generic form of primary matter constitutes them as a whole.[153] The first variation to appear in them, so as to make them specified by[154] by the species of the elements and so on, does not demand such divergence as to necessitate the nobility of one above another. Rather are they still subject to parity in rank and equality in potentiality.[155] But when mingling and involvement between elements become manifest, and when (in the measure of the compound's proximity to true equilibrium, which is ideal unity)[156] the mark is received of noble principles and forms, gradation and divergence appear in them. Thus, of solids, that whose matter is more submissive to the reception of forms is, from the standpoint of equilibrium of mixture, nobler than the others. This nobility possesses many ranks and numberless ascending degrees: and eventually a point is reached where the compound gains the faculty of receiving the Vegetative Soul, by which it is then ennobled. Several important properties[157] then appear in it, such as the ability to procure nourishment,[158] growth, the attraction of the wholesome and the shaking off of the unwholesome.[159] These faculties likewise occur variously in it in accordance with variation of aptitude.[160] That which is nearer to the region of the solids is in the same case as coral, which better resembles minerals. Next we come to things like those grasses which grow without sowing or cultivation, by the mere mingling of elements, the rising of the sun, and the blowing of the winds: in these the faculty for prolonged individual survival and the perpetuation of the species[161] does not exist. In the same sequence, virtue augments in just proportion[162] until we come to the seed-bearing grasses and the fruit-bearing trees, which have, to the limit of perfection, the faculty for individual survival and the perpetuation of the species. In the nobler of these, the individual males, which are the principles of the forms of progeny,[163] are distinguished from the individual females, which are the principles of the matters (involved).[164] Thus, until we arrive at the date-palm, which is particularized by certain of the properties of animals: this is to say that, in its constitution, one part is designated as having a greater innate heat,[165] corresponding to the heart in other animals, and stems and branches grow thence like arteries from the heart. Moreover, in fertilization, impregnation and conception, as well as in the resemblance of the odour of that by which conception is effected to the odour of animal semen, it is also like other animals. Again, when its head is cut off, or a pest touches its heart, or it is submerged in water, it dries up: (in these ways too) it is similar to certain animals. Some agriculturalists have recorded another property of the date-palm, the most remarkable of all, namely that one tree will show partiality for another, not conceiving from impregnation by any tree other than it; this property is close to that of affection and love[166] as found in other animals. In short, there are many similar properties in this tree, and it only lacks one thing further to reach (the stage of) an animal: to tear itself loose from the soil and to move away in quest of nourishment. In the Traditions of the Prophet (peace be upon him!) it is related that he called the date-palm the 'paternal aunt' of the human species, saying: 'Honour your paternal aunt, the date-palm, for she was created from what remained of Adam's clay.' This is surely an allusion to this (general) idea.

This station represents the acme of perfection in plants, the beginning of contiguity with the animal region. Beyond this degree are the degrees of animals, the first of which are adjacent to the region of plants: such are those animals which propagate like grass, being incapable of mating, multiplying and preserving the species, e.g. earthworms, and certain insects and animals appearing in one season of the year and vanishing in the opposite season. Their superiority over plants is in the measure of their capacity for voluntary motion and for sensation,[167] to the end that they may search for the wholesome and attract nourishment. Beyond this station are animals in whom the irascible faculty manifests itself, so that they may be on their guard against the repugnant: this faculty likewise varies in them, the organ of each being constructed and adapted in accordance with the faculty's dimension. Those which reach the stage of perfection in this respect are distinguished by fully developed weapons:[168] some of these, such as antlers and horns, are like javelins; others, such as teeth and claws, serve as knives and daggers; hooves and suchlike take the place of hatchets and clubs; finally, in place of darts and arrows, some birds and other animals have throwing instruments[169] in their feathers. Those who are deficient in this faculty are particularized by other means of defence, such as flight and the practice of ruses, as in the cases of the deer and the fox. If one reflects upon the different sorts of animals and birds, it will be observed that to each individual is assigned and disposed whatever is needed to effect and bring about freedom from anxiety.[170] This may take the form of strength and valour, or the organization of such instruments as has been mentioned; or it may be effected by inspiring observance of prudent measures inviting the perfection of the individual together with[171] the species: thus (we find) the requirements of mating, the quest to beget progeny, the care and nurture of children, the building of nests according to need, and the storing up of sustenance, the bestowal thereof on one's own kind,[172] and agreement with them or opposition to them. (In short, we have) caution, sagacity, deliberation and ingenuity directed to every matter, so as to leave the sage astounded, confessing the wisdom and might of his Maker: 'Holiness is His who gave every thing its creation, then guided (it)'.[1] The difference in the kinds of animals is greater than the discrepancy in the degrees of plants, on account of the proximity of the former to the simples[173] and the remoteness of the latter therefrom. The noblest of the species is that one whose sagacity and perception is such that it accepts discipline and instruction: thus there accrues to it the perfection not originally created[174] in it. Such are the schooled horse and the trained falcon. The greater this faculty grows in it, the more surpassing its rank, until a point is reached where the (mere) observation of action suffices as instruction: thus, when they see a thing, they perform the like of it by mimicry, without training or wearisome labour being expended upon them. This is the utmost of the animal degrees, and the first of the degrees of Man is contiguous therewith. Such are the peoples dwelling on the fringes of the inhabited world, like the negroes in the West[175] and others, for the movements and actions of the likes of this type correspond to the actions of animals.

Up to this limit, every gradation and discrepancy occurs in conformity with nature, but henceforth ranks of perfection or deficiency are determined according to will and reason.[141] Thus all men in whom these faculties are complete, and who are able (by use of organs and deduction of premisses)[176] to bring them from deficiency to better perfection, enjoy a greater virtue and nobility than those in whom such notions are less developed.[177] The first of such degrees is occupied by those persons who, by means of intelligence and the intuitive faculty,[178] bring forth noble arts and organize delicate skills and subtle instruments. Next comes a class who, by much utterance,[178a] reflection and meditation, engage with the sciences and the branches of knowledge and the acquisition of virtues. Beyond these, there are persons who, without the intermediacy of bodies, by revelation and inspiration,[179] receive knowledge of truths and laws from those brought close to Divine Majesty:[180] these are a comfort and an infallible cause of felicity to men of (all) climes and ages, in regard to perfection of disposition and the ordering of the affairs of this world and the next. This is the highest of the ascending degrees of the human species, the discrepancy in which is greater than in the species of animals in the same proportion as has been stated to hold between animals and plants. When this stage is reached, there is an inception of contiguity with the nobler world and of junction with the ranks of the sanctified angels and the abstract intelligences and souls. And so to the limit, where is the abode of Unity, and there the circle of existence meets, like a curved line beginning from a point and returning to the same point. Then intermediaries are set aside, gradation and opposition cease, *terminus a quo* and *terminus ad quem*[181] become one, and nothing remains but the Reality of Realities, the Ultimate of Quests, which is Absolute Truth:[182] 'And thy Lord's face abides, splendid and revered'.[183] After such an exposition, the nobility of Man's rank becomes obvious, likewise his virtue above the other existent beings in the world, and the particularity[184] which has been conferred upon him. Indeed, what becomes apparent is the nobility of rank of those persons whose minds[185] are the rising-place of divinity's light and the manifestation of oneness's abundance; whose existence is the acme of all acmes, the ultimate of all ultimates: the Prophets and Saints (peace be upon them!), who are the choicest of existent beings and the cream of generables.[186] The words 'Were it not for thee, I had not created the heavens' are a verification of this idea; rather is it this idea which confirms and gives sense to that allusion.[187]

Now the purpose of giving an account of these ranks is that it may be known that Man, in the beginning of the primal genesis, received a middle rank, falling among the ranks of generables. But he has a road, by will, to a higher rank, and by nature to a lower. Thus in the matter of externals, in accordance with a prudent purpose[188] nature has provided that which is needed by other animals, such as nourishment to replace what is dissolved,[150] and hair or wool to hinder the harmful effect of cold or heat, and instruments of defence by which to ward off the repugnant or the hostile. But while she has caused them to be relieved of their necessities,[189] what Man needs in this way has been entrusted to his management, his reason, his control and his will, so that he may contrive as best he knows: his nourishment is not procured without the organization of sowing, reaping, milling, kneading, baking and combining; his clothing is obtained only by application of spinning, weaving, sewing and dyeing; nor do his weapons come into being without art and polishing and measuring. Likewise, when we look to internals, the perfection of each of the species of vegetable and animal compounds was laid down in the beginning of primal genesis,[143] and rooted in its fundamental nature.[190] But Man's perfection and the ennobling of his virtue were entrusted to his reflection, reason,[148] intelligence and will; and the key of felicity and affliction, fulness and deficiency, was given into the hand of his own competence. If he moves in accordance with prudent purpose,[188] by way of the will, in a direct course, turning by degrees towards the sciences, the branches of knowledge, the arts and virtues,[191] the yearning for the attainment of perfection which is rooted in his nature will bring him, by a straight road and with a praiseworthy purpose, from rank to rank and region to region, until the divine light shines upon him, and he attains neighbourhood with the sublime assembly, joining those brought close to Eternal Majesty.[192] But if he choose to rest and abide in his original rank, passing the reins to nature's hand, nature will upset and capsize him, and bring him to face in a downward direction; a monstrous yearning and a corrupt inclination, like the depraved passions in the natures of the diseased, will be added to his original nature, so that he becomes daily, and momentarily, more defective, and decline and deficiency gain the mastery. Like a stone flung down from a height, he comes in the shortest time to the lowest degree and the basest rank, where is the place of his destruction and ruin. As has been said:

'This is the soul: neglected, it frequents the ignoble;
'But excited towards virtues, it devotes itself thereto'.

Since Man at the beginning of primal genesis[143] was adapted to these two conditions, there befell a need for prophets and philosophers, imams, guides, tutors and instructors,[193] who should—some graciously, others with severity—prevent his facing towards affliction and disaster (in which there is no need for great effort or movement, every rest and lack of movement being indeed sufficient in that sense); and who should turn his face towards eternal felicity (on which must be expended both effort and solicitude, this goal being unattainable without movement of the mind along the path of truth, and the acquisition of virtue). Thus, through leadership and direction, discipline and instruction, men arrive at the sublimest rank of existence. God prosper us in what He loves and approves, and lead us aside from the pursuit of passion!

## FIFTH SECTION

### SHOWING HOW THE HUMAN SOUL HAS A PERFECTION AND A DEFECT

Every existent being, refined or base, subtle 'or gross,[194] has a property in which no other existent being participates with it. Indeed, the determination and realization of its quiddity involve such a property.[195] But it may have certain other actions, in which other things besides itself participate with it. Thus a sword has the property of penetration and smoothness in cutting, and a horse that of obedience to the rider and fleetness in running, and no other thing could conceivably participate with them in this. It is true that a sword participates with the axe in hewing, and the horse with the donkey in load-carrying, but the perfection of each thing lies in the full issuing of its property from it, and its defect in the failing or want of such issue. So, the more perfect a sword be in penetration and smoothness of cutting (so that its action is achieved without its owner needing to employ excessive trouble and effort), the more perfect it is in its own affair; and the better runner a horse be, and the more tractable in serving its rider and obeying the bit and accepting schooling, the nearer it comes to its perfection. Likewise in respect of defect: if a sword cuts with difficulty, or even fails to cut at all, it will be used in place of another iron (tool), and this represents a decline in its rank; and if a horse does not run well, or is not obedient, it is turned into a pack-horse and made to share the donkey's lot, and this is charged to its clumsiness and meanness.[196]

Similarly, Man has a property by which he is distinguished from other existent beings. But he has other actions and faculties, in some of which the animal species share with him, and in some others the types of plants or the minerals and other bodies. (Something of this has already been explained.) However, the property to which none other has access with him, is the notion[197] of rationality,[135] on account of which he is called 'rational'.[32] This is not speech in act, for the dumb man also possesses this notion,[197] though not speech in act: rather does this notion[197] signify the faculty of perceiving intelligibles and the power of distinction and reason,[141] by which one discriminates between fair and foul, reprehensible and praiseworthy, and disposes of them according to the will. It is on account of this faculty that Man's actions are divided into good and bad, and fair and foul, and that he is characterized by felicity or affliction, as against the other animals and the plants. Thus, whoever applies this faculty properly, and by will and endeavour reaches that virtue towards which he was directed at creation, such a one is good and blissful; but one who neglects to tend that property, either by striving in an opposite direction or by sloth and aversion,[198] is evil and afflicted. As for what Man shares with the animals and other compounds, if this dominates him and he directs his aspiration thereto, he will decline from his own rank and arrive among the ranks of the beasts—or he may come even lower than that. For example, such a man may confine his desire to the attainment of pleasures and bodily appetites, favoured and yearned for by the senses and the corporeal faculties, such as foods, and drinks, and clothes and women,[145] which are the outcome of the dominance of the appetitive faculty;[89] or (he may confine himself) to the securing of conquest, domination and revenge, which are the fruit of the ascendancy of the irascible faculty.[90] But if he reflects, he will recognize that to confine one's aspiration to such ideas is sheer worthlessness and pure defect. Indeed, other animals in these respects are more perfect than he and more capable of effecting their design.[199] This can be observed in the avidity of a dog for eating, the intense urge of a pig to gratify its appetites, or the charge of a lion when overcoming and bringing down; similarly among other types of predatory animals, beasts, birds, water-dwellers and so on. So how should an intelligent man[200] be content to strive on a course where, even if he put forth a supreme effort therein, he cannot equal a dog; and whence should a man of high purpose[201] deem it permissible to seek something whereby, even if he spend a whole lifetime upon it, he is not to be compared to a pig? Likewise in respect of the irascible faculty: if Man relate himself to the least wild animal in that respect, the latter takes precedence over him. Man's virtue passes from potency to act only when he cleanses his soul from such monstrous vices, such ruinous defects; for the physician, so long as he removes not the sickness, can hold no hope of health; and the dyer, so long as he cannot find the garment free of the marks of filth and grease, will not deem it receptive of the colour intended. But when the inclination of the human soul is diverted from what must cause its deficiency and corruption, then of necessity the essential faculty[202] comes into motion; and it occupies itself with its own particular acts,[203] namely the quest of the true sciences and universal knowledge,[204] confining its aspiration to the attainment of felicities and the acquisition of good things. In proportion to the quest and to the close pursuit of congruents,[205] as also to the avoidance of the opposites and impediments thereto, so does that faculty increase. (In this it is) like a fire, which will not kindle unless it find a receptacle free from moisture; but once it has ignited, its ascendancy grows momentarily, and the faculty of burning increases within it, until it fulfils the requirements of its own nature.

Now deficiency possesses ranks: some are due to failure to apply the whole faculty of reason[141] in quest of an intention;[206] some arise from reason's being too weak to deal with impediments;[207] one group results from a turning towards that which is contrary,[208] on account of the authoritative position[209] of the faculties of concupiscibility and irascibility, an assimilation to beasts and wild animals, and a beguiling by the distractions of sensibles from attainment to those favours for which Man was created, so that he comes to everlasting destruction and eternal affliction. In the same manner, perfection possesses ranks, more numerous than the ranks of deficiency, which are spoken of at one time as Salvation and Felicity, at another as Grace and Mercy, or again as the Enduring Kingdom, True Joy and Refreshment to the Eye.[210] (As God has said (mighty be His name!): 'No soul knows what refreshment to eyes is hidden for them as a reward for what they used to do.'[211] In other places it is likened to *houris* and palaces, serving-lads and boys; elsewhere there is allusion to a pleasure which 'eye has not seen, nor ear heard, nor has it come to the heart of Man'.[212])

So it proceeds until he attains the neighbourhood of the Lord of the Worlds, and receives the ennoblement of observing His glory in sempiternal ease. But whoever, in deceit of his nature, turns aside from these noble, everlasting boons, striving after such inconstant contemptibles, which are truly 'like a mirage in a plain, which the thirsty man takes for water, but when he comes to it he finds it nothing':[213] (such a one) is deserving of his Master's hate and anger. What he gains is to merit, in this world, that lands and men should be relieved of him, his folly and corruption being taken from them; while, in the world to come, he earns loss and punishment, torment and destruction.[213a] God protect us from that by His favour and mercy! This is an exposition of the perfection and deficiency of the soul adequate for this place. In God is a fortunate issue.

## SIXTH SECTION

### SHOWING WHEREIN THE PERFECTION OF THE HUMAN SOUL LIES AND THE REFUTATION OF THOSE WHO HAVE OPPOSED THE TRUTH ON THIS SCORE

From the previous Section it has become obvious that the human soul has a perfection and a defect, and an account of that perfection has already been given in summary fashion. It has now become necessary to expatiate on that perfection in detail, so that once men become aware of its true nature, they will not grudge expending their supremest effort in quest of it. So we say: in the case of every existent being that is compound, its perfection is something other than the perfection of its parts or simples.[173] Thus, the perfection of oxymel is something other than the perfection of vinegar and of honey, and that of a house something other than the perfection of wood and of stone. Now since Man is compound, his perfection too is something other than that of his simples and parts; indeed, he has a perfection in which no single existent being participates with him; and the most perfect of men is the one who is the most capable of manifesting that particularity, and the one most attached to it, without exposure to the inroads of negligence or vacillation. The situation of virtue and perfection being known, that of vice and deficiency, which is its counterpart, is also obvious.

Man's perfection is of two kinds, inasmuch as his rational soul has two faculties, the Theoretical Faculty and the Practical Faculty. The perfection of the Theoretical Faculty lies in its yearning being towards the perception of all the sorts of knowledge and the acquisition of the sciences,[214] so that, conformable to the exigency of that yearning, it may gain (in the measure of ability) comprehension of the ranks of existent beings and an awareness of their realities; next (it is necessary that), it should be ennobled by knowledge of the True Quest and the Universal Goal,[215] wherein all existent beings culminate, thus to arrive at the World of Unitarianism,[216] nay, at the Abode of Unity[217] (itself). Then its heart will have rest and assurance, and the dust of perplexity will be wiped from the countenance of its conscience,[218] and the rust of doubt from the mirror of its mind.[219] Speculative Philosophy in its entirety comprises the detailed consideration of this kind of perfection.

The perfection of the Practical Faculty lies in organizing and ordering its own particular faculties and acts, so that they are in agreement and conformity, the one not seeking to dominate another. By their reconciliation its disposition grows in acceptability.[220] Next, it should come to the degree of perfecting things other than itself, which is to regulate the affairs of households and cities; so that it orders those states falling within the purview of association,[221] and all men arrive at a felicity shared by all. This type of perfection is what is sought in Practical Philosophy, and the present book will contain an indication thereto.

So the First Perfection is connected with speculation, and is (as it were) the form, while the Second Perfection can be regarded as matter. Just as form without matter, or matter without form, can possess no stability or permanence, so theory without practice is abortive, and practice without theory absurd. Theory is the starting-point and practice the conclusion.[222] The perfection which is composed of both, is that which we have called the 'purpose of Man's existence',[223] for 'perfection' and 'purpose' are approximate in sense, the difference between them being established by relationship: 'purpose' is that which is still in the confine of potency; when it reaches the confine of act it becomes 'perfection'. Thus a house, while its existence is still in the architect's conception, is a 'purpose', but when it is realized in external existence, it reaches the degree of 'perfection'. When Man reaches this degree, so that he becomes aware of the ranks of generables universally,[224] then are realized in him, in one way or another,[225] the infinite particulars subsumed under the universals;[226] and when practice becomes his familiar, so that his operations and acts are realized in accordance with acceptable faculties and habits,[227] he becomes a world unto himself, comparable to this macrocosm,[228] and merits to be called a 'microcosm'.[229] Thus he becomes Almighty God's vice-gerent[230] among His creatures, entering among His particular Saints,[231] and standing as a Complete and Absolute Man.[232] Complete and absolute is one who has the persistence and perseverance to aspire to blessedness in everlasting felicity and abiding, eternal ease, by His proof and command, and who makes ready to receive his Master's abundance. At length, between him and his Master no veil intervenes, but he receives the ennoblement of proximity to the Divine Presence. This is the sublimest degree and the remotest felicity possible to the species of Man. If it were not possible for some individuals of this species to reach this abode, this species' course would be like that of other animals and of the plants in respect of extinction and mutation,[233] and it would have no conceivable nobility of excellence over them.

Some people, whose intellects are unable to conceive such an idea, have declared for Man's utter extinction[234] after the annihilation of the body's frame [235] and the dispersal of the members. Having no regard for a material world-to-come,[236] they confined all aspiration to the attainment of pleasures and attachment to appetites. They have fancied that the Rational Soul exists for the contriving of actions and the cultivation[237] of things conductive to worldly pleasures. For example, they would say that the utility and purpose of recollection and reflection, which are two of the soul's faculties, are (respectively) to recall the pleasure derived from a food or a drink or a woman, and, by reflecting on the method of acquiring it, to arrive at the thing desired. Thus, they reckoned the precious soul[238] a servant and a hireling in the service of a base appetite, degrading that noble essence (associate of the Sublime Company)[192] to the lowest station, by placing it in the rank of servitude to the meanest of slaves,[239] the Bestial Soul[151] shared by the other animals. This is the opinion of the greater part of the ignorant and ignoble among men.

A nearly related view is that of a group who conceive the world-to-come as offering the same sort of pleasures and appetites as this world. From Eden's Paradise and proximity to the Divine Presence, they (only) ask excessive capacity to acquire pleasurable foods, or to have power over voluptuous women, or to get hold of much-coveted drinks.[145] In their devotions and their prayers they beg such things of their Master: they forsake the world and abstain from its delights on a business-like principle of driving a better bargain,[240] giving up a little of the present for much to come, and expending the contemptible and the transitory in quest of the imposing which endures. In truth, these people are the most avid of mankind for pleasures and appetites, not the most abstemious or the most moderate. Yet, in spite of all this, if mention is made in their presence of the World of Dominion or the Sublime Company,[192] or if they hear that the Angels, those brought close to the Presence of Sanctity, are sanctified and absolved from such impurities and from basenesses of the appetites, they still assert the eminence in rank of these beings; indeed, they recognize that the Maker (glorified and exalted be He!), who is the Creator of creatures and the Author[241] of all, is aloof and elevated above this degree, and that pleasure and enjoyment in such things is not proper to Him. In this respect, such people are the companions of the dog and the pig, not to say of beetles and worms, while in intelligence and distinction they are partners of the angels. Truly, the uniting of such a belief with the first opinion, in one mind, is one of the wonders of the world! If they would reflect a little, it would be obvious to them that so long as they be not first afflicted with the pangs of hunger, they will derive no pleasure from an appetizing morsel; and while they are not caught in the torture of thirst, they obtain no comfort from the drinking of cool water; if they are not prisoner to repletion of the seminal vessels, they are not eased by titillation of their channel of evacuation; and, not bearing the anguish of heat and cold, they can have no enjoyment from decking themselves with clothes. However, as they derive ease from all the varieties of this sort of treatment and care,[242] which effect relief from pains and immunity from their hurt; and since thereby they escape from enduring their severities, and the taste of such pleasure and comfort takes root in the palate of their imagination,[243] they form the idea that those pleasures represent perfection and utter felicity. Thus, they are heedless of the fact that if they yearn for the pleasures of eating, they will have first been afflicted with the pangs of hunger; if they seek the comfort of drink, they will previously have sought the anguish of thirst; and so on.

Galen says, concerning a group of such perverse men,[244] noted for the most corrupt behaviour, that when they find one to partner them in this course they set out, with his help and using his name,[245] to cast mankind into error, saying: 'We are not alone on this path.' In this way, they think that if they associate certain intelligent and virtuous persons with themselves therein, their exculpation will be manifest, and their imposture[246] will gain acceptance among others. Such persons corrupt young men and novices, casting into their minds the notion that virtues have no real existence;[247] or that if they do, they are impossible of attainment. Now, all men are naturally inclined towards the appetites, and ever-ready buyers of the sensuality we have described.[248] For this reason, the followers of this party are many.

Suppose one should censure them by arguing that these pleasures are in accordance with the necessities of the body, inasmuch as the body is compounded of opposite natures, such as hot and cold, moist and dry, and the dominance of one of these opposites over the others inevitably brings about the compound's dissolution. (Then one goes on to say) that care for eating and drinking is intended to ward off the latter state (necessitating, as it does, the body's dissolution), so that, as far as may be possible, the body will endure. But the treatment of disease cannot be an utter felicity, nor can relief from pain become a desired end or a pure good; for the utterly blessed is the one having no anguish at all, with the result that he can be neither concerned with, nor in need of, treatment therefor. The angels, who are brought close to the Divine Presence, are free and exempt from such diseases; and the Majesty of Might itself is aloof and exalted above description by such attributes.

(If you argue so), they will object that there are men more virtuous and more perfect than angels, while God (almighty and exalted be He!) cannot be related to His creatures at all. Thus they bring contention and wrangling into this matter, and ridicule the opinion of the one disputing with them, hoping to implant respect for their rootless uncertainties[249] in his mind. Yet a most remarkable thing is that, despite this line of argument and opinion, if they should hear of anyone that he has forsaken their path (i.e. the preferring of appetites), despising the enjoyment of pleasures, adopting contentment and frugality and a disregard of other desires, and limiting himself to the least mouthful and the most unwanted rag: for such a one they express much admiration and count him deserving of great favours from God.[250] Indeed, they will say that he is God's saint and elect,[251] there being none among men more angel-lived or illustrious than he. When they see him, they do not for a moment neglect to make him a show of humility and respect, reckoning themselves as among the wretched in comparison to him. The reason for such a situation, contrary though it be to their beliefs, is that, despite folly in opinion and viciousness in habit, there still remains in them some feeble trace of the Noble Soul's faculty. It is by this that they attain awareness of the merit of the virtuous and those who excel, so that they are compelled to honour and venerate them. They become involved in the contradiction of their way of life because they know no better.

A clearer pointer[252] to the weakness of their opinion and the feebleness of their argument[253] is as follows: although the Bestial Soul overcomes the Intelligent Soul,[254] and its owner engages with reprehensible appetites, yet because of the tiny measure of recovery[255] persisting in the Faculty of the Intelligence, he is ashamed to display these dealings, covering his action by such obstacles to the eyes as house-walls or the veil of darkness. Moreover, if someone observes him in such a situation he will be so beset by shame and embarrassment that he desperately wishes for death. There is an exception in the case of those whom baseness of nature has befallen to an extreme where humanity has completely departed from them, while shamelessness, which is one of the concomitants of surrender to deficiency,[256] has become a habit with them. There is no hope of reforming such a person's soul, and treatment can have no conceivable effect on his chronic disease, his established sickness.

As for the first group, however, in whom the trace of shame still endures, and for whom a restoration to health may be expected, they should reflect on the fact that shame is an indication of foulness, for all natures love to display a fair action. The reason for concerning oneself with whatever implies a foulness for which one must feel shame, can only be a defect concomitant with the nature of Man; and its removal, within the measure of ability's scope, is a necessary obligation.[257] So the more monstrous is the more foul, and the fouler, the more need for covering and burying; but there can be no covering or burying other than to eradicate the trace thereof from the nature.

If a person should wish to try to inform himself of the feebleness of such people's belief, let him put them the following question: If these actions are good actions, why do they account the concealment and pretended disapproval thereof a virtue and a generous gesture;[258] and why do they impute the display and free confession thereof to baseness and impudicity? When it becomes apparent that they have nothing to say and are at a loss to answer him, he will be adequately apprised of the depravity of their conduct and the perversity of their secret thoughts.

The intelligent man, then, should confine his aspiration to removing these faults and defects with which he is afflicted. He should content himself with sufficient nourishment to preserve equilibrium of temperament and maintain life.[259] In obtaining it, he should not seek to enjoy pleasures; rather should he seek health, that pleasure may follow, being realized accidentally.[260] It is proper for him to go a little beyond this limit, in order to preserve (a reputation for) generosity, to guard his dignity and rank among men, and to avoid (a charge of) avarice and meanness; but only on condition that this should not lead to any suffering or sickness; and he should not be tainted with a suspicion of any other motive. Of clothes, he should be satisfied with such quantity as will deflect the harm of cold or heat and keep covered his nakedness. It is proper for him to go a little beyond this limit, so far as will enable him to feel secure from contempt and reproach before his peers and his fellows, on condition that this should not lead to vainglory and pomp; and he should take no step to exceed the law of moderation. In sexual intercourse, he should confine himself to what is required for the preservation of the species and (the satisfaction of) the desire to beget offspring;[261] if he pass somewhat beyond this, he should not depart from the path of the *Sunna* or the principle of Wisdom,[262] stretching forth his hand to the womenfolk of others, or whatever else may lie outside his (rightful) grasp.[263] In the matter of dwelling and such other things as he may need, he should in the same way not transgress the limit. Thereafter let him strive in quest of felicity and the virtue by which his humanity is made entire, and which brings the Intelligent Soul to its desired perfection; and let him, in the measure of possibility, remove his defects. This, then, is virtue: shame does not demand its concealment, and there is no need of veils to bury it, or house-walls or the darkness of night.

To resume: Man, as we have said, is composed of three faculties, the meanest being the Bestial Soul, and the intermediate the Savage Soul, while the noblest is the Angelic Soul.[151] He is partner to the beasts in respect of the meanest, and diverges from them in the noblest; the predatory creatures he partners in the intermediate, again diverging from them in the noblest; and he partners the angels in the noblest, and diverges from them in the meanest. The bridle of choice and the rein of preference are in his hands: if he wishes, he dismounts at the stage of the beasts, and at length becomes one with them; if he wishes, he halts at the stopping-place of the wild animals, and at length becomes one with them; but if he so wishes, he may proceed to the angels' abode and become one of their number. Mention of these three souls is made in the Glorious Koran, under the titles of the Imperative Soul, the Reproachful Soul and the Peaceful Soul.[264] The Imperative Soul commands the indulgence of appetites and persists therein; the Reproachful Soul, after involvement in the necessary consequence of deficiency, causes such activity to appear foul in the eye of insight by repentance and reproach; the Peaceful Soul is satisfied only with the fair action and the acceptable operation.

Philosophers have said that of these three souls, only one possesses discipline and generosity in reality and in substance,[265] and that is the Angelic Soul; the second, although not possessed of discipline,[266] is receptive thereof, and is submissive to the instructor at the time of schooling, and this is the Savage Soul; the third is devoid of discipline and unreceptive thereof, and this is the Bestial Soul. The reason for the existence of the Bestial Soul is (to ensure) the endurance of the body, which is the subject and vehicle[267] of the Angelic Soul during the time in which it realizes its perfection and reaches its goal. Similarly, the reason for the existence of the Irascible Soul is to afflict and overcome the Bestial Soul, so as to ward off the corruption that may be expected from its ascendancy, for the bestial is not receptive of discipline. (Such a notion approximates to an interpretation of what has been transmitted in revelation.)[268] Plato says, in allusion to the Savage and the Bestial Souls: 'This one is like gold in softness and pliability, that one like iron in hardness and intractability.' Similarly, he says elsewhere: 'How hard it is for the man of appetite to become virtuous!' Thus, in the case of one who prefers the fair action, if he be not assisted by the Appetitive Faculty, he must seek aid against the latter from the Irascible Faculty, which excites ardour[269] to subdue and defeat it. But if, despite this seeking of aid and support, the appetite should still prevail, albeit its master (after giving prior place to its requirement) is importuned by regret and remorse, then the latter is still on the way to seeking improvement, and his reform is to be hoped for. But he must employ the express authority of resolution[270] to break the desire of the appetite for reversion[271] to anything like the former state. Otherwise, his case will be like that mentioned by the Ancient Philosopher,[272] when he says: 'I see that men profess to love fair actions, but turn away from shouldering the burden thereof, notwithstanding awareness of its virtue. Hence idleness and futility take hold of them, until there is no difference between them and one not marked by love of the fair action and knowledge of its virtue. If a sighted man and one who cannot see fall into a pit, both share in destruction, but the former is alone in meriting censure and reproach.'

The Ancient Philosophers[273] have also compared these three souls to three different animals brought together in one stable, a horse,[274] a dog and a pig, authority being exercised by whichever of the three is dominant. Some have said that Man stands towards these three souls like the rider of a powerful beast, who goes out in quest of game, with a hound or a cheetah up beside him. If authority lies with the human, he uses equitably[275] both quadruped and predator, respecting their well-being and his own in time of need, and arranging for the food and necessities of the whole group on a just basis. Thus all are well provided for[189] in the matter of food and drink and the other concerns of life. But if the beast have the upper hand, he will not recognize the rider's authority; thus, wherever from afar he sees better grazing, he will start to run in that direction, causing trouble both to himself and to his companions from unevenness of motion, in descent and rise, and by straying from the highway and hastening at the wrong time; and when he reaches his fodder, he leaves the others without provision, so that they weaken from hunger and are exposed to destruction. Sometimes it may happen that, in the course of his running, he comes to a tree, a thorn-bush,[276] a deep river or a dangerous water-course, destroying himself and them by a collision or a fall or some other calamity. Likewise, if the beast of prey is master, as soon as he observes a quarry, he will impel both rider and mount in that direction by virtue of his strength; and there result trouble and terror and ruin, the like of what has already been suggested. Indeed, it is likely that in the course of resisting and opposing the animal that is his quest, it is they who will receive a wound or an injury from which they perish. But if they are subject to a ruler who merits to rule,[277] i.e. the rider, they remain safe from such calamities and accidents.[278].

Now the condition of these three faculties, in the matter of reconciliation and intermingling, is contrary to that of bodies; for from regulation by the Angelic Soul there necessarily follows the union of the two other souls with it, so that you may say that all three are in reality one. Nevertheless, the faculties and operations expected from each proceed therefrom at the proper time, so that one might think each individually to be in its original state; and such is their agreement and peaceful relationship in that state that one might take the effective[280] to be the one faculty alone, having no antagonist or opponent. Hence the disagreement of scholars as to whether they are three faculties of one soul or three distinct souls.[281] However, if regulation be not entrusted to the Angelic Soul, antagonism and variance become manifest, increasing momentarily until they bring about the dissolution of the organ[282] and the destruction of all three. No state is more ruinous than that implying indifference to the Lord's government[283] and the dissipation of His benefits, for this is the meaning of unrighteousness;[284] or ingratitude for His bounties and a denial of His claims, for this is referred to as infidelity;[285] or the placing of things where they do not belong,[286] for this is what injustice really is;[287] or making the superior to be subordinated,[288] the emperor a servant, and the lord a slave, for the term 'upset of creation'[289] is a reference to this. Such a notion necessitates obedience to devils, and walking in the path of the Evil One and his hosts. We take refuge therefrom with God, asking Him for protection and prosperity.

## SEVENTH SECTION

### ON GOOD AND FELICITY, OR WHAT IS INTENDED BY ARRIVING AT PERFECTION

Since every act has an end and a purpose,[290] the perfection of the human soul can likewise be for a purpose. Such purpose, as has been said in the course of the argument, is its felicity which, relative to it, is identical with its good.[291] Thus, it may be more appropriate to make reference to a knowledge of the nature[59] of good and felicity, so that from awareness thereof, a yearning may arise in the deficient, inciting it to seek perfection: in the seeker, such nascent yearning may thus become dominant; in the perfect, joy and exultation at accomplishing the desired end may be increased.

The Philosopher Aristotle opened his book on ethics in this way, and truly the right view of the matter was the one taken by him: for the beginning of reflection is the end of action, and the end of reflection is the beginning of action,[292] as is borne out in all crafts. Thus, a carpenter, so long as he does not first conceive the use of a couch, will employ no thought on how to construct it; and so long as he fails to bring the mode of completion wholly within his fantasy,[134] he will not begin work upon it; finally, so long as the work is not completed, the use of the couch (which was the original thought) is not realized. Likewise, before the intelligent being conceives good and felicity (which are the result of the soul's perfection), the thought of attaining perfection takes no hold in his mind; but before such attainment be brought about, that good and that felicity will not be his.

Master Abū 'Alī (God have mercy on him!)[293] quotes Aristotle as saying, in his book of ethics, that young men, or such persons as have the nature of young men, will gain no great benefit from this book. Then he goes on to say: 'By young men, we do not mean young in age, for age has no bearing on this matter;[294] rather do we mean those persons whose conduct is entangled with sensible appetites, and whose natures have been overcome by inclination thereto.' For my part, I would say that I introduce into a book on ethics this Section (containing a discussion of felicity and good), not in order that young men may attain thereto, but that this idea may traverse their hearing: in this way they will recognize that Man enjoys such a rank, and that they may attain to it, and some yearning may accordingly manifest itself in them. Later, if divine aid assist them,[295] they may reach that degree. On his side, he[293] (God have mercy on him!) explains, at the beginning of the Section, the difference between good and felicity. Then he transmits the opinion of each category of philosophers, and finally he sets down the teaching of the moderns and whatever is in conformity with his intelligence.[296] The gist of these ideas will be expounded (here), if God almighty will.

I say, then, that according to the Ancient Philosophers[297] Good is of two kinds, absolute and relative.[298] Absolute Good is that which is intended by the existence of existent beings, [299] the end of all ends. Relative Good refers to things, in the attainment of which is a useful end.[300] Felicity is of the same order as Good,[301] but is relative to each individual, namely its attainment by voluntary, animated[302] motion to its own perfection. This being so, the felicity of each individual is distinct from that of another, whereas Good is uniform[303] in all individuals.

Some people have applied the word 'Felicity' to the other animals, but at base such a use is metaphorical,[304] for animals attain to their perfection, not through an opinion or reason[305] proceeding from them, but by an aptitude[306] they derive from nature; it is not, therefore, real felicity. What some animals do receive, by way of agreeable foods and drinks, and coverings, and comfort and ease, is likewise not in the category of felicity, these and their like being things dependent on chance and coincidence.[307] In mankind also it is thus.

The statement that Absolute Good is one idea in which all individuals are associated is based on the following reasoning. Every motion is in order to reach a requirement,[308] and similarly every action is in order to attain a purpose; but the intelligence does not allow that one should make motions and efforts to infinity in order to grasp a desired end or a purpose, for in any act the agent must possess something conceivable;[309] otherwise, an absurdity befalls, distasteful to the intelligence. But if such a purpose be Good in itself,[310] then it is Absolute Good; if, however, it be a cause of attaining a good whose goodness is a greater good, then the former is Relative Good and the latter good Absolute Good. Now, since the skills and the reasonings of all intelligent men are directed towards such a good, therefore

Absolute Good is one idea common in all; and such an idea must necessarily be known, so that all men may confine their aspiration to the quest for it, shunning orientation towards dispersed, relative goods,[311] and safeguarding themselves from error; likewise they will not account as good that which is no good.[312] Thus they may arrive at that rank or a rank nearer thereto, if God almighty will.

*The subdivision of goods*: The divisions of Good have been regarded in various ways. Porphyry[313] relates of Aristotle that he divided goods as follows: some are Noble, others Praiseworthy, some are Good in Potency, some useful as a means to Good.[314] Of the Noble, some possess nobility as essential, while others receive their nobility from these accidentally;[315] two things are involved here, Intelligence and Wisdom. The Praiseworthy Good refers to the various sorts of virtues and the categories of fair actions. Good in Potency means adaptation to these goods.[316] The useful in the way of Good applies to things that are desired, not for themselves but on account of some other things;[317] such are power and wealth.

Taking a different standpoint: goods are either ends or non-ends;[318] and ends are either complete or incomplete.[319] The complete (end) is felicity, for when it is realized, its possessor seeks no augmentation of it. The incomplete (end) refers to such things as health or affluence, to which, when realized, none confines himself: on the contrary, other goods are necessary thereto.[320] By non-ends are understood such things as the acquisition of learning, or treatment or exercise.[321]

Again, goods are either of the soul or of the body, or external to both.[322] Or they may be differentiated as intelligible or sensible.[323] Some have firmly located goods in the Ten Categories[324] that comprehend the classes[325] of existent beings, saying that Good lies in substances, like the 'substance' of intelligence which is the Prime Originator, in whom all existent beings culminate on the road to perfection, while *it* culminates in the Majesty of Eternality (mighty be His cause!); and in 'how much?', such as proportionate quantity and complete number; and in 'how?', such as psychical and corporeal pleasures;[326] and in 'relationship', such as hegemony and friendship; in 'where?', as in a secluded place; in 'when?', like a convenient time; in 'situation', like the conformity of parts;[327] in 'possession', as in the benefits of apparel; in 'action', such as the fulfilment of an order; or in 'passivity', as in the sensation of agreeable sensibles, like a pleasant sound or a beautiful form. These are the divisions of Good, according to the philosophers.

*The Subdivision of Felicity*: The divisions of felicity have likewise been regarded in several ways. One group of the Ancient Philosophers,[328] living in the early period (such as Pythagoras, Socrates, Plato and others, who all antedated Aristotle), referred felicity to the soul, accounting the body no share or portion therein. But all schools are united in the opinion that felicity comprises four kinds, called the Kinds of Virtues.[329] These are Wisdom, Courage, Continence and Justice,[330] and the greater part of the Second Division of this Discourse will comprise an account thereof. They went on to say that the acquisition of these virtues is sufficient for the attainment of felicity, there being no need of other virtues, whether of the body or otherwise[331] Thus, if the possessor of such virtues be obscure, or poor, or defective in his members,[332] or afflicted with every disease and trial, no harm results therefrom to his felicity; save from the sickness that restrains the soul from its proper operation,[333] such as corruption of the intelligence or viciousness of mind,[334] for when they are present, the attainment of perfection becomes impossible. Accordingly, they are further agreed to view the body as an organ to the soul, and they have placed the whole reality[59] of Man in his Rational[32] Soul.

However, a group coming after Aristotle (such as the Stoics,[335] and some of his followers, and some of the Naturalists),[336] who considered the body as one of the parts of Man, divided felicity into two, a psychical and a corporeal.[337] They said that so long as psychical felicity be not joined[338] with corporeal felicity, it cannot be called complete. The goods that are external to the body, and dependent on chance and coincidence,[307] they counted in the corporeal division. However, this opinion is regarded as feeble by the critical philosophers,[339] for chance and coincidence have neither stability nor permanence, and in attaining them reflection and reason have no point of entry or scope of operation.[340] But since felicity is the noblest and finest of goods, devoid of any semblance of change or decline, and since its attainment is vested in the reason and the intelligence,[341] how should it be exposed to the meanest of things?

Aristotle examined the matter, and he observed how different sorts of men disagreed and were perplexed in the matter of felicity. Thus, the pauper sees his felicity in affluence and wealth; the sick man in health and well-being; the humble in position and exaltation; the covetous[342] in being able to indulge appetites; the irascible[343] in overcoming and in violence of assault; the lover in being possessed of the beloved; and the virtuous man in pouring forth favour. This being so, he deemed it necessary, from the standpoint of philosophy,[6] to arrange the gradations of each class in accordance with the exigency of the intelligence; for anything, in its place and in its time, is a partial felicity relative to a given individual,[344] whereas the purview of the philosopher[345] must comprehend the verification of all realities.[346] Accordingly, he classified the totality of felicity under five heads: (1) that which is dependent on bodily health, soundness of the senses and equilibrium of temperament;[347] (2) that which depends on property and auxiliaries,[348] by recourse to which one effects the spread of liberality and comfort to men of good,[349] as well as other actions necessarily meriting commendation; (3) that which depends on fair speech and good repute, so that acclaim and appreciation are promulgated among men in accordance with one's well-doing and virtue; (4) that which depends on the prospering of one's purposes and the attainment of what reason demands, in accordance with hope and will;[350] (5) that which depends on excellence of opinion[351] and soundness of reflection, on awareness of what is right in deliberation,[352] and the immunity of one's tenets from error,[353] both as regards knowledge[354] in general and matters of faith[355] in particular. Thus, to whomsoever these five divisions accrue, such a one is felicitous, perfectly and absolutely;[356] on the other hand, he is defective in the measure of his deficiency in certain classifications or certain relationships.[357]

This same philosopher Aristotle says that it is difficult for noble actions to proceed from Man without material means,[358] such as munificence or a great number of friends or good fortune. This is the reason why Wisdom,[6] to reveal its nobility, has need of the art of Kingship.[359] For this reason, too, we have said that if ever a gift or a boon reaches mankind from almighty God, sheer felicity belongs thereto; for felicity is a gift and a boon from Him (blessed and exalted be He!) in the noblest stages and the highest ranks of goods. Such is proper to the Complete Man,[360] and the incomplete, e.g. infants, have no association with him therein.

In similar fashion, philosophers have differed as to whether the greatest felicity that Man enjoys is actualized in him[361] during the days of his life, or after his death. The earlier school of the Ancient Philosophers[328] are agreed that the body has no part in felicity; they say that so long as Man's soul is joined to the body, afflicted and defiled with the turbidity of nature and corporeal filth, its needs and necessities engrossed with many things—so long will it not be absolutely felicitous. Moreover, just as it is cut off, in the completest manner, from discovering the realities of intelligibles, by the darkness of primary-matter[362] and the deficiency and shortcoming of matter itself,[363] so, when it leaves this turbidity, it will be purified of ignorance; then, by the clarity and limpidity of its substance, it will become receptive of divine illuminations, attaining the title of Complete Intelligence. Thus, for such men, true felicity may exist after death.

However, Aristotle and a group of his followers assert that it is abominable and shameful to say that an individual should be in the world, holding right opinions, assiduous in actions of good, striving to unite the sorts of virtues, perfect in himself and perfecting what is other than himself, bearing the mark of vicegerency to the Lord of the Throne, and busily improving the classes of generables—

but being, despite all this honour and merit, poor and defective; and yet such that when he dies, and these operations and actions come to naught, he becomes felicitous completely! On the contrary, they hold to the settled opinion that felicity has ascending degrees and ranks, accruing gradually in the measure of endeavour, so that when one arrives at the farthest degree, one becomes felicitous completely, even though still within the confinement of life. Moreover, when Complete Felicity has been realized, it does not perish with the dissolution of the body. Such are the statements of the Ancients[297] on this topic.

When the moderns[297] considered these two approaches, comparing them with judicious rules and intellectual canons, they pronounced as follows: Man may have a spiritual virtue,[364] by which he is conformable to the angels in their illustriousness, and a corporeal vice, by which he becomes a partner to the beasts and the cattle;[365] and, in order to acquire that which brings about the perfection of the spiritual part, he resides a short while with the corporeal part in this lower world, cultivating it, giving it order, and endeavouring to gain virtues. Then, with the spiritual part, he removes to the upper world, where he holds converse with the sublime assembly for ever and evermore. By the upper and lower world, they are not referring to a local[366] 'upper' and 'lower' in conformity with sense; rather is everything sensible lower in this regard, even though it be upper in location; and everything intelligible is upper, albeit in location it be understood as lower.

Now, so long as Man is in this world, the term 'felicity' is applied to him conditionally on his striving to unite both virtues,[367] so that he may not only gain those things useful to attaining eternal felicity, but also, amid involvement with material things, become marked and moved by the study of noble and exalted substances, searching and yearning for them. This is the first of the ranks of felicity. But when he removes to the other world, he dispenses with bodily felicity, and his felicity becomes limited to observing the sanctified beauty of the Sublimities,[368] which is True Wisdom; thus he becomes immersed in the Majesty of Might, adorned with the attributes of the Splendour of Truth. Now he has reached the second of the ranks of felicity.

The holders of the first rank are again subdivided into two ranks. In the inferior rank are those at the stage of corporealities:[369] the virtues of the hither side are abundant in them, yet their minds, from overwhelming yearning for the mysteries,[370] are constantly moved towards the other world. In the superior rank are those at the stage of spiritualities:[371] the felicity of the other side is realized in them in fact, but, from overflow of perfection, they are concerned to perfect in essence those substances which are engaged with matter, while ordering the affairs of the world in accident. At the same time, they rejoice and are happy in beholding signs of the Divine Power, in surveying waymarks of the Infinite Wisdom, and in following them in the measure of ability and capacity.

Whoever of the human species falls outside these two classes, is numbered in the band of the beasts and the predators. 'They are like cattle, and even more lost (than they)',[372] for cattle have never been exposed[373] to such a perfection, nor turned away[373] therefrom through vileness of soul and meanness of aspiration; on the contrary, every class reaches its perfection in the measure of aptitude freely received in the beginning of genesis. Even this group has had the path to perfection opened to it, being called thereto with so much encouragement and admonition, and having the means of attainment and all necessary provisions[374] presented to them; but they have been remiss in effort and endeavour; indeed, they have openly adopted[375] a preference for the opposite side, spending their days in the employment of noble faculties for base gains. Thus, the cattle have a manifest excuse for not attaining the neighbourhood of the Sanctified Spirits or reaching the noblest felicity, whereas the persons in question necessarily merit reproach and blame, remorse and regret. It is as in the parable of the sighted man and the sightless, who stray from the highway and fall into a pit; though both are associates in destruction, the sighted man is blamed and the sightless forgiven.[376]

It is evident, then, that Man's felicity, so long as he is Man, is graded in two ranks. The first rank is not free from the blemish of pangs and remorse, either on account of failure to achieve the superior degree, or because of preoccupation with natural deceptions and sensible allurements; thus, such felicity is in reality defective. But complete felicity belongs to the people of the second rank, who are devoid of these things, but adorned with the effulgence of Divine Illuminations and the outpouring of infinite operations. Whoever reaches that stage, has reached the limit of the ascending degrees of felicity: for him is no solicitude at parting from a beloved, and no regret at the cessation of a pleasure or a favour. On the contrary, all possessions and benefits and worldly goods, even his body (which is the closest of things to him), become a handicap to him, and he accounts rescue and release from them as the greatest gift. If he does administer transient material goods,[377] in some small measure, it is in conformity with the need of this bodily frame[378] to which he is attached, he having no freedom of action or choice[379] concerning its dissolution or removal. Thus nothing proceeds from him contrary to the exigency of the will and desire of the Creator[380] (mighty and exalted be He!), while the deception of nature and the contrariness of passion and appetite can have no conceivable effect on him: he suffers no grief for the loss of a beloved, no tribulation at missing a thing desired; nor does he rejoice at accomplishing an ambition, or exult over the attainment of something agreeable.

There is a clear reference to these two states in a section of the Philosopher Aristotle's book on the virtues of the soul; Abū 'Uthmān Dimashqi[381] rendered it from Greek into Arabic with the greatest possible care, and Master Abū 'Alī[293] has introduced that same section into his *Book of Purity*. In the present instance, that section has further been put into Persian, and this is it:

'The first of the ranks of virtues which are known as Felicity is this: that Man should control his will, and his quest for his own interests in this sensible[382] world, as well as the sensory[383] things relating to soul and body, and whatever is joined to the one or associated with the other. Moreover, his control of sensible[382] states should not depart from an equilibrium agreeable to those states. But in this state Man's nature is still involved with passions and appetites, except he preserve the equilibrium and avoid excess. In such a position he is closer to what he should perform than to that from which he must refrain; for his affairs are directed towards a mean, regulatory rightness in virtue,[384] not falling outside the determining of reflection,[385] albeit mingled with the control of sensibles.[386]

'The second rank is that he should employ his will and aspiration in the more excellent matter of improving the state of soul and body, not being involved with passions and appetites and having no regard to sensory[383] requirements, save for what is necessary and unavoidable. Now, Man's virtue in this category develops additional gradation, for the ranks and stations of this category are many, some being higher than others. The reasons for this multiplicity are as follows: (1) because of the variance of natures; (2) because of the variance of customs; (3) because of the discrepancy in the ascending degrees of science and knowledge and understanding; (4) because of the variance of aspirations; and (5) in conformity with the discrepancy in yearning and in bearing the toil of the quest. It has also been said that variance of chance and coincidence lie behind the transition from the last of the ranks of this type of virtue to the virtue that is divine and pure;[390] for in that rank there is no regard for the expected, and no consideration for what is to come or for severance from the past; no inclination to a distant thing or grasping what is close; no fear or terror at any state, nor infatuation or yearning for any thing; and no desire for any corporeal or psychical[302] delights. Rather is he in control, by the intelligent part,[387] of the highest ranks of virtues, such control being an aspiration towards divine things, an eagerness and a questing for them without expectation of return; that is to say, his control thereof and his questing after it are for the sake of its essence and reality, not for some other thing.

This rank too occurs variously in individual men, in accordance with yearnings and aspirations, excellence, concern,[388] questing, strength of nature and soundness of belief. The assimilation of any person to the First Cause,[389] and his imitation of Its acts, are according to the station and rank of that person in these states that we have enumerated in this Section. The last of the ranks of virtue is that where Man's actions are all divine, pure.[390] Now, divine acts are Pure Good, and whenever an act is Pure Good, its agent does not perform it for any other purpose than the act itself; for Pure Good is an end sought for itself and intended for its own sake,[391] and that which is an end—particularly where such an end be highly valued—does not exist for the sake of any thing other. Therefore, Man's actions, when they all become divine and pure, proceed from the very pith and reality of his essence,[392] which is the Divine Intelligence; the other promptings of the bodily nature,[393] the accidentals of both the Bestial and the Savage Soul, and the imaginative accidentals[394] arising from both souls and from the promptings of the sensory[383] soul—all these are exorcized within him. At this point there remains to him no will or aspiration external to the act sought by him; indeed, his control of actions is without will or intention to any other thing, i.e. his purpose in any act is nothing but the essence of that act, as is the case with the act that is divine.

'Thus this state is the last of the ranks of the virtues in which Man imitates the acts of the First Principle, the Creator of All[395] (mighty and exalted be He!), i.e. in his actions he does not seek any portion or recompense or return or increase, his action itself being his purpose. His action is not for the sake of any other thing, for such a thing is other than the essence of the act and other than his essence, the essence of the act being the reality of the act, and his essence being his soul, which is the reality of the Divine Intelligence. The acts of the Creator[380] (exalted is He!) are likewise for the sake of His essence, not for something else external (thereto). So the action of man in this state is Pure Good and Pure Wisdom: its purpose is the manifestation of the act, not towards some other end which he desires should come into act. The acts proper to God almighty are in the same case,[396] for by primary intention[397] they are not directed towards something external to His essence, i.e. they are not for the sake of governing those things among which we are. If it were indeed thus, His acts would all be in the realization of external things, in the regulation of those things, in the regulation of the states of those things, and in intention towards them; thus external things would be the reasons and causes of His acts, which is abominable and repugnant: 'God is exalted above that to a great height'.[398] On the other hand, His concern[388] (mighty and exalted is He!) with externals,[399] and any act requiring regulation and gradation of such things, proceeds from

Him by secondary intention;[400] but even these He does not perform for the sake of such things, but likewise for His own sanctified essence, for the virtue[401] of His essence is in His essence, and not towards things that are recipients of virtue,[402] and so on.

'Similar is the course of the man who arrives at the ultimate end[403] in such imitation as is possible to him of the Creator[380] (glory to Him exalted!). Thus his actions too, by primary intention,[397] are for the essence, which is the Divine Intelligence, and for the act itself.[404] If he does perform an act which is the cause of advantage and benefit to something other, in primary intention[397] he does not perform it for that something other, the direction towards what is other being (only) in the secondary intention; for his act, in primary intention,[397] is for the sake of the act itself,[404] i.e. virtue itself and good itself,[405] his act being Pure Virtue and Good. So, his action is neither to attract an advantage nor to repel a harm, nor is it for the sake of vainglory, or a desire for authority or love of munificence. This is the purpose of wisdom[6] and the culmination of felicity. However, Man does not arrive at this degree until he entirely sets at naught his own will (dependent as it is on external things) and all psychical accidentals;[406] nor until the random thoughts arising from those accidentals[407] become totally obliterated and lost within him; nor until his inner self becomes charged with the divine character[409] and with infinite wisdom. But such a charge can come about (only) after it be purified of natural things, becoming utterly cleansed therefrom: then it is charged with divine knowledge[410] and infinite yearning, and becomes assured in divine things. That which is realized in Man's soul and in his essence (which is Pure Intelligence)—such as the Primary Propositions,[411] also called the Primary Intellectual Knowings[412]—is confirmed; however, the conception of divine things by his intelligence and his inner perception,[413] and his being assured of them, are in a nobler manner, subtler, more evident, more open and clearer, than by the Primary Propositions,[411] which are the Primary Intellectual Knowings.'[412]

This section, so far, comprises the argument of the Philosopher[414] and in these words are contained much of advantage on this topic. But God knows best!

Now, it must be understood that persons whose concern is limited to the improvement of certain faculties rather than others, or at one time rather than another, do not receive felicity; in the same way, it is impossible to effect the mangement of cities or the regulation of households by considering the state of one group rather than another, or the improvement of their affairs at one time rather than another. The Philosopher Aristotle coined a proverb to the effect that the appearance of one swallow is no harbinger of the season of spring, nor is one temperate day evidence of the return of the temperate season itself. Similarly, the way of the seeker of felicity is to seek pleasure in what lies in the course of wisdom, taking it for his standard,[409] and turning to nothing other, but letting that course be firm and constant. He will be felicitous absolutely[415] (only) when his felicity knows no decline or removal, is safe from upset or fall, and when the revolution of circumstances and the vicissitudes of time no longer have any considerable effect thereon. The possessor of felicity, so long as he is in this world, is subject to the control of the natural beings,[416] surrounded and encircled by the heavenly bodies[417] and the stars of his good- and ill-fortune,[418] and a participant with the rest of his fellow-men in adversities and calamities, trials and misfortunes; but such circumstances do not demean or defeat him, and in bearing them, he is not afflicted with the sufferings and distress which beset others, for he is not disposed (as they are) to receiving impression or domination;[419] neither alarm nor disquietude overcome him, nor do ingratitude or impatience proceed from him. Even if he be visited and tried with misfortunes and anguish like those of Job (peace be upon him!), he does not incline from the felicitous ones' confine of felicity[420] or commit base actions. What restrains him therefrom, distinguishing him from persons not marked by such virtues, is the preservation of courage, the prerequisites of fortitude and steadfastness which have become habitual[421] to him, and the confidence in a praiseworthy end, and unconcern for worldly accidentals,[422] that have become rooted in his mind.[423]

But the other group, either from weakness of nature[424] or by the domination of cowardice over innate disposition, [425] are so affected by these impressions[426] that they disgrace themselves, in monstrous perturbation and alarm at the sensation of pain, exposing themselves to the annoyance of strangers, the compassion of friends, and the abuse of enemies. Again, if they pretend to resemble the men of felicity, outwardly employing fortitude and calm in (the face of) trouble, they are inwardly pained and disturbed. From ill-will,[427] want of knowledge,[428] and lack of confidence in a secure end, improper motions[429] proceed from them; indeed, their actions and motions resemble those of a palsied member, which, from insubordination to the organ, moves left when impelled to the right and vice versa. In just this way, any man whose soul is not disciplined,[430] cannot feel safe against transgressing the boundary of moderation,[431] and inclining towards excess,[432] on the one hand, and neglect on the other.[433]

Aristotle further said that felicity is something constant and unchanging,[434] as we have already said. But mankind is exposed to conflicting changes: thus it may happen that one who is the happiest of men, becomes afflicted with great misfortunes, as has been related cryptically of Barnāmis[435] (this being the Greek form of the name of

Job the Prophet); and if such a person should pass away in the midst of that tribulation, men do not count him felicitous. If this be so, one cannot call men felicitous so long as their state at their lives' end be not known; but such an argument is detestable.

Then Aristotle goes on to say, in answer to this doubt, that if the course of Man's life be praiseworthy, he will prefer, in any state that may befall him,[436] the most virtuous act appropriate to that state:[437] such as fortitude in a time of adversity, liberality in a situation of wealth, and resignation in days of poverty. Thus he is felicitous in all states, and his felicity does not leave him. Moreover, this being so, if a great misfortune comes upon him, he meets it with fortitude and meekness,[438] so that his conduct necessitates an increase in felicity. If it be otherwise, his felicity becomes turbid and cloudy, griefs and cares being doubled, so that he is debarred from fair actions. But when the latter do proceed from a felicitous man in such states, his brilliance and beauty are augmented; for to bear great calamities, and to make light of painful happenings, is a most excellent course of life, so long as it be not due to want of feeling or deficiency of understanding, but arises from extreme nobility of essence,[439] greatness of soul,[440] and loftiness of aspiration. He continues by saying that since the basis[441] of conduct is a procession of acts (as we have said), no felicitous man falls into wretchedness, for at no time does he commit a faulty act;[442] in the same way, the felicitous man is always blissful,[443] even though he be visited by the calamities that befell Barnāmis,[444] because no disaster can remove the felicitous man from his felicity, he following his way of life and conduct in all states. Thus far extend the words of the Philosopher.[445]

Now, since we have said that felicity is realized when its possessor partakes of a pleasure lying on the course of wisdom, it seems necessary that we should append to these basic statements[446] an account of the divisions of courses[447] and an explanation of the pleasure which the felicitous enjoy; thus this topic will be completely covered in its own manner. So we say that the courses of the various sorts of creation are, taking a simple view,[448] three, just as the ends of their acts are of three kinds. First, the Course of Pleasure, which is the end of the acts of the concupiscible soul;[449] secondly, the Course of Generosity, which is the end of the acts of the irascible soul;[450] and thirdly, the Course of Wisdom, which is the end of the acts of the intelligent soul.[451] The Course of Wisdom is the noblest and most complete of the three, including within itself both Generosity and Pleasure; but an essential, not an accidental, Generosity and Pleasure, in contradiction of the other two courses (themselves). What proceeds from the wise man is wholly willed and commendable,[452] not departing from that state. But since everyone has pleasure in seizing the object of his desire, so the pleasure of the just man may lie in justice, and that of the wise man in wisdom. Likewise, since the supreme desire[453] of the virtuous soul is the attainment of virtues, so their realization is the most pleasurable of things to it, besides being, inasmuch as it does not remove, essential; whereas the pleasure of appetite, since it is by repetition[454] the cause of pain itself, is accidental. Similarly for Generosity.

As we have said, it is the opinion of this Philosopher[445] that while the Divine Felicity is the noblest of things and its course the most pleasurable of courses, nevertheless it has need of other, external felicities in order to manifest its virtue. Otherwise, such nobility remains concealed, and (in such case) its possessor is like a virtuous man sleeping, from whom no action of his becomes manifest. But if, realizing its true nature in nobility, he be empowered to manifest its workings,[455] his pleasure becomes a complete and actual pleasure,[456] and his joy true joy, purified from adulteration and absolved from inclination to vanities and follies. In that state, the love of perfection which is rooted in his heart verges on rapture and ecstasy;[457] and he becomes ashamed to subject the Sublime Authority to the demon of the belly and the privy parts,[458] or to serve his meanest members by his noblest, or to rejoice vainly in a pleasure in which the other animals share. Such a pleasure (he realizes) is sensory,[383] exposed to decline and removal, leading (by repetition and alternation)[459] to disgust and repugnance and resulting in pain. But intellectual pleasure[460] is the contrary of this; hence it is evident that intellectual pleasure is essential, but sensory (pleasure) accidental.

But where a person has not grasped true pleasure, how should he incline thereto? Or until he understand essential supremacy,[461] whence should he be a seeker thereof? Likewise, so long as he gains no awareness of Absolute Good and Complete Virtue,[462] joy and gladness remain impossible of realization. The Ancient Philosophers[463] had an adage which they used to record in temples and places of worship,[464] to the following effect: 'The Angel to whom the world is entrusted[465] says that there are in the world a good and an evil, and there is something that is neither good nor evil. Whoever recognizes these three as he should, will find deliverance from me and rest in safety; but whoever does not recognize them, I will kill him in the direst manner: not at one time, so that he escapes me, but by slow degrees over a long period of time.' If one meditates on this saying, one is made sharply aware of the import of the foregoing questions.[466]

To come to an exposition of the pleasure of felicity: we say that pleasure is of two kinds, active and passive.[467] *Prima facie*[468] active pleasure may be compared to the pleasure of males in sexual intercourse, while the passive pleasure is like that of females. Now, passive pleasure is swift to decline, removing and altering at the onset of varying states; but active pleasure is essential nor, by, reason of its inability to be acted upon,[469] is it subject to change. Thus, animal and sensory pleasures are in reality absolutely of the same order[470] as passive pleasure, for decline has access to them, and termination and substitution occur in them;[471] indeed, those selfsame pleasures, in a given situation,[472] are pains and regarded as unpleasant. But the pleasure of felicity is contrary to this, for it is essential, not accidental; intellectual, not sensory; and divine, not bestial. Thus, it is an active pleasure. It is for this reason that philosophers have described genuine[473] pleasure as bringing its possessor from deficiency to completeness, from sickness to health, and from vice to virtue.

Now, the states of these two sorts of pleasure vary in beginning and end.[474] Initially, the sensory pleasure is close to the nature of the thing desired,[475] and yearning grows within it in accord with the ascendancy of the animal faculty; but when prolonged indulgence[476] is realized, the effect on the nature[477] shows itself, so that it sometimes happens, as the force of the innate disposition is obliterated,[478] that one deems the repugnant agreeable, and thinks the loathsome to be fair; when the end[479] is reached, however, delight is banished, and the eye of insight makes plain its ugliness and disgrace, having regard to the harmfulness of its outcome. Thus it has no ultimate state.[480]

But intellectual pleasure is contrary to this pleasure, both initially and ultimately;[481] for in the beginning the nature has an aversion to it, it being acquired (only) by fortitude and discipline, perseverance and effort; but, once realized, the revelation of its beauty and brilliance, of its nobility and virtue, becomes evident; the pleasure beyond all pleasures shows itself, and we behold its praiseworthy outcome and true ultimate end.[482] This is the reason why the sons of men, in the spring of life, have need of schooling by father and mother; and later require to correct dispositions[3] and belief, and to straighten their course,[483] by the splendour of wisdom.[484] When a man reaches this rank, provided he faithfully follows such a course[485] (inasmuch as adherence to it brings about felicity, while running counter to it inevitably causes misery), he will have been educated (in the full sense of the word).[486]

Now, it is evident that the pleasure of felicity is active; but, just as a passive pleasure has to do with taking and receiving, so an active pleasure is dependent on giving and transmitting; hence it will be seen that felicity necessarily implies liberality.[487] The fulfilment of the pleasure of felicity consists in the display of virtue and the manifestation of wisdom, just as the highest pleasure of the author of a fair hand lies in exhibiting his calligraphy, while a musician's[488] utmost pleasure derives from application to his instrument. Moreover, since the liberality of the felicitous man is concerned with the most splendid of valuables, the noblest of prizes, namely the perfection of what is other (than himself), his pleasure is able to be greater than all (other) pleasures. What is remarkable, however, is that this liberality (which is true liberality, with nobility of station and eminence of rank) has a property[489] contrary to the property of metaphorical liberality:[490] for worldly wealth and endowments[491] are impaired by spending,[492] the dissemination thereof necessarily imposing a reduction in the affluence itself[493] and the whittling away of stores and provisions; but, with true liberality, the more expenditure and dissemination there be, the more the store grows and increases, and the more assured it is against deficiency and decline. Again, the materials[494] of metaphorical liberality[490] are exposed to conflagration and submersion, to pillage and to the domination of opponents, enemies and thieves; but the materials[494] of true liberality are secure against the influence of vicissitudes,[495] the approach of calamities, and the domination of the envious and the hostile.

The situation of the pleasure of felicity being understood, the pain of misery[496] (which is its opposite, the grief of regret and remorse at the loss of such a blessing)[497] can also be grasped. Now, the philosophers have disagreed as to whether felicity is deserving of praise[498] or not. The Philosopher Aristotle observes that one cannot praise things which are at the highest level of excellence,[499] though one may praise other things through them. He cites the instance of the Creator[380] (almighty and exalted be He!) and Pure Good, which is the emanation of His Sanctified Essence;[500] for there can be praise of other things either relative to His Majesty[501] or by characterization as 'good',[502] but His essence and attributes (glory be to Him!) are exalted above praise. Thus one glorifies, but does not praise Him.[503] Since, moreover, felicity is of the order of[470] good (for it is a divine thing), it is deserving of glorification, albeit exempt from praise. Man can be praised for felicity, or for an attribute leading to felicity, as he can be praised for justice, which necessarily produces felicity. Hence, it is evident that while felicity bestows praise, it does not merit it.[504] And God knows best!

# SECOND DIVISION OF THE FIRST DISCOURSE ON ENDS:[48] COMPRISING TEN SECTIONS

## FIRST SECTION

### ON THE LIMIT AND TRUE NATURE OF THE DISPOSITION, AND SHOWING HOW ALTERATION THEREOF IS POSSIBLE

DISPOSITION is a habit of the soul,[505] necessarily effecting the easy procession of an action therefrom, without need of any reflection or deliberation.[506] In speculative philosophy,[10] it has been made clear that those psychical qualities[507] which are quick to decline are called 'states',[508] while those slow to decline are known as 'habits'. Thus, habit is one of the psychical qualities, and it is the quiddity[59] of the disposition. As for its 'whyness',[509] i.e. the reason for its existence in the soul, two things are involved: nature and use.[510] We speak of 'nature' when the basic temperament[511] of a person necessitates his being adapted to one state or another: as in the case of the man whose irascible faculty is moved for the least cause, or who is overwhelmed by fear and alarm at a slight sound reaching his ear, or at some mildly disagreeable news[512] he hears; in another case, a man will be overcome by prolonged and uninhibited[513] laughter at a slight and surprising[514] motion; or again, for the slightest cause, a man may become subject to excessive dread and anxiety. 'Use' means that a person first elects an action by deliberation and reflection, then sets about it diligently,[515] until (by repeated application to it and laborious effort) he becomes familiar therewith;[516] and once complete familiarity is achieved, it proceeds from him easily and without deliberation, eventually becoming a disposition to him.

The Ancients[517] disagreed as to whether the disposition is one of the properties of the animal soul,[518] or whether the rational soul participates in its involvement.[519] Similarly they disagreed as to whether the disposition of any individual is natural to him (i.e. incapable of decline,[520] like the heat of fire), or other than natural. Some said that certain dispositions are natural, while certain others come into being[521] from other causes, and by application become fixed like them. One school took the view that all dispositions are natural, removal from them being impossible.[522] Yet another said that no disposition was either natural or opposed to nature, Man being so created that he adopts whatever disposition he wishes, easily or with difficulty: those in accord with the demands of the temperament (such as we have mentioned in the foregoing examples) (are adopted) easily, those contrary thereto, with difficulty. The cause of any particular disposition that may prevail over the nature of any of the sorts of men was originally an act of will,[523] which by perseverance and application had become a habit. Of these three schools, the last is in the right; for it is a matter of observation that infants and youths acquire a disposition from the upbringing and companionship of people characterized by it, or from involvement and close contact[524] with their actions, even though they may earlier have been noted for a quite different disposition. The first and second schools of thought lead to nullification of the faculty of distinction and reason,[525] the abandonment of all sorts of discipline and government,[526] the abortion of religious laws and observances,[527] and the neglect by the human race of instruction and education;[528] so that each man proceeds according to the demand of his nature, with a resultant removal of order and the impossibility that the species survive. The falsity and abomination of such a proposition[529] is only too obvious.

Among the adherents of the first school was a group of philosophers known as the Stoics,[335] who maintained that all men, in primal genesis,[530] were created good by nature; but, by association with the wicked, the indulgence of appetites, want of discipline and the impediment of immorality,[531] they reach a point where they do not reflect on the fairness or foulness of things, seeking to attain their desire and their lust in any way they can, until by degrees an evil nature takes hold in them.

Another group, earlier than they, asserted that Man was created of inferior clay and impure natures,[532] the turbidities[533] of the world having been converted into the matter of him. For this reason, evil is rooted in men at the foundation of their nature, but they are receptive of good by means of instruction and discipline; however, some of them, being extremely evil, are not susceptible of reform by discipline, while others, who are reformable, grow good if they frequent the virtuous and the good from their earliest existence;[534] otherwise, they retain their original nature.

Galen's opinion is that some men are by nature good, some bad by nature, and some in an intermediary position between the two, apt to incline either way. He refuted the first two schools of thought (mentioned above) by the following argument: if all men are good at genesis, passing to evil (only) by instruction, then they necessarily derive evil either from themselves or from other than themselves. If it be from themselves, then there is a faculty in them necessitating evil; hence they have not been good by nature, but evil. Moreover, if there be within them both the faculty of evil and the faculty of good, but the evil faculty prevailing over the good, then it again necessarily follows that they are evil by nature. If, on the other hand, they derive evil from other than themselves, then those 'good men' are by nature evil men. Thus, all men are not by nature good. He uses the selfsame proof to refute the argument that all men are by nature evil. Having refuted these two schools of thought, he affirms his own view thus: 'We can see, by the evidence of our own eyes, that the nature of some men necessarily implies good, from which they do not remove in any way, and they are few; the nature of others necessarily implies evil, such not being in any way receptive of good, and they are many; and the rest are in the middle, becoming good if they associate with good men, and evil from mixing with the evil.'

The philosopher Aristotle says, in the *Book of Ethics* and the *Book of Categories*,[535] that evil men become good by instruction and discipline; and although such a judgment is not of universal application,[536] nevertheless it cannot be doubted that some impression is made by repeated admonition and advice, continual correction and discipline, and chastisement by accepted punitive measures. Thus there is a class of men who receive the humane arts[537] with all alacrity, the effect of virtue becoming evident in them without delay or retardment; and there is another class, whose motion towards the assumption of virtues and discipline and rectitude is somewhat slower.

The argument of the modern philosophers,[538] that no disposition is natural, runs as follows: every disposition is receptive of change, but whatever is receptive of change is not natural, therefore no disposition is natural. Such a syllogism is valid in the form of the second mode of the first figure.[539] The minor premiss[540] (as has been demonstrated) is manifest from ocular evidence, from the necessity of disciplining young men, and from the excellence of the religious ordinances, which are Almighty God's governance.[541] The major premiss[542] is also self-evident,[543] for everyone necessarily knows that the nature of water, requiring it to tend downwards, cannot be changed so that it should tend in any other direction; likewise, the nature of fire cannot be diverted from burning, and similarly with other natural things. Moreover, if a disposition were natural, intelligent men would not issue instructions for the disciplining of infants, or for the correction of youths, and the righting of their dispositions and uses; nor would such instructions be acted upon.

If one reflects attentively on the states and dispositions of infants, particularly such infants as are carried from place to place in servitude,[544] this notion will be clearly understood. An infant, in his earliest days,[545] openly displays the requirement of his nature: his faculty of reason[546] is not sufficiently developed for him to conceal his states and his will by guile and deception, as do other classes, capable of distinction and reflection,[547] who carefully hide what they account foul, revealing (only) what they regard as fair. Moreover, in the case of infants, it is evident that some are adapted to the reception of the humane arts [537] with ease, but others with difficulty; while the nature of one group is (even) averse to their reception, so that the requirements of their temperaments (whether it be shame or impudence, generosity or meanness, harshness or delicacy, and so on through the rest of the states) proceed from them (without restraint). Again, some are easily led to receive the opposites of these states, while some are difficult to lead; one group has the possibility of reception, some have not; so that ultimately some emerge as good, one group as evil, and a (large) body as intermediate.

While it is true that the states of dispositions are alike,[548] yet, just as no form is similar[549] to another form, so no disposition is found congruous[550] with another. If discipline and government be neglected, each man's rein being placed in the hand of his nature, he will be left in the state required by his temperament fundamentally,[551] or by whatever may have occurred accidentally:[552] some in the bond of irascibility, some in the snare of appetite, one group a prisoner to greed,[553] and another body afflicted with pride.[554] However, the First Tutor,[555] to the whole community, is the Divine Edict in general;[556] while the Second Tutor,[557] to the possessors of distinction and the whole minds among them,[558] is Philosophy[6] in particular. So, by these degrees, they may arrive at the ascending ranks of perfection. Accordingly, it is incumbent on both mother and father to bring their children first of all into bondage to the Divine Edict,[556] and to reform their uses by various sorts of governance and discipline.[559] In the case of those deserving of blows and reproaches, they should recognize the required degree thereof as necessary in disciplining them; and with those who can be brought to reform by fair promises of favours and comforts, let them proceed thus in their regard.[560] In sum, they should, by compulsion or free choice,[561] so hold them to praiseworthy arts[537] and approved uses as to make them habitual. When they attain perfection of the intellect, they will enjoy the fruits thereof; and they will understand, in all cogency, that the straight path and the right road are the ones to which they have been held; and if they are prepared for a greater favour, a solider felicity, with ease they will arrive thereat: if Almighty God will, He being the Guardian of Success.

## SECOND SECTION

### SHOWING HOW THE NOBLEST OF DISCIPLINES IS THAT OF THE CORRECTION OF DISPOSITIONS

The nobility of any discipline[562] limited to the reform of any existent thing is likely to be[563] in accordance with the nobility of that existent thing in itself.[564] This proposition[529] is evident and open to the intelligence of intelligent men: for the discipline of medicine, whose purpose is to reform the body of Man, is nobler than the discipline of tanning, whose purpose is to try to reform[565] the skins of dead animals. Now, since the noblest of existent things is the human species, as has been proven in the Speculative Sciences (we having made reference thereto in the Fourth Section of the First Division), the existence of this species is dependent on the power and contrivance of the Creator[566] (exalted and sanctified be He!), but the improvement [567] of its existence and the perfection of its substance are entrusted to its (own) opinion and deliberation,[568] and the regulation of its will, as we have explained.

Now, the perfection of everything lies in the procession from it, in the completest manner, of the act proper to it; and its deficiency consists in the failure of such procession from it, as we have mentioned in respect of the horse (or the sword), which, if it be not the source whence proceeds its own particular property[569] in the completest manner, is fit (like a donkey) for the transport of burdens, or (like a sheep) for slaughter. Moreover, the manifestation of the peculiar property of Man (which requires the procession from him of the acts proper to him, so that his existence may reach perfection) can be effected only by means of the discipline under discussion; and a discipline whose fruit is to perfect this world's noblest existent being will tend to be[563] the noblest of disciplines practised by the inhabitants of this world.

It must, however, be recognized that just as there is an enormous discrepancy[97] between the individual members[570] of any class of animals, and even of vegetables[571] and minerals (for an Arabian race-horse cannot be equated[572] with a lumbering pack-horse, or a fine, polished Indian sword with a soft, rusty iron one), so there is a still greater discrepancy among individual[570] human beings. Indeed, in no one species of existent things are there the same difference and divergence as in this species. When the poet said:[573]

'I have never seen the likes of men for discrepancy
'In greatness, such that a thousand are counted as one'

he thought himself to be exaggerating, but in reality he was falling short of the mark; for in the human species one individual will be found to be the basest of existent things, while another will be the noblest and most virtuous of generables. But by means of this discipline it is possible to bring the lowest rank of Man to the highest degree of ascent, in accordance with his adaptation and fitness, albeit (as has been said) all men cannot be receptive of one sort of perfection. What a noble discipline, then, may be[563] the one whereby one can make the basest of existent things into the noblest of generables!

So much would seem to suffice on this topic if prolixity is to be avoided. God is the facilitator of good works, the One who prospers pieties!

## THIRD SECTION

### IN ENUMERATION OF THE CLASSES OF VIRTUES TO WHICH THE EXCELLENCES OF DISPOSITION REFER

In Psychology[33] it has been established that the human soul has three divergent faculties, with respect to which faculties it becomes the source of different actions and operations,[574] in association with the will; and when one of these faculties prevails over the others, the latter are overcome or lost. First is the Rational Faculty, also called the Angelic Soul, which is the principle of reflection and distinction, and of the yearning to see into the realities of things.[575] Second is the Irascible Faculty, also called the Savage Soul, which is the principle of irascibility and courage, of advancing to meet perils,[146] and of yearning to rule, to rise, and to gain increased status.[576] Third comes the Appetitive Faculty, also styled the Bestial Soul, which is the principle of the appetites, of the search for nourishment, and of yearning for pleasure by way of foods and drinks and women.[145] A reference to this classification has already been made in the First Division.[577]

Now, the number of the soul's virtues will tend to be in[563] accordance with the numbers of these faculties. Thus, whenever the motion of the Rational Soul is in equilibrium in itself,[578] and its yearning is for the acquisition of certain knowledges[579] (not that which is thought to be certain, while being in reality pure ignorance), from that motion the virtue of knowledge comes into being,[580] the virtue of wisdom being a necessary consequence.[581] Again, whenever the motion of the Savage Soul is in equilibrium (it being submissive to the Intelligent Soul, content with what the latter apportions to it, with no untimely excitation or infringement of limits in its states)[582] then from that motion the virtue of mildness[583] comes into being[580] for this soul, with the virtue of courage as a necessary consequence.[581] Yet again, whenever the motion of the Bestial Soul is in equilibrium (so that it is obedient to the Intelligent Soul, limiting itself to what the latter assigns to it, and offering it no opposition in the pursuit of its own passion)[584] from that motion the virtue of continence[585] comes into being,[580] with the virtue of liberality[586] as a necessary consequence.[581]

When these three classes of virtue accrue, all three being blended harmoniously,[587] there comes into being from their compounding a homogeneous state,[588] which represents the perfection and completion of those virtues; and that is called the virtue of justice. Hence the consensus and agreement of all philosophers, both modern and ancient,[589] on the fact that the classes of virtues are four: Wisdom, Courage, Continence and Justice; and no person is deserving of praise or apt to glory or take pride, save in respect of one of these four, or in all four together. Those who boast of nobility of lineage or family greatness, moreover, are ultimately referring to the fact that some of their forefathers and ancestors were noted for these virtues; and if a man glory in superiority and mastery, or in great wealth, men of intelligence show disapproval of him.

To put the matter in other words: it has already been stated that the soul has two faculties, one being perception by essence, and the other being movement by organs.[590] Furthermore, each of these has two further subdivisions: the faculty of perception into a speculative faculty and a practical faculty; and the faculty of movement into the faculty of repulsion (i.e. the irascible) and the faculty of attraction (i.e. the appetitive). Thus, from this point of view, the faculties are four; and when the control of each over its own objects[137] is in a state of equilibrium, as is necessary and proper (without excess or shortcoming),[591] then a virtue comes into being.

Accordingly, the virtues are likewise four: from training[237] of the speculative faculty comes Wisdom; from training of the practical faculty, Justice; from training of the irascible faculty derives Courage; and from training of the appetitive faculty, Continence. Now, perfection of the practical faculty signifies that its controls, over what pertains to action, are as they should be;[592] but the acquisition of these virtues pertains to action; hence the realization of justice is dependent upon the realization of the other three virtues, as has been mentioned in the first consideration (of this problem).[593]

Here, however, a difficulty emerges. We divided Philosophy[6] into speculative and practical, and practical philosophy into three sorts, one of them including the fourfold virtues among which is Wisdom; thus Wisdom is itself one of the parts of Wisdom.[594] But this is a false division.[595] The solution of this difficulty is as follows: just as action is connected with speculation (for which reason, in the division of the sciences, that part confined to knowledge of things whose existence depends on the control of the knower is characterized as the practical part), so speculation is connected with action; for speculation is one of those things whose existence depends on the control of the knower. Thus, from this standpoint, the acquisition of fundamental wisdom becomes one of the parts of practical philosophy, so that as Justice comes from Wisdom, so Wisdom comes from Justice. Or (one may say) that what is meant by 'wisdom' here is the use of the Practical Intelligence in the proper manner,[596] which is also called 'practical philosophy'. By considering the matter in different ways, confusion over the division disappears and doubt is removed.

Now, each one of these virtues necessarily entitles its possessor to praise, provided that it pass from him to other than himself; while the effect of that virtue is in his essence alone,[597] not communicating to other than himself, it does not necessarily entitle to praise. For example, in the case of a possessor of liberality, where his liberality does not pass from him to another, he is called a spendthrift,[598] not a liberal man; where a possessor of courage is in like case, he is called jealous,[599] not courageous; while the possessor of wisdom is called perspicacious,[600] not wise. But where the virtue becomes public, the effect of its good communicating to others, it obviously becomes a cause of fear or hope to others: so, liberality is a cause of hope, and courage a cause of fear, but (only) in this world, for these two virtues pertain to the animal, perishable soul. But knowledge[601] is a cause of both hope and fear, equally in this world and in the next, this virtue pertaining to the angelic, enduring soul; and when both hope and awe[602] (the cause of authority and respect)[603] are realized, praise becomes necessary.

These virtues have further been defined as follows:[604] 'Wisdom' means realizing the knowledge[605] of whatever tends towards existence;[606] but since existent things are either divine or human, wisdom is of two kinds, 'knowable' and 'do-able',[607] i.e. speculative and practical. 'Courage' signifies that the irascible soul should submit to the rational soul, so as not to become agitated in perilous affairs; and it should proceed in accordance with the latter's opinion,[608] so that the action it performs becomes fair, and the fortitude[609] it displays, praiseworthy. 'Continence' signifies that the faculty of appetite is obedient to the rational soul, its controls being in accordance with the exigency of the latter's opinion;[608] moreover, the operation of freedom[610] should be apparent in it, and it should be quit of bondage to the soul's passion[611] and of servitude to pleasures. 'Justice' signifies that all these faculties are in accord with each other, subordinate to the distinguishing faculty,[612] so that the conflict of passions and the opposite attractions[613] of the faculties cannot precipitate its possessor into the whirlpool of perplexity; and the operation of equity and impartiality[614] should be apparent in it. God it is, who prospers and assists!

## FOURTH SECTION

### ON THE SPECIES[50] SUBSUMED UNDER THE CLASSES OF VIRTUES

Below each of these four classes are innumerable species, of which we shall mention the better known.

The species subsumed under the class of Wisdom are seven: quick-wittedness, speed of understanding, clarity of mind, ease of learning, excellence of intellection, retention, and recall.[615] Quick-wittedness obtains when, from much concern with conclusive premisses,[616] the speedy production of propositions[617] and the easy derivation of conclusions[618] become habitual, comparable to the flashing of lightning. Speed of understanding applies when the movement from necessitating causes to consequences[619] has become habitual to the soul, so that there is no need therein for undue delay.[620] Clarity of mind signifies that the soul realizes an aptitude for extracting the desired result[621] without being befallen by any agitation or confusion. Ease of learning means that the soul acquires a sharpness of vision,[622] so as to direct itself wholly towards the desired object without the hindrance of random thoughts.[623] Excellence of intellection obtains when, in the examination and exploration of any reality, the proper limit and quantity is observed, so that there is no neglect of the internal and no regard for the external. Retention signifies a sound hold and grasp on those forms which the intelligence or the estimation have elucidated and elicited by the faculty of reflection or imagination.[624] Finally, recall applies when, by virtue of acquired habit, the conserved forms can be contemplated[625] by the soul, easily and at any time it desires.

The species subsumed under the class of Courage are eleven: greatness of soul, bravery, high-mindedness, perseverance, mildness, calmness, vigour, long-suffering, humility, sense of honour, and compassion.[626] Greatness of soul denotes that the soul does not regard favour or contempt, paying no heed to prosperity or the lack thereof, but showing itself able to bear both the agreeable and the unpleasant. Bravery implies the soul's confidence in its own perseverance, so that in a situation of fear no distress can touch it, nor do disordered motions[627] proceed from it. High-mindedness signifies that the soul, in quest of fair repute, has no eye for this world's felicity or misery, neither rejoicing thereat nor grieving, so much so that it fears not even the terror of death. Perseverance means that there is firmly established in the soul the power to resist sufferings and adversities, so that it is not broken when such things befall it.[628] Mildness obtains when the soul is assured that anger cannot easily move it, and that it will not lapse into tumult if something detestable overtakes it. Calmness applies when the soul, in hostilities or in wars necessary for the preservation of honour or the defence of the religious law,[629] displays no frivolity or levity; this is also known as 'un-giddiness'.[630] Vigour denotes that the soul is eager to win great matters in expectation of fair repute. Long-suffering signifies that the soul wears out the bodily organs by using them to acquire those things which are approved. Humility means that it assigns itself no merit over those lower in station. A sense of honour implies that no light attitude is taken towards the preservation of the community or of personal dignity[631] from such things as it is necessary to preserve them from. Compassion obtains when the soul is affected by observing the sufferings of its fellows, without any disturbance arising in its actions.

The species subsumed under the class of Continence are twelve: shame, meekness, right guidance, peaceableness, tranquility, fortitude, contentment, gravity, moderation, order, freedom and liberality.[632] Shame denotes the inhibition of the soul, when apprehensive[633] of committing foulness, in order to avoid meriting reproof. Meekness signifies the soul's supererogatory subordination to whatever may arise,[634] and this is also called mildness.[635] Right guidance prevails when there comes upon the soul a sincere desire[636] to perfect itself by praiseworthy stratagems.[637] Peaceableness means that the soul practises persuasion,[638] when there is dispute between varying opinions and divergent states, acting from capacity and habit,[639] unapproachable by disturbance. Tranquillity signifies that the soul is still when appetite is in motion, holder of its own halter. Fortitude applies when the soul resists passion, so that no subservience to foul pleasures proceeds therefrom. Contentment implies that the soul easily assumes[640] such matters as eating, drinking and dressing, being satisfied with whatever fills a gap[641] in any category that may arise. Gravity signifies that the soul, when aroused, takes a calm attitude towards desired objects, so that no immoderation[642] proceeds from it in hastiness; on condition, however, that the desired object be not lost to it. Moderation obtains when the soul adheres to good actions and approved deeds, admitting therein no shortcoming or slackness. Order means that it becomes habitual for the soul to preserve the disposal and arrangement of affairs in accordance with necessity and best interests.[643] Freedom signifies that the soul is empowered to acquire wealth[644] in fair ways, to spend it in approved fashion, and (also) to abstain from acquiring wealth by reprehensible methods. Liberality means that it finds the disbursement of moneys[645] and other gains easy and simple, so that (in proper manner and measure)[591] it may bring them to the place of deserving.[646]

Now Liberality is a species subsuming many (sub-) species, some of which may be detailed as follows. The species of virtues subsumed under the class of Liberality are eight: generosity, preference, forgiveness, manliness, attainment, charity, supererogation, and lenity.[647] Generosity means that the soul finds it easy to disburse great wealth on causes of general benefit and high value, as demanded by best interest. Preference signifies that it is easy for the soul to rise above every requirement proper to it,[648] expending it (instead) on one whose deserving thereof is clearly established. Forgiveness applies when it is easy for the soul to give up (both) retribution for evil and the quest of reward for good, albeit power and capacity[649] thereto be available. Manliness means that the soul has a sincere desire[636] to deck itself with the ornament of beneficence,[650] devoting thereto whatever is necessary, and even more. Attainment signifies the soul's delight in adhering to approved actions and persisting in praiseworthy conduct. Charity is assistance to colleagues,[651] friends and deserving persons in their daily life, allowing them to participate with one in sustenance and property.[652] Supererogation implies the cheerful expending of a modicum of certain things without the necessary obligation to do so.[653] Lenity is the voluntary leaving of a modicum of certain things, (also) without the necessary obligation to do so.

The species subsumed under the class of Justice are twelve: sincerity, amity, fidelity, concern, care of kin, requital, good fellowship, fair judgment, affection, acceptance, reliance, and devotion.[654] Sincerity is a sincere love, impelling one to concern oneself with all means of relieving a friend,[655] and to bestow on him whatever is possible. Amity prevails when the opinions and beliefs of a group coincide, in mutal assistance for the regulation of daily life. Fidelity signifies that one does not count allowable any deviation[656] from adherence to the path of charity and aid. Concern implies apprehension that an unpleasant situation may befall a person, and the concentration of one's purpose on the removal thereof. Care of kin demands that one allow one's relatives and connections a share in worldly goods. Requital is to meet a kindness done to one with the like thereof, or something more, and an offence with something less. Good fellowship prevails when one gives and takes equitably in transactions so as to be in accord with the natural inclinations[657] of others. Fair judgment means that the claims of others, when discharged by way of recompense, [658] should be void of favour grudged or regret.[659] Affection implies a quest for the love of one's peers[660] and of virtuous men, with pleasant countenance and fair speech, and whatever else evokes this notion. Acceptance signifies acquiescence in, and a cheerful, smiling reception of,[661] any action pertaining to the Creator[380] (glory be to Him!) or to those against whom opposition is not admissible[662]—despite the fact that this be not agreeable with natural inclination.[663] Reliance means that, in matters not entrusted to human capacity and competence, and where Man's opinion and reflection[413] has no conceivable scope for control, one should not seek to increase or diminish, to expedite or delay, nor incline to the opposite of things as they are.[664] Devotion refers to cultivation of the habit of venerating and glorifying the Creator[665] (mighty and exalted is He!) and those brought close to His majesty,[666] such as angels and prophets, imams and saints (peace be upon them!); likewise to obedience and subservience to the commandments and prohibitions of those exercising the religious law;[667] similarly, it implies that one should clothe oneself in piety,[668] the completer and perfecter of this concept.

This is an enumeration of the species of virtues; and from the compounding of some with others, numberless (further) virtues may be conceived, some of which have special names, while others do not. But God is the Guardian of Success!

## FIFTH SECTION

### IN ENUMERATION OF THE OPPOSITES OF THESE CLASSES, I.E. THE VARIOUS TYPES OF VICES[51]

Since virtues are enumerated in four classes, their opposites (which are the classes of vices) might also *prima facie*[669] appear four; namely Ignorance, the opposite of Wisdom; Cowardice, the opposite of Courage; Avidity, the opposite of Continence; and Tyranny, which is the opposite of Justice.[670] But, in accordance with deep regard and ample enquiry, (it becomes apparent that) each virtue has a limit, the transgression of which, in the direction either of excess or of shortcoming, leads to a vice. Indeed, whenever a regulation delimiting a virtue is neglected despite its repute,[671] or observed notwithstanding its lack thereof, that virtue becomes a vice. Thus every virtue is, so to speak, a middle-point, with the vices corresponding to it in the position of peripheries, like centre and circle;[672] just as on the surface of a circle, one point (which is its centre) is the farthest of (all) points from the circumference;[673] while of (all) other points round about, the number of which cannot be reckoned or computed, whether on the circumference or within it, each one (on whichever side it may lie) is nearer to the circumference than (is) the centre; so virtue likewise has a delimitation, which is at the farthest extreme from vices, and deviation from that limit (to whichever direction or side it may be) necessarily causes proximation to a vice. This is what the philosophers[674] mean when they say that virtue is at the middle-point and vices on the peripheries. Therefore, this being so, there are an infinite number of vices corresponding to every virtue, for the middle-point is defined, but the peripheries are not.

Adherence to virtue is (also) like motion along a straight line, while the commission of sins resembles deviation from that line. Now, it is obvious that there can be only one straight line between two limits, whereas non-straight lines may be infinite (in number); similarly, straightness of progression on the path of virtue is only conceivable along one course, while deviation from that course is unlimited. Hence the difficulty that befalls in adhering to the path of virtues, an idea expressed in certain allusions in the (Divine) Commandments[42] to the effect that 'the Path of Almighty God is slighter than a hair and sharper than a sword';[675] for the finding[676] of a true middle-point among (an) infinite (number of) peripheries is extremely difficult,[677] but its retention after finding [678] even more so. Philosophers[674] refer to the same idea when they say: 'To strike the bull's-eye is harder than to turn aside from it, but to continue on the mark thereafter, so as not to miss it, is (even) harder and more difficult.'[679]

It must be understood that one speaks of 'middle' in two senses; on the one hand, there is that which is in itself[680] the middle between two things—like four, which is the middle-point between two and six; and it is impossible that such should deviate from centrality. Then there is that which is relatively[298] the middle, like the specific and individual equilibria of the physicians;[681] the force of the word 'middle' in the present science is in the very same case,[682] and this is the reason why the conditions for each virtue differ according to each individual, necessarily varying with the variation of actions, states, times and so on. (Moreover, corresponding to each of the virtues of each given individual[683] are (an) infinite (number of) vices, as we have said; thus, the vices of any individual cannot be limited or numbered, for which reason the motives[684] for evil are very many, while those for good are few.) But the numeration of these individual items[570] and numbers is not incumbent on the master of a discipline,[562] whose task is to give fundamental principles and rules,[685] not to calculate particulars;[686] similarly, a carpenter or a goldsmith has a rule for the conception of a door or a ring (respectively),[687] by means of which he may actualize[688] (an) infinite (number of) individual specimens[540] of this class. In each situation,[689] however, they observe what is proper to that situation, as demanded by a particular[690] material, a particular[690] size, or the estimation of any need there may be.[691] It is not necessary that they should conceive the numbers of different doors and rings that can be brought into existence, or the numbers of spoilages[692] that may occur in the course of a discipline.[562]

Now, since deviations refer to two kinds, one necessarily arising from transgressing in the direction of excess[432] and the other necessarily arising from transgressing in the direction of neglect;[433] therefore, corresponding to every virtue are two classes of vice, the virtue standing at the middle-point and the two vices at two extremes. But it has already been explained that the classes of virtues are four; hence the classes of vices are eight. Two correspond to Wisdom, namely Ingenuity and Foolishness; two correspond to Courage, namely Foolhardiness and Cowardice; two to Continence, namely Greed and Sluggishness of Appetite; and two Correspond to Justice, namely Injustice and the Suffering of Wrong.[693]

Ingenuity, which is in the direction of excess, is the use of the reflective faculty on what is not obligatory[694] or beyond the obligatory extent; it is sometimes called 'cleverness'.[695] Foolishness, which is in the direction of neglect, is the disuse[696] of this faculty, voluntarily,[697] not out of natural disposition.[698] Foolhardiness, being in the direction of excess, denotes the undertaking of something when such undertaking is not decorous.[699] Cowardice, being in the direction of neglect, represents the avoidance of something when such avoidance is not praiseworthy. Greed, which is in the direction of excess, is avidity for pleasures beyond the obligatory[694] extent. Sluggishness of Appetite, which is in the direction of neglect, is rest (by free choice,[700] not from deficiency of natural disposition)[698] from motion in quest of those necessary pleasures[701] in which one is allowed to engage by both the religious rule and the intellect.[702] Injustice, being in the direction of excess, is the acquisition of the means of livelihood in reprehensible ways. The Suffering of Wrong, being in the direction of neglect, is allowing one who seeks the means of livelihood to possess them by force and plunder,[703] even submitting abjectly to their being taken without just claim. Moreover, since the means of obtaining property and sustenance,[704] and so on, are many, the unjust man and the treacherous are always well-endowed, while the oppressed is poorly off; but the just man is in an intermediate state.

Proceeding in just the same way, one must have regard to the species[50] subsumed under the classes of virtues, so to know the two vices corresponding to each, one at the extremity of excess[432] and the other in the direction of neglect.[433] It may be that for each one of these species and types[705] a particular[690] name has not been invented in every language; but once the idea is conceived, one may dispense with the term,[706] for the term is used to arrive at ideas. However, for the sake of example we will mention a necessary minimum corresponding to a few species, so that others may make analogies thereon.[707]

Thus we say: we enumerated seven of the species of Wisdom as follows: quick-wittedness, speed of understanding, clarity of mind, ease of learning, excellence of intellection, retention, and recall.[615] Now, quick-wittedness is a middle-point between malice and stolidity,[708] the former being towards excess and the latter towards neglect; and by 'stolidity' we mean that which arises from ill-will,[709] not from lack of natural disposition.[698] Speed of understanding is a middle-point between speed of imagination (occurring as a 'snatching',[710] without firmness of understanding) and slowness become habit from delay of comprehension. Clarity of mind lies between an inflammation[711] holding back the soul from the desired object by (very) excess of amount,[711] and a darkness arising within the soul, as a result of which there is delay in eliciting conclusions[712] Ease of learning is a mid-point between a precipitateness allowing no scope for the deduction of forms,[713] and a restraint leading to frustration.[714] Excellence of intellection lies between expending reflection[715] on the perception[716] of what is excess to the intellection of the desired object on the one hand, and a failure of reflection to intellect the totality of the desired object on the other hand. Retention is a mid-point between excessive concern to grasp[717] that the grasping of which is useless;[718] and a negligence in deducing forms,[713] which leads to a turning aside from that which it is important to retain. Recall is a middle-point between an examination[719] requiring a waste of time and a blunting of the instrument (employed), and a forgetfulness that necessarily arises from carelessness of what it is incumbent[694] to observe.

In just the same way, one may speak of the species[50] relating to the other classes. It may be that some vices have a well-known name, as in the case of Impudence and Bashfulness,[720] which lie on either side of the virtue of Shame;[632] or Prodigality and Stinginess,[721] on either side of the virtue of Liberality;[632] or Arrogance and Self-Abasement,[722] as situated to the virtue of Humility;[626] or Impiety and Scrupulosity,[723] lying on either side of the virtue of Devotion.[654]

It may also be that a virtue is positive,[724] relative to the middle-point, like Liberality and Courage,[725] so that its direction of excess[432] is obscure to certain short-sighted persons, who make no distinction between such a vice and the virtue itself; thus, the more Prodigality[721] and Foolhardiness[693] they behold, the more perfect they fancy the virtue to be. In the direction of neglect,[433] however, this confusion does not arise, as with Stinginess[721] and Cowardice:[693] for this direction is negative,[726] and the divergence of the positive[724] and the negative is obvious indeed. But, with the virtue which, relative to the middle-point, is negative,[726] the opposite of this rule obtains: thus, with Humility[626] and Mildness[626], it is their direction of neglect[433] that is obscure, while there is no obscurity surrounding their direction of excess,[432] for the latter is positive.[724] With a virtue unmarked by a preponderance in any one direction,[727] like Justice,[728] both directions are clear (to see).

This is a brief exposition of the types[705] of vices; from some of them certain classes of sickness befall the soul, and an account will be given later of their causes, signs and treatments, if God Almighty will.

## SIXTH SECTION

### A DISTINCTION BETWEEN VIRTUES AND THOSE STATES THAT RESEMBLE VIRTUES

Earlier, in the chapter confined to an exposition of Good and Felicity,[729] we recalled that the necessary causes[730] of Felicity signify the perfection of defective faculties;[731] and we explained that the perfection of the faculties proceeds by acquisition of the Fourfold Virtues. Thus, the necessary causes of Felicity are the Four Classes of Virtues and the species[50] subsumed under them; and the felicitous man is he whose essence unites these attributes.[732] Now, since one class of these Virtues depends on the Speculative Faculty,[733] namely Wisdom,[6] while the three remaining classes depend on the Practical;[734] therefore, the scene of the operations[735] of Wisdom is the Rational[32] Soul, while that of the operations of the three remaining is the Body. Moreover, since actions proceed from men resembling the actions of the virtuous, and the necessity arises to distinguish between virtue and what is not virtue, by a knowledge of the true nature[736] of each action, and a distinction between that which has virtue for a principle,[737] and that which has another state for its principle, not virtue; therefore, in this Section, we propose to expound this idea at length.

Now, in the field of Philosophy[6] there is a group who collect and retain the problems of the sciences, producing in the course of dialogue and dispute an exposition of every point of those truths they have picked up by way of imitation and appropriation,[738] in such manner that their listeners are filled with admiration, and bear witness to the ample learning and the perfect virtue of such people. But in reality self-confidence and cool certainty,[739] which are the fruit of Wisdom,[6] are not to be found in their minds,[740] the essence of their beliefs and the net result of their knowledge being (only) doubt and perplexity. Indeed, in their account[741] of the sciences they may be compared to certain animals mimicking human actions, or to children who try to imitate adults.

Thus, the operations of this group and their like are similar to the operations of the wise,[742] and since the source[743] of Wisdom[6] is the soul, awareness of this sort of imitation is somewhat rare. Similarly, the practice of continent men[744] proceeds from persons not continent in soul, like those who turn away from worldly appetites and pleasures (for various reasons): either because they expect something of the selfsame class in nature,[745] and greater in quantity, whether in this world or in the world to come; or because they have remained deprived[746] of the sensation of some of these classes, not acquiring the taste thereof and being unaware how to exercise or try[747] them, as in the case of certain dwellers in open country or mountains, in deserts or rural areas, who have largely lost contact[748] with cities. Or again, from continual indulgence and intemperance,[749] their veins and vessels[750] have become afflicted with repletion, so that fatigue and lassitude have made inroads on both sense and organ.[751] Or (such abstention may be) because of sluggishness of appetite[693] or defect of nature,[752] appearing in primal genesis[753] or as the result of an upset in the composition of the bodily structure;[378] or again, it may be because of an apprehension entertained as to the result of indulgence, such as fear of the sufferings and diseases which are the consequences of excess[432] and of persistence (in such courses); or because of any other impediment whatsoever. At any rate, the practice of continent men[744] proceeds from such people and their like without their essences being qualified by the attribute of 'continence'; for the continent man, truly speaking, is the person who observes the limit and the claim of continence, this (alone) being his incentive[754] to prefer this virtue; it is the ornament of the Appetitive Faculty (without which there can be no continuance of the individual or of the human race) that it should be adorned (solely) with this adornment, without the suggestion[755] of any other purpose, such as the attraction of a benefit or the repulsion of a harm. Having given precedence to this acquisition,[142] however, it proceeds to partake of every kind of thing desired by the appetite[756] in the measure of need, as is necessary and proper,[591] in accord with the requirement of best interest.

Likewise, the practice of liberal men proceeds from persons devoid of true liberality. Such are those who—seeking to enjoy appetites, desiring affectation,[757] eager to increase their status[758] or their proximity to the ruler, or trying to repel harm from themselves, their property, their honour, or their family[759]—show favour to people unmarked by the title of merit, e.g. evil men, or those renowned for impertinence, absurdities and all manner of buffooneries.[760] Or (sometimes) they spend in expectation of more, as is the practice of merchants and profit-seekers.[761] Thus, the reason for the expenditure of substance[762] in the likes of this class (and for the procession from them of the acts of liberal men) is that some are afflicted by a nature inclined to eagerness and avidity[94] others by one tending to boasting and affectation, while yet others have a nature adapted to labour[763] and commerce. There is also a group whose expenditure should rather be considered as prodigality,[764] and this arises from failure to appreciate the worth of money; such a state mostly befalls heirs and persons unacquainted with the toil of gain and the difficulty of accumulation, for, where wealth is concerned, income is hard to acquire, but disbursement is easy. To illustrate this idea, the philosophers[765] have cited the legend of the man who carries a heavy stone up a steep mountain and thence lets it down again; for arduous acquisition is like carrying a heavy stone up a mountain, while easy expenditure resembles letting that stone down again.

The requirement of money is a necessary one[766] for the regulation of one's daily life, and advantageous for the manifestation of wisdom[6] and virtue; but to acquire[142] it in praiseworthy ways is most difficult,[677] fair occasions of acquistion[767] being few and the pursuit of the way thither arduous for the noble,[768] albeit easy for the ignoble, who care not for the method of acquisition.[142] This is the reason why most men who wear the ornament of nobility[769] are poorly endowed with wealth,[770] and complain of chance and fortune;[771] while their opposites, who amass wealth in treacherous fashion and by disapproved methods, are open-handed and easy-living, emulated and envied by the common people.[772]

But the intelligent man, rather than the advantage and ease that will be his in return for such actions, prefers that his court should be free from reproach[773] and his honour exempt from criticism; he is on guard against the uncleanness of treacheries and larcenies, and he refrains from injustice towards equals or subordinates; he keeps aloof from anything calling for disgrace, reproof and shame, such as deceiving the inexperienced[774] or pandering to sinners,[775] giving currency to impure enjoyments among the rich and the royal,[776] and abetting them in impious and detestable practices; likewise, giving approval to villainies and shameful doings in accord with the inclination of their natures; and (finally) the gratituitous carrying of defamation, slander, calumny and detraction,[777] and all the other sorts of evil and mischief committed by seekers after wealth. Thus, he neither blames chance nor complains of the turn of fortune; nor does he envy such wealthy and favoured ones as these.

The truly liberal man is the one who does not alloy the expenditure of wealth with any other purpose beyond the fact that liberality for its own sake[778] is a fair thing; if his consideration does touch upon the advantage of another, it is accidental and by secondary intention.[779] In this way he comes to resemble the First Cause (who is Pure Beneficence)[780] and achieves true perfection.

In an exactly similar manner a practice resembling courage proceeds from certain men in whom courage is not (really) present. Such are those persons who go forward to engage in wars, and to bestride anxieties and terrors and dangers, in quest of wealth or dominion, or any other of the various species of desires impossible to enumerate; for the motive for such advances is an avid nature, not a virtuous one,[781] and fortitude and constancy in the face of such terrors come not from abundance of courage, but from an extreme of eagerness and greed.[782] Indeed, to expose the noble soul to danger, and to advance against monstrous abominations in quest of wealth or whatever may be equated with wealth[783]—this may bespeak the utmost baseness of aspiration and feebleness of nature.

It frequently happens, too, that impostors[784] contrive to resemble continent and courageous men, albeit they be the remotest of all mankind from excellence and virtue; so much can this be the case that there proceed from them (such acts as) an aversion from appetites, the endurance of punishments by the ruler,[787] whether they take the form of cuts with the lash, or the severing of limbs, or various kinds of wounds and injuries that do not heal. It may be that they attain the utmost degrees of fortitude, allowing hand or foot or ear to be cut off, or eye to be put out, or submitting to any of the various sorts of suffering, torture, mutilation, gibbeting and execution;[785] and all in order that their name and reputation may endure and spread abroad among men, their fellows and companions, who are like them in ill-will[709] and deficiency of virtue. Similarly, a man may show courage when he is on guard against the reproach of the world or of his kin,[786] or for fear of authority[787] or of falling from his station.[788] Again, there are persons who by coincidence have been victorious over their peers[789] on several occasions, and who are impelled to bring about such situations again and again by the confidence implanted in their imagination[790] from habitual repetition, and from lack of realization that the attainment has resulted from chance occurrences.[791] Yet again, lovers in quest of the beloved, from excess of desire to debauch[792] or from extreme eagerness to behold, will cast themselves into terrifying labyrinths, and prefer death to life.

The 'courage' of the lion, the elephant and other animals, albeit resembling courage, is not courage (in the true sense); for the lion is confident in his own strength and superiority, and can easily foresee his victory,[793] so that his advance is in the nature of ascendancy and power and strength, not in the nature of courage. Moreover, in most cases his quarry[794] is devoid of any instrument of resistance, so that, in relation to his prey, he may be compared to a fully-armed warrior attacking an unarmed weakling. Thus, that which is the condition for the virtue is lacking in him.[795]

The truly courageous man is the person whose wariness of committing anything foul and abominable exceeds any anxiety over the severance of life, for which reason he prefers fair dying to reprehensible living.[795] While the pleasure of courage may not be sensed in the initial stages[796] (for these, in courage, involve a fear of destruction), ultimately[797] it is so sensed, either in the mansion of this world or after one's departure therefrom; this is especially true where the soul has been expended in the defence of Truth, in the Way of the Creator (mighty and exalted is He!),[798] and for the temporal and eternal benefit of oneself and the faithful;[799] for the man caught up by such a course knows that his duration in this transient world is but for a few numbered days, with death as the inevitable end of the affair, whereas his opinion in the love of Truth and his precedence in quest of virtue are constant and direct. Hence he chooses to defend the faith and the community,[800] and to protect his honour from the enemy, thwarting the designs of the subjugator on friends and kin, as also on men of faith and action in the Way of Almighty God;[801] to flee he is ashamed, knowing that the coward, in choosing flight, seeks the perpetuation of something that will in no way endure; indeed, truly speaking, such a person is in quest of an absurdity.[802] Again, if he finds a few days' respite, his existence is made miserable and his life troubled, and he passes his days exposed to contempt and humiliation, hostility and reproach. Hence, he will prefer to expedite death, with the virtue of courage, a lasting reputation and an eternal reward, rather than to delay it with so much trial and tribulation. The words of a man universally agreed to be courageous,[803] the Commander of the Faithful 'Alī b. Abī Ṭālib (God be satisfied with him!), which proceed from pure courage—are a confirmation of this idea: 'O people! If you are not killed, you will certainly die; by Him in whose hand is the soul of Ibn Abī Ṭālib, are not a thousand sword-blows on the head a lighter matter than death upon a couch!'[804]

The disposition of a courageous man, in resisting the soul's passion and refraining from (the indulgence of) appetites, is in accordance with what has already been said. Whoever has formed a conception of the definition of courage as we have previously recorded it, will recognize that the actions we have enumerated, although similar to courage, nevertheless lie outside the (true) sense[805] thereof; it will be obvious to him that not everyone who faces up to perils,[146] and shows no anxiety before abominations, is a courageous man. Indeed, persons who have no fear of losing honour or shaming modesty, or who are unafraid of perilous visitations (such as violent earthquakes or incessant thunderbolts), or of chronic diseases or painful sicknesses, or of the loss of companions and friends, or of the waves and turbulence of the sea, when exposed to such calamities—such persons are closer to madness and impudence than to courage. Similarly, a person who, in a situation of safety and leisure, casts himself into danger by jumping from a great height by way of experiment,[806] or climbing a wall or a steep and perilous mountain, or throwing himself into a whirlpool with no skill in swimming, or exposing himself without necessity to an enraged camel, a wild ox or a swift, unschooled horse, competing in courage and demonstrating to others his measure of manliness and strength—such a person is more nearly related to vainglory and folly than to courage.

As for the actions of persons who hang themselves,[807] or take poison, or throw themselves into a pit, for fear of poverty or dread of losing a high station[788] or the endurance of something abominable, these are more fittingly attributed to cowardice than to courage; for the cause[808] of such actions is a cowardly nature, not a courageous one, inasmuch as the courageous man is long-suffering[809] and able to bear tribulations. Whatever circumstance arises,[810] an action proceeds from him appropriate to that circumstance. Accordingly, it is incumbent on all men of intelligence to venerate one marked by courage; and wisdom[6] demands that the king, or whoever directs the affairs of the faith and the realm,[811] should emulate such a person and press hard upon him,[812] recognizing his worth and distinguishing between his position and that of those who would resemble him while having no part of courage. The courageous man is a rare treasure,[813] manifestly scornful of hardship in praiseworthy causes, long-suffering of disagreeable events, and making light of matters which the vulgar account serious, such as violent death. He neither grieves over an unpleasantness impossible to retrieve, nor is he disturbed by an alarm suddenly arising; when he lapses into anger, his anger is of a necessary degree, against one deserving of vexation, and at a time that is appropriate; when he exacts revenge, he proceeds to do so according to the selfsame conditions.

The philosophers[765] have said that when a man is liable to vengeance[814] but is prevented therefrom, a dejection[815] invades his soul, which cannot conceivably be removed without an act of revenge. But when he has attained his desire, the cheerfulness which is rooted in his nature makes its return. Such vengeance, if it be in accordance with courage, is praiseworthy; otherwise, it is reprehensible. There have been many persons who have proceeded to exact vengeance from an oppressive ruler or an overwhelming opponent, so as to cast themselves thereby in the gulf of destruction, without any harm or deficiency having come to their affairs: such vengeance is a mischief[816] in its author, bringing about (only) an increase in his degradation and impotence.

Thus, it is evident that continence, liberality and justice are good only when proceeding from a wise man; likewise, the conditions therefore are fulfilled only by wisdom, which employs each species in its place, in its time, and in the measure required in accordance with best interest. So, not every 'continent' man or every 'courageous' man is wise, but every wise man is both continent and courageous.[817]

In like manner, a practice similar to justice proceeds from persons in whom justice does not exist; they manifest the actions of just men for the sake of affectation and reputation,[818] hoping to derive thereby a property or a position[788] or something (otherwise) desired; or it may be for some other purpose, such as has already been mentioned in the case of the other virtues. But the actions of such as these should not be ascribed to justice; for the truly just man is the one who begins by balancing his psychical faculties,[819] and adjusting[820] the actions and words which proceed from those faculties, so that no one dominates another; thereafter, too, he regards in the very same style whatever is external to his essence, such as transactions and favours, and so on.[821] At all times his eye is to the acquisition of the virtue of justice, not on any other purpose. The result then is that there accrues to the soul that psychical form which is demanded by total propriety,[822] so that its actions and operations are drawn into the thread of order.

In respect of the other virtues the same consideration must be observed in order to recognize their true natures from what is (only) similar thereto. God is the Inspirer of right judgment.

## SEVENTH SECTION

### SHOWING THE SUPERIORITY OF JUSTICE[52] TO OTHER VIRTUES, AND AN EXPOSITION OF ITS STATES AND DIVISIONS

As regards signification,[823] the word 'Justice' denotes the idea of equivalence;[824] but to conceive of equivalence without regard to unicity[825] is impossible. Now, inasmuch as unicity is particularized and distinguished as the remotest rank and the highest degree of superiority and perfection—the permeation of its operations from the First Principle (which is truly One)[826] throughout all numerables[827] being like the diffusion of the lights of existence from the First Cause (which is absolutely Existent)[828] throughout all existent things—so, the nearer one is to unicity the nobler one's existence. This being so, no relationship is nobler than that of equivalence, as has been established in the Science of Music;[20] and, among virtues, none is more perfect than the virtue of Justice, as is obvious in the discipline of Ethics,[829] for the true mid-point is Justice, all else being peripheral to it and taking its reference therefrom. Now, just as unicity necessarily implies superiority (indeed, is the cause of permanence and consistence in existent things), so multiplicity necessarily implies inferiority (indeed, is the cause of corruption and abortion in existent things). Equilibrium[830] is the umbra[831] of unicity, which obliterates the azimuth[832] of paucity and multiplicity, deficiency and excess (these being some divergent types), bringing it by the device[833] of unicity from the nadir of deficiency and the vice of corruption to the zenith of perfection and the virtue of permanence. Were it not for equilibrium, the circle of existence would not be complete, for the generation of the three generables[834] from the four elements[835] is dependent on equable mixings.[836]

In short, there is much to be said on this subject, and this could lead to prolixity. Rather should we proceed straight to our purpose, saying that justice and equivalence necessarily imply the ordering of diversities.[837] Now, in music any proportion that is not one of equivalence refers to a proportion of equivalence by some process or other of dissolution—otherwise, it falls outside the bounds of proportionate relationship[838] (altogether). In other matters, whenever a thing has order, in some manner or another justice is found therein; otherwise, its reference is (merely) to corruption and confusion.

This may be shown as follows. Equivalence itself is present wherever similitude[839] (which is synonymous with unicity)[840] accrues in a substance or a quantity; where similitude is lacking, it is as when one says: 'The relation of the first to the second, is as that of the second to the third, or that of the third to the fourth'. The first (of these two latter categories) is called a continuous relationship, the second a discrete relationship.[841] In the various classes of things that can be related,[842] different terms are used, such as 'numerical relationship', 'geometrical relationship', 'synthetic relationship',[843] and other relationships such as have been explained in the sciences.

The Ancients gave very great importance to the matter of proportion in eliciting the superior sciences by means thereof.

Now, when justice is considered in respect of matters necessitated by the ordering of daily life,[844] and into which the will has entry, three categories are involved; first, what pertains to the division of possessions and favours;[821] secondly, what pertains to the division of transactions and exchanges;[845] thirdly, what pertains to the division of things into which enters compulsion,[846] such as corrections and chastisements.[847]

As for the first division, one says that since the relation of this person to this favour or possession is like the relation of a person in similar rank to a favour or possession in like measure,[848] therefore this favour or possession is his right, and must be secured to him. If there be an excess or a deficiency, this must be compensated. Such a proportion is similar to the discrete.[841]

In the second division the proportion resembles at one time the discrete and at another the continuous.[841] Discrete is as when one says that the relation of this draper to this cloth is as that of this carpenter to this bench, so that there is no inequity in exchange. Continuous is as when one says that the relation of this cloth to this gold is as that of this gold to this bench, so that in the exchange of the cloth and the bench there is no inequity.[849]

In the third division a relationship obtains similar to the geometrical,[843] as when one says: the relation of this person to his rank is as the relation of another person to *his* rank; if he nullifies the equality[851] by an inequity[849] or a harm caused to the other person, he should himself be caused an inequity or a harm corresponding thereto, so that justice and equity returns to the former state.

The just man is the one who gives proportion and equivalence[850] to disproportionate and inequivalent things. For example, if a straight line is divided into two variant parts, and it is wished to bring them within the bounds of equivalence,[824] one must inevitably reduce the longer by a certain amount, adding it to the shorter, so that equality[851] results while paucity and abundance, deficiency and excess, are removed. Such a person finds it easy to apprise himself of the nature of the middle-point so as to repel the peripheries therefrom. The same applies in respect of lightness and gravity, profit and loss, and (all) the other declinations.[852] In the case of the former, if something is put onto the light and taken away from the heavy, equity results; but if they be equal, when one side is reduced it becomes light, and if the other be increased it becomes heavy. In profit and loss, if one takes less than is due one incurs a loss, but a profit if one takes more. The determiner of the middle-point in every case, so that by knowledge thereof the repulsion of (other) things may be effected in equilibrium, is the Divine Commandment.[853] Thus, in reality, the positor of equality[851] and justice[854] is the Divine Commandment, for God (exalted be mention of Him!) is the source of unicity.[855]

Now, Man is by nature a citizen,[856] whose day-to-day life would not be possible without mutual assistance, as will be more fully stated later. But mutual assistance depends on some serving others, and on a taking from some and a giving to others, so that compensation, equivalence and proportion shall not be lost.[857] Thus, when a carpenter gives his work to a dyer, and a dyer gives his to a carpenter, equity results; but it may be that a carpenter's work is more or better than a dyer's, and vice versa, so that a requirement necessarily befalls for a mediator and an adjuster—namely, money.[858] Now, money is a just mediator between men, but it is silently just,[859] and the requirement for a rationally[32] just being remains; if the adjustment between exchangers does not result by money (the silently just), aid is sought of a rationally[32] just being, who assists money so that order and adjustment in fact come about. The rational being[32] is a man, so that the requirement is for an arbitrator.[860] From this discussion, it is obvious that the preservation of justice among men cannot be effected without these three things, viz. the Divine Commandment, a human arbitrator, and money.

Aristotle said that money is a just law, 'law' in his language signifying regulation, administration, and similar notions.[861] (This is the reason why the *sharī'at* is called the Divine Law.)[853] In the *Nicomachean Ethics*[862] he says that the greatest law may be from God, that the second is of the order of the greatest,[863] while the third is money. Thus, the Law of Almighty God is an exemplar of other laws;[864] the second law is an arbitrator, who must follow the Divine Law,[853] while the third law follows the second. In the revelation of the Koran, this very same idea is to be found, when He says: 'And We sent down with them the Book and the Scale so that men might hold the balance; and We sent down iron, containing great harm and also benefits to men.'[865]

Money, which is the equalizer of diversities,[866] is required for the reason that if there were not adjustment of diversities by diverse prices, association and negotiation in the various aspects of taking and giving could not be determined and organized. When money, however, is diminished for some and increased for others, equilibrium results, and the negotiation of the dyer with the carpenter becomes equitable. This has to do with civic justice,[867] about which it has been said: The prosperity of the world lies in civic justice, but its ruination in civic tyranny.[868] It frequently happens that a little labour is equal to many (other) labours, like the sighting of a surveyor,[869] which counts for much in comparison with the toil and tribulations of the labourers; or as in the case of an army-commander's planning, which cannot be measured as against the fighting of the combatants (themselves). Corresponding to the just man is the tyrant,[870] the one who nullifies equality.[851]

In accordance with Aristotle's observations and the foregoing principles,[871] the tyrant is of three kinds. The first is the Most Monstrous Tyrant,[872] and he is the person who will not follow the Divine Law;[853] the second is the Average Tyrant,[873] who does not obey the arbitrator;[860] and the third is the Petty Tyrant,[874] the one who does not proceed in accordance with the monetary law.[875] The mischief resulting from the tyranny of this last grade consists in the seizure and plunder of properties, and in all manner of theft and treachery; but graver than these is the mischief arising from the tyranny of the other two grades.

Aristotle further said that whoever adheres to the Divine Law acts in the nature of equivalence,[876] acquiring good and felicity in just ways. The Divine Law[853] bids only to the praiseworthy, for from Almighty God proceeds only the fair; so the command of the Divine Law is to good and to things leading to felicity, while it issues prohibition against civil mischiefs.[877] Thus, it bids to courage, to the keeping of order in lines of battle, and to a combative spirit;[878] likewise to continence and the preservation of self from improprieties,[879] restraining from iniquity and slander, abuse and evil speech. In short, it urges one to virtue and withholds one from vice. The just man, moreover, practises justice first in regard to himself,[880] and then towards his associates among the citizens.[881]

Thus, he has said[882] that justice is not a part of virtue, but all virtue in its entirety, while tyranny (which is its opposite) is not a part of vice, but all vice in its entirety. However, some kinds of tyranny are more apparent than others: for example, that which takes place in respect of buying and selling, pledges and loans,[883] is more apparent to the citizens than thefts and debauchery and pandering, or the desertion of slaves and the giving of false witness,[884] for these latter are closer to injustice.[885] Some others are closer to domination,[886] as with torture in bonds and fetters, and the like.

Now, the just ruler is an arbitrator in equality,[887] removing and nullifying these mischiefs; likewise, in preserving equivalence,[824] he is the vice-gerent of the Divine Law.[888] Thus, of goods he does not award himself more than others, nor less of evils; hence the saying that 'The Vice-gerency is a Purification'.[889]

Next (Aristotle) goes on to say: The common people recognize the degree of a man's authority[890] by his reputation for nobility of person and lineage,[891] or by his being supported by great opulence. But men of reason and discernment realize that wisdom and justice make up the conditions of aptitude for such rank, for these two virtues are the instruments of true sovereignty and rule,[892] classifying every man's rank in its proper grade.[893]

The causes of every kind of harm may be limited to four. First, appetite, a consequence of which is depravity;[894] secondly, malice, a consequence of which is tyranny;[895] thirdly, error, a consequence of which is grief;[896] fourthly, anguish and perplexity associated with baseness, a consequence of which is anxiety.[897] When appetite impels a man to harm others, it is inconceivable that he should have any pleasure or preference in such harms; but he acquiesces therein when they befall accidentally in the course of endeavouring to reach the object of appetite. It may even be that he feels repugnance and pain at such harms, but the force of appetite leads him to commit what he detests. As for the malicious man,[898] who deliberately harms others, he does so by preference, deriving pleasure therefrom. Thus is the case of one carrying slanders and calumnies to unjust men,[899] so as to lessen another's well-being, without himself deriving any benefit therefrom other than the pleasure accruing to him from the other man's disagreeable situation, inasmuch as he is relieved of envy—or for some other reason.

As for error, when it becomes the cause of another's harm, it is not by way of intention or preference, nor does it necessarily give rise to pleasure;[900] rather is the intention towards another action, which action itself leads to harm, as in the case of an arrow striking someone unintentionally. Inevitably, grief and anxiety are a consequence of such a situation. As for anguish, it is the principle of an action the cause of which is external to the essence of the one associated therewith,[901] he having no preference or intention in the matter. For an example one may take the case where someone is injured, and even killed, by colliding with an unschooled animal ridden by a person who holds him in affection. Such a person (as the rider), suffering anguish,[902] is to be pitied in this incident, not blamed. But where a person, out of drunkenness or rage or jealousy, proceeds to some abominable act or other, he may not escape punishment and reproof; for the principle of such acts (i.e. the partaking of an intoxicant, or subservience to the irascible or the concupiscible faculty,[89–90] so that the procession of the abomination is a necessary consequence thereof) has lain within his will and choice.

This is an account of Justice and the cause thereof. As to its divisions into acts, we say thus:

The First Philosopher[903] divided Justice into three categories. First comes that which Man must perform in respect of what is due to Almighty God, who is the bestower of goods and the effecter of favours;[904] nay, He is the (very) cause of the existence of every grace consequent on existence (itself). Thus, justice demands that, in the measure of his ability, God's servant should follow the better path in regard to those things that lie between him and the One he serves, putting forth his utmost effort to observe the conditions of the obligation.[905] The second category concerns that which Man must perform in respect of the rights of his fellow-men, the honouring of princes, the discharge of trusts, and fair-dealing in transactions.[906] Thirdly, there is that which he must perform to discharge the claims of predecessors,[907] such as the payment of their debts, the execution of their testaments, and similar duties.

Thus far we follow the sense of the Philosopher's words.[908] The proof of his observations on the necessary obligation[905] to discharge the claims of Almighty God (magnified be His magnificence!) is as follows. The condition of justice must be apparent in the giving and taking of possessions and favours; hence, corresponding to the gifts and infinite graces of the Creator (mighty be His name!) that reach us, there must be a constant claim, to the discharge of which, in one way or another, (all) our capacity must be devoted. If someone be singled out by another for (even) a trifling favour and fail to requite it in some way, he is charged with the reproach of injustice; how, then, when he is singled out for infinite gifts and numberless graces, reinforced thereafter, successively and continuously, from moment to moment, by all the adjuncts of benefactions; and yet he, in return, will not concern himself with the thought of gratitude for grace, the discharge of what is due, or the payment of a kindness? Indeed, the course of justice demands that he confine his (whole) effort and endeavour to requital and compensation, not holding himself excused for any oversight or shortcoming. Why should he not be virtuous as the just ruler?[909] As an effect of *his* governance, roads and realms are tranquil and well-maintained; his justice is apparent and renowned in distant parts and local territories; he lets no second pass in waste or negligence, in his defence of women and the protection of the kingdom's integrity,[910] in preventing men from oppressing one another, and in facilitating the means to Man's best interest in this world and the next. All this is to the dual end that his good may encompass all subjects and subordinates, while his beneficence reaches everyone in particular, whether weak or strong; and, again, in order that he may acquire the merit of having everyone in his realm, individually, obliged to undertake some form of compensation, remissness in which would demand characterization by the stigma of injustice.

It is true that, by reason of his independence of the doings[911] of his subjects, their recompenses can consist only in sincerity of prayer, the spread of praise, the recital of virtues and glories, and the exposition of strivings and splendours; likewise, in fair thanks, disinterested affection, the free giving of obedience and counsel, and the renunciation of recalcitrance in private or in public; or, again, in the endeavour to complete his course (in the measure of capacity and the degree of ability), and in the adoption of his example in the organization of the household and the regulation of family and kindred—towards which they stand as a king towards his realm. Nevertheless, their neglecting to perform these observances or to fulfil these conditions, according to capacity and choice, is nothing but outright unfairness and inequity,[912] and divergence from the practices of justice;[913] for taking without giving falls outside the fundamental law of fair-dealing.[914] Moreover, the greater the provision of grace and the outpouring of favour, the more monstrous an injustice in return therefor; for although injustice is abominable in itself, yet some instances are more abominable than others, just as one cancellation of a grace, or one denial of a claim, may be viler than another.

Now, if it be recognized how grievous is the abomination of failing in one's requital of the claims of kings and princes,[915] as regard the free-giving of obedience, gratitude for grace, and affection and just endeavour:[916] consider, then, how reprehensible and unlawful may be oversight and negligence in fulfilling the claims of the true Possessor of Empire,[917] from whose lavishness and liberality, every hour (nay, every moment), such infinite graces and bounties reach our souls and bodies as not to be brought within the boundary of reckoning or the field of computation.

If we speak of the first grace, which is Existence, no substitute can be conceived therefor. If we speak of the composition of the physical frame or the refinement of forms[918]—why, more than 1,000 pages have been covered by the author of the *Book of Anatomy*[919] or the compiler of the *Book on the Uses of the Members*,[920] and this merely in reckoning what is accessible to feeble human conjecture, without bringing into the area of presentation one drop from the ocean (in its entirety); nor have they discharged the obligation to know (even) one point as it ought to be known, or reached the fundamental reality[921] of one minute detail. If, again, we speak of souls and faculties and habits and spirits, desiring to give an account of the support reaching our soul from the outpouring of His Intelligence and Light and Splendour and Glory and Brilliance[922] and Blessing and Benefits, we can discover no scope on that topic for either expressions or allusions; and we (must) account our tongue and power of exposition, our understanding and conjecture, impotent and defective in mastering the realities and subtleties thereof. Or let us speak of the grace of everlasting life, of eternal dominion and proximity to the Unique Presence, He having brought us into range of acquiring these and gaining them, and of possessing aptitude and merit therefor; in the result, we find only impotence and perplexity, shortcoming and bewilderment. 'Verily, by my life, only cattle are ignorant of these graces.'[923] Albeit the Creator[380] (almighty and exalted is He!) has no need of our strivings, nevertheless it were most shameful and base that we should not undertake to discharge a due or put forth an effort by means of which we may erase from ourselves the reproach of inequity and the stigma of deviation from the conditions of justice.

The Philosopher Aristotle, in his exposition of the service that servants should perform,[924] says as follows: Men disagree as to what the creature[925] should perform on behalf of the Creator[925] (exalted be He!). Some have said that one must practise fasting and formal prayer, the service of temples and shrines,[926] and propitiation by sacrifices.[927] Others have said one should confine oneself to admitting His lordship and confessing His favour and magnificence, in accordance with ability. Yet another group have said one must approach His presence by well-doing,[928] either to oneself by purification and good governance,[929] or to one's own kind by aid and wise counsel and admonition.[930] Another opinion is that one should be eager to reflect and meditate on divine things,[931] and to master such studies[932] as will bring about an increase in knowledge of the Creator[380] (praised be He!); for by means of such knowledge one may attain to perfection, and the affirmation of His unity will eventuate within the boundary of realization. Still others have said that what is due[257] to God (mighty and exalted be He!) from creatures is not one specified thing[933] to which they should apply themselves, nor is it of one type or mode;[934] rather does it vary according to the classes and ranks of men in respect of (their attainments in) the different sciences. The argument, up to this point, is related in Aristotle's words, as transmitted;[935] but no indication has been handed down of his preferring[936] one of these opinions rather than another.

A later group of philosophers[937] take the view that the service of Almighty God may be comprehended under three heads. First comes that pertaining to bodies, such as formal prayer and fasting, and standing in noble stations with regard to invocation and silent prayer.[938] Second is that which pertains to souls, such as sound convictions,[939] e.g. the affirmation of unity, magnification of the Almighty Truth, and reflection on the manner in which His liberality[940] and wisdom is diffused upon the world, and matters of like purport. The third category is that which is obligatory[257] in the associations of men, such as fair-dealing in transactions, crop-sharing agreements and marriages;[941] the discharge of trusts, the counselling of one's fellow-men, striving against the enemies of the faith,[942] and the defence of womenfolk. Of these (philosophers), a group more akin to the men of discernment,[943] have said that service of Almighty God consists in three things: true belief, correct utterance, and upright action.[944] The detailed implementation[945] of each item, at any moment of time and on any occasion, and in any connection or regard, will vary as the prophets or the jurisconsults[946] (who are the heirs of the prophets) may expound; and the mass of mankind,[947] to keep the Commandment of the Truth (glorified be His glory!), is under the obligation[257] to submit to them and to conform to their course.

It should be known that the human species, in proximity to the presence of divine things,[931] has stages and stations to the number of four. First comes the station of the people of certainty, called the Assured Ones,[948] and this is the rank of the great philosophers and the outstanding scholars;[949] second is the station of the people of well-doing, called the Well-doers,[950] and this is the rank of those who, besides perfect knowledge,[951] are adorned with the ornament of action and characterized by the virtues we have enumerated; the third station is that of the Dutiful Ones,[952] a group engaged in the reform of land and people,[953] whose endeavour is confined to perfecting created beings;[954] the fourth station is that of the people of attainment, called the Attainers and also the Sincere Ones.[955] The culmination of this rank is the stage of Union,[956] beyond which there is no conceivable station or stage for the human species.

Aptitude for these stages lies in four qualities:[957] first, eagerness and vigour in seeking; secondly, the acquisition of true sciences and sure forms of knowledge;[958] thirdly, shame at ignorance and at the deficiency of capacity[959] resulting from negligence; fourthly, assiduity in following the path of virtues in accordance with capacity. These four are called the means of conjunction with the presence of the Truth.

The means of separation from that presence, another name for which is 'anathema',[960] are likewise four. First comes a fall[961] causing evasion,[962] with contempt [963] as a necessary consequence; second is a fall demanding concealment,[964] with slight esteem[965] as a necessary consequence; thirdly, there is a fall causing rejection,[966] with hostility[967] as a necessary consequence; and fourth comes a fall causing banishment,[968] i.e. removal from the presence, with hatred[969] as a necessary consequence.

The causes of eternal torment,[970] which lead to these separations, are likewise four. First comes sloth,[971] a consequence of which is idleness and waste of life; second comes ignorance and foolishness,[972] arising from abandonment of insight[973] and failure to train the soul by education;[974] thirdly, we have the impudence[975] which is born of neglect of the soul and of barefaced shamelessness[976] in following appetites; fourth is complacence[977] about those vices which necessarily follow from persistence in abominations and from abandonment of repentance.[978] In the Revelation[979] occur the four terms 'deviation', 'impure deposit', 'veil' and 'seal',[980] which approximate in sense to that of these four causes. Each of these torments has a treatment,[981] of which summary mention will be made later, if God Almighty will.

These are the words of the philosophers[742] about service to Almighty God. Plato the Metaphysician[982] has said that when justice accrues, the light of the faculties and the parts of the soul shine upon each other; for justice necessarily produces all virtues, and the soul is thus able to discharge its special function[983] in the most excellent way possible. This state is the ultimate approximation of the human soul to Almighty God.

Plato has also said that the centrality[984] of justice is not like the centrality of other virtues, because both peripheries of justice are tyranny,[985] whereas in no other virtue do both peripheries coincide in one vice. His exposition is as follows: tyranny is both the quest for excess and the quest for deficiency, for the tyrant[870] seeks excess for himself and deficiency for others, in respect of whatever is beneficial; again, in the case of what is harmful, he seeks deficiency for himself and excess for others. But justice is equality,[851] and on the two peripheries of equality lie excess and deficiency; therefore both peripheries of justice are tyranny. Moreover, whereas each virtue, from the standpoint of centrality, requires equilibrium,[830] justice is general, comprehending[986] all equilibria.

Justice is a psychical affection,[987] from which proceeds strict adherence to the Divine Commandment;[853] for the Divine Commandment is the determiner of quantities, the specifier of positions and middle-points.[988] Thus, the dispenser[989] of justice has no manner of opposition or contrariness in nature[990] to the dispenser[989] of the Commandment; rather is his whole aspiration devoted to observing accord with the latter, assisting him and following after him,[991] for he derives the equivalence[824] from him which his nature[992] seeks. Now, the minimum equivalence between two persons is in respect of something common[993] between both, or in respect of two things; hence the elements[54] of a continuous or a discrete[841] relationship are established.

It should be understood that this psychical affection is something other than act, or knowledge, or faculty; for an act proceeds without this affection, as we have said in the case of the acts of just men proceeding from the unjust;[994] while faculty and knowledge assume a uniform[303] attachment to opposites, for knowing two opposites, or being capable of two opposites, is one thing. But every affection that is receptive of one opposite[995] is other than an affection receptive of another opposite. This notion must be kept in mind[996] in respect of all virtues and habits, for it is one of the secrets of this science.

Justice is associated with liberality[997] in respect of transactions and giving and taking, for justice is present in the acquisition of wealth on the aforementioned conditions,[998] while liberality is present in the disbursement of wealth on the same conditions. Acquisition is a taking, and is thus closer to effect;[999] but disbursement is a giving, and is thus closer to act. It is for this reason that people love the liberal man more than the just, notwithstanding the fact that the order of the universe depends more on justice than on liberality. Now, the characteristic[1000] of a virtue is to do good, not (merely) to abandon evil; and the characteristic of the love of men is that they should speak praise for lavish kindness,[1001] not for the amassing of wealth; but the liberal man amasses wealth not for wealth's sake, but in order to expend and disburse; he may appear poor,[1002] for he is acquisitive[1003]—albeit by fair means—and does not slacken in acquisition, since his attainment to his (particular) virtue is by means of wealth; but he is on guard against both waste and prodigality, niggardliness and cheeseparing. Thus, every liberal man is just, but not every just man is liberal.

Here a doubt is introduced, to which an answer has been given; and it is as follows.[1004] Since justice is a matter of free will,[1005] acquired in order to win virtue and merit praise, then injustice[985]—which is its opposite—must also be a matter of free will, acquired in order to win vice and merit blame; but it would seem improbable[1006] that a rational man[72] should choose vice and blame; thus, the existence of injustice is impossible of realization.[115] The answer is that whoever commits an act resulting in a harm becomes a tyrant towards his own soul, inasmuch as the will,[1007] though capable of benefit in the soul, prefers to choose evil and abandon the counselling of reason.

Master Abū 'Alī (God have mercy on him!)[1008] has provided another, and a better, answer than this, as follows: since man has diverse faculties, it is possible that the one may motivate an act contrary to what is required by another faculty; thus, an angry man, or one excessively given to appetite, or one who is quarrelsome in drink, freely chooses acts, without the counselling of reason, which—once indulged in—he subsequently regrets. The reason why this is so is that where the upper hand is held by the faculty demanding the act in question, that act seems fair; moreover, since that faculty has striven to subjugate the reason and to make use of it,[1009] the reason has no scope to criticize; but once the assault of that faculty dies down, the (real) abomination and corruption become apparent. As for those people characterized by the felicity of virtue, their reason is never overcome, and the procession of a fair act becomes habitual to them.

Another question is propounded, more difficult than the first, and this is as follows: favour[1010] is praiseworthy, but it has no part in justice, for justice is equivalence,[824] while favour is augmentation. We have said that justice is the uniter[1011] of virtues, and has the rank of middle-point; and, just as deficiency from the middle-point is blameworthy, so is augmentation also. Thus, favour is blameworthy, but this is a contradiction.[1012]

The answer is as follows: favour is circumspection[1013] in justice, so as to be secure from the occurrence of deficiency; but the centrality[984] of virtues cannot be according to one manner, for while generosity is a middle-point between prodigality and niggardliness, augmentation thereof is nearer to circumspection than deficiency;[1014] and while continence is a middle-point between greed and sluggishness,[1015] deficiency therein is nearer to circumspection than augmentation. Moreover, favour cannot be realized without prior observance of the conditions for justice, which first fulfils the obligation of merit[1016] and then, out of circumspection, adjoins an augmentation thereto. But if, for example, one gives all one's wealth to an undeserving man, leaving the deserving at a loss,[1017] one is not showing favour, but behaving as a spendthrift,[1018] for justice has been neglected.

Thus, it is evident that favour is justice in augmentation, while the one showing favour is a just man, circumspect in justice. His conduct is such that he gives himself less and others more of what is beneficial; and of what is harmful, he gives himself more and others less—and this in opposition to injustice.[985] It is also evident that favour is superior[1019] to justice inasmuch as it is taking justice to extreme lengths,[1020] not in the sense that it lies outside justice. The reference by the Custodian of the Law[1021] to 'justice' is a universal, not a particular,[1022] reference; for justice, which is equivalence,[824] may sometimes lie in substance, sometimes in quantity, and sometimes in quality;[1023] likewise with the other categories.[1024] This may be shown as follows: water and air are correspondent[1025] in quality, but not in quantity;[1026] if they were correspondent in quantity, the measure[1027] of both would be equal,[1028] but contention[1029] would arise in respect of quality; thus, in quality, the superior would prevail over the inferior,[1030] which would corrupt. Likewise, in the case of fire and air; if the elements were not correspondent, but could annihilate and corrupt each other, the universe would become naught in the least space of time. However, the Creator[380] (mighty and exalted is He!), by His favour and providence,[1031] has so ordained that all four should be correspondent and equal in force[155] and quality, so that they may not totally annihilate each other; but where a part falls to one side,[1032] the part surrounding it does annihilate it, so that all the ways of Wisdom[6] may become apparent.

A reference to this idea is contained in the words of the Custodian of the Religious Law[1033] (blessing and peace be upon him!) when he says: 'By justice[1034] stand the heavens and the earth'. What is intended by this is that the Law[1035] commands by universal justice that one should follow the divine course, but it does not command by universal favour, for universal favour cannot be encompassed. Justice can be encompassed inasmuch as equality[851] has a prescribed limit, whereas augmentation is unlimited, inviting to favour and instigating and urging thereto; but favour cannot be general and all-embracing, as justice is general and all-embracing.[1036] Our remark that favour is a circumspection[1013] and a going to extreme lengths[1020] does not apply to justice in a general way,[1037] for such circumspection can belong to the just man only in respect of his own portion: for example, if he becomes an arbitrator between two contestants he can show favour to neither side, since it comes ill from him to observe anything but pure justice and absolute equality.[851]

Again, when we said that justice was a psychical affection,[987] this in no way contradicts what we said to the effect that justice is a psychical virtue, for such a psychical affection is regarded in three ways: first, in relation to the essence of that affection; secondly, with respect to the one possessed of that affection; and thirdly, with respect to the person having occasion to do with that affection. With regard to the first, it is called a psychical habit; and with regard to the second, a psychical virtue; while with regard to the third, it is called justice. In all moral states[1038] and habits, these considerations must be observed.

It is incumbent upon the rational man to employ universal justice in such a way as first to apply it to his own soul, namely in the adjustment of the faculties and the perfection of habits, as we have said. If he does not adjust the faculties through justice, appetite will move him to something consonant with its own nature, but anger to something opposed thereto; so, through diverse impulses, he seeks all manner of appetite-gratifications and all sorts of favours,[1039] with the result that, from the perturbation and upheaval of these states and the counter-attraction of the faculties, all kinds of evil and harm befall. The situation is also thus wherever one postulates a multiplicity without a subduing head[1040] to order it, giving it stability and arrangement through the felicity of unity, which is the shadow[831] of God.

Aristotle has compared the man whose state is subject to the counter-attraction of the faculties, as described above, to a person being pulled on both sides so that he is split in two; or on different sides so that he is torn to pieces. But when he makes the faculty of distinction[1041]—which is the vice-gerent of God (mighty and glorified is He!)[1042]—the arbitrator[860] of the faculties within the human essence,[1043] so that it safeguards the conditions for equilibrium[830] and equality,[851] then each one attains its due, and the disorder to be expected from multiplicity is relieved. Next,[1044] when he has completed the adjustment of the soul in this way, he is obliged[694] to concern himself with the adjustment of friends and family and kin in like manner; then with the adjustment of strangers and distant persons; and finally, with the adjustment of animals, until the superiority[1045] of such a person over his fellow-men becomes apparent and his justice is fulfilled. The person who attains this limit in justice is God Almighty's friend,[1046] His vice-gerent,[1042] and the best of His creation. Corresponding to him is the worst of God's creation, the person who first does injustice[985] to himself, next to his friends and relatives, and then to the rest of mankind and the classes of animals, by neglecting chastisements.[1047] (It is obvious what sort of man this must be) for the knowledge of two opposites is one thing: thus, the best of men is the just man, and the worst of men is the unjust.[870]

One group of philosophers[742] have said that the arrangement of existent things and the ordering of generables are effected by love,[1048] and that man's compulsion to acquire the virtue of justice is due to losing the nobility[1045] of love; for[1044] if people concerned with transactions are marked by love of one another, they will deal fairly with each other, so that opposition will be removed and order result. However, since such a discussion is more appropriate to political and economic philosophy,[1049] it behoves us to rest in our exposition of the question of love. God knows best!

## EIGHTH SECTION

### IN CLASSIFICATION OF THE ACQUISITION OF VIRTUES AND THE DEGREES OF FELICITY

It is an established fact in the philosophical sciences[1050] that the principles of the various classes of motions, which are necessitated by orientation[1051] towards the species of perfections, are (ultimately reducible to) one of two things, nature or discipline.[1052]

An example of nature is the principle which moves sperm, through the degrees of classified mutations and diversified conversions, to the point where it reaches the perfection of an animal; an example of discipline is the principle which moves wood, by means of tools and instruments, to the point where it reaches the perfection of a couch. Moreover, nature takes precedence over discipline, both in coming into existence and in rank;[1053] for it proceeds from Divine Wisdom alone,[1054] whereas discipline proceeds from human desirings and willings by enlisting the assistance and participation of natural things. Thus, nature is in the position of a teacher and a master, while discipline holds the place of a student and a pupil. Again, since the perfection of any thing lies in the assimilation[1055] of that thing to its own principle, so the perfection of discipline lies in its assimilation to nature. Its assimilation to nature means that it follows nature in the advancement or the relegation of causes, in putting everything in its place, and in the observance of gradation and classification; so that the perfection towards which Divine Omnipotence[1056] has directed nature, by way of subjection,[1057] may be realized from discipline by way of regulation.[1058] However, the virtue necessary to discipline, which is to acquire such perfection in accordance with will and desire, becomes an adjunct to that perfection.[1059] For example, when men place the eggs of birds in a heat corresponding to the heat of the latter's breast, the same perfection to be expected in accordance with nature, namely the bringing forth of young birds, is brought about by this regulation;[1058] but another virtue is adjoined thereto, i.e. the emergence of many birds at the same time, such that it would seem impossible[677] that the like thereof should come into being by way of (normal) incubation.

Following these prefatory observations, we would say that since the correction of dispositions[3] and the acquisition of virtues, which we have proposed to study,[1060] form a matter of discipline, it becomes necessary in this connection to follow nature. This means that we consider in what sequence, and according to what classification, the faculties and habits came into being in the beginning of creation; and then observe that same gradation in the correction (of our dispositions).

It is a well-known fact that the first faculty to appear in infants is that of seeking nourishment and striving to obtain it: for when the infant is separated from its mother's womb, it seeks milk from her breasts without any prior study,[1061] and when its faculty increases, it makes demands by shouting and crying. Later, when its faculty of imagination[1062] becomes able to retain a likeness, it craves those things whose similitudes it has derived through the senses,[1063] such as the mother's shape, and so on. Then the irascible faculty[90] becomes evident in the child, so that he is on his guard against hurtful things, and begins to resist, and to struggle with, anything that obstructs his attainment to benefits. If he be able to carry out retaliation and defence on his own, he does so; otherwise, he seeks aid by crying and weeping, looking for help from mother and nursemaid. Still later, these faculties and longings which are the principles moving the organs, increase to the point where the operation of his most peculiar soul, namely the faculty of distinction,[1064] becomes apparent therein. The beginning thereof is a manifestation of the faculty of shame,[1065] an indication of a sense of fair and foul. Eventually, this faculty also tends to increase.

As each one of these faculties reaches a perfection possible according to the individual, he concerns himself in any way feasible with the observance of that perfection in the species. As to the first faculty, which is the principle of the attraction of what is agreeable, and the one entrusted with the nurture of the individual, when it has brought the individual (by nourishing and development) close to the perfection towards which he is directed, he becomes excited to preserve the species; hence arise a passion for mating and a longing for procreation.[1066] As for the second faculty, namely the principle of repelling whatever is repugnant, when it becomes fully able to preserve the individual, it proceeds to protect the species; thus becomes apparent a yearning for favours and all manner of ascendancy and dominion.[1067] As for the third faculty, the principle of reason and distinction,[1068] when it has found skill in the perception of individuals and particulars, it occupies itself with the intellection of species and universals,[1069] receiving the name of 'intelligence'. In this state, it becomes in very fact a recipient of the name 'humanity', and the perfection entrusted to the regulation of nature becomes complete.

Next it is the turn of discipline to regulate, so that the humanity which has achieved complete existence by means of nature may find true persistence through the agency of discipline. Thus, the seeker after virtue must follow this same usage[1070] in attaining the perfection towards which he is directed, observing, in his correction[237] of the faculties, the sequence and classification that he has derived from nature: he should begin by adjusting the faculty of appetite, next the faculty of irascibility, and finally the faculty of distinction.[1041]

If it should so chance that he has been reared in infancy on the principle of wisdom,[1071] he should give thanks for a great gift and a substantial grace, as will hereinafter be explained; for most of his vital concerns are provided for,[1072] while his motion along the path of virtue-seeking is a smooth one. But if, in his initial growth, he has been reared contrary to his own best interest, he must strive by degrees to wean his soul of bad customs and unpraiseworthy habits, not despairing at the difficulty of the way; for neglect calls for everlasting misery, while the making good of what is lost grows daily more difficult and nearer to improbability,[1073] until, when it reaches the stage of utter impossibility,[1074] nothing results but regret and lamentation. May God give us refuge from His displeasure and lead us to that which pleases Him, by His mercy!

It should be known that no one is innately created in a state of virtue,[1075] just as no creature is created a carpenter or a scribe or a craftsman: as we have said, virtue is a matter of discipline.[1076] However, it is often the case that a person is by constitution[1077] more easily receptive of virtue, having the conditions of aptitude more fully within him; but just as a student of writing or of carpentry[1078] must apply himself to the trade in question, in order that there may become fixed in his nature that affection which is the principle whereby such an act proceeds from him in a proper manner, so that in respect of that habit he is called a craftsman and referred to that trade: so, in like manner, the student of virtue must advance to the acts demanded by that virtue, in order that an affection and a habit may appear in his soul represented by his ability to cause such acts to proceed perfectly and with ease: at that moment he is marked by the brand of the virtue in question.

As has been said, in discipline one must follow nature; and the art most nearly corresponding to this discipline[1079] is the art of medicine, which is limited to making the body well, just as this discipline is limited to perfecting the soul. Thus, the way in which one should follow nature in the present discipline resembles the way in which the physician follows nature in the art of medicine. For this reason, some philosophers call this discipline 'spiritual medicine'.[1080] Moreover, just as medicine falls into two parts, one of which brings about the preservation of health, while the other effects the removal of sickness: so this science likewise has two branches, one of which brings about the preservation of virtue, while the other effects the removal of vice. And we propose, if God Almighty wills, to expound each branch with the utmost endeavour.

Following these arguments, it becomes clear that the student of virtue must first examine the state of the faculty of appetite, and then that of the faculty of irascibility, ascertaining whether either is naturally disposed in accord with the law of equilibrium or divergent therefrom.[1081] If it is in accord with the law of equilibrium, he must strive to preserve that equilibrium and to make habitual the procession therefrom of that which is fair relative to the faculty; if it be divergent from equilibrium, he must take steps first to restore it to equilibrium, and then to acquire the habit in question. When he is acquitted of the correction[237] of these two faculties, he must occupy himself with perfecting the speculative faculty,[1082] observing (due) classification therein.

When he first begins to learn, he must concern himself profoundly with that branch which keeps the mind from straying, and guides it on the way to procuring knowledge (of all sorts);[1083] next with the branch in the usages of which estimation[1084] assists reason, while perplexity and aberration[1085] have no scope therein, so that the mind gains the taste of certainty, and adherence to truth becomes a habit. Thereafter, he should restrict his investigation to knowing the concrete essences of existent things[1086] and discovering the true natures and states thereof.[1087] He should start from the principles of the sensibles[1088] and terminate his investigation at knowledge of the principles of existent things.

When he arrives at this stage, he has acquitted himself of the correction[237] of these three faculties. Next he should show zeal in preserving the articles of justice,[1089] determining works, states and transactions in accordance therewith relative to nature. If he observes this minute point also, he has become a human being in very fact, and the title of wisdom and the mark of virtue are his. If thereafter he should wish to take thought for external and bodily felicity, that is all to the good; if not, at least he has not abandoned vital concerns[1090] or busied himself with superfluities.[1091]

Felicity is of three kinds: psychical felicity, bodily felicity, and civic felicity,[1092] the last pertaining to assemblage and civilization.[1093] Psychical felicity is as has been already explained; its degrees are classified in a fivefold manner: first, the science of the Correction of Dispositions;[3] second, the science of Logic; third, the science of Mathematics; fourth, Natural Science; and fifth, Divine Science.[13] We mean by this that instruction must be given in this sequence, so that the benefit thereof may speedily accrue in both worlds.

As for bodily felicity, it has to do with those sciences which refer to the ordering of the body's state (such as the application of remedies, the preservation of health, and the science of the toilet),[1094] and which are collectively called 'Medicine'. Also included is the Science of the Stars, for advance knowledge confers advantage.[1095]

Civic felicity has to do with the sciences pertaining to the ordering of the state of the community and the realm,[1096] and the affairs of daily life and society:[1097] these may be the sciences of the religious law, such as Jurisprudence, Scholastic Theology, Tradition, Exegesis and Interpretation;[1098] or they may be exoteric[1099] sciences, like Literature, Rhetoric, Grammar, Calligraphy, Reckoning, Surveying and Accounting,[1100] and the like. The use of each is in accordance with its place; and God best knows what is right!

## NINTH SECTION

### ON PRESERVING THE HEALTH OF THE SOUL, WHICH IS BUT THE RETENTION OF VIRTUES

When the soul is good[1101] and virtuous, zealous to attain virtue and acquire felicity, and obsessed[1102] with the winning of true sciences and certain knowledge (in all its forms),[1103] its owner is obliged to take thought for those things which invoke the retention of these conditions and the maintenance of these prescriptions. Now, just as, in medicine, the rule for preserving the body's health is to use that which is wholesome to the constitution, so the rule for preserving the health of the soul is to prefer association and intercourse with such persons as are congenial and collaborative in respect of the aforementioned qualities. Nothing has a greater effect on the soul than a companion or close friend: for this reason, one must be on one's guard against the intimacy or fellowship of persons not adorned with these talents, and especially against intercourse with men of evil and defective character, such as those who have achieved notoriety for tomfoolery and impudence,[1104] or expended their aspiration on attaining (the fruits of) foul appetites or winning lewd pleasures; for the avoidance of this class is the most important condition and the thing most necessary for one who would preserve this health. Moreover, just as it is necessary to guard against intercourse with them, so it is necessary to guard against lending an ear to their tales and anecdotes, or listening to their reports and discussions and poetry-recitals and idle stories, or attending their gatherings and receptions, especially when such occasions are alloyed with the approval of the inner self and the inclination of nature;[1105] for from attending one gathering, or listening to one pleasantry, or reciting one line of poetry in such a way, so much filth and impurity attaches itself to the soul that it can be purified therefrom only by lapse of days and severe remedies. It often happens that such situations have become the occasion of corrupting men of outstanding virtue,[1106] the means of leading astray those both shrewd and learned;[1107] what, then, can one expect in the case of young men still in training or tyros seeking their way as yet?[1108]

The reason for this is that a love of bodily pleasures and a yearning for physical comforts are fixed in human nature by virtue of the defects innate to it according to its primary disposition.[1109] Moreover, if it were not for the halter of intelligence and the fetter of philosophy,[1110] the whole species would be afflicted with this calamity, and it would not come about that the virtuous moderated themselves to the necessary amount, or that the felicitous and the eminent contented themselves therewith. It should be understood, however, in the case of the intimacy of true friends or participation with congenial companions in pleasant jest, agreeable narration and acceptable good-cheer, invoking pleasure, that these are lawful and permitted[1111] so long as intelligence, not appetite, be the determinant,[1112] and that one does not eventuate from the confine of moderation to the degree of prodigality or the rank of deficiency, so as to penetrate into that against which we have enjoined being on one's guard. Gladness[1113] also, like other dispositions, has two peripheries: one is in the direction of excess,[432] and is marked by tomfoolery and impudence and lewdness;[1114] while the other (in the direction of neglect)[433] is known and deplored under the titles of dullness, gloom and severity.[1115] The middle rank, comprehending the conditions of equilibrium,[830] is celebrated for a cheerful manner, openness and good-fellowship;[1116] the entitlement to be known as 'elegant'[1117] is confined to the holder of this degree.

Among the means of preserving the health of the soul is a strict adherence to the obligations of praiseworthy acts, whether of the class of speculatives or that of actives;[1118] and this in such manner that the soul is day by day called to account for its discharge of the obligation relating to each one, infringement or oversight thereof being in no way reckoned allowable. Such a concept corresponds to bodily exercise in 'physical medicine';[1119] indeed, the physicians of the soul go to greater lengths in the importance they attach to the present exercise than do those of the body in the weight they give to the benefit of the former. This is because the soul, as it grows careless of its attention to speculation,[1120] turning aside from its reflection on realities and its immersion in ideas, inclines to foolishness and stupidity,[1121] being cut off from the material goods of the world of sanctity;[1122] and when it is stripped of the ornament of action, and grows intimate with sloth,[1123] it draws near to destruction; for such divesting and abandonment necessarily produces a shedding of the form of humanity and a reversion to the rank of beasts; and this is veritable inversion,[1124] from which we take refuge with God.

But when the novice-student[1125] acquires the habit of exercise in reflective matters and strict adherence to the fourfold sciences,[1126] and grows intimate with veracity,[1127] he makes light of the rigour of speculation[1120] and reflection;[1128] and he becomes accustomed to truth, while his nature recoils from the false, as does his ear from lying. Thus, when he draws closer to the degree of perfection, betaking himself with minute speculation[1120] to the study of philosophy,[6] he achieves mastery of that science's deposits and treasures, its secrets and abstrusenesses, and reaches the farthest degree. However, if such a student becomes, for knowledge and excellence,[1129] unique in his day, a leader among his contemporaries, he must not be prevented by conceit in his knowledge from attending to his customary obligation and (even) seeking to increase it, having a clear realization that knowledge is infinite: 'Over everyone possessed of knowledge is One Knowing'.[1130] Indeed, in rehearsing his study, he should not be neglectful (even) of that which is evident to him, but rather make it habitual by repetition and committing to memory, for the bane of knowledge is forgetfulness. Let him, too, remember at all times the words of Ḥasan of Baṣra: 'Curb these souls of yours, for they are wayward; and renew them, for they are quick to dull!'[1131] These words, with their few vocables, their extreme eloquence and their fulfilment of the conditions for effective rhetoric,[1132] contain much valuable matter.

One preserving the health of the soul must have a clear realization that he is guarding noble graces, magnificent treasures and infinite gifts: if, without lavishment of wealth or the shouldering of difficulties or the taking on of troubles, a man is marked out for such favour and grace, and then (by turning away and closing his eyes, and by slothful and neglectful courses) allows it all to go for naught, remaining naked and empty—such a one is truly deluded and deserving of reproach, destitute and deprived of right guidance and divine aid. This is more particularly so when one sees how, in quest of accidental graces and addressing themselves to metaphorical gains,[1133] men willingly burden themselves with the difficulties of long journeys, crossing fearsome deserts and traversing agitated oceans, and exposing themselves to all manner of distasteful things and causes of self-destruction, such as wild beasts and highway-robbers and so on; moreover, in most cases, though enduring such terrors, they remain disappointed and without profit, being afflicted with excessive regrets and consuming remorse such as to stop the breath and root out the spirit. Even if they attain a grasp of some part of their quests, damage from decline and removal follows after, and there can be no confidence or trust in the endurance thereof; for the materials involved are composed of external things and accidental causes,[1134] and externals have no immunity from calamities but offer access to the inroads of time.[1135] Moreover, infinite are the fear, the timidity, and the weariness of soul and mind that—even while it does endure—go to the preservation of the incidental.[1136]

If the seeker after this latter species be a prince,[1137] or one of the elect and such as are admitted to his presence,[1138] the varieties of unpleasantness and tribulation are multiplied in his case: in addition to the rivalry of opponents and the contention of the envious, whether near or far, they are compounded by the pressing requirement of plentiful materials and supplies, which are necessary both to equip servants and retinue, and to take the part of[1139] friends and enemies as well. Moreover, what with demands for more, protests, and imputations of failure and defect, proceeding from relatives and connections (of whom he can satisfy not one, let alone the whole community), he must listen to such words, in unbroken train and succession, constantly and continually, from the most select few[1140]—nay, from children and womenfolk, and even retainers and servants—that he most earnestly desires death itself, as a relief from such tribulation and suffering, and from the stirring of rage and anger, which he may not, for observance of best interests, display or assuage. Withal, he feels insecure from the jealousies and disputes of his helpers and supporters, as from the wiles and collusions of his enemies and opponents.

Again, the more numerous his subjects and his armies, the greater his concern on their account to guard their welfare and assure their means of support; for such people, having taken no trouble to fend for themselves financially,[1141] become the means of increasing his solicitude and perplexity and aversion. Such a person, though imagined by men to be wealthy and lacking in nothing,[1142] is in reality the poorest of all, inasmuch as poverty connotes need, and need is in proportion to the object of need.[1143] Thus, the more worldly materials employed to fill a man's want, the greater his poverty; and the less a man's want of worldly benefits and materials, the greater his wealth. Hence God Almighty is the Most Independent of those having no dependence,[1144] for He has no need of anything or anyone; as princes,[1145] however, are the neediest of mankind in the matter of acquisitions and possessions, so they are the poorest of mankind. The Commander of the Faithful, Abū Bakr the Veracious,[1146] said in a sermon: 'The most wretched of men, in this world and the next, are princes'; thereafter, he went on to characterize princes, saying that when a man attains the degree of kingship, Almighty God diverts his desire from that which is within his own control, so that he grows avid in quest of that which is under the control of others. Likewise are multiplied the means by which his life may terminate, and apprehension overwhelms his heart, so that he is envious of little and enraged by much. For salvation he has forebodings,[1147] and he remains at a loss to perceive the pleasure of beauty and serenity;[1148] he takes example from nothing, and relies on no one. Like a brass-coated dirham,[1149] or a deceitful mirage, he is outwardly joyous but inwardly sad. When his reign comes to its end, and the source of life[1150] is cut off, Almighty God makes minute reckoning with him,[1151] as justice demands, showing him scant pardon.[1152] 'Assuredly, kings are the ones who are deprived.' Thus run his words, and he has indeed hit the target of accuracy in describing the states of kings.[1153]

Master Abū 'Alī[1154] (God have mercy on him!) says that, among the greatest rulers of the age, he observed 'Aḍud al-Daula[1155] repeating these words and inwardly wondering at the correspondence of such notions to his own conditions. People who regard the outward states of kings, and see their ornaments and cushions and thrones and carpets and robes, their pages and slaves and deputies and chamberlains and servants and retinues, their mounts and led-horses and insignia and drums[1156]—these persons imagine that, with such pomp and circumstance, they must have unending gladness and delight, enjoyment and pleasure. I do assure you, it is not so:[1157] for, amid such states, they are heedless of the thoughts of onlookers and taken up with necessary concerns for the regulation and arrangement of their own affairs, as has already been partially explained. If a man will, he may argue from the circumstance of the property-owner and his property (small though this be) to that of the king and his empire (even though it be great); and by experiment and analogy[1158] he will take example from this notion, so that what we have said will become clear to him.

It may be that if a person attains unexpectedly to dominion or kingship, he will at first derive pleasure therefrom for a few days; but when his eye settles to observing such chattels,[1159] he later accounts them as natural as other things, and he casts his sight on things lying outside the circle of his control, becoming avid to acquire them; so much so that if, for example, he be given the world and what is in it, his (only) desire is to find another universe; or else his aspiration seeks to ascend to the quest of everlasting duration and real possession, so that all the affairs of kingship and the chattels of empire become a pestilence to him. In short, the custody of property and the rule of empire are matters of extreme difficulty—and this on account of the dissolution pertaining by nature to this world, the annihilation and dispersal consequent on the accumulation of treasures and valuables and the levying of armies and legions, and the disasters and vicissitudes that befall all the other many sorts (of possessions) and wealth. Such is the state of those who seek metaphorical graces.[1160]

As for real graces, which are to be found in the essences of the excellent and the souls of those possessed of virtues,[1161] it is impossible to conceive of parting with them on account of any calamity whatsoever, for that which is given by the Majesty of Lordship is preserved from the blemish of retraction. As the wise Sanā'ī has said:[1162]

> 'The Wheel (of Fate) takes away what it has given,
> 'But God's design remains forever.'

The Giver of these goods has so ordained, regarding the usufruct[1163] thereof, that if we do but conform, a fresh grace each moment bears fruit, until at length everlasting affluence[1164] results. If, however, we let them go to waste, we shall have acquiesced in our own misery and destruction. What deception and loss are greater than to call forward the wastage of those substances that are precious, enduring and essential,[1165] while absenting oneself in quest of those purposes that are inferior, transitory and accidental?[1166] Moreover, if after much ado such a one obtains, or still seeks, something thereof, the inevitable outcome can only be (respectively) that it is taken away before he is, or he before it.

The Philosopher Aristotle has said that one who has a sufficiency[1167] at his disposal, and is capable of living moderately,[1168] should not occupy himself with the quest of superfluity;[1169] for to that there is no end, and the seeker thereafter experiences unpleasantnesses without limit. We have ourselves frequently referred to sufficiency and moderation, saying that the true purpose thereof is to cure pangs and indispositions such as hunger and thirst, as well as to avoid falling into calamities and catastrophes; it is not to pursue pleasures, which are in reality pangs and indispositions, albeit they outwardly appear pleasurable. Indeed, the fullest pleasure is health itself, which is one of the concomitants[1170] of moderation. Thus, it is evident that in turning aside from such pleasure there are to be found both health and pleasure, while in pressing on towards it is neither pleasure nor health.

When a person does not dispose of enough to satisfy bare necessity[1171] and must therefore needs strive and seek, let him not go beyond the amount of his need. Let him rather beware of the ascendancy of greed and the hurt of inferior acquisitions;[1172] and let him observe the way of courtesy in his dealings with others,[1173] making evident that he is obliged (only) by necessity to engage in contemptible activity. Let him consider, too, the other animals, who, when their bellies are full, refrain from effort to obtain more: some kinds of animals spend their days in procuring carrion and some in procuring dung, but they are satisfied and content with the portion which falls to their lot; nor do they shun or avoid one another's foods, save for the sustenance of their opposites (as in the case of the dung-beetle and the honey-bee).

Thus, since the relationship of each animal to its particular food is as the relationship of other animals to their foods; and as each is satisfied and pleased with that amount which assures the preservation of his continued existence; so men, who need sustenance by virtue of their participation in the animal soul, should also regard foods and sustenances in the same way,[1174] not according them any more virtue or merit than they would to the residue which must be evacuated and expelled as a matter of necessity. Rather should they reckon the occupation of the intelligence in the preparation of meals, and the using up of life in the enjoyment thereof, to be as abominable as indolence and reluctance in seeking such quantity as is necessary; and it should be certainly understood that superiority of the matter taken in to that expelled,[1175] and the favourable regard shown for exertion on behalf of one rather than the other, is one of the necessary requirements of nature, and is not based on intelligence. Nature has a favoured concern with matter taken in inasmuch as it will produce therefrom the replacement of solubles;[1176] and since the matter taken in includes that which will become a part of the body, nature reckons it congenial.[1177] But the matter expelled it rejects and abhors, both because it has lost any usefulness of this sort,[1178] and also in order to evacuate the location and empty the site of replacement.[1179] If, however, the intelligence follows nature in this sense, this is of the category in which the inferior makes use of the superior—as we have several times said.[1180]

One preserving the health of the soul must not in any situation excite the faculties of concupiscence or irascibility,[1181] rather leaving the impulsion[1182] thereof to nature. This is because it frequently happens that by the recollection of a pleasure felt when gratifying an appetite, or when in a position of exalted rank, a man acquires a longing to repeat such a situation; then this longing becomes the principle of a motion, so that one must use reflection[1183] in obtaining the object of the longing,[1184] and employ the faculty of reason[1185] in relieving the needs of the animal soul,[1186] it being impossible to conceive of any other way of winning one's purpose. Such a state is similar to that of someone who excites a spirited mount or a ravening dog, and then grows concerned to devise an escape therefrom. It is obvious that only madmen would proceed to such motions. But if the intelligent man will leave the exciting of these two faculties to the constitution,[1187] the claims of nature alone will undertake to deal adequately with this matter,[1188] for they have no further need, on this score, of the assistance or aid of thought and recollection.[1189] Moreover, if at the time of excitation one determines, by careful thought and recollection,[1189] the amount to which is assigned the preservation of the body's health, and which is necessary to perpetuate the species, so that no excess need arise in use, then divine governance and the requirement of His will will have been discharged.

Likewise, such a one must keep before him a minute regard to all manner of motions and rests, words and actions, regulations and dispositions,[1190] in order that nothing contrary to the intelligent will may proceed from him by reason of customary practice.[1191] If, however, such custom occasionally gains precedence, and an action contrary to resolve[1192] arises from him, he must impose a punishment corresponding to the fault. For example, if the soul rushes upon a harmful food at a time when it is urgently necessary to abstain, he should chastise it by refraining from (all) food and imposing a fast, as he sees fit, sparing no lengths in the way of reproof and castigation and all manner of torment. Likewise, if the soul fly into an inappropriate anger, it should be disciplined by the importuning of a fool[1193] (who will humiliate its prestige), or by vows and alms-giving[1194] such as come hard to it. Philosophers relate in their writings[1195] that Euclid, the author of the *Geometry*, secretly paid the idiots of his city to reprove him publicly, whereby his soul was chastened.

If, on the other hand, one feels in the soul an inappropriate sluggishness,[1196] one should compel it to its wonted course by the labour of increased good works and the suffering of additional fatigue.[1197]

In short, let him set before himself those things which give no scope for either disorder or indulgence, in order that the soul may renounce opposition to the intelligence, not accounting transgression of its prescription as allowable. At all times he should be circumspect as to involvement with vices or aid to the vicious. Nor let him account minor wickednesses[1198] as insignificant or seek indulgence in committing them, for such an attitude gradually inspires to the commission of grave sins.

If a person, in earliest youth, acquires the habit of restraining his soul from the gratification of appetites, exercising self-control[1199] when assailed by anger, and guarding his tongue and showing forbearance with his colleagues:[1200] in such a case, it will not come hard to him to persevere in such manners.[1201] Thus, retainers afflicted with the service of fools[1202] become hardened to folly and abuse and disregard; so easy does it become for them to listen to all sorts of abominations that they are not affected thereby. Indeed, it sometimes happens that, in response to such utterances, there proceed from them unaffected smiles;[1203] and they meet them with cheerfulness and jocularity, albeit they have not heretofore reckoned forbearance allowable in such circumstances, or recoiled from retaliation in speech or vengeance by retort. In like case is the situation of one who becomes intimate with virtue and avoids the society and conversation of fools.

A man should, moreover, acquire support and provision[1204] by equipping himself with long-suffering[609] and self-control[1199] in anticipation of the motion of concupiscence and anger; in this he follows the example of prudent princes, who prepare to resist their enemies, with all manner of engines and by the fortification of strongholds, before the latter attack, in a period of leisure while it is possible to give play to reflection.[1183]

He who would preserve the health of the soul must seek out his own faults with the utmost thoroughness. Nor should he confine himself to this alone, for (as the wise Galen says, in the book he composed to introduce men to their own faults)[1205] since every person loves his soul its faults remain concealed from him, and he fails to perceive their mark, evident though it may be. So, to regulate such a disorder, (Galen says), one should choose a perfect and virtuous friend,[1206] telling him—after prolonged and intimate acquaintance with him—that a sign of his sincere affection would be for him to consider himself obliged to advise the former of his soul's faults, so that he may avoid them henceforth. In this connection, moreover, he should place him under a binding injunction,[1207] not acquiescing in his saying that he sees no fault in him: let him rather come at this friend with reproaches and make plain to him how much he detests such a statement, charging him with treachery, and returning to the original question and bringing much insistence to bear. If the friend persists in declaring nothing, let him make a show of utter grief at such behaviour and of a manifest coolness towards him, until he admits something recognizably demanded by the need to denigrate.[1208] When this stage is reached, he will certainly manifest no disapproval, nor will he let himself be overcome, in the other's presence, by resentment or displeasure; on the contrary, he will receive what is said with cheerfulness, gladness and joy, giving thanks therefor for many a day, whether privately or in company, until that friend counts his gifts and presents themselves a mark of his faults. Eventually, he proceeds to treat his faults with whatever will necessarily obliterate the mark thereof and expunge their impress; this results in a strengthening of the friend's confidence in his word and in the fact that his purpose is limited to the mending of his soul, so that the former shows no reluctance to give the same advice again.

Thus far the words of Galen.[1209] However, such a friend may be hard to find, and most often the desire to profit by such people will be lacking. In such a case, it may be that an enemy will prove more useful than a friend, for an enemy will observe no restraint in publicizing faults, not confining himself to what he knows, but going beyond all bounds and serving his ends by grasping at all manner of calumnies and slanders. In this way, men are alerted to their faults, even to regarding their souls as arraigned on the charges he has invented, and exercising circumspection in the face of the disorder that may be expected.

The same Galen,[1209] in another discourse, said that good men have profit from their enemies, the sense being the same as that which we have set down.

Ya'qūb al-Kindī,[1210] who was one of the Philosophers of Islam, says: the seeker after virtue should make a mirror of the manner[1211] of his companions, so as to take advantage of the state of each manner as leading to an evil action, and thus become informed of his own evil deeds. This is to say, he should search out the evil deeds of men, but censure himself, with reproach and rebuke, for each one thereof, so that you might imagine that the action in question had proceeded from him. Moreover, at the conclusion of each day, he should carry out an examination of every action performed during that day, thoroughly and without overlooking any single one: for it is unseemly that we should strive to preserve that which is expended casually[1212] (such as tiny pieces of stone and little bits of dry herb, the lack of which in no way makes us defective), while neglecting to preserve that which is expended from our very essences;[1213] for our continued existence implies[1214] the abundance thereof, while our annihilation is confined (only) to its diminution. So, when we become aware of an evil action, we must regard it as necessary to go to any length in censuring the soul, establishing a punishment for the same and allowing indulgence no way to bring it to naught. If we do thus, the soul will abstain from evil courses and form an attachment for good works. Moreover, abominations must be always present before our regard, so that we may not forget them; likewise we must observe the same condition in respect of good deeds, so that they may not escape us.

Later, he goes on to say that we should not be content, like documents and books, to instruct others in wisdom[6] while ourselves remaining without it; or to be like a whetstone, which sharpens iron but itself is unable to cut. Rather should we be like the sun, diffusing[1215] light from our essence upon a moon, so as to lend it a likeness to ourselves, albeit its light falls short of the sun's own: this is exactly our state as regards the diffusion of virtues.

Thus far the words of Kindī, who express this idea more emphatically than other writers.[1216] God best knows what is right!

## TENTH SECTION

### ON TREATING THE SICKNESS OF THE SOUL, IMPLYING[1214] THE REMOVAL OF VICES

Just as, in the science of physical medicine,[1217] sicknesses are removed by an opposite, so in psychical medicine too[1218] one must remove vices by the opposite of those vices. We have already numbered the classes of Virtues and reckoned up the classes of Vices,[1219] which are (so to speak) peripheries to those middle-points. Now, since the Virtues are four and the Vices eight, and inasmuch as one thing can have no more than one opposite (for opposites are two existent beings at the remotest distance one from another): so, in this regard, one may not call vices the opposites of virtues, save in a figurative sense.[1220] However, in the case of each pair of vices (which are of one order,[1221] one being at the extreme of excess[432] and the other of neglect),[433] these may be termed opposites of one another.

It must be understood that the professional rule[1222] in treating diseases is as follows: first, to know the classes of diseases, then to recognize their causes and symptoms, and finally to proceed to treatment thereof. Moreover, diseases are constitutional declinations from (a state of) equilibrium,[1223] while their treatment is the restoration of such constitutions to equilibrium by technical skill.

Now, since the faculties of the human soul are confined in three species, as we have said:[1224] the faculty of discrimination, the faculty of repulsion and the faculty of attraction;[1225] since, again, the declinations of each occur in two kinds, either through a disorder in the quantity of the faculty, or through a disorder in its quality; and since, moreover, the disorder in quantity represents either a departure from equilibrium in the direction of excess, or a departure from equilibrium in the direction of deficiency:[1226] therefore, the diseases of each faculty may be of three sorts—in conformity with excess, with neglect, or with depravity.[1227]

Excess in the faculty of distinction signifies such things as guile and cleverness and ingenuity[1228] in what pertains to action; in what relates to theory, it signifies such things as going beyond the limit of speculation and judging abstractions by the faculty of estimation and the senses, as one would judge the sensibles.[1229] On the other hand, neglect therein signifies such things as foolishness and stupidity[1230] in practical matters; and in theoretical matters, inadequacy of speculation, as when the judgments of sensibles are effected upon abstractions.[1231] Depravity of the faculty is represented by a yearning for sciences that do not yield certainty or perfection of the soul, as for the science of disputation, and for argument and sophistry[1232] in the case of a person employing them in place of the certainties;[1233] or as for the science of divination and omen-taking, conjuring and alchemy,[1234] in the case of a person who designs thereby to attain to the gratification of base appetites.

As for excess in the faculty of repulsion, it signifies such things as violent rage, vindictiveness and inappropriate jealousy, and (generally) displaying an affiinity with wild beasts. Neglect therein connotes, for example, lack of self-regard, weakness of nature, faintheartedness,[1235] and (generally) displaying an affinity with the characters of women and children. Depravity of the faculty is represented by a yearning for perverse vengeances, such as wreaking wrath on lifeless objects or beasts, or even on the human species where it is for a reason not necessitating anger in most natures.

As for excess in the faculty of attraction, it signifies such things as gluttony and greed for food and drink, and a passion and lust for persons not the proper objects of this appetite.[1236] Neglect thereof, on the other hand, implies such things as being too languid to seek necessary sustenance or preserve the race, and a (general) sluggishness of appetite.[693] Depravity of the faculty signifies such things as a relish for eating dirt, an appetite for pederasty,[1237] or a use of the appetite in any way lying outside the incumbent law.[1238]

These are the classes of simple diseases occurring in the faculties of the soul, of which there are many species; and many other diseases arise from compounds thereof, all of which derive, however, from these classes. Among these diseases there are some which are called 'fatal',[1239] and most of the chronic[1240] diseases have their origins therein: these cover such cases as perplexity and ignorance in the speculative faculty,[1241] while in the case of the other faculties, such things are involved as anger, faintheartedness, fear, sadness, envy, desire, passion and sloth.[1242] The harm these diseases inflict on the soul is all the more serious, and their treatment (accordingly) more important and more generally beneficial.

Following this explanation, each will be discussed in its proper place, if God Almighty will!

The causes of the declinations[852] are twofold, one psychical[302] and the other corporeal. The reason for this is as follows: Divine Providence[1243] has created the human soul attached to a corporeal frame,[378] making the separation of the one from the other dependent on His Will (mighty is His Name!); so, when either is affected by the advent of a reason or a cause,[1244] this necessitates a change in the other. Thus, when the soul is affected by excess of anger, or the dominance of passion, or constant grief, this necessarily brings about a change in the body's form in all sorts of ways, such as agitation, trembling, pallor or emaciation; likewise, when the body is affected by diseases and illnesses (especially when they occur in a superior member,[1245] like the heart or the brain), these necessarily bring about a change in the state of the soul, such as deficiency in distinction, corruption of the imagination, and failure in the employment of faculties and habits.[1246]

This being so, one treating the soul must first endeavour to know the state of the cause, so that if there shall have been a change in the physical frame,[378] he may administer thereto all manner of treatments as contained in the medical books. If, on the other hand, it is the soul that has been affected, he shall occupy himself with removing what is amiss by all manner of treatments as contained in the books of this (present) discipline.[562] When the cause is relieved, the disease is necessarily relieved as well.

General remedies[1247] in medicine are effected by the use of four categories: diet, drugs, poison, and cauterization or surgery.[1248] In psychical diseases too, one must have regard to the same system, inasmuch as one first recognizes the foulness of the vice one seeks to ward off and remove, in such fashion that doubt has no scope for ingress; one takes cognisance, furthermore, of the corruption and disorder to be awaited and expected from the access of such vice, whether in matters of the faith or in worldly affairs, fixing them firmly in the imagination. Then, as the next stage, one eschews that vice by (the use of) the intelligent will: if one's purpose is attained, well and good; if not, one must constantly concern oneself with application to the virtue corresponding to that vice, going to great lengths to repeat, in the most excellent way and the fairest manner, the acts pertaining to that faculty. Such remedies, generally speaking, correspond to treatment by diet as practised by physicians.

If, however, by this sort of treatment the sickness is not removed, one must proceed to chide and revile, to humiliate and reproach, the soul for the act in question, either in thought or by word or deed. If this does not produce the desired result, and one's object is to adjust[1249] one of the two animal faculties (i.e. the irascible or the concupiscible), then one must effect this adjustment and assuagement[1250] by the use of the other faculty; for whenever one is dominant, its fellow is dominated. Moreover, as originally created,[1251] just as the purpose of the concupiscible faculty is to preserve alive the individual and the species, so the purpose of the irascible faculty is to defeat the onslaught of appetite; thus, when they are compensatory,[1252] the rational faculty has scope for distinction. This category of treatment is analogous to the medicinal remedies of the physicians.

If, again, the disease is not removed by this method, the vice being extremely firm and deep-rooted, then, in order to crush and suppress it, one must seek aid from embarking on the occasions of the vice that [1253] is the opposite of the vice in question. But one must always observe the condition of adjustment:[1249] that is to say, when the vice goes into decline and approaches the degree of the mid-point (which is the abode of the virtue), one must abandon the course on which one is embarked, in order not to incline from equilibrium[830] to the other periphery, and thus to fall into another disease. This category of treatment corresponds to the poisonous remedy, to which the physician does not put his hand unless he is compelled to do so; and when he does, he recognizes the obligation to full circumspection, lest there be any declination of the temperament towards the other periphery.

If this type of treatment too proves insufficient, the soul constantly betaking itself to the repetition of a deep-rooted wont, then it must be schooled by chastisement and mortification;[1254] arduous actions must be imposed upon it, and it must be charged with toilsome tasks; furthermore, one should set about making vows and covenants that are difficult to implement after a prior observance of the prescripts of the wont.[1255] This category of treatment is like the cutting off of limbs in medicine, or the cauterization of the extremities. 'The final remedy is cauterization.'[1256]

These are the general remedies[1247] for the removal of psychical diseases: their use in any particular disease will not prove too difficult for anyone who has followed attentively from the beginning of the book until this place, informing himself about virtues and vices. However, we shall give further indications in detail concerning the treatment of certain fatal diseases (which are the most destructive of psychical diseases), so that it may be easy by analogy to remove other diseases, having regard to remedies. God it is who prospers and assists!

As for the diseases of the Speculative Faculty, although they have many degrees, whether simple or compound, yet the most destructive thereof may be classified as three: (1) perplexity; (2) simple ignorance; and (3) compound ignorance.[1257] The first class is of the order of excess, and the second of the category of neglect; while the third has reference to depravity.[1227]

*The treatment of Perplexity*: Perplexity arises from the contradiction of arguments[1258] in difficult questions, and the inability of the soul to ascertain the truth and refute error. The way to remove this vice, the most fatal of vices, is as follows: first, one acquires the habit of recollecting the primary proposition[1259] that to unite, or to remove, both negation and affirmation[1260] in one state is impossible; in other words, in any question wherein one is perplexed, one must make a decisive judgment for the invalidity of one of two contradictory extremes.[1261] Next, one must practise close adherence to the laws of logic, scrutinizing premisses and investigating the syllogistic form[1262] with an extreme degree of curiosity and a full measure of circumspection, so as to become aware of the fault's location and the error's origin. Indeed, the general purpose of the Science of of Logic, and especially of the *Book of Sophistical Syllogisms*[1263] (which deals with the recognition of specious arguments),[1264] is the treatment of this disease.

*The treatment of Simple Ignorance*: The true case of this ignorance is that the soul is devoid of the virtue of knowledge, without being contaminated by the conviction that it has acquired knowledge. Such ignorance, initially, is not blameworthy, for it is a condition of learning that the former should be present: inasmuch as one who knows, or thinks he knows, has finished with learning. Moreover, the genesis of the human species occurs in this state. What is blameworthy is to dwell in such ignorance, not moving along the road of learning; and if one becomes complacent and content with such (a state), one is stigmatized by the most destructive vice. Treatment thereof is governed by meditation on the state of man and the other animals, so that one becomes aware that the virtue of the human being over other animates lies in reason and distinction,[1265] whereas the ignorant (who is lacking in this virtue) is to be numbered among the other animals, not among the former species. The confirmation of these (last) words will be found in the fact that when such a one is present in a gathering held to discuss the sciences, he utterly relinquishes the property of the species (i.e. speech)[1266] and behaves like the other animals, who are incapable of articulation.[1267] If he reflects on such a state, it will come to his attention that the words which he is able to utter when this group (i.e. the men of science) is not present are more analogous to the noises of the other animates than to human speech.[1266] If his concern were with speech, he would be able to employ it in dialogue[1268] with a group whose humanity (i.e. distinction) is the greater.

Nor should such a one fall into error, when considering thus, on account of the application to him of the name 'Man', for green wheat is called 'wheat', and sour grapes are called 'grapes', but only by way of metaphor,[1269] the sense being that the former is apt to receive a wheaten form (and so on). Likewise, the effigy of a man is described as 'a man', figuratively speaking,[1270] that is to say that it resembles a man in form. Rather, if he does himself justice, will he realize that he is in degree lower than the various categories of animals: for every animal is capable of the amount of perception[716] needed to order the concerns of its daily life and to preserve its line, and it has regard for the perfection which is the ultimate end of its existence. But it is otherwise with the ignorant man.

Moreover, just as with regard to the properties of his own species (which he finds missing in himself) he must see himself as more closely resembling the other animals, so with regard to the properties of the other animals he will find himself nearer to the minerals; indeed, relative to the various categories of minerals, and with due observance of the conditions governing them, he will fall below that rank as well. And so on, to the lowest of the low.[1271] Eventually, when by such reflection he becomes aware of the deficiency of his degree, the meanness of his substance and the feebleness of his nature (this being the meanest of existent beings),[1272] then—if there be left in him any urge whatsoever to recovery—he will start to move in quest of the virtue of knowledge. 'Everything is aided to do that for which it is created.'[1273]

*The treatment of Compound Ignorance*: the true case of this ignorance is that the soul is devoid of the form of knowledge, but preoccupied with the form of invalid conviction[1274] and with the certainty that it does in fact know. No vice is more destructive than this one. Just as physicians of the body are incapable of treating certain bad diseases and chronic sicknesses, so also physicians of the soul are incapable of treating this particular disease; for, despite the distorted form[1275] (to which the soul is attached) there is no awareness (of what is wrong), and where there is no awareness there is no quest (for amelioration). This is the knowledge 'to which ignorance is preferable a hundred times.'[1276]

Now, the most advantageous policy to employ in this connection is to excite the victim of such ignorance to acquire the mathematical sciences, such as geometry and arithmetic, and to train himself in accordance with the proofs thereof. If he accepts such guidance, going deep into those fields of knowledge, he will become apprised of the pleasure of certainty and the perfection of truth, and also of the apathy of his soul,[1277] so that an urge to recovery arises in him. Then, when he adverts to his own convictions, and finds the pleasure of certainty to be banished therefrom, some access is allocated to doubt. Next, if he observes the stipulation of equity, he will become apprised in but a short time of the confusion of his own belief, so that he reaches that degree of being ignorant where his ignorance is Simple Ignorance. At that point he attends to the prescriptions for learning.

Now since these diseases relate to the Speculative Faculty, and inasmuch as Speculative Philosophy[10] includes the removal of diseases from that faculty, we shall confine ourselves to this much concerning this discipline. However, we shall employ further explanation in respect of the treatments of the diseases of the other faculties such as are peculiar to this discipline.

The diseases of the Faculty of Repulsion[1278] are beyond computation, but the most destructive of them are three in number: Anger, Cowardice and Fear.[1279] The first derives from excess, the second from neglect, and the third is related to a depravity[1227] of the faculty. Here follows a detailed account of the treatments thereof.

*The treatment of Anger*: anger is a motion of the soul, having as its principle the appetite of vengeance.[1280] When this motion becomes violent, the fire of rage is ignited, the blood begins to seethe, and the brain and arteries are filled with a dark vapour, so that the intelligence is cut off by a veil and its action grows feeble. As the philosophers have said,[1281] the human frame becomes as a mountain cave, filled with a blaze of fire and choking with flame and smoke, from which are recognized only noise and sound, tumult[1282] and the dominance of conflagration. In such a state it is virtually impossible[1283] to treat this deterioration or to quench this blaze, for everything (normally) used to extinguish a conflagration (now) becomes the source of its power and the reason of its augmentation. If one clutches at admonition the rage only grows greater; and if one resorts to a ruse in order to placate, flames and burning brands are but multiplied thereby. Moreover, this state differs in individuals in accordance with the variability of constitutions;[1284] thus, there may be a composition,[1285] like the composition of sulphur, which ignites at the least spark; or a composition corresponding to that of oil, which requires a greater cause of ignition; similarly, through compositions like those of dry wood and wet, until one arrives at a composition that it is virtually impossible[1283] to ignite at all. This classification, with respect to the state of anger, applies while the principle of the motion is still in its first stages.[1286] But when the cause is continuous, the different degrees appear equivalent: in just the same manner, by a tiny fire, arising in a piece of wood from light but continuous friction, there are consumed mighty forests and trees all together, both dry and wet.

Again, one should consider the state of the mist and the thunderbolt, whereby from the mutual friction of two vapours, wet and dry, there arise the ignition of lightning-flashes and the projection of thunderbolts, which pierce rugged mountains and flinty rocks; and one must regard in the same way the state pertaining to the excitation of anger and the havoc it wreaks, even though its cause may be the merest word.

Isocrates the philosopher[1287] says: I have more hope for the safety of a ship—driven, as it may be, by fierce winds and the violence of turbulent seas into a deep that surrounds mighty mountains and beats on cruel rocks—than for the safety of an inflammatory and irascible man; for sailors have scope for the employment of various subtle devices to save such a ship, whereas no ruse avails to still the flame of anger, once it is ablaze. Indeed, the more one employs exhortation or humility or supplication, the fiercer it appears, like a fire onto which is cast dry firewood.

The causes of Anger are ten: Conceit, Pride, Contention and Quarrelsomeness, Jesting, Arrogance, Scorn, Treachery, Unfairness, and the Quest of Precious Things[1288] (which in their rarity become the necessary cause of rivalry and envy); a yearning for vengeance is the end of these causes all together.[1289]

The consequences of Anger, or the accidents of this disease, are of seven categories: regret, the expectation of requital in this world and the next, the hatred of friends, the scorn of the ignoble, the rejoicing of enemies, disturbance of the constitution, and physical suffering[1290]—and these all together. Anger is a momentary madness; as the Prince of Believers, 'Alī[1291] (God ennoble his countenance!) has said: 'Vehemence is a species of madness, for its author has regrets, and if he does not regret, then is his madness firmly established.' Sometimes, moreover, it effectively chokes off the heat of the heart, producing one of those grave diseases that result in destruction.

The treatment of the causes of Anger effects the treatment of Anger itself, for the removal of the cause necessarily effects the removal of the thing caused, and the cutting off of the sources[1292] necessarily makes the disease to disappear. If, however, after treatment of the cause some touch of the disease should happen to appear, it will be easy to repel it by the management of the intelligence.[1293] The treatment of the causes of Anger is as follows:

In the case of *Conceit*: this is a false presumption[1294] in the soul, inasmuch as it accounts itself deserving of a station to which it is not entitled. When, however, it becomes aware of its own faults and deficiencies, and recognizes that virtue is common to all men, it becomes secure from conceit; for whoever finds his own perfection in others will not be conceited.

In the case of *Pride*: this is a vainglory in external things, which are exposed to calamities and to all manner of decay, so that a man can have no confidence in their permanency and stability. Thus, if his pride is in wealth, he is never safe from its being seized and plundered; if it be in lineage, then the justest instance in this category[1295] occurs where someone among his ancestors was characterized by virtue; and then let it be supposed that that virtuous ancestor of his appears and says: 'This honour to which you lay claim, belongs absolutely[1296] to me, not to you; what virtue do you have in your own soul, in which you can take pride?' Such a one will be incapable of rendering him an answer. A poet has put the same idea in verse:

'If you take pride in ancestors who passed on long ago,
'Men will say: "You speak true, but how poorly they begat!" '

And the Prophet (blessing and peace be upon him!) said: 'Do not bring me your genealogies: bring me your (own) actions!' It is also related that one of the Greek princes was boasting to a slave-philosopher; the latter said: 'If the reason of your boasting to me lies in these fine clothes with which you have adorned yourself, then the beauty and the ornament is in the clothes, not in you. If, however, the reason of your superiority lies in this horse on which you are mounted, then the agility and sprightliness are in the horse, and not in yourself. If it be the superiority of your fathers, it was they, not you, who possessed that superiority. Moreover, since of these virtues none is yours by right, if the owner of each should ask for the return of his portion—nay, if no single virtue had been handed down from him to you, for there to be any need of restoration—then who would you be?'

It is likewise said that a philosopher was in the home of a wealthy man, who was boasting of his ornaments and furniture, and of the abundance of his property and gear. In the course of the conversation the philosopher felt the need to expectorate; he looked to right and left, but could find no place suitable for his purpose, so he cast the spittle he had collected in his mouth into the face of the owner of the house. Those present upbraided and reproached him, but the philosopher said: 'Is it not proper to expectorate into the meanest and vilest of places? I looked to left and to right, but I could find no place meaner and viler than the face of this person, stigmatized as it is by ignorance.'

In the case of *Contention and Quarrelsomeness*: they necessarily cause familiarity[1297] to disappear, producing cleavage and mutual dislike and hostility.[1298] But the good order[441] of the universe depends on familiarity and love,[1299] as will be explained hereafter. Thus, contention and quarrelsomeness are among those corruptions that necessarily remove the order[1300] of the universe; these are the most destructive attributes of vices.

In the case of *Jesting*: if it be employed in a measure of equilibrium,[830] it is praiseworthy. 'The Apostle of God (God bless him and give him peace!) used to jest, but not to play the fool.'[1301] The Prince of Believers, 'Alī (God be pleased with him!) was given to jesting to a point where people held it against him, saying: 'If it were not for the fact that he is given to joking. . . .'[1302] Salmān the Persian once said to him about a jest he played on him: 'This (habit of yours) held you back to fourth place (when the Caliph was being chosen).'[1303] However, to stand on the boundary of equilibrium is an extremely difficult matter. Most men aim at equilibrium, but, once under way, they overpass the boundary by such an encroachment that it becomes a reason for alarm;[1304] latent anger[1305] is made apparent, and rancour[1306] takes firm root in men's hearts. Thus, to one who cannot observe moderation,[1307] jesting is prohibited. As has been said: 'Many a grave matter has been brought on by playfulness', and 'A remark may be a source of conflict.'[1308]

*Arrogance* comes closer to Conceit: the difference is that the conceited man lies to his own soul in the opinion he has of it, while the arrogant man lies to others, albeit he be devoid of such opinion. The treatment thereof is close to that for Conceit.

*Scorn* belongs among the acts of people given to impudence and tomfoolery.[1309] The person who engages in such a course is one who recks nothing of himself enduring the like thereof, even making his means of livelihood out of humiliation and abasement and the commission of vices necessarily provoking the laughter of the wealthy and the comfortably-off. On the other hand, anyone marked by liberality and superiority[1310] will hold his own soul and honour too dear to expose them to even one impertinence from a saucy fellow;[1311] yea, even though he be given in return the contents of the treasuries of kings.

*Treachery* has many aspects, for it may be employed in respect of property, or position, or affection, or a man's womenfolk.[1312] However, none of these aspects of treachery is well-considered by anyone possessing the smallest measure of humanity, and this is why no one will admit to it. This characteristic[1313] is greater among the Turks than among other groups of peoples, whereas loyalty[1314] (which is the opposite of treachery) is greater among the Byzantines and the Abyssinians. The vice of Treachery is too great to need further explanation.

*Unfairness* means to impose the burden of injustice on another by way of vengeance, and its abominable character is recognizable by that pertaining to Injustice and the Suffering of Wrong,[1315] which have already been discussed. The intelligent man[72] should not engage in vengeance until he knows that an even greater harm will not result therefrom: that will be (only) after consulting the intelligence and regulating the opinion,[1316] a state which may itself be attained (only) after attainment to the virtue of mildness.[583]

The *Quest of Precious Things*, which becomes the necessary cause of rivalry and altercation, includes both grave error on the part of persons marked by abundance of capacity and, at the other end of the scale, a proportionate situation for average men.[1317] Thus, every ruler in whose treasury lies a precious hoard or a noble jewel is exposed to the fear of loss or to the grief that is a necessary consequence of loss. But the nature of the world of Becoming and Corruption, which is posited upon alteration and conversion and vitiation,[1318] is satisfied with nothing less than the supervention of calamities to the categories of compounds.[1319] Thus, when a ruler is afflicted by the loss of something rare, the same state as befalls unfortunates becomes apparent in him; friend and foe become aware of his impotence and grief, and his poverty and need in seeking (once more) the like thereof become manifest, so that his respect and dignity grow less in the hearts of men.

It is related that a crystal bowl[1320] was taken to a ruler as a present. It was exquisitely pure and clear, characterized by perfect finish and roundness, with all manner of legends and figures[1321] raised in relief thereon, by precise craftsmanship and utter ingenuity, so much so that in refining the designs and polishing the concaves it had repeatedly been exposed to danger. When the ruler's glance fell upon it, he expressed measureless wonder and admiration at it, and ordered it to be placed in his private treasury. Constantly he took pleasure in observing it, until after a short while time effected the (inevitable) conclusion of its nature by destroying[1322] it. At this, such grief and regret overwhelmed the mind of the king that he forbore to manage the realm, to study matters of importance, and to give audience to the people. His retainers and nobles put forth their best endeavour to seek some rarity similar to the bowl in question. But when the ultimate end of their efforts was frustration and disappointment, realization of the virtual impossibility of finding such a thing only resulted in a redoubling of the king's grief and sorrow; so much so that it was feared that the rein of self-possession would pass from the grasp of his control.

So much for the states of kings. As for the average of mankind, if they gain possession of a fine piece of merchandise, or a unique pearl, or a noble jewel, or rich dress, or a sprightly mount, or a handsome slave: in all such cases, the domineering and insolent ones inevitably concern themselves with the desire and quest (of material things).[1323] If, however, there are those who pursue the way of lenity,[1324] they are afflicted with grief and sorrow; again, if they concern themselves with refusing and averting (access thereto by others), then they cast themselves into the whirlpool of destruction and extirpation. But if, from the very first, they have no eagerness to acquire the like of such valuables, they will be quit and secure of these sore trials.

Consider again: Precious stones (such as ruby and jacinth) may be made away with by all manner of trickery and guile and theft, so that it becomes anything but easy to profit immediately from their existence in order to cover some need. This is especially so where their owner is in a position of dire necessity,[1325] an eager man open to bargaining. It has frequently happened that great rulers, when the supplies to their treasuries have been cut off and they have chanced to incur excessive expense, have fallen under the necessity to sell jewels unique of their kind. But, on casting them into the open market for bidding by auction, surrendering them into the hands of brokers and merchants, they have found no one who would help them out for their (true) value or anything approaching it. Even where there has been someone disposing of such a degree of opulence, he has been apprehensive of admitting it in that situation; thus, the only result has been that the common people have learned of the helplessness and the need of the individual in question. Again, if merchants do manifest eagerness to possess such an article, they will not be safe, (even) in a time of security and quiet, from depreciation and loss; for the (only) seekers and bidders for such things are deluded rulers, having more wealth than worry,[1326] and such a class is not often to be found. At the same time, in a situation of insecurity and upheaval, their very lives are in danger on account of such things.

These are the causes of Anger and the treatment thereof. Anyone observing the condition for Justice,[52] making this disposition[1313] the habit[421] of his soul, will find the treatment of Anger an easy matter; for Anger is tyranny[1327] and a departure from equilibrium[830] in the direction of excess.[432] Anger should not be characterized by fair attributes, as when some people suppose that violent anger springs from an abundance of manliness,[1328] so that they impute it, by false imagination,[1329] to courage. How can one relate to a virtue a disposition that is the source of foul acts, such as tyranny to one's own soul, as well as to one's friends and connections, one's slaves and servants and womenfolk? The man with such a disposition constantly torments these people with the scourge of punishment, neither overlooking their stumbles, nor having compassion on their helplessness, nor accepting (the fact of) their being without fault. On the contrary, for the slightest cause he lets loose tongue and hand against their honour and their person. Indeed, the more they confess to sins not committed (striving to be humble and submissive, in the hope of quenching the fire of his rage and quietening the ferocity of his malevolence), the greater the lengths to which he will go in respect of unseemly behaviour, irregular motions[627] and molestation of them, Furthermore, if in the substance of anger,[1330] depravity[1331] be joined to excess,[432] he passes beyond this degree and metes out the same treatment to tongue-tied beasts and inanimate objects[1332] such as vessels and furnishings, seeking relief by trying to strike donkeys and cows, or to kill pigeons and cats, or to break implements and tools.

Often it will happen that people of this class, having ascribed to them an excess of foolhardiness,[1333] will vent their rage on cloud, wind and rain, when these do not suit their fancy; or if the nib of a pen does not produce script conforming to their will, or a lock be not opened in accordance with their sense of haste, they will break them and gnaw at them, soiling their tongue with abuse and incoherent speech.

Among the kings of ancient times, it has been said of a certain person that when his ships came in somewhat late from a sea voyage, his perturbation was such that he became enraged at the ocean, and would threaten it with a draining away of its water and a filling up with mountains (in their place)! Master Abū 'Alī (God have mercy on him!)[1008] says of a certain saucy fellow of his own day that because he became melancholy whenever he slept at night in the light of the moon, he grew enraged at the latter, tongue-lashing it with insults and reproaches. Indeed, he composed poems lampooning it, and his satires on the moon are well known.[1334]

On the whole, such actions, while greatly to be abominated, are ridiculous, and their author merits derision rather than the attribution of manliness;[1335] nay, he deserves shame and disgrace rather than honour and esteem. Consideration will show that this mode (of conduct) is more to be found among women and children, and the old and infirm, than among men and youths and those in good health.

The vice of Anger can also arise from the vice of Greed,[1336] which is its opposite; for when a greedy man is restrained from the object of his appetite, he flies into a rage, venting ill-humour on those singled out as responsible for such matters,[1337] such as women and servants, and so on. Likewise, the miser, when he loses some part of his belongings, behaves in just the same way towards his friends and associates, and casts suspicion upon trustworthy persons. The fruit of such courses can only be the loss of one's true friends and the defection of faithful counsellors, together with overwhelming regret and painful reproof; the man who adopts them remains cut off from pleasure and gladness, happiness and joy, so that his life is constantly made wretched and his days beclouded, and he is characterized by the mark of misery.[1338] The possessor of courage and manliness,[1335] on the contrary, if he suppresses this nature by mildness,[583] turning aside from its causes by (the use of) knowledge, in whatever situation he becomes involved (whether one for forgiveness and connivance[1339] or one for calling to account and vengeance), will hold to the course of intelligence and respect the condition for Justice,[52] which necessarily produces equilibrium.[830]

They relate of Alexander that a saucy fellow proceeded to injure his honour by recounting his faults and deficiencies. One of the nobles said: 'If the king will give the command for him to be punished, he will desist from this behaviour, thus becoming an example to others.' Alexander replied: 'Such an idea is remote from (sound) opinion; for if, as a consequence of the punishment, he grows even more insolent, busying himself with criticizing and publishing my faults, then I shall have given him material for chatter and led others to find some excuse for him.' Again, one day, they captured and brought before him a domineering person, who had rebelled against Alexander and stirred up much sedition and mischief. Alexander signed for him to be pardoned. One of his boon companions, in an excess of rage, remarked: 'If I were you, I would kill him,' to which Alexander replied: 'Then I, since I am not you, will not kill him!'

These are the greater part of the causes of Anger, which is the gravest of the sicknesses of the soul; and we have also given an introduction to the treatments thereof. Once the material sources of this disease have been cut off, it is easy to remove its accidents and consequences;[1340] for reflection,[1341] in choosing the virtue of mildness[583] and employing either retribution or indulgence[1342] (as opinion deems correct), finds scope for salutary speculation and adequate thought.[1343] God it is who prospers and assists!

*The treatment of Faintheartedness*:[1344] The knowledge of one opposite necessitates knowledge of the other opposite; and we have said that Anger is the opposite of Faintheartedness.[1345] Thus, Anger is a motion of the soul by virtue of the appetite of vengeance,[1280] whereas cowardice is a quiescence of the soul, through vitiation of the appetite of vengeance,[1280] in a situation where motion would be more fitting. The consequences and accidents[1346] of this disease are several: abasement of the soul;[1347] unease;[1348] wrong desire on the part of the base and others among one's family and children, and those with whom one has dealings; inconstancy in affairs; idleness and a love of ease, which inevitably give rise to many vices; the fact that the unjust are enabled to practise injustice; complacency about ignominies[1349] befalling one's soul, one's family and one's property; listening to abominations and obscenities in the form of abuse and calumny; not being ashamed of that which is a necessary cause of shame;[1350] and, finally, remissness in important affairs.

The treatment of this disease and its accidents consists in removing the cause, as we have explained in the case of Anger. This implies alerting the soul to its deficiency, and impelling[1182] it by irascible motives,[1351] for no man is devoid of irascibility; however, when it becomes deficient and weak, it can (like a fire) regain force, igniting and catching flame, from constant excitation.[1182]

They recount of certain philosophers[674] that they used to betake themselves to perilous situations and onto battlefields, casting their soul into grave dangers, and embarking in ships when the sea was disturbed—and this in order to acquire constancy and fortitude,[1352] to avoid the vice of idleness and its consequences, and to set in motion[1182] the faculty of Irascibility, of which faculty Courage is the virtue.[1353] Furthermore, they will even indulge in contention and hostility with one who is secure against any misfortunes in this connection—again, in order that the soul may move from periphery to mid-point; but when the soul feels, of itself, that it approaches that limit, it must not overpass it so as to fall away to the (other) periphery. God knows best![1354]

*The treatment of Fear*: Fear arises from the apprehension of something unpleasant or the expectation of something dreaded,[1355] which the soul is incapable of repelling. Now, apprehension and expectation may relate to an occurrence, the coming into existence[676] of which lies in future time; and this event may belong to grave matters, or to slight ones.[1356] On both suppositions, it will be either necessary or possible,[1357] and what gives cause to possibles[1358] is either the action of the one who fears or the action of another. But for none of these categories is fear an exigency of the intelligence,[1359] so that it is not fitting that an intelligent man should be afraid for any one of these reasons. This may be explained as follows: since he recognizes that the repulsion of the necessary[766] is outside the bounds of human capacity and ability, he will realize that the only result of being apprehensive[1360] thereof is to hasten calamity and to attract misfortune; at the same time, if he renders melancholy (by fear and dread, agitation and distress) the amount of life at his disposal before the occurrence of the redoubted happening,[1361] he will remain deprived of (the possibility of) regulating worldly interests or acquiring eternal felicity; he will combine loss in this world with exemplary punishment in the next, thus becoming a luckless one in both. On the other hand, if he will comfort and calm himself, conforming his heart to those things that must be,[1362] he will both find safety in this transitory world and take (sound) measures with regard to the hereafter.

As for that which is possible: if its cause be not by the action of the person marked by fear, he should consider to himself that the true nature of the possible is that both its existence and its non-existence are admissible;[1363] thus, to be certain that the thing dreaded will happen,[1364] and to experience[1360] fear (accordingly), can only result in hastening the suffering—with the same necessary conclusion as in the preceding category.[1365] If, on the other hand, he lives serenely (by fair presumption and powerful hope, and by abandoning thought for what will not necessarily occur),[1366] he can give attention to matters of importance, both spiritual and worldly.

Again, if its cause be the action of this person himself, he must refrain from evil choice[1367] and from treachery towards his own soul, not embarking on actions having a bad end and an unwholesome outcome: for the commission of abominations is the action of a person who is ignorant of the nature of 'the possible'.[1368] Thus, if a man knows that the appearance of an abomination calling for ignominy is possible, that when it appears his calling to account therefore is also possible, and (finally) that the occurrence of whatever is possible is not to be wondered at:[1369] assuredly, he will not embark on such an action. To summarize: the reason for fear, in the first category, is that he judges the possible to be necessary, while, in the second category, he judges the possible to be impossible.[1370] If he observes the (proper) condition for each in its own place, he will remain secure from these two types of fear. And God knows best!

*Treatment of the Fear of Death*: Since the fear of death is the most common and the direst of fears, it is necessary to comment adequately thereon. We say: everyone has the fear of death, not knowing what death is; or because he does not know where will be the ultimate abode of his soul; or because he supposes that, with the dissolution of the parts of the body and the break-up of the composition of his frame,[1371] the non-existence of his essence necessarily follows,[1372] so that the universe remains existent, but he is unaware of it; or he supposes that death is accompanied by great pain, more severe than the pain of the diseases leading thereto; or he fears punishment after death; or he is perplexed, not knowing how will be the state of his soul after death; or because he regrets the loss of the property and the children remaining after him.

The majority of these presumptions are vain and without reality,[1373] their source being sheer ignorance.[1374] This may be demonstrated as follows.

Anyone not knowing the true nature[736] of death should recognize that death may be interpreted as the soul's non-employment of the bodily organs,[1375] as when the master of a craft[562] does not use his tools and implements. He should further realize that, as is elucidated in books on philosophy,[6] (and as we have indicated at the beginning of the book), the soul is an enduring substance, which does not disappear and become annihilated at the dissolution of the body.

If, on the other hand, a man's fear of death is because he does not know where will be the ultimate abode of the soul, then his fear is of his own ignorance, not of death. It is anxiety to avoid this ignorance that has inspired scholars and philosophers[674] to endure the labour of the quest, so that they have given up physical pleasures and bodily comforts, choosing sleeplessness and hardship that they might find salvation from the hardship of this ignorance and the trial of this fear. Since real comfort is to find escape from the hardship of the body, while real hardship is ignorance; therefore, real comfort is knowledge. The men of knowledge derive ease and comfort from knowledge, for the world and what is in it seem in their eyes contemptible and undeserving of esteem. Moreover, since they have found everlasting permanence and eternal continuance in that comfort which they have attained through knowledge, while finding that only rapid decline and removal, the calamity of disappearance and impermanence, and abundance of cares and all manner of trouble, are associated with worldly matters; this being so, they have contented themselves with a necessary modicum,[1377] detaching their hearts from the superfluities of life,[1378] for the superfluities of life never reach an end beyond which lies no other end. Death in reality is such an avidity as this, not the thing (most men) try to avoid.

For this reason, philosophers[674] have said that death is of two types, voluntary and natural;[1379] and the same is true of life. By 'voluntary death' is meant the putting to death of the appetites and abandonment of the obstacles they offer.[1380] By 'natural death' is meant the soul's departure from the body. 'Voluntary life' refers to transient and worldly life, contingent on eating and drinking, while 'natural life' is everlasting permanence in gladness and joy. The Philosopher[8] Plato has said: 'Die by will, and you will live by nature!', while Sufistic sages[1381] have put it thus: 'Die before you die!'.

Consider again: whoever is afraid of natural death is afraid of the concomitant of his own essence[1382] and the completion of his quiddity;[59] for man is living, rational[32] and mortal,[1383] so that a dying man,[1383] as part of a living one, is a completion of quiddity.[59] What ignorance can be greater than that a person should suppose that his disappearance[109] is in his living[1384] and his defectiveness in his completion?[1385] The intelligent[72] man must, on the contrary, estrange himself from defectiveness and become familiar with perfection, always seeking that which will make him complete and noble and enduring,[1386] and at the same time bring him forth and liberate him from the fetters and captivity of nature.[1387] Let him recognize further that when the noble and divine substance wins release from the gross and obscure substance[1388] (this being a release of clarity and purity, not of mingling and turbidity),[1389] it gains possession of its own felicity, attaining to dominion of the universe, proximity to its Lord, and intercourse with the Pure Spirits;[1390] and it obtains release from contraries and calamities.[1391] This being so, it is evident that the (truly) unfortunate person is the one whose soul, before leaving the body, inclines and yearns towards corporeal organs and psychical pleasures;[1392] fearing to leave them; for such a one is at the farthest extremity from his (true) abode,[1393] and is on his way to an even more painful location than the one he is in.

As for the person who is fearful of death because of a presumption he entertains as to the pain thereof; the treatment for him is to recognize that that presumption is false.[1394] Pain pertains to the living being receptive of the soul's operation;[1395] so that whenever a body is not affected by the soul, it has no sensation of pain, the sensation of pain occurring by the intermediacy of the soul. Thus, it is evident that death is a state the existence of which is not accompanied by any sensation on the part of the body: accordingly, the latter does not suffer pain on account of it, for that which suffers pain has departed.

As for the man who fears punishment, he does not fear death, but the punishment that comes after death. Now, punishment is executed upon something that endures,[1396] so that he is acknowledging the endurance of something of himself after death, while at the same time confessing to the sins and evil deeds by which punishment is merited. This being so, his fear is of his own sins, not of death; the conclusion is, therefore, that he should not rush upon sins. As we have already explained, the necessary cause of rushing upon sins lies in destructive habits in the soul,[1397] and we have offered guidance for the eradication of the workings[455] of these latter. Thus, what is feared in this category has no effect, while that which does have an effect is neglected and even ignored. The treatment of ignorance, however, is knowledge.[601]

Similar is the situation of the one who does not know how will be the state of his soul after death, for whoever admits to any state after death, admits to endurance.[1398] When he says that he does not know what that state is, he is admitting to ignorance: once again, the treatment for this is by way of knowledge, so that when he attains confidence,[1399] the fear leaves him.

As for the person who is fearful and regretful at leaving behind family and children, wealth and property: he should realize that grief simply tends to hasten pain and unpleasantness, while at the same time being of no avail in the situation in question. We will set down later the treatment for grief.

After these prefatory observations, we go on to say that Man is one of the generables,[1400] and it is established, according to Philosophy,[1401] that every generable is corruptible.[1402] Therefore, whoever does not wish to be corruptible, will not have wished to be a generable; while whoever wishes his own existence, has wished his own corruption:[1403] thus, his not wishing corruption is (the same as) his wishing corruption, and his wishing existence is (the same as) his not wishing existence: but this is absurd, and the intelligent man pays no attention to the absurd.[1404]

Moreover, if our ancestors and forefathers had not passed away, our turn to exist would not have come; for if permanence[1398] were possible, it would also be possible for our predecessors, and if all men who have ever been, were to endure (allowing, too, for the fact of generation and propagation), they would not find room on earth. Master Abū 'Alī (God have mercy on him!)[1008] has given us a very lucid passage in explanation of this idea. He says: Let us suppose that an illustrious man of former times, whose offspring and descendants are well known and clearly designated (e.g. the Prince of Believers, 'Alī, God ennoble his countenance!)[1291] were still to be living, together with all his race and lineage, both from within his own lifetime and after his death over the space of the last 400 years.[1405] Assuredly, their number would exceed 10,000,000; for their residue at the present time, as scattered throughout the lands of the inhabited quarter (of the earth), and bearing in mind the monstrous slaughter and the various forms of extermination that have overtaken the members of this family,[1406] numbers close on 200,000 persons. Consider, then, what their number would be if one were to take into account, together with this total, all the members of past generations and the infants who died in their mothers' wombs![1407] Moreover, for every person who lived in 'Alī's time, the same quantity must be added to the original over the space of the last 400 years if one is to realize the extent to which the number of persons would grow, on the assumption that death is taken away from among men during the same 400-year period, while propagation and generation remain in force. Again, if this 400-year period be multiplied,[1408] the multiplications of people, as with those on the squares of a chessboard, pass beyond the boundary of record and the area of computation.[1409] If the surface of the inhabited quarter (which has been measured and assessed by surveyors) were shared out among such a company, the portion of each would not be sufficient for him to step upon it and stand upright. Thus, even if all this mass of people attempted to stand straight, with their arms held aloft, in the closest proximity to each other, there would not be room for them on the face of the earth—much less when it is a question of lying or sitting down, or moving about and going their different ways.[1410] No place would remain free for building or cultivation or the disposal of waste-matter. Such a situation, moreover, would come about in only a short period: how then, if with the prolongation of time, and by numberless multiplications in the same reference, they were reduced to sitting on one another's heads!

From the foregoing it is evident that to wish for enduring life in the world, to have a loathing of death and demise, and to conceive that hope can have any relation to such a longing:[1411] these things belong to the fancies of the ignorant and the absurd notions of the simple-minded. Intelligent men, however, and sagacious persons[1412] hold their minds and hearts[1413] free of such thoughts, recognizing that no man can conceivably win any addition to that which is required by Perfect Wisdom and Divine Encompassing Justice:[1414] and that Man's existence in this (present) predicament and situation[1415] is one beyond which no end[1416] can be conceived.

Thus, it is apparent that death is not mean, as the common run of people suppose: on the contrary, what is mean is the fear which is a necessary consequence of ignorance.

Take now the case of one who is aware of the necessity of death, and does not long for everlasting continuance, but (as the extent of his hope) confines his aspiration to length of life in such measure as may be possible. Such a one should be reminded that whoever desires long life is desiring old age; and in old age, as a matter of course, there occur deficiency of the natural heat,[165] wasting of the original moisture,[1417] and weakness of the principal members;[1418] and a necessary consequence, also, is a diminution of movement, and likewise loss of vitality,[1419] disorder of the organs of digestion, falling-out of the organs of mastication,[1420] and a deficiency of the faculties, such as the nutritive, and of the fourfold ancillaries.[1421] Such states may be referred to as 'sicknesses and sufferings'. But a further consequence of this state lies in the death of loved ones and the loss of those held dear, and a constant succession of afflictions and befalling of adversities, and poverty and need and all the other varieties of hardship and trial. Yet the one who fears all this, from the very first moment[737] when he hoped and wished for length of life, was seeking such states as these: longingly he sought, and looked for, the likes of these abhorred misfortunes. But when he attains certainty that death means that Man's essence and core and quintessence depart from the metaphorical, figurative body, which has been put together from the four natures by way of distribution,[1422] and then been placed in the net of the soul's control,[1423] for a few numbered days, so as to attain its perfection by means thereof; but that the soul then escapes from the impediment of place and time, attaching itself to the Presence of Divinity[1424] (which is the dwelling of the pious[952] and the abode of the good), and becoming safe from death and conversion and extinction—(when, we say, he attains this certainty) he assuredly no longer allows himself to suffer any apprehension[1360] on account of this state. No longer does he trouble himself for any acceleration or delay (thereof) that may occur, nor does he acquiesce in the gaining of misery or inclination to the darknesses of Purgatory,[1425] the end of which will be the descending slopes to Hell,[1426] the wrath of the Creator[1427] (glorious be His Name!), the abode of the lewd, and the point of repair of the wretched and the evil. He is the One whose aid is to be sought![1428]

*The treatment of the diseases of the Faculty of Attraction*: while they pass beyond the area of computation, the most destructive of them are excess[432] of appetite, love of idleness, and grief and envy.[1429] Of these diseases, one belongs to the area of excess,[432] the second to that of neglect,[433] and the third and fourth to the area of depravity of the quality.[1430] The respective treatments of them are as follows.

*Treatment of Excess of Appetite*: earlier, in foregoing chapters, we have commented briefly on the reprehensibility of that avidity and eagerness which is directed towards a quest for pleasure derived from things eaten and drunk. The debasement of aspiration, the demeaning of nature[1431] and other vices accruing in consequence of this state (such as abasement of the soul,[1347] gluttony, the humiliation of sponging, and loss of respect)[1432] stand in no need of commentary or exposition, being evident to both high and low in estate. Moreover, the various diseases and pains arising from dissipation and the transgression of (due) bounds[1433] have been set out and expounded in books of medicine, and their treatments likewise registered and recorded. As for the sexual appetite,[1434] eagerness to gratify it is among the gravest causes of deficiency in piety, emaciation of the body, waste of property, damage to the intelligence, and the reckless outpouring of personal honour.[1435]

Ghazālī (God have mercy upon him!)[1436] has likened the Appetitive Faculty to a tyrannical revenue-agent. He says that if the latter have a free hand to collect men's wealth, without any restraining or inhibiting force in the shape of punishment by the ruler or fear of God or a compassionate nature, he will seize all that the tenantry possess,[1437] afflicting everyone with destitution and poverty; likewise, the Appetitive Faculty, if it find full scope and should not chance to be assuaged by the correction of the Faculty of Discrimination, the mortification of the Faculty of Anger and the attainment of the virtue of Continence,[1438] will consume on its own account all the materials of nutrition and the beneficial chymes,[1439] thus rendering all limbs and members thin and feeble. If, on the other hand, in accordance with the demands of justice, it employs only the necessary quantity for the preservation of the species, it resembles the agent who justly collects the required sum from the taxpayers, and expends it on the maintenance of the frontiers and other projects of benefit to the community.

One troubled with this avidity should ascertain for himself that the similarity of women one to another in respect of enjoyment is (even) greater than the similarity of foods in filling a need. Thus, just as it is reckoned detestable that a man should leave deliciously prepared and cooked foods (behind him) in his own house and go begging at the door of other houses in search of that which will stay the assault of his hunger, so it is also reckoned detestable that he should go outside his own womenfolk and his lawful spouse[1440] and busy himself in deceiving other women. If, however, the passion of his soul within him[1441] should trick out the qualities of a woman who passes by him veiled, so that he conceives excessive pleasure to lie in close relationship and acquaintance with her,[1442] he must employ his intelligence, not being deluded by the falsehood and deception of such a fancy; for, on examination and inspection, it is frequently to be observed that from beneath the covering there come forth the most ruinous form and ugliest aspect. In most situations, moreover, that which lies within the net of his control[1423] is more effective in stilling the appetite than is the expenditure of effort and exertion that is made in quest of the woman. If, again, he follows up his eager inclination, it will picture in his mind so much fairness and beauty, so much allure and coquetry, at every form wrapped in the covering of veils and forbidden to his gaze, as to render his days melancholy in the quest thereof. Nor will such a man pay heed to the experience and example of others, who have earlier been subject to the same presumption, only to become aware (once the covering was taken off) of the manifestation of deception and illusion.[1443] One might go so far as to say that if in the whole world (so to speak) only one woman were left, he being deprived of the enjoyment of her, he would still fancy that she offered a pleasure the like of which was not to be found in the others. So much eagerness and guile[1444] does he employ, in order to gain a taste from the banquet of beauty, that he becomes cut off from his own best interests in both this world and the next; and this is the utmost folly, the final extreme of aberration.[1445] The person, however, who restrains his soul from the pursuit of passion,[1446] contenting himself with lawful measure,[1447] finds deliverance from the fatigue and affliction that are the consequence of so much vice.

The most destructive of all the varieties of excess[432] is that of Love,[1448] which is the consumption of all one's aspiration, on behalf of the authority of appetite,[1449] in quest of one particular person. The accidental aspects[1450] of this disease are at the very extreme of depravity,[1227] and it may sometimes lead to the verge of the soul's ruination and the loss of this world and the next. The treatment thereof consists in diverting the thoughts from the loved one, as far as one has the power to do so, by occupying oneself with exact sciences and subtle disciplines such as are peculiar to the reflective virtue;[1451] furthermore, such a one should associate with virtuous boon companions and discerning comrades,[1452] whose engagement is with such things as do not necessarily bring about the recollection of corrupt imaginings;[1453] and he should remain aloof from tales of lovers and recitals of poems relating to them; and, finally, he should endeavour to still the Appetitive Faculty either by coition or by the use of depressants.[1454] If these treatments are of no avail, it will be found profitable to undertake a lengthy journey, to burden oneself with arduous enterprises, or to embark upon difficult tasks. Also prescribed for the removal of this disease is abstinence from food and drink, in such measures that weakness overtakes the physical faculties but without leading to collapse and excessive damage.[1455]

*Treatment of Idleness*: the love of idleness[1456] demands that one be deprived of both worlds; for neglect to observe what is proper to daily life leads to the destruction of the individual and the cutting off of the species, and what weight can attach to the other varieties of vices in the face of these two calamities? At the same time, to be heedless of attaining ultimate felicity conduces to a nullification of the purpose of causing to be;[1457] for the latter is called for by the outpouring of the liberality of the Necessarily Existent,[1458] while this (state) is one of open animosity and contention with that Majesty (we take refuge with God therefrom!). Now, since idleness and sloth[971] comprehend such corruptions, there is no need for further prolixity in expounding their abomination and reprehensibility.

*Treatment of Grief*:[1456] grief is a psychical pain[1459] arising from the loss of a loved one or failure to attain a desired object; its cause is avidity (to satisfy) corporeal demands and eagerness for (the gratification of) bodily appetites, together with regret for the loss and escape thereof. Such a state befalls the person who deems it possible for sensibles to endure and for pleasures to be constant;[1460] who reckons it not impossible[1461] that it should be within his control to arrive at all the objects of desire and attain all things purposed. If, however, the person afflicted with such diseases has recourse to the intelligence, observing the conditions of equity, he will recognize that it is out of the question[1462] for there to be constancy and persistence in whatever is in the world of Becoming and Corruption.[1463] Constant and enduring are the things belonging to the world of the Intelligence, which are outside the control of contraries.[1464] So, then, such a one will not covet what is out of the question; and when he no longer covets it, he will not be grief-stricken over an expected loss; rather will he confine his aspiration to the attainment of enduring desires, expending his effort in quest of beloved objects that are unalloyed,[1465] and avoiding that which, by its nature, necessitates the corruption of his essence. If he does mingle himself[1466] with anything, he will content himself with the amount of his need and with meeting urgent necessity, counting it obligatory[257] to avoid accumulation and the wish for great possessions (which afford incentives[684] to vainglory and boasting), so as not to be regretful at leaving them or pained by their removal and departure. Matters being thus, he will attain benefit without dread and receive joy without distress, he will win a gladness with no regret, and he will gain the fruit of a certainty that has no perplexity. If it be otherwise, however, he will be for always a prisoner of grief without cessation and of pain without end; for at no time will he be exempt from failure to obtain a desire or from the loss of a loved one, inasmuch as in the World of Becoming and Corruption[1463] there can be no becoming without corruption,[1467] so that the man who desires it will suffer disappointment and loss. As the poet says:[1468]

'He who is rejoiced not to see what hurts him,
'Let him not take up anything whose loss he fears!'

A fair[699] custom to follow is to be content with what is available,[1469] while not lamenting or regretting that which is lost,[1469] so that one remains always delighted and in a state of felicity. Should a person have some doubt as to whether adhering to this custom and profiting by this disposition[1313] is to be branded with the mark of facility, or characterized by the attribute of extreme difficulty,[1470] let him reflect on all the sorts of men,[65] the variety of their aims and modes of life,[1471] the acceptance by each of his portion and lot, and the joy and happiness he displays in the discipline and craft peculiar to him[1472] (such as merchants in commerce and the woodworker in carpentry, the rogue in lawlessness, the hermaphrodite in effeminacy, and the procurer in pandering). So much so, that each will regard as truly defrauded the one lacking that discipline, terming 'utterly insane' the one who is heedless of that state; for each recognizes happiness and ease as attached to the existence of that pleasure, and total deprivation as linked to the loss of that mode of life. As the text of the Revelation[1473] expresses it: 'Each party rejoices in what is theirs'.

The reason for such confidence is adherence to this custom and assiduous practice therein. Thus, if the seeker after virtue will follow this path, in his choice of a course and a way, not trying to turn aside from walking the highways and winning the benefits of the perfection which is the goal of this expedition, he will be worthier of the joy of felicity than are that company who are caught in the bonds of ignorance and the captivity of error. He is a speaker of truth, while they say false; he enjoys certainty and accuracy, while they are astray and without clear purpose;[1474] and they are sick and wretched, while he partakes of health and felicity; indeed, he is the friend of God, but they are His enemies. 'Surely, no fear lies upon the friends of God, neither do they grieve!'[1475]

Kindī[1476] (God's mercy be upon him!) says in his book *The Warding Off of Griefs*: It may be shown as follows that grief is a state which men attract to themselves by their own bad choice, being external to natural things. Let one who has lost anything wished for, or been disappointed in any object of desire, reflect with the eye of wisdom[6] on the causes of his grief; or let him take example by those persons who have been deprived of that very thing wished for and object of desire, but have come to accept and acquiesce in such deprivation; it will become clear to him that grief is neither necessary nor natural.[1477] At this, the one who attracts and acquires it will inevitably return to the natural state and find tranquillity and solace (therein).

We have ourselves observed a class of people who have been afflicted by some disaster to their children or dear ones or friends, so that griefs and sorrow have befallen[1136] them, overpassing the boundary of moderation;[830] yet, after the lapse of but a little time, they have come across something to make them laugh and be glad and joyful and happy, whereupon they have forgotten the matter entirely. Likewise, persons losing wealth and possessions and other acquisitions (have been known to) live miserably for a few days in all manner of sorrow and anxiety, and thereafter their despondency is exchanged for sociability and peace of mind. Announcing the same idea is the saying of the Prince of Believers, 'Alī (God ennoble his countenance!): 'Show fortitude after the manner of the noble-minded, or seek forgetfulness as do the beasts'.[1478]

The intelligent man,[72] regarding the state of mankind, will recognize that he is not distinguished from them by any remarkable disaster or untoward trial. If he allows this disease (taking, as it does, the same course as other sorts of depravity)[1479] to gain a hold, he will still ultimately incline to consolation and find recovery therefrom. Thus, in no sense does a conventional disease find acceptance with him,[1480] nor is he acquiescent to the depravity of any person whatsoever. He will realize, too, that the situation of one desiring the persistence of worldly benefits and advantages is like that of one present at an entertainment, when a pastille[1481] is being circulated from hand to hand among the company; who, while each one for a moment enjoys its fragrant scent, longs to possess it when his turn comes, thinking himself of all the party singled out for ownership thereof, the pastille being placed by way of gift within his control.

Thus, when it is taken back from him, he is left with embarrassment and confusion, or regret and remorse. Likewise, all categories of acquisitions are the pledges of Almighty God,[1482] who has allowed men to participate therein, while retaining (mighty and magnificent is He!) the power of recall whenever, and at the hand of whomsoever, He wishes. Blame and reproach, disgrace and ignominy are not directed at the person who returns the pledge willingly,[1483] whose hope and desire are severed therefrom. But as for one who does desire it, showing distress when it is taken back from him, he brings down on himself disgrace and blame, while at the same time incurring guilt of ingratitude for the grace received; for the least degree of gratitude involves the cheerful[1484] return of a loan to the lender, with even a show of alacrity to answer the call. This is especially true where the lender leaves the noblest part of what he has given and recalls only the meanest. By this 'noblest part' is meant the intelligence and the soul, as well as the virtues which the hand of the importunate cannot reach, and in which the domineering have no desire to participate.[1485] These perfections have been conferred upon us in such wise as to be inaccessible to requests for return or restitution; while, as to the meaner and baser part which is asked back from us, the purpose of this is both the observance of honour towards Him[1486] and the guarding of justice among our fellows.[1487] If for the passing of everything lost we allow ourselves to be overcome by grief, we must always be grieving.

Thus, the intelligent man[72] should not expend his reflection on matters that both harm and give pain, taking as little as possible of such acquisitions ('the believer is sparing of provisions')[1488] so as not to be afflicted with grievings. A certain great man said: 'If the world had no further fault than the fact that it is on loan,[1489] it would still be proper that the man of noble purpose should pay it no heed, equally as such men are ashamed to borrow all manner of splendid adornment.' Socrates was asked the reason for his abundant cheerfulness and absence of grief. He replied: 'It is because I set my heart on no thing so as to become grief-stricken when it is lost.'

*Treatment of Envy*: Envy[1429] is present when, through an excess of greed, one wishes to be distinguished by the advantages and acquisitions of other men: thus the aspiration of such a one is confined to removing them from others and attracting them to himself. The cause of this vice derives from a compounding[1490] of ignorance and avidity, for it is out of the question[802] for one person to hope to amass the worldly goods designated as essential deficiency and deprivation.[1491] Indeed, even if such a possibility be supposed, it is inconceivable that he could derive enjoyment from them. Thus, both ignorance of the true fact of this situation[1492] and excess of avidity are an instigation to envy; and since the object desired by the envious man is impossible of realization,[1493] the only profit accruing to him is grief and suffering. The treatment of these two vices, then, constitutes the treatment for envy, and it is because of the connection of envy with grief that it has been discussed in this place; otherwise, it would be more appropriate to refer envy to the compound diseases.[1494]

Kindī[1495] describes envy as the most abominable of diseases and the most odious of evils. This is the reason why the philosophers[765] have said that whoever loves to have an evil befall his enemy is a lover of evil, and a lover of evil is (himself) evil. More evil, again, than he is the person who wishes that an evil may befall someone not his enemy. Moreover, whoever does not wish that good should befall a person has wished evil to that person; and if it is friends he treats thus, so much the more destructive and the uglier it is. Thus the envious man is the evillest person; and he is always grief-stricken, for he is overcome with distress at the good of other men—indeed, the good of mankind runs contrary to what he desires. However, since good will never be removed or cut off from mankind (at large), it is inconceivable that his distress and his grief can have any termination or conclusion.

The most destructive of the kinds of envy is the one accurring among men of knowledge.[1496] The very nature of worldly benefits (having regard to restriction of area, want of scope, and the straightness that is a concomitant of matter)[1497] is a cause[808] of envy: this is to say that the one who desires suffers his will to be accidentally attached to the removal from others of what he desires,[1498] even though such a notion be not approved by him essentially.[1499] The philosophers[742] have compared the world to a short blanket cast over himself by a tall man: if he covers his head with it, his feet are left bare, while if he will not leave his feet deprived, his head will remain so. Likewise, if one individual be singled out for the enjoyment of a benefit, another is prevented therefrom. Knowledge,[601] however, is removed from this taint;[755] for its disbursement and expenditure, allowing one's fellow-men to share in its benefits, can only require[1500] an increase of pleasure and a perfection of enjoyment. In this case, therefore, envy arises from the nature of absolute evil.[1501]

It should be recognized that there is a difference between emulation[1502] and envy, for emulation is a longing to acquire a perfection or a desired object, sensed as in another by the essence of the one spurred to emulation,[1503] without any wish for its removal from him; whereas envy is accompanied by this wish for removal from the other person. Emulation, moreover, is of two kinds, one praiseworthy and the other reprehensible; praiseworthy emulation occurs where the longing is directed towards felicities and virtues, the reprehensible where the longing is directed towards appetites and pleasures. It is thus in the same case as avidity.[1504]

So much for envy; whoever acquaints himself with all that we have set forth, marking it right well, will find it an easy matter to treat other vices and to recognize their causes and any such accidents as may arise.[1505]

For example, if he reflects upon falsehood, he will recognize that Man is distinguished from other animals by speech;[1266] that the purpose of manifesting the virtue of speech is to inform others of something of which they are unaware. But falsehood runs contrary to this purpose; therefore, falsehood nullifies the property of the species.[1506] The cause thereof is an urge to seek wealth or prestige[788]—in short, eagerness for anything in this category. Among its consequences are loss of personal honour, the ruination of great matters, engagement in detraction, calumny, defamation and slander, and the arousal of the unjust.[1507]

If he reflects upon pretentiousness,[1508] he will recognize that its cause is the domination[787] of irascibility and the imagining[790] of a perfection not found in oneself. Among its consequences are ignorance of gradations, failure to observe dues, coarseness of nature, ignobility[1509] and tyranny.[985] As regards the notion itself, pretentiousness is compounded of conceit and falsehood.[1510]

If he reflects upon parsimony, he will recognize that its cause is fear of poverty and need, or love of high position (to be attained) through wealth, or wickedness of soul, or the quest to deprive mankind of good things. If he reflects upon hypocrisy,[1511] he will recognize that it is falsehood both in word and in action.[1512]

In short, if he knows the true nature of each, being aware of its causes, it will be easy for the seeker after virtue to subdue and guard against those causes, in the same way as for other abominations. God it is who prospers and assists!

Here ends the First Discourse, to be followed by the Second, praise being accorded to God and He prospering us to good effect.

SECOND DISCOURSE

# *Economics:*[1513] *in Five Sections*

## FIRST SECTION

### THE REASON OF THE NEED FOR HOUSEHOLDS,[53] AN ACCOUNT OF THE BASES[54] THEREOF, AND THE PRESENTATION OF WHATEVER IS IMPORTANT IN THIS SENSE

WHEREAS mankind needs food for the preservation of the individual; and the food of the human species cannot be procured without the organization of techniques,[1514] such as sowing, harvesting, cleaning, pounding, kneading and cooking; and the arrangement of such processes cannot conceivably be effected save by the collaboration of helpers, and the application of tools and utensils, and the consumption therein of long periods of time; (this being contrary to the case of the food of other animals, which is produced and prepared naturally,[1515] so that their urge is limited to the search for fodder and water, in accordance with the demand of nature; and when they have stilled the access of hunger and thirst, they refrain from further motion); and since the restriction of mankind to the amount of their day-by-day need would inevitably bring about the exhaustion of supplies and a dislocation of their mode of life, it being impossible to contrive in one day the quantity of food which forms a daily ration:

This being so, the need has befallen to store the necessaries of life and to keep them safe from the rest of one's fellows, who are partners in necessity; but safeguarding cannot be effected without a location, in which food and sustenance will not spoil, and which—at the times of sleep and waking, by day and night—will restrain therefrom the hand of both the unjust and the predator.[1516]

Thus the necessity has arisen for the building of houses. Since, however, mankind must occupy itself with the contrivance of a technique[1517] that will encompass the acquisition of food, it will (tend to) remain heedless of the safekeeping of that amount which is already stored away. Accordingly, there has been a need for helpers who would reside in the houses, as deputies,[1518] for most of the time, occupied with the custody of the stores of sustenance and food. This necessity is in accordance with the preservation of the individual.

But, in accordance with the preservation of the species, there is also need for a mate,[1519] on whose existence procreation and generation are dependent. Accordingly, Divine Wisdom[6] has required that every man should take a mate, one who will both attend to the custody of the house and its contents, and also by means of whom the work of procreation is fulfilled. Moreover, the condition for economy of provision[1520] is observed by the investment of one person with two offices.[1521] Now, once generation is accomplished, and (it becomes apparent that) the child will not survive and grow without the upbringing and nurture of father and mother, there arises the further obligation[257] to assume responsibility for its affairs; but as soon as a company is assembled—that is to say, man, wife and children—the contriving[1522] of their sustenance, and the fulfilment of their wants[374] may be hard for one person. Thus, the need for auxiliaries and servants becomes manifest. With this company, who are the bases[54] of the household, the organization of a state of life[1523] is effected; hence, from this argument it is clear that the bases of the household are five: father, mother, child, servant and sustenance.

Now, since the organization of any plurality[1524] may be effected by some manner of combination,[1525] demanding a kind of unity,[1526] there likewise arose the need, in organizing the household, for the devising of a technique[1514] to bring about such a combination. Of all the company aforementioned, the master of the household was most fitted to give attention to this task; accordingly the government of the group[1527] was settled upon him, and the chastisement of the company[1528] entrusted to him, so that he might advance the regulation of the household in a manner demanding the organization of its inhabitants.

Just as the shepherd grazes a flock of sheep in a proper manner, taking them to suitable pastures and watering-places, protecting them from harm by wild beasts and from celestial and terrestial calamities, and arranging stopping-places for summer and winter, midday and night-time, in accordance with what is properly required by each particular time—and all this so that there may accrue both the business of his livelihood and the organization of their condition; so, likewise, the regulator of the household[1529] attends to what is appropriate in respect of foodstuffs and provisions, arranging the affairs of daily life and managing the circumstances of the community by encouragement and intimidation, promises, prevention and imposition,[1530] courtesy and criticism, and kindness and severity—and this so that each one may reach the perfection towards which he is directed as an individual, while all participate in an order of circumstance that necessarily produces ease of livelihood.

It should be recognized that the meaning of 'household'[1531] in this place is not that of a house, made out of brick and mortar, stone and wood. Rather does it refer to a particular combination[1532] between wife and husband, begetter and begotten, servant and one served, and the possessor of property and property itself; this, irrespective whether their dwelling be of wood and stone, a tent or a pavilion, the shade of a tree or a cave in the mountains.

Thus, the technique of regulating a household (which is called

Domestic Philosophy)[1533] consists in supervising the state of this community in such a way as necessarily produces general best interest, by facilitating the means of livelihood and of attainment to the perfection which is sought in accordance with association. Now, since all individuals of the species, whether king or subject, superior or subordinate,[1534] stand in need of this sort of combination and regulation; and since each person, in his own degree, is charged with assuming responsibility for the affairs of a community, so that he is their pastor and they are his flock;[1535] therefore the usefulness of this knowledge is general and indispensable, and its benefits encompass both the affairs of the faith and those of this world. This is why the author of the Sharī'a (peace upon him!) enjoined: 'You are each a shepherd, and each is responsible for his flock'.[1536]

The Ancient Philosophers[273] have much to say in this connection, but their writings on this subject have not chanced to be rendered from the Greek into the Arabic language. However, there is a compendium of the observations of Bryson,[1537] which is extant in the hands of the Moderns.[1538] The Moderns themselves have expended the utmost effort, by accurate opinions and pure intellectual exercises,[1539] to polish[237] and arrange this discipline and to deduce its laws and basic principles[1540] in accordance with the exigency of the human intelligence;[1541] and (their work) has been recorded in book-form. The Principal,[1542] Master Abū 'Alī al-Ḥusain b. 'Abdallāh Ibn Sīna, has a treatise on this subject, which (while perfect in its eloquence) observes the condition of conciseness. The present Discourse has taken the essential part of that treatise and decked it out with homilies and moral examples derived from both Ancients and Moderns. If God will, it will be honoured by the favourable regard of men of merit! He is the Guardian of Success.

It should be understood that the general basic principle[1543] for the regulation of a household may be expressed as follows. Take the case of a physician, who considers the state of Man's body with regard to the equilibrium[830] resulting to the whole composition in accordance with the compounding of the members. Such equilibrium necessarily effects the body's health and is the source of acts in a manner of perfection. Therefore, if that equilibrium be present he preserves it, while if it be lost he tries to recover it. If a disorder arises in a certain member, by treating that one he safeguards the best interests of all members; in particular, he safeguards by primary intention[397] the interest of the principal member[1544] adjacent to it, and then by secondary intention[400] the interest of that member itself. So much so, that if the welfare of all members lies in the amputation and cauterization of that one, he abandons all idea of mending it, thinking nothing of cutting it off or removing it, so that the corruption should not spread to the other members.

In just the same way, it is incumbent[257] on the regulator of the household[1529] to observe the welfare of all the inhabitants of the household. His regard should be confined, by primary intention,[397] to the equilibrium obtaining in the combination; the preservation or restoration of that equilibrium should be posited on sound method;[1545] and in regulating the state of each separate individual he should imitate the treatment accorded by the physician to each separate member. Each one of the bases[54] of the household, relative to the household itself, may be likened to each one of a man's members relative to the whole human frame:[378] some rule while others are ruled, and one group is noble while another is base. Moreover, although each member has its own particular equilibrium[830] and act, nevertheless the act of all members in association and collaboration is the end of all acts.[1546] Likewise, each individual among the inhabitants of a household has a nature and a property in isolation,[1547] and his motions are directed towards a particular purpose,[1548] that from the acts of the group may result the order desired in the household. The regulator of the household (who may be likened to the physician from one point of view, and to one member—the noblest of members—in another regard) must be aware of the nature, property and act of each individual among the inhabitants of the household, as also of the equilibrium resulting from the combination of those acts; this is so as to bring them to the perfection necessarily effected by the ordering of the household;[1549] and if a disease occurs he removes it.

Although, as we have said, the consideration of the state of a household lies outside any principle of technique,[1550] nevertheless (it may here be remarked that) the ideal states of a household *qua* dwelling[1551] are as follows. Its foundations should be solid, its ceilings inclined to loftiness, and its doorways wide, so that there be no necessity for inconvenience in passage to and fro. The dwellings of the men should be separated from those of the women; the place of residence for each term and season should be adapted to the time in question; the location of stores and possessions should be characterized by impregnability; precautions should also be taken to ward off disasters, such as fire and flood, the incursions of thieves and the molestations of pests. Again, in the dwellings of men attention should be paid to such things as necessarily effect a safeguard against earthquakes, such as spacious courts and raised supports;[1552] and in all the abundance of amenities and spaces, one should preserve the conditions of the compatibility of situations.[1553]

Most important of all is to have regard to the state of one's neighbourhood, so as not to be afflicted with the proximity of evil and corrupt persons and those of troublesome nature, and yet (at the same time) to be secure from the calamity of solitude and isolation.

The Philosopher[8] Plato had taken a house in the goldsmiths' quarter.[1554] When asked the reason for this, he said: 'If sleep overcomes my eyes, preventing me from thinking and studying, the noise of their tools will wake me up!' God best know what is right.

## SECOND SECTION

### CONCERNING THE GOVERNMENT AND REGULATION OF PROPERTY AND PROVISIONS[55]

Since the human race is under the compulsion to store up provisions and supplies (as we have mentioned in the foregoing Section), and inasmuch as it is not possible for some foods to last for any length of time, accordingly the need arose to collect what was indispensable and to gather what was required of every kind. Thus, if certain kinds should be exposed to waste, others less liable to perish would still remain. Next, because of the necessity for transactions and the aspects of giving and taking, there was (as we have said in the previous Discourse)[1555] a need for money, which is the preserver of justice, the universal adjuster and the lesser law.[1556] In virtue of its existence,[1557] and by equating a little of its kind with a great amount of other things, one is able to accomplish the labour of transporting provisions from dwellings to more remote dwellings: this, inasmuch as the transportation of a little of it (being of the value of a quantity of provisions) serves for that of a quantity of provisions, and it is therefore possible to dispense with the inconvenience and trouble of carrying the latter. Likewise, in view of the solidity of its substance, the firmness of its constitution, and the perfection of its composition[1558] (which called for permanence), it was possible to conceive of the stability and fixity of acquired gains;[1559] for if it were to change or to disappear, this would necessarily nullify the trouble taken to gain supplies and to gather acquisitions. Moreover, with its acceptance by the various peoples, its full usefulness was organized for all. By such minutiae, the providence of the perfection dependent on nature in the affairs of daily life brought Divine Grace and Godly Favour from the boundary of potency to the region of act;[1560] at the same time, that which was dependent on discipline[562] (such as other technical matters)[1561] was entrusted to the insight and regulation of the human species.

Having said so much by way of preface, we continue thus:

A consideration of the state of wealth[1562] may be under three aspects: first, with regard to income; secondly, with regard to custody; and thirdly, with regard to expenditure.[1563] As for income, its cause is, or is not, connected with competence and management,[1564] the first case being that of such matters as crafts and commercial enterprises, the second referring to inheritances and gifts. Now, commerce (inasmuch as it is conditional on stock,[1565] while stock is exposed to molestation by the means of destruction) falls short of a craft[562] or a trade in reliability and permanence.

In acquisition, it is necessary to observe on the whole three conditions: avoidance of tyranny,[985] avoidance of disgrace,[1566] and avoidance of meanness.[1567] Tyranny is present, for example, when one obtains things by domination,[886] or by discrepancy in weights and measures, or by deceit and theft. Disgrace is involved when one acquires things by stooping to impudence and tomfoolery and abasement of soul.[1568] Meanness involves gain by a base craft when one is able to perform a noble one.

Crafts are of three kinds, noble, base, and intermediate.[1569] Noble crafts are those coming within the range [1570] of the soul, not that of the body; and they are called the crafts of liberal men and of the polite.[1571] The greater part of them come within three classes: that which is dependent on the substance of the intelligence, such as sound opinion, apposite counsel, and good management—and this is the craft of ministers;[1572] that which is dependent on cultivation and learning,[1573] such as writing and rhetoric, astrology and medicine, accounting and surveying[1574]—and this is the craft of men of letters and of culture; and that which is dependent on strength[155] and courage, such as horsemanship, military command, the control of frontiers and the repulsion of enemies—and this is the craft of chivalry.[1575]

Base crafts are also of three classes: that which is repugnant to the best interest of the generality of mankind, such as practising a monopoly or engaging in sorcery—and this is the craft of the mischievous;[1576] that which is repugnant to one of the virtues, such as tomfoolery, minstrelsy and gambling—and this is the craft of the ingenious;[1577] and that which exacts a revulsion of nature,[1578] such as cupping, tanning and street-sweeping—and this is the craft of the abject. [1579] However, since the judgments of nature[663] are not acceptable to the intelligence, the last of these kinds is not abominable to the intelligence itself; from the standpoint of necessity a certain group must perform these tasks, whereas the first two kinds are indeed abominable, and men should be prevented from engagement therein.

The intermediate crafts comprise the other classes of livelihoods and kinds of trades. Some of them are necessary,[766] like agriculture, and some unnecessary, such as dyeing. Again, some are simple, like carpentry and the work of the blacksmith, while others are compound, such as scale-making and the cutler's trade.

Now, all who are characterized by a trade should make advance and seek perfection therein, not showing contentment with an inferior degree or acquiescing in meanness of aspiration. It should be recognized that men have no finer ornament than an ample subsistence,[1580] and the best means of acquiring a subsistence lies in a craft; for the latter not only comprehends justice, but is near to continence and politeness, while being remote from avidity and desire, the commission of lewd practices and the omission of important tasks.[1581] One must eschew all wealth obtained by domineering and overweening attitudes, hatred of others and persecution,[1582] or by disgraceful and disreputable means, through the expenditure of personal honour, the loss of polite standards,[1583] and the pollution of one's good repute, or through the distraction of others from their serious affairs—and this, even though the wealth be considerable. What is not defiled by such taints, however (despicable though it be in amount), should be reckoned purer and more fraught with blessing.

As for the custody of wealth, it is hardly feasible without accretion,[1584] for expenditure is necessary. In this matter, three conditions: first, that disorder does not find its way into the daily lives of the inhabitants of the household; secondly, that disorder makes no inroads on piety and good repute, for if the necessitous, notwithstanding their affluence, are left deprived of piety, it is an unfitting state of affairs, while if they turn aside from showing generosity to their equals[660] as well as to those who humbly present petitions,[1585] it is a far cry from (noble) aspiration; thirdly, one should not commit any vice thereby, such as parsimony or greed.

If these three conditions be observed, the custody (of wealth) may be effected upon three (further) conditions: first, that expenditure should not correspond to income, but be less; secondly, that there should be no expenditure on anything which it is virtually impossible[677] to turn to productive account,[1584] such as a property which cannot be cultivated or a jewel desired only by a very rare[813] person; and thirdly, that a brisk business should be sought, and a constant gain (albeit small) be preferred to great profits occurring haphazardly.[1586]

The intelligent man[200] should not neglect to store up provisions and property, so as to consume them in time of need or when it becomes hard to acquire them, as in years of famine and disaster and in periods of sickness. It has been said that it is preferable to have part of one's property in cash and the proceeds of merchandises;[1587] part in commodities, furnishings, provisions and (general) goods;[1588] and part in landed holdings, estates and livestock.[1589] In this way, if a breach be made on one side it is possible to repair it from the other two sides.

As for expenditure and disbursement, four things should be guarded against therein. The first is meanness and cheeseparing,[1590] which imply a tight restraint on one's own expenditures and those of one's family, and also abstention from giving freely in a good cause.[1591] The second is extravagance and dissipation,[1592] which involves spending on redundant purposes such as (the gratification of) appetites and pleasures, and also immoderate disbursement on an obligatory end. [1593] The third is affectation and vainglory,[1594] and involves spending wealth, pridefully and ostentatiously, in an occasion of contention and boasting. The fourth is bad management, i.e. the application in some places of more than a moderate amount,[1307] and in others of less.

The objects on which wealth is spent are confined in three categories. First comes that which is given by way of piety and in quest of the things pleasing to God, such as alms and the poor-rate;[1595] next is that which is given by way of generosity and favour and in a good cause,[1596] such as gifts and presents, pious offerings[1597] and donations; thirdly, there is that which is disbursed out of necessity, or in quest of the congenial,[1177] or in order to repel harm. The quest of the congenial refers to such things as household expenditures on items of food, drink and clothing; repulsion of harm comprises giving to the unjust[899] and the ingenious[1598] so as to preserve one's soul, one's property and one's good repute intact from them.

In the first category (the purpose of which is to seek proximity to the Majesty of Might) four conditions must be observed: first, that what is given be given in a willing spirit and with an expansive heart,[1599] without repining or regret, whether in private or openly; secondly, that one who would be sincere[1600] should give as seeking to please the Object of worship,[1601] not with expectation of gratitude or an eye to recompense, or in solicitation of renown and fame; thirdly, that the greater part be given to the poor who conceal their need,[1602] for although one should (as far as may be) not disappoint the asker, nevertheless it is more appropriate to count this division (of giving) as part of the second category, inasmuch as it is better to draw near to the Majesty of Might through something motivated from within rather than from without; fourthly, that the veil of the deserving should not be rent by divulging and publicizing their receipt of charity.

In the second category (which is numbered among the acts of the virtuous) five conditions must be observed. First comes despatch,[1603] for despatch renders matters pleasanter; secondly, concealment, for with concealment one is closer to success, apart from its being more appropriate to generosity; thirdly, belittling and disdaining (one's own part), even though it be great in terms of weight and worth; fourthly, constant giving,[1604] for interruption brings forgetfulness; fifthly, applying one's benefit in the proper place, lest it come to nothing, like seed sown in sterile ground.

In the third category only one condition must be observed: that of moderation.[1307] In that which is the means of one's seeking what is congenial,[1177] one should be closer to extravagance than to cheeseparing, at least to an extent sufficient to effect the preservation of one's good repute; for that is of the order[470] of repelling harm rather than of pure extravagance.[1605] Indeed, if one fulfils the conditions of taking the middle course[1606] in all respects, one will not escape the aspersions of the slanderer or the disparagement of the detractor. The reason for this is that equity and justice[1607] are missing in most natures, while desire and envy and ill-will are firmly rooted. Thus, relying in one's expenditure on the opinions of the common people may more readily save one's good repute than reliance on the rule of conduct followed by the elect:[1608] for the inclination of the former is to dissipation, just as that of the latter is to cheeseparing.

These are the universal laws required in the matter of handling property:[1609] their particular applications[1610] will not escape the intelligent man,[72] God Almighty so willing!

## THIRD SECTION

### CONCERNING THE CHASTISEMENT AND REGULATION OF WIVES[56]

The motive[754] for taking a wife[1611] should be twofold, the preservation of property and the quest of progeny; it should not be at the instigation of appetite or for any other purpose.

A good wife is the man's partner in property, his colleague in housekeeping[1612] and the regulation of the household, and his deputy[1613] during his absence. The best of wives is the wife adorned with intelligence, piety, continence,[585] shrewdness,[1614] modesty, tenderness, a loving disposition, control of her tongue, obedience to her husband, self-devotion in his service and a preference for his pleasure, gravity, and the respect of her own family.[1615] She must not be barren, and she should be both alert and capable in the arrangement of the household and in observing a proper allotment of expenditure.[1616] In her courteous and affable behaviour and in her pleasantness of disposition,[1617] she must cultivate the companionship of her husband, consoling him in his cares and driving away his sorrows.

A free woman is preferable to a slave, as possessing greater intimacy with both strangers and kinfolk,[1618] being better able to enlist the support of relatives and to conciliate enemies, rendering greater co-operation and assistance in the matters of daily life, and being more apprehensive of degradation in respect of society, progeny and offspring.[1619] A virgin[1620] is preferable to one who is not, for she will be more likely to accept discipline,[1621] and to assimilate herself to the husband in disposition and custom,[1622] and to follow and obey him. If, over and above these attributes, she wears the adornments of beauty, race[1623] and wealth, she unites in herself all the varieties of merits and nothing can conceivably be added thereto.

If, however, some of these qualities be lacking, (at least) intelligence, continence[585] and modesty should be present; for to prefer beauty, race and wealth to these three qualities is to invite trouble and ruin and disorder in matters spiritual and temporal. Let not a woman's beauty, above all, be an incentive[754] to ask for her in marriage: beauty is seldom allied with continence,[585] for a beautiful woman will have many admirers and suitors;[1624] at the same time, the weakness of women's intelligences offers no obstacle or hindrance to their compliance, so that they embark upon disgraceful proceedings;[1625] so, the outcome of addressing oneself to them in marriage is either lack of self-respect[1626] and endurance[609] of their disgraceful conduct (which involves wretchedness in both worlds) or the dissipation of property and wealth and the suffering of all manner of griefs and cares. Thus, as regards beauty, one should confine oneself to symmetry[830] of frame,[378] and even in this respect one should observe the exact requirement of moderation.[1627]

Likewise, a woman's property should not become a reason for desiring her, for when women own property it invites their domination and authority, a tendency to use others and to assume superiority.[1628] Even if the husband controls the wife's property, the wife accounts him as in the position of a servant and an assistant,[1629] according him no regard or esteem; thus, absolute upset follows as a necessary consequence,[1630] until, with the corruption of affairs, household and livelihood lapse utterly.

Once the bond of union[1631] is effected between husband and wife, the husband's procedure in ruling his wife should be along three lines: to inspire awe, to show favour, and to occupy her mind.[1632]

Inspiring awe means that he maintains himself as a formidable figure[1633] in the eyes of the wife, so that she would not account it allowable to be remiss in heeding his commands and prohibitions. This is the foremost condition for ruling womenfolk,[56] for if any upset befall this one condition, the way is open for the wife to follow her fancy and her will.[1634] Nor will she confine herself to this, but rather bring the husband into subjection, making him the means of attaining her desires and realizing her purposes by reducing him to subjugation and servitude. Thus the one who should command is commanded, the one who should obey is obeyed, and the regulator is regulated; and the end of such a state is the realization of shame and disgrace, of reproach and destruction to both, for so many ignominies and villainies result that it becomes inconceivable to make reparations and amends therefor.

As for showing favour, this means that one confers on the wife those things that call for love and sympathy,[1635] so that when she feels apprehensive as to the removal of that state, she solicitously undertakes the affairs of the household together with submission to her husband; whereby the desired organization results. The various categories of favours in this connection are six in number.

First, to keep her fair of aspect.[1636] Secondly, one should go to extreme lengths to keep her veiled and secluded from those having no right of entry to the female quarters,[1637] so contriving that no outsider ever learns of her marks or qualities or reputation.[1638] Thirdly, one may consult her in the early stages of household affairs, provided that this does not give her the desire to be obeyed. Fourthly, she may be given a free hand in control of provisions in the best interest of the household, and in the employment of servants on important tasks. Fifthly, one should establish close ties[1639] with her relatives and members of her family, considering it a necessary obligation to observe the exact requirements of co-operation and mutual support.[1640] Sixthly, when the husband senses the effect of her integrity and propriety,[1641] he should not prefer another wife to her, albeit the former be her superior in beauty, property, race[1623] and family; for women are impelled,[754] by the jealousy rooted in their natures, operating together with their deficiency in intelligence, to give way to abominations and ignominies, and to such other acts as necessarily bring about the corruption of the household, evil association, a disagreeable existence, and a want of order. Indeed, no indulgence[1642] is allowed in this regard to any save kings, whose purpose in taking a wife[1611] is the quest of progeny and numerous descendants, and in whose service wives are virtually slaves.[1643] Even in their case, caution is to be preferred; for the man in the household is like the heart in the body, and just as one heart cannot be the source of life in two bodies, so one man cannot easily organize two households.

As for occupying the mind, this means that one should keep the wife's mind constantly busy with the assumption of responsibility for the important affairs of the household, for consideration of its best interests, and for the performance of those things that inevitably effect the organization of daily life; for the human soul will not suffer idleness,[1644] and lack of concern with necessities inevitably leads to a regard for unnecessary matters.[1645] Thus, if a wife have no part in the arrangement of the household or the rearing of children or concern with the welfare of the servants, she will confine her attention to matters inevitably bringing disorder into the household: she will busy herself with excursions,[1646] with decking herself out for excursions, with going to see the sights, and with looking at strange men, so that not only are the affairs of the household disordered, but her husband even comes to enjoy no esteem or awe in her eyes. Indeed, when she sees other men, she despises him and holds him of little account, and she is emboldened to embark on abominable courses, and even to provoke admirers to quest after her; so that in the long run, in addition to disorganization of daily life and loss of manhood and the acquisition of disgrace, destruction and misery supervene in both this world and the next.

However, in the matter of ruling a wife, a husband must be on his guard against three things. First comes excessive love[1647] of the wife, for if this be present, it necessarily follows that the wife will become dominant and that her fancy will be preferred to his own best interests. If he is, however, afflicted with the trial of love for her, he should keep it concealed from her and so contrive that she never becomes aware thereof. Then, if he cannot contain himself, he must employ the remedies prescribed in the case of Love.[1648] In no case should he remain in that state, for such a calamity inevitably produces the aforementioned corruptions. Secondly, the husband should not consult the wife on affairs of universal importance,[1649] and certainly not inform her of his own secrets. He should, moreover, keep hidden from her the amount of his property and his capital,[1565] for women's inaccurate opinions and their want of discrimination in such matters can only invite numerous calamities. Thirdly, he should restrain the wife from foolish pastimes,[1650] from looking at strangers, and from listening to tales about men from women characterized by acts of this kind. Certainly he must never give her any easy way thereto, for such notions[197] inevitably bring grave corruptions. The most destructive (activity of all in this respect) is the frequentation of old women who have been admitted to male gatherings and retail stories from these (experiences).

There is a Tradition to the effect that women should be prevented from learning the Joseph Sūra,[1651] inasmuch as listening to such narratives may cause them to deviate from the law[1070] of continence.[585] From strong drink[1652] they should be restrained totally, for this, in however small an amount, may be the cause of impudent behaviour and of excitation of appetite;[1653] and in women, no characteristics[957] are worse than these two.

The way by which women may become worthy of their husbands' satisfaction, and gain esteem in their eyes, comprises five heads: the practice of continence;[585] a display of efficiency;[1654] standing in awe[1632] of them; compatibility in marriage and avoidance of disputes;[1655] and, finally, a minimum of scolding, with a courteous manner in their society. The philosophers[742] have said that a worthy wife will take on the role of[1656] mother, friend and mistress,[1657] while a bad wife will adopt [1656] those of despot,[1658] enemy and thief.

As for the worthy wife's attempt to assimilate to[1656] a mother, this means that she desires the husband's proximity and presence, while hating his absence; and that she will bear the burden of her own suffering in the course of attaining his desire and satisfaction, for this is the very course followed by a mother with a child. Assuming the part[1656] of a friend means that the wife should be content with whatever the husband gives her, while excusing him for whatever he withholds from her or does not give to her; at the same time, she should not grudge him (the use of) her own property, and she should conform to him in character.[1659] Playing the part of [1656] a mistress involves humbling herself in the manner of a maidservant, giving a pledge of service, and enduring the husband's sharp temper; she must also endeavour to publicize his praiseworthy side and to conceal his faults; let her, further, give thanks for his graciousness, while forbearing to scold him for whatever (in him) is uncongenial to her nature.

When the unworthy wife becomes like[1656] a despot, this means that she loves sloth and idleness,[696] utters foul abuse, frequently makes false accusations, and gives way to violent rages; at the same time, she is heedless of those things that necessarily bring about her husband's satisfaction or enragement, and she inflicts much distress on the servants, both male and female. When she behaves like[1656] an enemy, she shows contempt for her husband and treats him lightly; she displays a harsh temper, and disavows his benevolence; she becomes rancorous towards him, complains of him and repeats his faults. When she assumes the part of[1656] a thief, it means that she betrays him with respect to his property, asking from him without need and making little of his kindness; she likewise persists in courses which he detests, falsely affects friendship, and places her own advantage above his.

The prudent course[1660] for one afflicted with an unworthy wife is to seek release[1661] from her, for the proximity of a bad wife is worse than that of wild beasts and serpents. If, however, release be virtually impossible of attainment,[1662] four sorts of stratagem may be applied to the situation.

First, the expenditure of wealth, for the preservation of one's soul and manhood and good repute is better than the preservation of wealth; indeed, if it is necessary to spend a great deal of wealth to redeem oneself from her,[1663] that wealth should be accounted of little consequence. Secondly, one may resort to disputes, displays of bad temper, and a separation of sleeping-quarters, albeit in such a manner as not to lead to any mischief. Thirdly, one may adopt subtle wiles, such as encouraging old women to inspire her with an aversion to oneself and a desire for another husband, at the same time oneself outwardly professing desire for her and unwillingness to leave her—so that it may come about that she herself conceives an eagerness to leave the husband; in short, one may use, as one sees fit, all manner of connivance or obstruction, encouragement or deterrence,[1664] in order to effect a separation.[1665] Fourthly, and after finding oneself unable to implement the other measures, one may leave her, choosing to go on a far journey, so long as one shall have made arrangements to prevent her from embarking on any ignominies: this, to the end that she may lose hope, and herself choose separation.[1666]

The wise men of the Arabs[1667] have said that one should be on one's guard against five types of woman: the lamenting widow, the wife who trades on her wealth, the wife bemoaning her fallen estate, the one who is like a brand on the back of the neck, and the one who is like vegetation growing on a dunghill.[1668]

The lamenting widow is the woman who has children by another husband, and who is continually showing them favours with the wealth of that husband. The wife trading on her wealth is the well-endowed woman who by means of her wealth places her husband under an obligation. The wife bemoaning her fallen estate is the woman who, before the time of her present husband, enjoyed better circumstances or had a more eminent husband, and is continually complaining and moaning about (the loss of) those circumstances and that husband. The wife like a brand on the back of the neck is the incontinent woman:[1669] whenever her husband leaves a gathering, men speak of her in such a way as to affix a mark to the nape of his neck. The wife like vegetation on a dunghill is the fair woman of bad origin,[1670] who is accordingly compared to herbage on a midden.

Whoever is incapable of fulfilling the conditions for the chastisement of wives should rather remain a bachelor, drawing his skirt clear of contact with their affairs; for the mischief of associating with women, quite apart from its disorder,[1671] can only result in an infinite number of calamities: one of these may be the wife's intention to bring about the man's destruction, or the intention of another with regard to the wife. God it is who prospers and assists!

## FOURTH SECTION

### CONCERNING THE CHASTISEMENT AND REGULATION OF CHILDREN

When a child comes into the world, one must begin by bestowing on him a fine name; for if an inappropriate name be given to him, he will be sick at heart on that account his whole life long. Next, a nurse must be chosen, who is neither stupid nor diseased, for bad customs and most diseases are transmitted by the milk from the nurse to the child:[1672]

'Beware of approving for the child a nurse diseased and mean of mind:
'The nature that enters the body with the milk leaves it only when the soul does!'

When once his suckling is complete, one must concern oneself with the discipline and training of his character[1659] before destructive dispositions[1659] gain a hold; for the infant is apt, and inclines the more to reprehensible dispositions by virtue of the deficiency and the need in his nature. In correcting his dispositions, however, one should follow nature: that is to say, the more a faculty emerges in the infant frame,[1673] the more the perfection of that faculty should be promoted. The first of the operations[455] of the faculty of discrimination[1674] to become apparent in the infant is that of shame; accordingly, it must be observed that if shame gains the mastery over him, so that he most often behaves submissively and betrays no impudence,[975] it is an indication of his good breeding,[1675] inasmuch as his soul is averse to the abominable and inclined towards what is fair. This is, moreover, a sign of his being apt to accept discipline:[1676] if such be the case, therefore, one must show all the greater consideration for his disciplining and pay all the greater attention to his good upbringing, not showing indulgence to any negligence or omission therein.

The first principle of discipline is to keep him from mingling with the contrary-minded,[1677] for frequenting them and playing with them must inevitably corrupt his nature. The soul of an infant is malleable[1678] and all the quicker to accept form from its peers.[789] He must be awakened to a love of nobility,[1679] especially such nobilities as he can attain merit to by intelligence, discrimination and piety[1680]—not those dependent on property and race.[1623]

Next, he should be taught the practices and duties of the Faith,[1681] inspired with an assiduous devotion to them and chastised for abstention from them. Let good men be praised before him and evil men taken to task. If a fair action proceeds from him he may be praised therefor, while if it be some minor foulness, he should be intimidated by reprimand. He should be led to look favourably on contempt for eating, drinking and the wearing of splendid clothes; let him likewise be made to take delight in the soul's superiority to greed and to exclusive preference for[1682] foodstuffs and drinks and other pleasures. Again, it must be brought home to him that brightly coloured and embroidered clothes are fitting for women, while noble and eminent persons[1683] pay no heed to such things. (All this) to the end that when he has listened to it sufficiently, and his hearing becoming replete therewith from constant repetition and recital, he may adopt it as his customary practice. Whoever speaks against such ideas, especially among his coevals and peers,[789] should be kept at a distance from him. Let him be chided for bad manners,[1684] for an infant in his early days of growth and increase commits many foul actions, most often being greatly given to lying, envy, theft, tale-bearing and quarrelling; he will also tend to be a busybody,[1685] guilty of bringing down malice and harm upon himself as well as others. Later, with discipline, age and experience he will turn away from such things, but it is necessary to call him to account for them in childhood.

Thus, let his discipline be begun; and let him be given to learn by heart improving stories and poems,[1686] discoursing of noble manners, so that he becomes firmly convinced of the ideas already imparted to him. He should first be introduced to the *rajaz* and then to the *qaṣīda*;[1687] but he must be kept away from frivolous poetry, with its talk of odes and love and wine-bibbing, such as the poems of Imru' al-Qais and Abū Nuwās. No attention should be paid to those people who regard the learning of this sort of verse as a mark of elegance, claiming that tenderness of nature is to be acquired thereby; for such poetry can only be the corruption of youth.

For every good trait of character proceeding from him he should be praised and made much of, for the opposite he should be upbraided and rebuked. However, one should not openly reveal that he has committed any foul act, charging him only with negligence, so as to avoid his further embarking upon a show of insolence. Rather, if he keeps the matter to himself, let others also keep it so. But if he resumes (his course of action), let him be privately upbraided, the foulness of his behaviour being much emphasized: let him be admonished against repetition and warned against adopting it as a customary practice. Once again, however, one should be careful not to display any open hostility,[1688] for this will produce impudence[975] and incite to repetition: 'Man eagerly desires whatever is forbidden.'[1689] Indeed, he will scorn even to listen to reproaches, engaging in foul pleasures by way of bravado.[1690] In this matter, therefore, one should employ subtle wiles.

When one first begins to discipline the appetitive faculty,[89] one should instruct in the manner of eating food, in the way that we shall indicate. The child should be made to understand that the purpose of eating is health. not pleasure; for sustenance is the source of life and health, and may be regarded as drugs used to doctor hunger and thirst; just as medicine is not taken for pleasure or by desire, so likewise with food. Let the worth of food be depreciated in his eyes, and let him be made to see the foul form of the greedy man, the gormandizer and the glutton. At the same time, he should not be encouraged to desire varieties of foods, but persuaded to limit himself to one; and his appetite should be controlled, so that he restricts himself to the coarser food and feels no eagerness for that which is more pleasant. Let him also from time to time adopt the custom of eating dry bread. Such manners, albeit good in poor men, are even better in the rich.

The child should be given an ampler supper than breakfast, for if he eats a large breakfast he will become indolent and incline to sleep, and his understanding will be dulled. If he be given less meat, it will avail him in sharpness of movement, alertness, lack of dullness, and an arousal to be brisk and sprightly. Let him be kept from eating sweetmeats and confectionery, for such foods are not easily convertible.[1691] He should be accustomed not to drink water while eating, and he should on no account be given wine and intoxicating drinks before he reaches early manhood, for they will harm both his body and his soul, exciting[754] him to anger and foolhardiness, impulsiveness, impudence and giddiness.[1692] He should not even be allowed to be present in a gathering of wine-drinkers, unless the company be virtuous and polished men,[1693] from whose society some advantage accrues to him.

Let him be kept from hearing obscene remarks, and from games and idle sports and tomfoolery. He should not be given his food until he has discharged his disciplinary duties[1694] and is thoroughly tired. He should be restrained from any act performed clandestinely, for the motive[754] for concealment is an apprehension of foulness—so that (if he be not allowed to continue, in the long run) he will not become emboldened to commit what is foul. Let him be prevented from much sleep, for this brings with it grossness of understanding, deadness of mind, and languor of the members. Nor must he be allowed to sleep by day; and let him also be kept from soft clothing and the means of enjoyment, so that he grows up properly and makes hardness[1695] his habit. Let him be brought to avoid light clothing and the cool room in summer, and the heavy cloak and the fire in winter. Walking and movement, riding and exercise should be made his customary pursuits. He should, again, be kept from the contrary-minded,[1677] and taught the manners of movement and rest, rising, sitting and speaking, as we shall later indicate.

His hair should not be arranged, nor should he be decked out in the garments of women. Let him be given no ring until the time of necessity arrives. He should, moreover, be prevented from boasting to his peers[789] about his ancestors, or his wealth and possessions, and the things he has to eat and to wear; and he should instead be taught to be humble with all and gracious with his peers, and restrained from arrogance towards his inferiors and obstinacy and covetousness[1696] with his equals.[789]

He will be kept from lying and not allowed to swear oaths, whether truthfully or otherwise: oaths come ill from anyone, and even if grown men may sometimes have need of them, children assuredly never do. Let him choose to be silent, not speaking save in answer; and let him be brought to look pleasantly on occupying himself with listening before adults, avoiding obscene remarks and curses and idle conversation, and accustoming himself to good, fair and elegant speech. He should be urged to show respect to his own soul, his tutor,[1697] and anyone senior to him in age. Older boys have even greater need of such manners.

The child's tutor should be intelligent and religious, well versed in the training of dispositions and the education of the young, with a reputation for fair speech and gravity, an awe-inspiring manner, manliness and purity; he must also be aware of the characters of kings, the manners[537] involved in associating with them and addressing them, and (indeed) how to converse with every class of man. He should further be on his guard against the dispositions of the vicious and the mean.

Let the child be accompanied in the schoolroom by other well-born[1698] children, themselves adorned with good breeding and fair habit, so that he does not become bored, rather learning his manners from them: thus, as he sees other scholars, he will emulate them and contend with them, and conceive an eagerness to learn. Again, when the tutor, in the course of disciplining, proceeds to administer a beating, they will refrain from crying out and seeking intercession, for such is the act of slaves and weaklings. The first beating should be short but thoroughly painful,[1699] so that he takes warning thereby and is not emboldened to repeat his offence. Let the tutor be restrained, however, from reviling the children foully or in an ill-bred manner, being rather urged to show affection towards them, and effecting a fair retribution, so that the child comes to adopt as his own customary practice the doing of good to his fellow-men.[1700]

Let gold and silver be presented to him in a contemptible light, for the calamity arising from these is greater than that from the venoms of serpents. At times he may be given permission to play, but let his games be gentle[1701] ones, not involving excessive fatigue or pain; thus he will become rested from the fatigue of his discipline, and his mind will not be blunted. He should be accustomed to obey his father, his mother and his tutor, and to regard them with the eye of veneration, so that he goes in fear of them. Such a manner comes well from all men, but so much the better from the young.

An upbringing in accordance with this law inevitably brings about a love of virtues and an absention from vices. Let him, moreover, have his soul restrained from (the indulgence of) appetites and pleasures, and equally from the expenditure of his thought thereon, so that he may rise to higher things.[1702] He should, indeed, be led to spend his days in pleasant state and wholesome living, with fair commendation, and few enemies but many friends, both noble and virtuous.

When he passes from the stage of childhood and reaches understanding of the purposes[1703] of men, he should be made to realize that the purpose of wealth and estates and slaves, of retainers and horsemen and the spreading of carpets,[1704] is the comforting of the body and the preservation of health, so that he remains equitable of constitution[1705] and falls not into diseases and calamities, but rather wins aptitude and preparedness for the abode of eternity. Let it be brought home to him also that the true sense of 'bodily pleasures'[1706] is release from sufferings and rest from fatigue, so that he may adhere closely to this principle.

At length, if he be among the learned, let him begin gradually (as we have indicated) to learn the sciences, beginning with the science of Ethics and proceeding to the sciences of Speculative Philosophy;[1707] in this way, that which he first acquired on authority[1708] will become proven to him, and he will give thanks and rejoicing over the felicity which, in the early stage of his growth, was provided for him without any act of voluntary choice.[1709]

It is to be preferred, however, that the nature of the child should be considered and his circumstances taken into account, using physiognomical insight and discernment,[1710] in order to determine his innate fitness and aptitude for any craft or science.[1711] Only when this has been done should he be set to concern himself with the acquisition of that category; for not everyone is apt to every craft: if it were otherwise, all men would occupy themselves with the nobler craft.[1712] Indeed, beneath this discrepancy and divergence that are deposited in men's natures,[1713] there lie an obscure secret and a subtle device, on which may be dependent the ordering of the universe and the support of the descendants of Adam. 'Thus is the ordaining of the Mighty One, the Knowing One'.[1714] However, when someone is apt for a craft, let him be directed towards it (without more ado), for he will the sooner attain its fruits and wear the ornament of a calling;[1715] otherwise, his days will have been let go to waste and his life made useless.

In every branch, the candidate should be urged to a full study of what pertains to that branch in the way of compilations of the sciences and the humanities.[1716] Thus, if he wishes to learn, for example, the craft of secretaryship, he must make an intensive study of calligraphy and polished discourse, and he must memorize treatises, orations, proverbs, poems, anecdotes, dialogues, elegant stories and witty novelties, while at the same time learning the keeping of accounts, and the other literary sciences.[1717] Nor should he content himself with knowing some and ignoring the rest, for the failure of aspiration in acquiring a calling[1715] is the vilest and most destructive of characteristics.

When a child's nature is found to be unsuitable for the acquisition of a particular craft, inasmuch as he lacks favourable equipment and apparatus,[1718] let him not be forced thereto: there is wide scope in the varieties of craft, so let him transfer to another. However, this is on condition that having made a considerable advance and start therein, he should practise assiduity and constancy, not throwing everything into upset and confusion and moving from one ill-learned calling[1719] to another. In the course of application to any branch one becomes accustomed to training, which moves the natural heat,[165] and this necessarily effects the preservation of health, the banishment of sloth and stupidity, the sharpening of wits, and the arousal of cheerful attitudes.[1720]

When one of the crafts has been learned, let him be enjoined to win his livelihood and earn his daily bread thereby; so that, perceiving the delight of acquirement, he may take it to its farthest extent, even employing speculative virtue to master the finer points thereof.[1721] (There is also the practical consideration) that he should be capable and skilled enough to seek his means of subsistence and accept responsibility for matters pertaining to this; for most children of rich men, deluded by wealth and cut off from crafts and a knowledge of appropriate behaviour,[1722] tend to fall, after a reverse of fortune, into humiliation and poverty, and to become a source of annoyance to their friends and of unholy satisfaction[1723] to their enemies.

Once a boy is earning by means of a craft, it is better that he be made to take a wife, and that he should be set up in a separate home.[1724] It was a practice among the kings of Persia not to have their children reared among retainers and servants, but to send them away with trustworthy persons, so that they should grow up used to hard living and to rough fare and clothing, and averse to luxury and splendour: the cases of these persons are well known. In Islamic times, the rulers of Dailam have had the very same custom.[1725]

When a person has been brought up, however, contrary to the ideas set forth above, he will find it difficult to accept discipline, especially when age has left its mark upon him; an exception may be made if he is aware of his abominable character, apprised of the manner of rooting out established custom, intent and painstaking to that end, and inclined to the company of good men. Socrates the Philosopher,[8] being asked why he consorted most with young men, replied: 'Because it is conceivable that moist and tender branches may be straightened, but there is no tendency towards straightness in withered sticks that have lost their freshness and had their bark dried out.'

So much for the chastisement of sons. In the case of daughters, one must employ, in the selfsame manner, whatever is appropriate and fitting to them. They should be brought up to keep close to the house and live in seclusion,[1726] cultivating gravity, continence,[585] modesty and the other qualities we have enumerated in the chapter on Wives. They should be prevented from learning to read or write,[1727] but allowed to acquire such accomplishments as are commendable in women. When they reach the bounds of maturity they should be joined to one of equal standing.[1728]

Having completed our account of the way to bring up children, we will conclude this Section by mentioning those classes of manners[537] which we have promised, in the course of the argument, to expound in detail. In this way, children may learn them and adorn themselves therewith. Nevertheless, it behoves all categories of men to pay close attention to them, not regarding themselves as able to dispense with them: the singling out of this one category in the present Section is not because children stand in greater need thereof, but for the reason that they may be more receptive of these matters, and better able to persevere in them. God it is who best prosper and assists.

*The Manners[537] of Speech*: One should not speak much, nor interrupt the speech of another by one's own. Whenever someone is relating a story or a tale of which one already has knowledge, one should not reveal one's knowledge thereof, so that the person in question may complete his discourse. Let no man answer to a matter that is asked of another. If a question be put to a group of which he is one, let him not try to outstrip the others. If someone be already occupied with making answer, and he be capable of giving a better, he should be patient until that answer is completed, then giving his own in such a way as to offer no affront to his precedent.[1729] Let him not plunge into any discussions being carried on by two persons in his presence; and if they should conceal their remarks from him, let him not try to overhear; above all, so long as they do not for their part invite him to join them therein, let him make no move to interfere.

When dealing with his superiors[1730] a man should not speak in allusions;[1731] nor should he keep his voice high or low, but observe a mean.[830] If some obscure idea occur in his argument, let him endeavour to expound it by means of clear examples: otherwise, let him observe the requirements of brevity. He should not employ uncommon terms or unusual allusions.[1732] When others are developing an argument before him, he should not take it upon himself to reply until the argument is complete. When he does speak, he should not make any pronouncement before first fixing the idea in his mind. Let him not repeat his remarks unless there be need to do so.

A man should not betray agitation or anguish, nor utter obscenities or abuse. If, however, he finds himself compelled to mention something obscene, let him allude to it indirectly.[1733] He should not make improper jests.[1734]

In any gathering let him make discourse appropriate to that gathering; and in the course of his speech, let him not gesture with hands and eyes and eyebrows, unless what he is saying demands some delicate gesture, when he may perform it in the approved manner. He should not engage in argument and dispute, with the members of any gathering, over what is true and what false: especially, let him not dispute with superiors[1730] or with the ingenious,[1735] or with anyone with whom it is not profitable to dispute. When the case of one opponent finds favour with him in a debate or a controversy, he should nevertheless see justice done. Let him be, as far as possible, cautious in addressing common people,[1736] children, women, madmen and drunken persons. Let him not use subtle language with one who does not understand. In controversy, let him observe delicacy: he should not maliciously[1737] mimic the movements, actions or words of any person, nor should he use language likely to cause alarm.[1738] When he comes before a superior, let him begin with a remark that may be taken as an acceptable omen.

Slander, calumny, false accusations and lying are to be avoided: indeed, in no circumstance may one engage therein. One should have nothing to do with the authors of such things, being loth to give ear to them. Listening should be practised more often than speaking: a wise man[8] was asked why his listening exceeded his utterance, to which he replied: 'Because I have been given two ears, but only one tongue—that is to say, you must listen twice as much as you speak!'

*The Manners*[537] *of Movement and Rest*: In walking one should not move quickly or in haste, for that is a sign of frivolity;[1739] nor, however, should one go to exaggerated lengths in dawdling and slowness, for that is a mark of sloth.[971] One should not strut like the arrogant, or move the shoulders in the manner of women and effeminate men.[1740] The dangling and the movement of the hands are also to be guarded against, equilibrium[830] being preserved in all situations.

When walking, a man should not much look behind, for such is the action of loutish persons.[1741] Nor, however, must the head be held constantly forward, for this is an indication of grief and overwhelming anxiety. In riding, likewise, equilibrium[830] is to be preserved.

When sitting, the feet should not be put forward, nor should one be placed on the other. One should kneel[1742] only in subservience before kings, a master, a father, or anyone comparable to these persons. The head should not be rested on the knees or the hands, for that is a mark of grief or sloth.[971] One should not hold the neck bent, or play with the beard or the other members. Let not the finger be placed in the mouth or the nose, and let no noise be produced with the fingers, the neck[1743] or the other members. Yawning and stretching are to be avoided; nor should one blow the nose or spit in the presence of others, but if the necessity should befall, these things should be done in such a way that the noise thereof does not reach those present. At the same time, they should not be done with the bare hand, the edge of a sleeve, or a clean skirt. The expectoration of saliva (in particular) is greatly to be avoided.

When he goes into an assembly, let a man look to his rank, not sitting above his own delimitation, nor below. But if he be the senior among those who have taken their places, the obligation to preserve his rank lapses from him, since wherever he sits, there is the place of honour. If he be a stranger and have not sat in his due place, let him come thither as soon as he becomes aware of this. Should he not find his place to be vacant, however, he should endeavour to return without allowing any agitation or reluctance to become apparent.

Before others, let him bare only his face and hands. Before superiors,[1730] he should not bare his forearms or his legs; while in no circumstances, whether privately or in the presence of another, should he uncover the area between the knee and the navel. Let him not go to sleep before others; nor should he sleep on his back, especially if he snores in his sleep, for taking this position causes the noise to become louder. If drowsiness overcomes a man in the midst of a gathering, he should either rise (supposing he is able to do so) or banish sleep by conversation or thought. When, however, he finds himself in the midst of a gathering who themselves fall asleep, he should either suit himself to them or leave them, so long as he does not stay there awake.

In general, he should so act as not to produce annoyance or revulsion in others, behaving churlishly[1744] to no man and in no circle.

Should some of these customs come hard to him, let him consider to himself that such blame and reproach as must necessarily be his lot, as the result of neglecting one point of good manners,[1745] will greatly exceed the tribulation he has to bear in abandoning that to which he is accustomed. In this way, it will become easy for him.

*The Manners*[537] *of Eating*: First, hands and mouth and nose should be cleansed, and then one may appear at table. When one takes one's seat at table, one should not proceed to eat directly, unless one be the host. The hand and the clothing should not be soiled, not more than three fingers should be employed in eating, and the mouth should not be opened wide. The eater should not take up large morsels, nor should he swallow quickly or keep his mouth full. Let him not lick his fingers. At the same time, he should not inspect the different varieties of food, or sniff at them, or make a selection from them. If the best dish be scant in amount, let him not fall upon it greedily, but rather offer it to others. Grease should not be left on the fingers; bread and salt should not be made damp. One should not look at one's fellow-diners, nor inspect the morsels they take, but eat with one's face forwards. That which is taken to the mouth (we refer to such things as bones) should not (afterwards) be placed on the bread or the table-cover;[1746] when there is a bone or a hair in a morsel of food, let it be removed from the mouth in such a way that no one else is aware.

Let a man beware of committing that which he finds repulsive in others. Let him, too, so keep what is before him that if someone conceives a desire to take up the remains of his food, such a person is not (in the event) repelled thereby. Nothing from the mouth and no morsel of food should be dropped into one's cup or onto the bread.

A man should not withdraw his hand (from eating) some considerable time before the other guests: rather, if he feels himself satiated, should he while away the time until the others also finish. If, however, the assembly as a whole withdraw their hands, he should do likewise, even though he be hungry; an exception may be made where he is in his own home or in a place where there are no strangers present. If, in the course, of a meal he feels the need for water, let him not drink it hastily so as to produce noises from mouth and gullet. When a man picks his teeth, he should go to one side: that which drops onto the tongue from the teeth he should swallow down, while that which he brings out with the toothpick he should throw away in some place where other people will not be disgusted by it; if he find himself in a group, however, he should cease picking his teeth. When he washes his hands, he should be at great pains to cleanse the fingers and the roots of the nails, and likewise while cleaning the lips and the teeth; but he should not gargle, or spit into the basin. (If water does run from his mouth, he should conceal it with his hand.) Let him not try to wash his hands before others can; if, however, hands are washed before the meal, it is proper that precedence should go to the host, in this, over the others present.

*The Manners*[537] *of Wine-drinking*: When wine is brought on at a gathering, one should sit next to the most virtuous of one's fellow-men, taking care not to sit beside anyone noted for inconsiderate behaviour.[1747] The (atmosphere of the) party should be kept agreeable with witty anecdotes and attractive poems having some appropriateness to time and circumstance. Sourness of countenance and a mood of depression[1748] are to be avoided.

If a man be the junior member of the gathering, by age or in rank, he should occupy himself with listening. If a musician be present, one should not embark upon the telling of stories. Let a man not interrupt the discourse of his boon companion.[1749] In all circumstances one should pay attention to the senior member of the party, giving ear to his observations, but without totally disregarding others.

In no case may one stay so long as to become drunk, for nothing is more harmful than drunkenness to one's concerns in this world and the next, just as no virtue or nobility exceeds that of good sense and sobriety.[1750] Accordingly, if a man have a poor head for wine,[1751] he should drink little, or he should dilute it, or he should leave the party earlier. If, again, his companions become drunk before he reaches the stage of circumspection,[1752] he should endeavour to get away from them, or so contrive that the drunken man leaves the gathering. Let him not become involved in the conversation of drunken men or busy himself in mediation between them; however, where matters eventuate in hostility, he should restrain them from (attacking) each other. If he be capable in wine-drinking, let him show no excessive concern with what circulates, nor force his companions thereto. If one of the boon companions be incapable of wine-drinking, he should not bear hard upon him. Again, should a malaise[1753] overwhelm him, let him fight it off in the midst of the assembly in such a way that his companions do not become aware thereof, or let him go outside without delay; once he has vomited, he may return to the party.

He should not pick up fruits and sweet-herbs from before his friends, nor should he consume quantities of sweetmeats. Let him single out each one of his fellows with the greeting appropriate to him. He should not alone become the source of the party's sociability, cheerfulness and liveliness, for such a notion leads to lack of respect. Let him not rise frequently from the assembly. If a handsome person[1754] be present, he should not constantly look at him, even though the latter be bold towards him, and he should not speak to him much. Let him not be asking the instrumentalists for the tune which he naturally favours. When he reaches the limit that he recognizes, let him rise and endeavour to go to his accustomed place; but if he cannot, he should (at least) go to a location remote from the party and there lie down.

So far as he is able, let him not appear at parties given by princes, or persons who are not his peers,[660] or those with whom he is not on easy terms. In cases of necessity, let him (at least) quickly leave again. At no time should he go to parties given by 'clever' people.[1755] If at any time he be afraid of drunkenness, while his boon companions press him to stay, it is proper for him to get away from the party by pretending to be drunk, or by some other stratagem.

This is as much as we promised to relate on the subject of Manners.[537] This category transcends the limit of computation, varying according to situations and times; nevertheless, it is not difficult, for an intelligent and virtuous man who has mastered the laws and the fundamental principles of fair actions,[1756] to observe the conditions and the finer points[1757] of each matter in its own place. From universals it is easy for him to deduce the particulars, intelligence itself being a just arbiter in every case. And God best knows what is right!

### *Supplementary Section on observing the Rights of Parents*

This Section was appended, after the publication of the work, some time in the year 663.[1758]

Thirty years after the publication of the present book, there arrived in these parts, (coming) from the Presence of the Emperor of the World (God eternalize his reign!)[1759] a certain great man, outstanding among mankind in most of the branches of virtues: namely, the one served and revered, Prince of Amirs in this world,[1760] Glory of State and Faith, Pride of the World, 'Abd al-'Azīz al-Nīshāpūrī (God strengthen his supporters and prolong his glorification!). And, ennobling this work with his august perusal, he observed that from among the virtues to be found mentioned therein, one great virtue was missing—namely, observance of the rights of parents, which naturally follows[1761] from worship of the Creator,[665] as He has Himself ordained (mighty is His Name!):'Thy Lord has decreed that thou shouldst worship none save Him, but to thy parents show kindness!'

'Accordingly', (the great man went on to say) 'it is fitting that there should also be some indication urging men towards this virtue and warning them away from the vice corresponding to it, i.e. filial disobedience.'[1762] The writer of the present book had (in fact) made some mention of this idea in several places, allusively and indirectly; however, since this omission does occur at the proper location, he has appended a few lines on the subject as an addendum to the Fourth Section of the Second Discourse, which itself deals with the Chastisement and Regulation of Children. It is as follows.

The course to be followed by children in seeking to please their parents, as also the obligation to observe the latter's claims upon them, have been referred to by Almighty God in several places in the Revelation.[1763] At the same time, these things may be known in the present work also, by way of the intelligence, from what we have set down in the Seventh Section of the Second Division of the First Discourse, which is confined to an exposition of the superiority of Justice to the other virtues and an account of its divisions and states. Thus, mention having been made of the graces of the Creator[380] (exalted is He!), and it having been explained how there is an obligation to offer Him gratitude and worship in the measure of one's capacity, as required in the course of justice: (it is then observed that,) next to the graces of the Creator[380] (exalted is He!), no good can be compared with those received by children from their parents. In the first place, the father is the first of the contingent causes[1764] bringing about the child's existence. Next, he is the cause of the child's being reared and brought to perfection. Thus, on the one hand, from the physical advantages attaching to the father he achieves physical perfections (such as growth and increase and nourishment, and so on), which are the causes of the enduring and perfecting of the child's person; while, on the other hand, from the father's psychical[302] management he attains psychical perfections (such as manners,[537] education, virtue, skills, sciences, and a way of earning his livelihood),[1765] which are the causes of the enduring and perfecting of the child's soul. Moreover, by all manner of toil and trouble and the shouldering of burdens, the father makes a worldly accumulation, which he stores up for the child's sake, looking favourably on his succession after his own death.

Secondly, the mother, at the beginning of the child's existence, associates and participates with the father in causality,[1766] inasmuch as she is receptive to the operation effected by the father.[1767] Again, she endures the toil of carrying the child for nine months, the tribulations of the peril of birth-giving, and the pangs and sufferings of that state. She is an even closer cause,[1768] in the matter of supplying food to the child, for she is the source of its very life; and she is for a long time directly concerned with its physical nurture,[1769] attracting beneficial things to the child and repelling harms from it. Indeed, in her excess of compassion and affection, she will place the child's life above her own.

All this being so, justice demands that, after the Creator's[665] claims have been met, nothing should take precedence over observance of the rights of parents, (the expression of) gratitude for graces received from them, and the effecting of their contentment. Moreover, in one sense, this category (of duty) is more proper to be observed than the former, for the Creator[665] is able to dispense with requital for His graces, while parents stand in such need thereof that they expect and look for a child all their days in order that he may serve them and discharge his obligations towards them. This, then, is the reason for the juxtaposition of 'kindness to parents' with the profession of unicity and the obligation to worship.[1770] The purpose of the custodians of the religious ordinances[1771] in urging men to do this is to the end that they acquire this virtue.

Observance of the rights of parents lies in three things:

First, in a sincere love for them in the heart, and the aim to please them in word and deed, by such things as veneration, obedience, service, softness of speech, humility, and all such things as do not lead to conflict with the satisfaction of the Creator[380] (exalted is He!) or to any prohibited and disorderly course. Where a conflict does result, it should be by way of humane behaviour, not through open hostility or strife.[1772]

Secondly, in rendering assistance to them in all their requirements, before they themselves ask for it, without any taint[755] of conferring a favour or seeking a return,[1773] and in the measure of possibility: this again, so long as it does not lead to anything seriously prohibited, for this one is bound to avoid.

Thirdly, in displaying a benevolent attitude towards them, both privately and publicly, in this world and the next, carefully guarding their injunctions and the works of piety for which they have given directions—and all this both while they are still alive and also after their deaths.

As will be explained in the Second Section of the Third Discourse (which is devoted to an account of the virtue of Love),[60] the love of parents for their children is a natural love, while that of the children for their parents is voluntary. This is why, in the religious ordinances,[1774] children are more frequently exhorted to show kindness to their parents than are the latter to show kindness to their children.

From what we have said, the difference between the rights of the father and those of the mother will be evident. The rights of the father are more spiritual,[1775] and for this reason children become aware of them only after intellectual consideration.[1776] The rights of the mother, on the other hand, tend rather to be physical,[1777] and for this reason children understand them when they first begin to feel, showing a readier inclination towards their mothers. This being so, the claims of fathers are to be discharged rather by offering obedience, and by kindly mention, benediction and commendation (which are more spiritual[1775] concerns); and those of mothers by offering money and bestowing the means of livelihood, and by all the various sorts of kindness that tend to be more physical.[1777]

As for filial disobedience,[1762] which is the vice corresponding to this virtue, it also is of three kinds:

First comes hurt to the parents by a deficiency of love,[60] or by words and deeds leading to some degree thereof, e.g. by showing contempt for them, or being 'clever' at their expense,[1747] or holding them up to mockery, and so on. Second comes stinginess and quarrelling with them about money matters and the means of livelihood, or offering while seeking a return or with an admixture of patronage,[1778] or regarding any kindness done them as burdensome. Third come such things as despising them and showing them no compassion, whether privately or publicly, in life or after death; and also holding of little account their counsels and injunctions.

Just as kindness to parents naturally follows from sound conviction, so filial disobedience[1762] naturally follows from corrupt conviction.

Those persons who may be compared to[1779] parents (such as masters, grandparents, paternal and maternal uncles, elder brothers, and the parents' own true friends) are on the same footing as [1779]they in respect of the obligation to observe reverence towards them, to give to them and assist them in times of need, and to avoid anything leading to their displeasure.

From other Sections of this book, offering as they do an exposition of the mode of intercourse with the various categories of mankind,[65] one may obtain full information on the ends in view[48] in the present connection. If God Almighty will, He being the Guardian of Success!

## FIFTH SECTION

### CONCERNING THE GOVERNMENT OF SERVANTS AND SLAVES[57]

It should be understood that, within the household, servants and slaves occupy the same position as hands and feet and other members in relation to the body. Thus, anyone undertaking to do for another something requiring the assistance of the hand takes the place of the other person's hand; and whoever exerts himself in a task in which the foot should labour, accomplishes toil proper to the foot; while the one who observes with the eye anything on which a look should be expended, spares this trouble to the sight (of the other person).

Where this class of people does not exist, the doors of ease are fast shut, for through their constant rising and sitting, their various motions and rests, and their successive advances and withdrawals[1780] (which impose fatigue of body, lapse of severity, and loss of gravity) important functions[1090] may be discharged. Accordingly, due thanks should be offered for the existence of this company: they should be regarded as the pledges of Almighty God, and all manner of benevolence, affability, gentleness and encouragement should be used in their employment. The limbs and members of this class of people are (after all) also subject to weariness and lassitude, languor and exhaustion, and the impulses[684] of necessities and voluntary choices[1781] are likewise implanted in their natures.[657] Therefore, one should observe the punctilio of equity and justice,[1782] and refrain from oppression and tyranny, so that Almighty God's governance may be advanced and gratitude rendered for His grace.

When taking servants, one should gain a thorough knowledge and experience, and an acquaintance with a person's circumstances, before putting him to work. If, however, this cannot well be done, one should have recourse to physiognomical insight, and intuition and conjecture.[1783] Let a man, however, feel bound to keep away from persons of irregular form and incongruous proportion, for in most cases the disposition will follow the physical shape.[1784] As the Persian proverb has it, 'the nicest thing about an ugly man is his face!' And the Tradition says: 'Seek good among the pleasant-faced!' One should, too, avoid the afflicted, such as the one-eyed and the crippled and the leprous, and the like. To rely, at the same time, on the quick and ingenious person[1785] is not to behave circumspectly, for it often happens that deception,[695] guile and trickery are allied with these two qualities. Modesty and small intelligence are to be preferred to great vigour of mind[1786] together with impudence,[975] for modesty is the best of qualities in this connection.

When the servant is successfully acquired, he should be employed at the craft for which he is designated as fitted, and his wants attended to. Let him not be transferred from one sort of work to another and from craft to craft, but let him rather be made content with that to which his nature inclines, and for which the equipment[1787] is available to him; for every nature has a particularity[1000] for a particular craft. If this law[1070] be transgressed, one behaves like the man who ploughs with the horse while making the ox to run. However, when a servant objects to a certain sort of work, his objection should not be the essential reason for taking him away from it,[1788] for such is the behaviour of the despondent and the restless; whenever the master does take such a man away from his work, he will stand in need of a better replacement, and the same will apply to the replacement himself, so that one remains deprived of the advantage of service altogether.

The master must have firmly established in his servants' hearts (the conviction) that there is no manner or means for them to leave him, in any way or for any cause whatsoever. Such a course is not only closer to courtesy[1789] and appropriate to loyalty and generosity, but it leads the servant to observe the requirement of compassion and affection, conformity and carefulness; for such behaviour proceeds from the latter (only) when he recognizes himself as a partner and a participant in the grace and wealth of the one he serves, and when he is secure from dismissal or transfer.[1790] When he conceives, however, that his master is weak in judgment and feeble of purpose, being likely to discharge him for any single offence, he will reckon himself as (so to speak) loaned[1489] to his service, and his situation will be like that of a transient: he will give no thought to any task, nor will he observe the requirement of compassion, limiting his aspiration rather to collecting and storing away against the day of departure and the ill-treatment received from his master.

The basic principle governing the service of servants is that what impels[754] them thereto should be love,[60] rather than necessity or hope or fear: in this way, they perform the service of good counsellors,[1791] not the inferior service of slaves. No disorder of any kind whatsoever should be committed in anything pertaining to the servants' livelihood, whether in matters of food or dress or in any other respect: on the contrary, one should put these matters before one's own indispensable needs, seeing that they are provided for[374] in respect of everything necessary. Let times of rest and ease be appointed for them, it being thus contrived that the tasks entrusted to them are undertaken cheerfully and diligently, not in an attitude of languor and sloth.

In correcting[1792] servants, degrees must be observed, various types of discipline and rectification[1793] being employed in accordance with the different categories of crimes and offences; but the path of forgiveness must not (in any case) be entirely closed off. Where a person reverts to his offence after repentance, he should be given a taste of punishment, and a measure of severity may even be employed; but one should not despair of his taking the right road, so long as he has not removed the fetter of modesty or professed self-will[1794] and impudence.[975] If, however, he become contaminated with any lewd offence or vile iniquity (in which it is reprehensible to continue), and will not accept reform[1792] through discipline and correction,[1795] then the right course is to banish him with all speed. Should this not be done, the other servants will be ruined by his proximity, inasmuch as the corruption passes from him to others.

A slave is better fitted for service than a free man, for a slave is more inclined to accept obedience to the master and training in accordance with his dispositions[1659] and manners;[537] he is also more apt to despair at (the prospect of) separation from the master. When choosing slaves, one should take for one's personal service[1796] the more intelligent, the wiser, the more eloquent, and those with a greater share of modesty and piety. For commercial enterprises, one needs those who are more continent, more capable and more acquisitive. The cultivation of estates calls for those with a tendency to strength, toughness and the capacity for hard work; while the grazing of flocks is best carried on by those with stout hearts and loud voices and no great inclination to sleep.

Slaves may be placed in three categories according to their nature:[1797] the freeman by nature, the slave by nature, and the slave by appetite.[1798] The first group should be treated like children and encouraged to acquire a proper mode of conduct.[1799] The second should be used like beasts and cattle and kept in training.[1800] The third category should be allowed to indulge their appetite in accordance with need, and kept at work by scornful and slighting treatment.

Among the classes of nations, the Arabs are distinguished for their speech,[1266] their eloquence and their ingenuity,[1801] but they are also noted for harsh nature and powerful appetite.[1802] The Persians, on the other hand, are distinguished by intelligence, quickness,[1803] cleanliness and sagacity,[1804] albeit noted for cunning and greed. The Byzantines are distinguished for loyalty, trustworthiness, affection and competence,[1805] but noted for stinginess and meanness. Indians are distinguished for strength of feeling, and of intuition[1806] and understanding, but noted for conceit, malevolence, guile and a tendency to fabrication. The Turks are distinguished by courage, worthy service and fine appearance, but noted for treachery, hardness of heart and indelicacy.[1807]

This is the complete argument on this subject. And God best knows what is right!

THIRD DISCOURSE

# *On Politics:*[1513] *comprising eight Sections*

## FIRST SECTION

### ON THE REASON OF MAN'S NEED FOR CIVILIZED LIFE,[58] AND AN EXPOSITION OF THE NATURE[59] AND VIRTUE OF THIS BRANCH OF SCIENCE

WE remarked earlier that every existent being has a perfection: in the case of some existent beings, this perfection is conjoined with existence at genesis;[1808] in others, the perfection is subsequent to[1809] existence. An example of the first category is to be found in the heavenly bodies, while the second is represented by terrestrial compounds. Furthermore, whatever has a perfection subsequent to its own existence, must inevitably have a motion from deficiency to perfection; and that motion cannot occur without the aid of causes, some of which are 'perfecters' and some 'disposers'.[1810] The 'perfecters' are such things as the forms that emanate from the Bestower of Forms, by way of succession,[1811] onto the sperm, with the result that it passes from the boundary of 'sperm-ness'[1812] to human perfection. By the 'disposers' are denoted such things as sustenance, which becomes matter in relationship,[1813] so that growth may reach the end that is possible.

Aid is basically of three kinds. First comes that which is a partial aid[1814] to the thing in need of aid, such aid being matter. Secondly, there is the aid intermediate between the thing in need of aid, on the one hand, and its act on the other: such aid is an instrument. Thirdly, there is the aid having an act on its own account,[1815] such act being a perfection relative to[1816] the thing in need of aid: this aid is a service.[1817] This last category has two divisions: that which aids essentially, i.e. the end[1416] of its act is aid itself; and that which aids accidentally, i.e. its act has some other end, and aid results in consequence.

An example of aid as matter is that rendered by the plant to the animal, which derives sustenance therefrom. An example of aid as instrument is that rendered by fluid[1818] to the nutritive faculty[124] in bringing sustenance to the members. Aid as essential service[1819] is represented by that of the slave to the master, and as accidental service,[1819] by that of the shepherd to the flock.

The Second Philosopher, Abū Naṣr Fārābī,[1820] from whose *dicta* and aphorisms[1821] the greater part of the present Discourse is derived, says that snakes essentially serve the elements,[1822] for they themselves derive no advantage from biting animals, and thus bringing about the dissolution of the latter's composition; wild beasts, on the other hand, serve accidentally, for their purpose in hunting prey is their own advantage, and dissolution into elements[1822] necessarily follows as a consequence.

Having said so much by way of preface, we go on to observe that elements,[1822] plants and animals—all three—render aid to the human species, and this whether as matter, as instrument, or by way of service. But Man renders them no aid, save in the third way, and that accidentally; for he is nobler, while they are baser, and although it is proper for the baser to serve the baser as well as the nobler, yet it is not proper for the nobler to serve the baser, but only its own like. Man aids his own kind by way of service, not as matter or instrument. Indeed, as matter he cannot render aid to anything if he be considered as a human being,[1823] for, so considered, he is an abstract substance.[1824]

Now just as Man needs elements[1822] and compounds to aid him in all three categories, so he needs his own species also to render mutual aid by way of service. Animals have need both of the natural elements[1825] and of plants, but their need of their own kind varies: thus, certain animals, such as those spontaneously generated[1826] and most aquatic animals (which have no need in propagation for union of male and female), are able to exist without mutual aid, and there is no conceivable profit in their coming together. In the case of certain others, however, such as most of the procreative animals,[1827] the individual males and females have need of each other to preserve the species; whereas to preserve the individual, after the period of nurture, they stand in no need of mutual aid or association; thus they come together at the time of mating and during the days of growth, but thereafter each one separately goes about his business. Others again, such as bees and ants and certain classes of birds, need to give mutual aid and to come together, both for the preservation of the individual and also for that of the species.

As for plants, they need the elements[1822] and the minerals[1828] in all three categories. The need, as matter, is obvious; as instrument, the need may be like that of the seed for something to keep it covered and protected from the blight of cold and heat until it grows; as service, one may instance its need for mountains containing springs of water. Plants may have need of one another for preservation of the species, as in the case of the palm-tree,[1829] where the female will not bear fruit without the male. For the preservation of the individual, however, they have no need of each other, save in rare instances: one may cite the example of the gourd-plant, the existence of which is exposed to destruction if it have no support, and similarly with the vine and certain other plants.

The compounds have need of the elements[1822] in all three categories. It may be that within these four degrees—i.e. elements,[1822] minerals,[1828] plants and animals—some render service to others coming after them in rank, as we have mentioned in the case of the snakes;[1830] in that respect, the former are (to be regarded as) more base.

To summarize: the purpose of this detailed exposition is to show that the human species, which is the noblest of existent beings in the universe, needs both the aid of the other species and the co-operation of its own kind to ensure the survival of the individual as well as that of the race. The demonstration of its need for the other species is surely evident, and there is no further necessity to develop it in this place. The demonstration of its need for the co-operation of its own kind is as follows: Let us suppose that each individual were required to busy himself with providing his own sustenance, clothing, dwelling-place and weapons, first acquiring the tools of carpentry and the smith's trade, then readying thereby tools and implements for sowing and reaping, grinding and kneading, spinning and weaving, and the other trades and crafts, and only then concerning himself with these weighty undertakings themselves. Clearly, he would not survive without food during all this time; and if his days were to be divided up among several occupations, he would not be capable of doing justice to any one of them all.

But when men render aid to each other, each one performing one of these important tasks that are beyond the measure of his own capacity, and observing the law[1070] of justice[52] in transactions[1831] by giving greatly and receiving in exchange of the labour of others: then the means of livelihood are realized, and the succession of the individual and the survival of the species are assured and arranged: as is the case in fact. Surely there is an allusion to this idea in the Traditions, where it is said that when Adam (peace be upon Him!) came into the world and sought sustenance, he had to perform a thousand tasks until bread was baked, the thousand and first being to cool the bread, which he then ate. The same idea is to be found expressed by the Philosophers[765] in the following way: a thousand hard-working individuals are required before one morsel can be put into the mouth.

Now, since the work of Man pivots[1832] on mutual aid, while co-operation is realized by men undertaking each other's important tasks fairly and equally,[1833] it follows that the diversity of crafts, which proceeds from the diversity of purposes, demands (a measure of) organization; for if the whole species were to betake themselves in a body to one craft, there would be a return of the situation against which we have just been on guard.[1834] For this reason, Divine Wisdom[1835] has required that there should be a disparity of aspirations and opinions, so that each desires a different occupation, some noble and others base, in the practice of which they are cheerful and contented.

Likewise, it has been ordained that there should be diversity in their states in such matters as wealth and poverty, quickness and stupidity; for if all be wealthy, they will not serve one another, as equally they will not if all be poor: in the first case, this is on account of their being independent of each other, in the second because of inability to pay anything in return for the service of one to another. Again, since crafts vary in nobility and baseness, if all men be equal in the faculty of discrimination,[1836] they will choose one class (of employment), whereby the other classes will remain vacant and the desired end will not be realized. This is what the Philosophers[765] mean when they say: 'If men were equal, they would all perish'.[1837]

However, since some are distinguished by correct management and others by superior strength, one group by great dignity of manner and another by abundant capability (while some, devoid of discrimination and intelligence, are virtually tools and instruments for men so endowed), all tasks are determined in the manner as observed; and from each undertaking his own important duty, the ordering of the universe and the organization of Man's daily life becomes act.

Now, since it is impossible to conceive the species to exist without co-operation, while co-operation without combination[1838] is an absurdity,[802] therefore the human species is naturally in need of combination. This type of combination, of which we have already given an account, is called 'civilized life'.[58] The term is derived from 'city', a city being a place of combination for individuals carrying on, by their various trades and crafts, the co-operation which is the means of procuring a livelihood. Just as we said, concerning Economics, that what was meant by 'household' was not a dwelling, but the combination of the inhabitants of a dwelling in a particular way:[1839] so here also, what is meant by 'city' is not the dwellings of the inhabitants of a city, but a particular association[1840] between the inhabitants of a city. This is what the Philosophers[765] mean when they say that Man is naturally a city-dweller,[1841] i.e. he is naturally in need of the combination called 'civilized life'.[58]

Now, the motives[684] for men's actions differ, and their movements are directed to varying ends, e.g. the intention of one will be to attain a pleasure, whereas that of another will be to acquire an honour: thus, if they be left to their own natures,[657] no co-operation can conceivably result among them, for the domineering man[1842] will make everyone his slave, while the greedy[342] will desire for himself all things that are acquired; and when strife befalls among them, they will concern themselves (only) with mutual destruction and injury. Necessarily, therefore, one requires some type of management[1843] to render each one content with the station which he deserves and bring him to his due, to restrain each man's hand from depredation[846] and from infringement of the rights of others, and to concern itself with the task for which it is responsible among the matters pertaining to co-operation. Such a management is called 'government'.[1844]

We observed in the First Discourse, on the subject of Justice,[1845] that in government there is a need for the Law,[1035] for an arbitrator[860] and for money. Thus, if such management be in accordance with the obligation[905] and principle of Wisdom,[1071] leading to the perfection which is in potency in species and individuals, it is called Divine Government;[1846] otherwise, it is related to whatever else may be the reason for such government.

The Philosopher[8] Aristotle has divided simple types of government[1847] into four: government of a king; government of domination; government of nobility; and government of the community.[1848]

Government of a king is the management of a community in such a way that virtues accrue to them, and this is (also) called 'government of the virtuous'.[1849] Government of domination denotes the management of the affairs of the base, and this is also called 'government of baseness'.[1850] Government of nobility is the management of a community noted for the acquisition of nobility.[1851] Government of the community denotes the management of different factions[1852] according to a rule[1070] established by the Divine Law.[853]

The government of a king distributes[1853] these other types of government to those concerned therewith, calling each category to account for its particular government in order that their perfection may pass from potency to act. Thus this form of government is the Government of Governments.

The connection between government of a king and government of the community is to be explained as follows: the government of some depends on enactments,[1854] as with contracts and transactions; while that of others depends on intellectual judgments,[1855] as in the case of the management of a kingdom or the administration of a city. But no one would be able to undertake either of these two categories without a preponderance of discrimination and a superiority in knowledge,[1856] for such a man's precedence over others without the occasion of some particularity[184] would call for strife and altercation. Thus, in determining the enactments[1854] there is a need for a person distinguished from others by divine inspiration, in order that they should follow him. Such a person, in the terminology of the Ancients,[517] was called The Possessor of the Law,[1857] and his enactments the Divine Law;[853] the Moderns[1858] refer to him as the Religious Lawgiver, and to his enactments as the Religious Law.[1859] Plato, in the Fifth Discourse of the *Book of Politics*, has referred to this class thus: 'They are the possessors of mighty and surpassing powers'.[1860] Aristotle, again, says: 'They are the ones for whom God has greater concern'.[1861]

Now, in determining judgments,[1862] there is need (also) for a person who is distinguished from others by divine support,[1863] so that he may be able to accomplish their perfection. Such a person, in the terminology of the Ancients,[517] was called an Absolute King,[1864] and his judgments the Craft of Kingship;[1865] the Moderns[1858] refer to him as the Imam, and to his function as the Imamate.[1866] Plato calls him Regulator of the World,[1867] while Aristotle uses the term Civic Man,[1868] i.e. that man, and his like, by whose existence the ordering of civilized life[58] is effected.

In the terminology of some, the first of these persons is called the Speaker, and the second the Foundation.[1869]

It must be established that the sense of the term 'king' in this place is not that of someone possessing a cavalcade, a retinue or a realm: what is meant, rather, is one truly deserving of kingship,[1870] even though outwardly no one pays him any attention.[1871] If someone other than he be carrying on the management of affairs, tyranny and disorder become widespread.

In short, not every age and generation has need of a Possessor of the Law,[1857] for one enactment suffices for the people of many periods; but the world does require a Regulator in every age, for if management ceases, order is taken away likewise, and the survival of the species in the most perfect manner cannot be realized. The Regulator undertakes to preserve the Law and obliges men to uphold its prescriptions;[1872] his is the authority of jurisdiction[1873] over the particulars of the Law[1035] in accordance with the best interest of every day and age.

From this it is evident that Politics[1874] (which is the science embraced in this Discourse) is the study of universal laws[1875] producing the best interest of the generality inasmuch as they are directed, through co-operation, to true perfection. The object of this science is the form of a community,[1876] resulting by virtue of combination and becoming the source of the members' actions in the most perfect manner.

Now the master of any craft considers his craft in a manner relevant to that craft, not whether it is good or evil. Thus, the physician regards the treatment of a hand from the standpoint of acquiring for that hand an equilibrium[830] by means of which it becomes capable of grasping, without regard as to whether such grasping be of the order of good or evil things. But the master of the present craft considers all the actions and works of the masters of (other) crafts from the standpoint of their being good things or evil. Thus, this craft is supreme above all crafts,[1877] and its relationship to them is like that of theology[13] to the other sciences.

Now, since the individual members of the human species need each other for the survival of both the individual and the species, and inasmuch as their attainment to perfection is impossible[115] without survival, therefore they need each other in order to attain perfection. This being so, (it follows that) the perfection and completion of each individual is dependent on the other individuals of his species. Accordingly, it is incumbent upon him to associate and mingle with his own kind in a co-operative manner; otherwise, he has deviated from the principle of Justice[728] and become characterized by the mark of Tyranny.[985] However, association and mingling in this way can only occur when he has become aware of the circumstances governing those modes that lead to order and those that lead to corruption, and when he has acquired the science that assures a knowledge of each separate species. But this science is Politics.[1874] Thus, every person is compelled to study this science in order that he may be capable of attaining virtue. If it be otherwise, his transactions and associations will not remain free from Tyranny,[985] and he will become a cause of the world's corruption in accordance with the measure of his rank and station. Once again, the all-embracing character of the benefit deriving from this science becomes obvious.

Just as the master of the science of medicine, being skilled in his craft, becomes capable of preserving the health of Man's body and removing disease: so the master of the present science, being skilled in his craft, becomes capable of preserving the health of the world's constitution (which is called 'true equilibrium')[830] and removing therefrom any deviation. In reality, he is the world's physician.

In short, the fruits of this science are the diffusion of good things in the world, and the removal of evils, in the measure of human ability.

We have said that the object of this science is the form of combination among human individuals;[1878] but the combination of human individuals varies both generally and in particular; thus, it is necessary that one should know the sense of the term 'combination of individuals' in each separate regard. We say: the first combination occurring among individuals is that of the household, and this has been explained already; the second combination is that of the people of a locality;[1879] this is followed by the combination of the inhabitants of a city; next comes the combination of great communities;[1880] and finally the combination of the inhabitants of the world. Again, just as each individual forms part of the household, so each household is part of the locality, each locality part of the city, each city part of the community, and each community part of the inhabitants of the world.

Each combination has a head,[1881] as we observed in relation to the household: but the head of the household is subordinate[1882] relative to the head of the locality, the latter is subordinate relative to the head of the city, and so on until one reaches the head of the world, who is the Head of Heads;[1883] and he is the Absolute King.[1864] His consideration of the world's state and the state of its parts is like the physician's consideration of the individual and the parts of the individual, or like the householder's consideration of the state of the household and its parts.

Whenever two individuals are associated in a craft or a task, some form of headship establishes itself between them; that is to say, the one who is more perfect than the other in that craft becomes the head, while the other individual must obey him in order that he should become directed to perfection. Eventually, all individuals terminate in one individual, who is by merit the Absolutely Obeyed One, the one imitated by the species;[1884] or in a number of individuals in like case with that one individual[1885] as regards the unity of their opinions on the best interest of the species. Moreover, just as the Head of the World[1883] considers the parts of the world in accordance with his attachment to the generality of the parts, so the head of any combination has a regard for the generality of that community of which he is the head, and for the parts of that combination, in such a manner as effects their well-being first and in general, while also effecting the well-being of each part secondarily and in particular.

The attachment of combinations one to another is of three kinds. First comes the case where one combination is part of another combination, as with household and city; secondly, where one combination includes another combination, as with community[1886] and city; and thirdly, where one combination is the servant and aid of another combination, as with village and city (for the combinations of the inhabitants of villages are defective, inasmuch as each one, in a different category, renders service to the complete civic combination). In these three modes, the aid of combinations to each other is by way of matter, instrument and service, as with the aid rendered to each other by the species—and of this we have already spoken.[1887]

Since the synthesis[1887a] of the world's inhabitants has been determined in this wise, (it follows that) those persons who forsake the synthesis, inclining to isolation and loneliness, will remain without part in this virtue; for it is sheer Tyranny and Injustice[1888] to choose loneliness and solitude, and to turn away from co-operation with the rest of mankind, when one has need of the things they have acquired. There are, however, some such who account this behaviour a virtue, as with the class who isolate themselves by cleaving to their cells or by dwelling in mountain-clefts; this they call 'abstention from the world'. Another group will sit looking to other men to help them, while themselves totally blocking the road of aid; this they call 'resignation'. Then there are those who go touring from cities to cities, nowhere taking up their abode or contracting any association likely to bring about an intimate relationship: they claim to be deriving a lesson from the state of the world and regard this as a virtue. Such people, and those like them, use the provisions which others have acquired by co-operation, while giving them nothing in return or requital; they eat their sustenance and they don their clothing, but they make no payment for these things, having turned away from that which effects the ordering and the perfection of the human species. Yet since, by the fact of their solitude and loneliness, they do not bring into act the vices of those characteristics that they naturally have in potency, some shortsighted people fancy them to be persons of virtue. Such an estimation is erroneous; for Continence[585] does not mean abandonment of the appetite of belly and privities in all respects, but rather observance of the limit and due proper to everything, and the avoidance of both excess[432] and neglect.[433] Again, Justice[728] does not mean not being unjust to men one cannot see, but rather conducting one's transactions with men according to the principle of equity.[1889] But so long as a person does not mingle with other men, how should Liberality[1890] proceed from him? And if he never falls into exposure to any peril, when will he make application of Courage?[1890] And, should he never see a desirable form, how should the operation of Continence become apparent in him? If the matter be considered, it will be evident that this class of people tend to resemble solids and corpses, not those possessed of virtue and discrimination;[1891] for the latter do not seek to deviate from what has been determined by the First Determinant[1892] (mighty is His Name!), imitating His Wisdom,[6] in the measure of capacity, in conduct and customs, and asking success from Him in this connection. He it is who best grants success and assistance!

## SECOND SECTION

### ON THE VIRTUE OF LOVE,[60] BY WHICH THE CONNECTION OF SOCIETIES[61] IS EFFECTED, AND THE DIVISIONS THEREOF

Men need each other, then, and the perfection and completion of each one lies with other individuals of his species. Moreover, necessity demands a request for aid, for no individual can reach perfection in isolation, as has been explained.[1893] This being so, there is an inescapable need for a synthesis,[1887a] which will render all individuals, co-operating together, comparable to the organs of one individual. Again, since Man has been created with a natural direction towards perfection, he has a natural yearning for the synthesis in question. This yearning for the synthesis is called Love. We have already alluded to the preference (that may be shown) to Love above Justice.[1894] The reason for this idea is that Justice requires artificial union,[1895] whereas Love requires natural union;[1895] at the same time, the artificial in relation to the natural is like an outer skin,[1896] the artificial imitating the natural.

Thus, it is obvious that the need for Justice (which is the most perfect of human virtues) in preserving the order of the species, arises from the loss of Love;[60] for if Love were to accrue between individuals, there would be no necessity for equity and impartiality.[614] Etymologically, the word 'equity' derives from 'equal share',[1897] i.e. the dispenser of equity divides the disputed object equally with his colleague;[1898] but division into halves is one of the consequences of multiplicity,[1899] whereas Love is one of the causes of union. In these regards, the virtue of Love over Justice is obvious.

One school of Ancient Philosophers[1900] went to extreme lengths in magnifying the position of Love, saying that it is the cause of the ordering of all existent things, so that no existent thing may be devoid of some Love, just as it may not be devoid of some measure of existence or unity.[1901] However, they say, Love has degrees, and because of its gradation existent things are graded in degrees of perfection and deficiency. Moreover, just as Love effects ordering and perfection, so domination effects corruption and deficiency; when it befalls existent things, it may be according[563] to the deficiency of each category. This group is known as the School of Love and Domination.[1900]

Other philosophers,[742] too, while they have not proceeded to declare such a doctrine openly, have nevertheless admitted to the virtue of Love and explained how ardour[1902] spreads to all the generables.[1903]

Now, since the true nature[736] of Love is the quest for union with that thing with which the seeker conceives it perfection to be united; and as we have said that the perfection and nobility of each existent thing is in accordance with the unity that has been effused upon it;[1904] therefore, Love is the quest for nobility and virtue and perfection, and the more one is moved by this quest the greater one's yearning for perfection, and the easier it is for such a one to attain thereto. Thus, in the terminology of the Moderns,[1905] the word "Love" and its opposite are used in a context in which the Rational Faculty[1906] participates. (It is true that) the elements[1822] necessarily have an inclination towards their own centres[1907] and a flight from other directions.[1908] The compounds also necessarily have an inclination towards each other by virtue of the affinities[1909] that have arisen in their mixing; (and they have these), in specified and limited relationships,[1910]—such as the numerical, the superficial and the synthetic[1911]—so that they may thereby be the principle of remarkable acts[1912] (called 'properties' and 'secrets of natures'),[1913] such as the inclination of iron to the lodestone. There are also the opposites (of these), which arise by virtue of constitutional repulsions,[1914] like the repulsion from vinegar of the acetic-detesting stone.[1915] None of these, however, are reckoned of the order of Love and Detestation,[1916] but are referred to as Inclination and Flight.[1917] The mutual agreement and hostility of non-rational animals[1918] likewise lie outside this order, being referred to as Affection and Aversion.[1919]

The divisions of Love in the human species are of two kinds: natural and voluntary. An example of natural love is that of the mother for the child: if this class of love were not innate[174] in the mother's nature, she would not give nurture to the child, and the survival of the species could not conceivably be effected. Voluntary love falls into four classes: that which is swift to contract and to dissolve;[1920] that which is slow to contract and swift to dissolve; that which is swift to contract and slow to dissolve; and that which is slow to contract and to dissolve.

Now, the ends[48] of the different types of men, in respect of the things they seek,[1921] diverge at the level of simplicity[1922] into three branches: Pleasure, Profit and Good.[1923] From the compounding of these three together a fourth branch comes into being. These ends require the love of those persons who will assist and help in attaining to perfection of the individual or the species, and these are the (whole) human race. Thus, each of these motives[1924] is a cause of one of the classes of voluntary love.

Pleasure may be a cause of the love which is soon contracted and soon dissolved[1925] for pleasure, despite its all-pervasive existence,[1926] is characterized by swiftness of alteration and passing away, as we have said; and persistence or decline spread from the cause to the thing caused. Profit is a cause of the love that is slowly contracted and soon dissolved, for the bringing of profit—rare though it be—[1927] is swift to pass away. Good is the cause of the love which is soon contracted and slowly dissolved: soon contracted by virtue of the essential affinities[1909] between men of good, slowly dissolved because of the true union necessary to the nature[59] of good, which renders dislocation impossible.[1928] That which is compounded of all three is a cause of the love which is slowly contracted and slowly dissolved, for seeking to join both causes, i.e. Profit and Good, necessarily brings about both states.

Love is more general than Friendship,[1929] for Love is conceivable amid a swarming throng, but Friendship does not reach this degree of comprehensiveness. In rank, Affection[1930] is closer to Friendship. Passion,[1931] which is an excess of Love,[60] is more particular than Affection, for Passion occurs only between two people. The reason for Passion may be either an excessive quest for Pleasure or an excessive quest for Good, Profit having no possible access to the production of Passion whether on the basis of simplicity or by virtue of being compounded. Thus, Passion is of two kinds: one reprehensible, arising from an excessive quest for Pleasure, the other praiseworthy arising from an excessive quest for Good. The difficulty of distinguishing clearly between these two causes results in the diversity of men's attitudes towards praising or blaming Passion itself.

The reason for the friendship of young men, and persons of like nature, is the quest of Pleasure, and this is why they are continually striking up a friendship and separating again; indeed, it occasionally happens that they will become friends with each other and part again several times in the course of a short period. If their friendship be based on endurance, it will be a reason for their confidence in the endurance of the pleasure and its repetition time and again; when such confidence declines, however, such friendship is immediately removed.

The reason for the friendship of old men, and persons of like nature, is the quest of Profit. Since they find common advantages, which happen to be prolonged in most cases, a friendship proceeds from them, enduring as the profit endures. When, however, the link of hope is cut, that friendship is removed.

As for the friendship of the men of good: since it is sheer good, and good is something constant, unchanging, accordingly the affection[1930] of those associated with it is preserved from change and decline.

Again, since men are compounded of opposite natures, so that the inclination of each nature is contrary to that of another: therefore, the pleasure congenial to one nature is contrary to the pleasure of another nature. For this reason, no one of all the various classes of pleasures can be free and devoid of the stains of the torments to be found in parting from the other pleasures.

In Man, however, there is to be found a simple, divine substance[1932] having no affinity with other natures, and he can enjoy thereby a class of pleasure having no similarity to other pleasures. The love producing this pleasure is excessive in the extreme, being like to distraction,[1933] and it is known as Utter Passion and Divine Love.[1934] Certain of those who assimilate themselves to God[1935] lay claim to this love. The First Philosopher,[903] on this subject, has reported of Heraclitus[1936] that he says: 'Divergent things can have no complete affinity[1937] or synthesis[1938] with each other, but concordant[1937] things are gladdened and inspired with yearning the one to the other.'

The following remarks have been made as a commentary on these words. Simple substances, being concordant[1937] and yearning one to another, form a synthesis,[1938] so that a true unity results between them and discrepancy is removed; for discrepancy is one of the concomitants[1170] of material things, and material things cannot enjoy this type of synthesis.[1938] If a yearning does result in them, so that they incline to some sort of synthesis,[1938] they meet (only) at extremities and surfaces, not in essences and realities;[1939] such a meeting, however, not attaining to the degree of conjunction, necessarily calls for discontinuity.[1940]

When the substance deposited in Man is purified of the turbidity of nature,[533] and love for the various sorts of appetites and favours[1941] is banished from it, there accrues to it a sincere yearning for its like, and it occupies itself in contemplating, with the eye of perception, the Majesty of Pure Good, the source of (all) goods; and the illuminations of that Presence are effused upon it.[1942] Then there results to it a pleasure that cannot be related to any (other) pleasure, and it attains to the aforementioned degree of union. (At such time) it knows no further disparity between using and forsaking the bodily nature; however, it is more fitted to that lofty degree after total separation, for complete purity[1943] can result only after departing this transient life.

One of the virtues of this class of Love,[60] i.e. the love of men of good one to another, is that deficiency can have no access to it, nor calumny any conceivable effect upon it; for weariness there is no scope to make inroads on its type, nor can evil men have any share or part therein. Love for the sake of Profit or Pleasure, however, may be held by evil men for evil men, as well as for good, albeit it is swift to pass away and dissolve[1944] inasmuch as the profitable or pleasurable thing is desired accidentally, not essentially. If often happens that what calls forth such loves as these is an association[1945] befalling among the authors of these loves in unusual places, such as on shipboard or during journeys and the like. The cause of this is a (sense of) fellowship[1946] which is rooted in the nature of Man: indeed, Man is called 'Man' for this reason, as has been established in the discipline of polite letters (for the person who said 'you are called man because you are forgetful', fancying that 'Man' was derived from 'forgetfulness', was in error in his supposition).[1947] Now, since natural fellowship[1948] is one of the properties of men, and inasmuch as the perfection of any thing lies in the manifestation of its property[489] (as we have repeatedly said in several places), so the perfection of this species too lies in the manifestation of this property to its own kind. This property, moreover, is the principle of the love calling forth civilized life[58] and the (social) synthesis.[1938]

True Wisdom,[1949] then, requires that this property be (regarded as) superior, but religious laws and commendable manners also invite one thereto. Hence, men have been urged to combine in both devotions[1950] and convivial entertainments, for in society[1945] the above-mentioned fellowship comes from potency into act. It may be for this reason, too, that the Islamic Religious Law[1951] has given pre-eminence to the communal prayer over prayer in isolation:[1952] thus, when men come together five times daily in one place, they may feel (a sense of) fellowship one with another, and their participation in devotional acts[1950] and other dealings with each other[1953] may become the cause of confirming such fellowship. It may even be that they will progress from the degree of fellowship to that of Love.[60]

A verification of this argument lies in the following consideration. While these devotions are prescribed[1954] for the inhabitants of a quarter or locality who do not find it unduly difficult[677] to come together five times daily in a mosque, it would be unfitting to deprive of this virtue the inhabitants of a town to whom such combination seemed arduous. Accordingly, another form of devotion was ordained, namely that once in the week the inhabitants of (the various) quarters and localities should assemble, all together, in one mosque capable of holding the whole community; in this way, the inhabitants of the city are enabled to participate in the virtue of assembly in just the same way as do the inhabitants of a locality. Again, since for the inhabitants of country districts and villages to form a society[1945] weekly with each other and with the townsmen would seem to demand the abandonment of important tasks, two occasions in the year were designated for a devotion to comprise the combination of the whole community;[1955] and for their place of assembly the open country was ordered, as being capable of accommodating the multitude, for it might seem to lead to difficulties to lay out a building in which there were room for all the community, yet which at the same time would be used only twice in the year. Moreover, in the amplitude of a space where all the people can be present, they are able to see each other and renew the bond of fellowship, and their motivation to love[60] and familiarity[1946] towards each other is thereby increased.

To proceed one stage further: all the inhabitants of the world have been put under the obligation of combining together, once in a lifetime, in one location. However, there is no attribution here to any specified time in one's life such as might cause excessive hardship and trouble: the intention was, rather, that by making matters easy the inhabitants of distant lands might come together, acquiring some share of that felicity to which the inhabitants of cities and the localities have been made receptive, and making a display of that natural fellowship[1948] to be found in their innate disposition.[1956] It is the more fitting that the place designated should be the territory in which the Possessor of the Religious Law[1957] resided, for observing his relics[455] and performing his observances and ceremonies impose respect and veneration for the Religious Law[1958] in men's hearts, producing a speedy response and obedience to the calls[684] of goodness.

In short, from the way these devotions are conceived and interlocked one with another,[1959] the purpose of the Religious Lawgiver[1859] in summoning to the acquisition of this virtue becomes evident: for (the act of) fixing the pillars[54] of devotion upon the law[1070] of best interest is itself a cause of the combination of both felicities.

Let us return to our discussion of Love.[60] We say: as for the causes of the aforementioned loves (apart from Divine Love),[1934] since they are common between those concerned with the loves, it may be that these in one situation are contracted on both sides, and in another subject to dissolution; it may also be that one endures while the other is dissolved.[1960] Take, for example, the pleasure common to husband and wife, which is the cause of their love: it may be on both sides a cause of their loving each other, but it may also happen that the love ceases on one side while enduring on the other; for pleasure is characterized by swiftness of alteration, and alteration on one side does not necessarily produce alteration on the other. Similarly with the benefits common to wife and husband in respect of domestic goods: if both co-operate therein, these become a reason for common love. But consider where one of them falls short in his prescribed duty: for example, the wife looks to the husband to acquire these goods, and the husband to the wife to guard them, but if one fails the other, love grows contrary and complaints and reproaches result, in daily-increasing measure until the link is severed; or, alternatively, the bond slackens, or endures for a while in conjunction with complaining and scolding. In the case of other loves, one should take an analogous example.

The causes of some loves are diverse, such as the love whose cause on one side is Pleasure and on the other Profit: an instance is that between a singer and a listener, where the singer loves the listener by reason of profit, while the listener loves the singer for pleasure. The same situation obtains between lover and beloved,[1961] where the lover expects pleasure from the beloved, while the latter expects profit from him. In this sort of love, there are frequent complaints and charges of injustice: indeed, in no one of the classes of Love[60] do such scolding and complaints arise as in this sort. The reason for this is that the seeker after pleasure tries to hasten the thing desired, while the seeker after profit delays his attaining thereto, so that equilibrium[830] is inconceivable between them save in rare instances. Hence, lovers are continually complaining and charging injustice, whereas it is in reality they themselves who are unjust, for they seek to advance fulfilment of their enjoyment of the pleasure of beholding and union, while delaying, or not even discharging, recompense therefor. This class of Love is called 'reproachful love',[1962] i.e. love conjoined with reproach; nor are all the classes thereof encompassed within this one example, albeit they all derive from this same idea as mentioned above.

The love between ruler and subject, superior[1881] and subordinate,[1882] and rich man and poor, is also liable to complaints and reproaches, inasmuch as each expect from his opposite something which is most often not available. At the same time, non-availability combined with expectation brings about a corruption of intent,[1963] from corruption of intent there results a sense of dilatoriness,[1964] and the latter invites reproach as a consequence. By observance of the condition of Justice,[728] however, these corruptions may be dispelled. Likewise slaves look for more than they merit from their masters, while the masters account them deficient in service and sympathy and counsel, with the result that they give themselves up to reproaches. Yet, so long as there accrue no satisfaction with the measure that is merited (this being one of the concomitants of Justice), so long will such love not be brought into order. There is no need to comment (further) on the difficulty in the way of its becoming all-embracing.[1965]

The love of good men, however, will not have arisen from the expectation of Profit or Pleasure, being brought about by correspondence of substance,[1966] inasmuch as their goal is Pure Good and the quest of virtue; hence, it remains removed from the taint[755] of discord and altercation, and there result in consequence the mutual good counsel and justice of transaction[1831] which are demanded by union. This is what the Philosophers[765] mean when they say of the friend: 'Your friend is the individual who is yourself in reality, but someone other than you as individual'.[1967] It necessarily follows for the same reason that such friendship is a rarity, that it is not to be found at all among the masses, and that no confidence can be placed in the friendship of young men; for when a man is not acquainted with good, being heedless of right purpose, his love may be a result of the expectation of some pleasure or profit. Rulers make a display of friendship for the reason that they account themselves condescending and beneficent,[1968] and accordingly their friendship is not complete and deviates from Justice.[728]

When a father loves a child for the reason that he considers himself to have a great claim upon him, then his love is close to this (type of) love from one point of view. In another regard, however, he has an essential love[1969] for the child, by which he is peculiarly distinguished: namely, that he regards the child as in reality his second self,[1970] fancying that the child's physical existence[1971] is a copy made by nature from his own form, while she has transferred a likeness of his essence to (become) that of the child. And indeed, this is a conception not without justification, for Divine Wisdom[1835] by inspiration moves[754] the father to produce the child, making him a secondary cause in its creation.[1972] This is why the father wishes the child every perfection that he wishes for himself, and why he devotes his own aspiration to ensuring that there accrue to the child every good and felicity that he himself has missed. It does not come hard to him that men should tell him his son is more virtuous than he, while the same remark made about another he does find hard to accept; in this sense, his is like the case of a person progressing towards perfection, who does not find it hard that people should say: 'Now you are more perfect than you were earlier'—indeed, such words are pleasing to him. Another reason for the excessive love of the parent is that he recognizes himself as the cause of the child's (physical) existence:[1971] he has been gladdened by him from the beginning of his coming into being, his love has increased and taken firm root with the child's nurture and growth, he has accounted him a means to hopes and joys, and through his existence he has taken confidence to heart for the endurance of his own form after the passing away of matter. Such notions, among the common people, are not so refined[1973] that they can express them (in this way), but in their inmost hearts[185] they have a sort of awareness thereof, as with a person who sees a vision behind a veil.[1974]

A child's love falls short of that of a father, for the former is the thing caused and effected,[1975] and it becomes aware of its own existence and of that of its cause only after an extended lapse of time. Indeed, if it does not come to know the father in life, and does not enjoy the benefits of him for any while, it will never acquire love of him; and should it not be blessed with a full share of understanding and insight, it will show no great veneration for him. For this reason, children have been enjoined to show kindness to their parents, while the latter have not been so enjoined in respect of the children.[1976] The love of brothers for one another derives from participation in one cause.

The love of a ruler for a subject should be a paternal love, while that of the subject for the ruler should be filial; the love of subjects for each other should be fraternal,[1977] so that the conditions of order may be preserved among them. What is meant by these attributions is as follows: that the ruler, in dealing with the subject, should model himself on the sympathetic father in respect of sympathy and compassion, solicitude and graciousness, nurture and indulgence, and in his quest for best interests, his warding off of unpleasantnesses, his attraction of good and his prohibition of evil; that the subject, on the other hand, should follow the example of an intelligent[72] son in giving the father obedience and good counsel, esteem and veneration; and, finally, that (the subjects) in their generosity and kindness to each other should behave like brothers in agreement. (In all this) each one (should conduct himself) in the measure of his proper merit and worth, as time and situation demand, so as to uphold justice[728] by fulfilling each one's share and due; thus order and stability will result. Otherwise, if excess and deficiency make inroads, and justice be removed, corruption manifests itself, the governance of the realm becomes one of domination,[1978] hatred is substituted for love,[1979] discord for agreement, wrangling for familiarity, and hypocrisy for affection. Everyone wishes his own good, even if it include the harm of others, so that friendship is nullified and chaos (the opposite of order) becomes apparent.

The love that is exempted from the impressions and turbidities of (all) misfortunes[1980] is that of the creature for the Creator.[665] Such love can belong only to the man of Divine Learning,[1981] the claims of all others being characterized by vanity and falsification; for love is based on knowledge,[605] so how can there be love in one who has no knowledge[1982] of Him and is unaware of His diverse continual graces and manifold successive favours reaching both soul and body? It may well be that such a one, in his own imagination,[1983] sets up an idol, which he recognizes as his Creator and Object of worship;[1984] and that he concerns himself with loving and obeying it, reckoning this to be Pure Monotheism and Uncluttered Faith![1985] By no manner of means, God forbid! 'For most of them do not believe in God without attributing partners (to Him)'.[1986]

The pretenders to love of God are many, but the true practitioners among them[1987] are few, nay fewer than few. Obedience and veneration are never absent from such true love: 'Few of My servants are grateful'.[1988] Love of parents follows[1761] this love in rank, and no other love attains the rank of these two, save that of the teacher[1697] in the student's heart, this latter love being intermediate in rank between the two aforementioned loves. The reason for this is as follows: the first (type of) love is at the very extremity of nobility and grandeur inasmuch as the Object of love[1989] is the cause of existence and of the grace consequent on existence; the second (type of) love is related to this in that the father is the sensible reason and the proximate cause (of these);[1990] teachers, however, in the nurture of souls, may be equated with[1779] fathers in the nurture of bodies; again, from the standpoint that they are the completers of existence and the perpetuators of essences,[1991] they imitate the Primary Cause,[1992] and from the standpoint that their nurture is a branch on the root of existence, they may be likened to fathers. Thus, love of them is inferior to the first (type of) love, but above the second, for their nurture is a ramification upon the root of existence, but nobler than the nurture of fathers. In truth, the teacher is a corporal master and a spiritual master,[1993] his rank in veneration being below that of the Primary Cause[1994] but above that of human fathers.

Alexander was asked whether he loved his father or his teacher the more, to which he replied: 'My teacher, for my father was a cause of my transitory life, whereas my teacher was a cause of my life everlasting'.[1995] Thus, the right of the teacher over that of the father is in the measure of the superiority in rank of the soul over the body, and this proportion must be preserved in the love and veneration shown to him as compared with the father. Likewise, the love of the teacher for the student in the way of good is superior to that of the father for the son in the same proportion, for the teacher nurtures on complete virtue and sustains with pure wisdom,[1996] so that his relation to the father is like that of the soul to the body.

Now, so long as the gradations of the (various) loves are not conceived of by the just man, he is not able to fulfil the conditions of justice.[728] Thus, where the love due to[257] God is concerned, to associate any other therewith is sheer polytheism.[1997] Again, to venerate a superior as one would a parent, to show honour to a ruler[787] as for a friend, or to show love appropriate to a child when dealing with relatives and parents: such courses represent mere ignorance and absolute lack of judgment,[1998] and the confusions involved bring about disturbance and disarray and necessarily lead to reproaches and complaints. But when each one's measure is fulfilled in respect of love and service and good counsel, this promotes familiarity of companions and intimates, needful association,[1999] and just observvance of the dues of everyone deserving.

Treachery in friendship is more ruinous than betrayal in respect of gold and silver. In this connection, the First Philosopher[903] says: 'False love is soon dissolved, as false moneys, large and small, are soon spoiled'.

The intelligent man,[72] therefore, must in each category have the intent of good,[2000] observing the limits of the gradation of that category. Thus, he will recognize friends as being in the position of his own soul and account them partners in his own goods; acquaintances and familiars he will hold as like to hands and feet,[2001] striving to bring them—within the measure of possibility—from the boundary of acquaintanceship to the degree of friendship; in this way, he will have held to the course of good for his own soul, as well as for superiors, for his immediate family and the wider family[2002] circle, and among friends.

As for the evil man, however, who shies away from this course, being overcome with love of idleness and sloth, and heedless of the distinction between good and evil, he holds to be good that which is not good; and the perversity of aspect that is established in his essence[2003] becomes the principle of his shunning his own soul, for perversity is naturally something to be fled.[2004] But if he flees from his own soul, he will also flee from anyone having an affinity[1937] to his soul. Thus, he is continually in quest of something to distract him from concern with himself, and he becomes intent on things such as games and the means of accidental pleasures, which will put him beside himself;[2005] for it necessarily follows, given his leisurely condition, that he *will* be concerned with himself, and when he is so concerned, he becomes annoyed at himself. His love, therefore, is for friends who will keep him remote from himself, and his pleasure is in things that put him beyond himself: felicity he reckons to lie in passing his life in these and their likes, for they keep him unaware of the disturbance and perturbation arising in his soul from the conflicting attraction of appetites and the quest of unmerited honours, to say nothing of the diseases—like grief, anger, fear and the rest—that necessarily follow from such conflicting attraction.[2006] The reason for this is that the synthesis[1887a] of opposites in one state is inconceivable, while movement from one to another, in which disturbance consists, is vexatious: hence, by mixing and consorting with his likes, and by applying and devoting himself to games, his imagination is diverted from sensing that state, so that he instantly perceives an escape from that vexation and grows heedless of the punishment and the torment ultimately to follow. So, he takes joy in that state and considers it to be felicity.

Such a person, in reality, is no lover of his own essence, or he would not seek to leave it; nor is he, indeed, a lover of any person else, for love of others is based upon love of self. Moreover, since he loves nobody and nobody loves him (in return), he lacks both counsellor and well-wisher, to the degree that his own soul likewise does not wish him well; the outcome of such a state is unending regret and remorse.

As for the good and virtuous man, however, who enjoys his own essence and is rejoiced by it, he inevitably loves his own essence, and others love his essence likewise, for the noble man is beloved; and loving him, they choose to be friends with him and to unite with him, so that not only is he his own friend, but others are his friends too. Such a course is inseparable from kindness[2007] towards others, whether intentionally or unintentionally. The reason for this is as follows: his actions are pleasurable and beloved in themselves; at the same time, the pleasurable and the beloved are that which men choose;[2008] thus, he wins many disciples and followers,[2009] and his kindness encompasses them all. Such kindness, moreover, is preserved against decline and annihilation,[109] being constantly in augmentation; in this it contrasts with the kindness which is accidental, the principle of the latter being an unaccustomed state,[2010] so that the decline of that state demands the cessation of the kindness, and such cessation brings on reproaches and complaints. This is why the author of accidental kindness is enjoined and commanded to regularize it: 'To do something regularly is more difficult than to start it.'[2011] The love which is accidental to this kindness is (accordingly) 'reproachful love'.[1962]

As for the love existing between the author of kindness and its recipient,[2012] there is a discrepancy between them: that is to say, the love of the former for the latter is greater than that of the recipient for the kind person himself. The proof of this is as given by the First Philosopher:[903] one who lends or one who does a kindness[2013] has a concern respectively for the state of the borrower or the person receiving the kindness, confining their (whole) ambition to the well-being of these people. In the case of the lender, it may be that he wishes the welfare of the borrower in order that he may recover his property, not (simply) for love of him, i.e. he prays for his well-being and survival, his enrichment and prosperity, in order that perchance he himself may attain his due; but the borrower does not have this concern for the lender, and does not pray for him in this way. In the case of one doing a kindness,[2013] however, he loves the recipient of the kindness, albeit expecting no advantage from him; the reason for this is that whoever does a praiseworthy act loves what he himself has done, and since his deed is direct his love reaches the goal.[2014] As for the recipient of the kindness, again, his inclination is to the kindness itself, not to its author, so that the latter is loved by him (only) accidentally. The love, furthermore, which is acquired by doing a kindness, and which is regularized with time, is in the same case as advantages won by much fatigue and toil: that is to say, just as a person acquires wealth by the endurance of hardships and the fatigue of journeyings, and then is cautious and even parsimonious in the expenditure thereof (unlike the one who gains wealth easily, such as an heir), so also the man who has acquired a love by assuming a measure of trouble is more tender thereof and more fearful of its decline than is the person who has not needed to be at any great pains in its acquisition. This is why the mother loves the child more than the father, yearning towards him and doting on him to a greater degree, for her tribulation in rearing him has been the greater. The poet too loves his poetry and admires it more than does anyone else; and similarly with every craftsman who has taken excessive pains in the exercise of his craft. Moreover, it is evident that the toil of the patient is not to be compared to that of the agent, but the taker is the patient and the giver the agent.[2015]

From these considerations, then, it is clear that the love of one doing a kindness is greater than that of the recipient of the kindness.[2012] Now, it may sometimes be that the former does a kindness out of freedom;[2016] at other times it is in order to win fair mention, or again for reasons of affectation.[1511] The noblest of these categories is where the action is based on freedom, for a consequence thereof is in fact fair mention and lasting commendation and the love of the generality of mankind, even though these things were not the object of the kind man's intention.

We have already said that each person loves his own soul, and at the same time wishes to do kindness to the person whom he loves; thus, each person wishes to do kindness to his own soul. However, since the causes of love are Good or Pleasure or Profit,[2017] the person who makes no distinction between these classes, being unaware of the superiority of one over another, will not know how he should do a kindness to his own soul. This is the reason why some men choose a course of pleasure for the soul, some a course of profit, and some one of ennoblement,[1851] for they have no knowledge of the nature of the course of good and so go astray. That person, on the other hand, who is aware of the pleasure of good, is not content with external, transient pleasures, but chooses the highest, the most complete, and the grandest of the various categories of pleasures. This is the pleasure of the Divine part,[2018] and the one adopting this course is following the acts of God (mighty and exalted is He!), enjoying true pleasures, benefiting friends and others by supererogation and munificence and charity,[2019] and being capable of such excess of vigour and greatness of soul[2020] as is beyond his peers.[660]

Since we are speaking of Love,[60] into a discussion of which enters love of Wisdom[6] and of Good, some reference to these latter is also necessary (at this point in our argument). We say thus: love of wisdom, the preoccupation with intellectual concerns, and the employment of divine opinions[2021]—all these are particular to the Divine part[2018] to be found in Man; and they are safeguarded against the disasters likely to befall other types of love. Detraction can make no inroads against them, nor can the evil man make any intervention therein, for their cause is Pure Good, and Pure Good is exempt from matter and the evils of matter. So long as men employ human dispositions and virtues,[2022] they are debarred from the true nature of this Good and excluded from Divine Felicity. In acquiring this latter virtue there is assuredly need for those other virtues; but only if, after acquiring those virtues, a man busies himself with the Divine Virtue, will he truly have concerned himself with his own essence, becoming free of the struggle with nature and its pangs and the struggle with the soul and the disciplining of its faculties, and finding intercourse with the Pure Spirits and the Favoured Angels.[2023] Thus, when he passes from transient existence to enduring existence, he attains to everlasting grace and perpetual joy.

Aristotle says that complete and unalloyed felicity belongs to those allowed to approach the Divine Presence.[2024] Nor must we append human virtues to the angels; for they have no dealings[1831] one with another, place no pledges with each other and have no need of commerce, so as to require Justice;[728] they fear nothing for Courage to be commendable in them; they are exempt from disbursement and untainted by gold and silver, so that it is meaningless to attribute Liberality to them; and their freedom from appetites leaves them with no requirement of Continence;[585] and not being composed of the four elements,[2025] they have no yearning for sustenance. Thus, these Purified and Holy Ones,[2026] among all God's creatures, are independent of human virtues. But God (mighty and majestic is He!) is greater than the angels and worthier of sanctification and exaltation than (of reference to) the likes of such notions as these. Indeed, it is more appropriate to characterize Him as something simple to which assimilate—albeit by a remote assimilation!—intellectual concerns and the various categories of goods.[2027] One fact about which there can be no dubiety whatsoever is that He is loved only by the felicitous and the good among men, who are aware of True Felicity and Good and try to approach Him in the measure of ability; who seek to please Him according to capacity, and who follow His acts in the degree of capability; so as to draw near to His mercy and satisfaction and neighbourly protection, and to acquire the right to be said to love Him.[2028]

Then (Aristotle) employs a term not used in our language,[2029] saying that whomsoever God Almighty loves, him He 'cares for',[2030] as friends care for friends, and to him He shows kindness. This is the reason why the philosopher[8] enjoys wonderful pleasures and strange delights; so that anyone attaining the reality of Wisdom[6] knows that the pleasure thereof is above all pleasures, and hence pays no heed to any other pleasure, nor abides in any state other than Wisdom. Since it be thus, the Philosopher[8] whose Wisdom[6] is the most complete of all wisdoms is Almighty God; and only the felicitous philosopher[8] among His servants loves Him in reality, for like rejoices in like. In this respect, this Felicity is the loftiest of all the aforementioned felicities. This Felicity, moreover, is not human, since it is removed and absolved from natural life and the psychical faculties,[2031] being at the extreme of divergence and remoteness from them. Rather is it a Divine gift, which God Almighty confers on the one He has selected from among His servants;[2032] and subsequently on the person who (himself) strives to find it, restricting his whole life-span to its quest and enduring fatigue and adversity on that account. Whoever will not persevere in fatigue is (in reality) a yearner after play, inasmuch as play resembles ease,[2033] and ease is neither the purpose[1416] of felicity nor one of its causes. The one inclined to ease is a person natural of form and bestial of race,[2034] such as slaves, infants and beasts; but such categories cannot be characterized by the term 'felicity', whereas the intelligent[72] and virtuous man devotes his aspiration to the highest ranks thereof.

The First Philosopher[903] also goes on to say that Man's aspiration should not be (merely) human,[2035] although he himself is human; nor should he become content with the aspirations of dead animals,[2036] although his own ultimate end[2037] will be death; on the contrary, with all his faculties he should be roused to discover the Divine life; for while Man is insignificant in the body,[2038] yet is he great in wisdom[6] and noble in intelligence. The intelligence, moreover, is the most illustrious of all created things, being a Chief Substance,[2039] predominant over all by the Creator's[380] command (almighty and sanctified is He!). Again, although men, so long as they be in this world, stand in need of outwardly fair estate, yet should they not devote their entire aspiration thereto or greatly exert themselves to amass wealth and affluence, for property does not bring one to virtue, and there is many a poor man doing the works of the generous. This is why philosophers[742] have said that the felicitous are those whose portion of external goods is moderation,[1307] and from whom proceed only the acts demanded by virtue, small though their resources[2040] be.

All the argument so far is that of the Philosopher.[8] Next he goes on to say that knowledge of virtues is not sufficient, the need being for competence[1805] in their practice and use. Among men, there are those who desire virtues and goods, and on whom exhortation has an effect; but they are few in number, abstaining (as they do) from perverse and evil things by their innate purity and the goodness of their nature.[2041] Others refrain from these things on account of threats and reproofs, admonition and disapproval, as also because of their fear of Hell with its torment and punishment.

Thus, some men are good by nature, while others are good by religious legislation.[2042] The instruction of this latter class in the Religious Law[2043] is like administering water to a person who has a morsel stuck in his throat: if they be not disciplined in accordance with the Religious Law, then like that person they will surely perish, for no stratagem is effective in reforming them. Thus, the man good by nature and virtuous by innate disposition is a lover of Almighty God; his affairs are not accomplished at our hand or by our management, God Almighty Himself being the administrator and manager of that which is his concern.

From these preliminaries it is evident that the felicitous are in three classes. First comes the person in whom, from the beginning, the operation of high-mindedness[2044] is evident: he is modest and has a generous nature, and is marked out by a propitious upbringing;[2045] he inclines to consort and mingle with good men, and to cultivate and frequent the virtuous, at the same time avoiding their opposites. Second is the person who did not originally possess these characteristics, but seeks the right[2046] through effort and endeavour; seeing how men differ, he is assiduous in his quest of the right, in order to arrive at the degree of the philosophers,[742] i.e. in order that his knowledge may be sound and his action proper; this is achieved by concerning oneself with philosophy and rejecting prejudice.[2047] To the third category belongs the person who is constrained to such courses unwillingly, either by the discipline of religious legislation or by sententious instruction.[2048]

It will be evident that of these divisions the one to be desired is the second, for the principles underlying the occurrence of felicity from very birth (on the one hand) and compulsion to acquire discipline (on the other) do not belong to the essence of one seeking strenuously, but relate to externals, whereas complete and true Felicity is his (alone). He is the one who enjoys the love of Almighty God, and the wretched man, who perishes, is his opposite. And God best knows what is right!

## THIRD SECTION

### ON THE DIVISIONS OF SOCIETIES, AND AN EXPOSITION OF THE CONDITIONS OF CITIES

Every compound has a rule, a property, and a form[2049] by which it is particularized and made unique, but its parts do not share with it therein. A combination of human individuals likewise, by virtue of being synthesized and compounded,[2050] also has a rule, a form, and a property unlike those to be found in each one of the individuals themselves. Now, since human and voluntary acts are divided into two classes, good and evil, so societies are also divided into the same two classes: first comes the one whose cause is of the order of goods, and second that whose cause is of the order of evils. The first is termed the Virtuous City, the second the Un-Virtuous City[2051]

The Virtuous City is of one type only, for right[2046] is removed from multiplicity, and there is only one road to goods. The Un-Virtuous City, however, is of three types: first, the one whose parts, i.e. the human individuals, are devoid of the use of the rational[32] faculty, so that what brings them to adopt civilized life[58] is their adherence to one of the other faculties, and this is known as the Ignorant City;[2052] secondly, that where they are not devoid of the use of the rational faculty, albeit the other faculties render it subservient and themselves become the effecter of civilized life,[58] and this is known as the Impious City;[2053] thirdly, that where, because of deficiency in the reflective faculty,[2054] they have conceived a law in their own fancy,[2055] calling it 'virtue' and basing civilized life[58] upon it, and this is known as the Errant City.[2056] Each one of these Cities has an infinite number of ramifications, for there is no limit to the erroneous and the evil. Moreover, even in the midst of the Virtuous City itself, Un-Virtuous

Cities may come into being, for reasons to be mentioned later, and these are known as Growths.[2057] The purpose of such Cities is to make known the Virtuous City, in order that the other Cities may by exertion be brought to the same rank.

The *Virtuous City*, then, is a combination of people whose aspirations are fixed on the acquisition of goods and the removal of evils; inevitably, there is participation among them in two matters, opinions and acts. Their agreement in opinions means that their convictions as to Man's beginning and end,[181] as well as to the states intermediate between these two, are in accordance with right[2046] and in agreement with each other. Their agreement in acts signifies that they are all uniform[2058] in the attainment of perfection, the acts proceeding from them being cast in the mould of wisdom[6] rectified by intellectual correction and guidance,[2059] and determined by the laws of justice and the conditions of governance;[2060] so that, despite the difference in individuals and the divergence of states, the end[1416] of the whole community's acts should be one, and their ways and courses consonant one with another.

It should be understood that the faculty of discrimination[1041] and reason[135] has not been created identical in all men, but graded in varying ranks, from the end[1416] beyond which nothing can be, to the limit below which is the degree of the beasts; this diversity, as has been observed, becomes one of the causes of order. Now, since the faculty of discrimination is not equal, the whole community's perception of beginning and end[181] (which, with other objects of perception, diverge to the utmost) cannot be of one mode. On the contrary, certain persons alone rightly (in the measure of such capacity as may belong to their like) arrive at a knowledge of beginning and end,[181] and of the mode by which mankind proceeds from the First Principle and all terminate therein: and they are those who are particularized by perfect intelligences, sound natural dispositions and correct usages,[2061] and whose right guidance is guaranteed by Divine support and Lordly direction[2062]—and they may be in number extremely few.

Now, since the human soul has perceptive faculties,[2063] by which corporeal and spiritual things are perceived (such as estimation, reflection, imagination and sense),[2064] and which themselves are arranged and graded in purity and turbidity[533] (as is established in the Science of Philosophy);[6] since, moreover, no one of these faculties, at any time whatsoever, whether sleeping or waking, is ever idle or disengaged; and since, finally, knowledge of beginning and end[181] pertains particularly to the substance of the noble soul, no other faculty entering or participating with the latter therein:

Accordingly in the state where the pure essence of the aforesaid community is occupied with observation of beginning and end, and matters pertaining thereto, it inevitably follows that these faculties (which are subordinated to the soul) should be characterized by the conception of forms appropriate to that state. But what is known by the soul[2065] is at the extremity of distance and remoteness from any delineation on the corporeal faculties, which can perceive only exemplars and fantasies and forms;[2066] therefore, such exemplars are likewise of the same order.[470] As for the noblest and subtlest exemplars possible in corporealities,[369] they are realized in each faculty in accordance with its rank and degree of proximity or remoteness in relation to the soul; but the intellectual faculty has adjudged with true knowledge that the thing known (in this case) is sanctified and stripped of such forms.

This class (of which we have been speaking) comprises the most virtuous philosophers.[2067] The group next below them in rank are those who remain incapable of sheer intellectual knowledge[2068] and whose utmost perception is image-wise (in character),[2069] by an estimation like that of the philosophers, albeit the latter hold it necessary[694] to 'remove' from it.[2070] Now, since this class is debarred from knowledge[605] in the true sense,[736] they are permitted to apply the judgments of this form to beginning and end, but they feel obliged to remove it from the judgments of the form represented in their fantasy,[2071] which is lower in rank than the estimative form and nearer to the corporealities;[369] so they deem it concomitant[1170] that they should reject and deny its connection with that estimative form, while at the same time admitting and confessing that the knowledge of the former class is more perfect than their own types of knowledge. This class is called the People of Faith.[2072]

A class lower still than these, incapable even of estimative conceptions, content themselves with imaginative forms, conceiving beginning and end in corporeal exemplars, while considering it necessary[694] to reject any corporeal positions and consequences[2073] thereof and professing the knowledge of the first two classes. These are the People of Assent.[2074] The persons of limited vision below them in rank limit themselves to even more remote exemplars, holding fast to some of the judgments of corporealities. They are the Negligible Ones.[2075] It may further be that if one observes the ranks in the same sequence one reaches the Image Worshippers.[2076]

In short, these divergences occur in accordance with (varying) aptitudes. It is, for instance, as though one person is aware of the true nature[736] of a thing, another of its form, and a third knows the reflection of that form as it falls on a mirror or in water, while a fourth is familiar with an effigy made by a sculptor to that description; and so on.

Now, since the utmost capacity of each person suffices only for him to maintain himself in one of these ranks, he cannot be characterized as falling short: on the contrary, he is directed towards perfection, and his face is turned, in the world of knowledge, to the orientation-point[2077] of God (great is His glory!). Moreover, the Possessor of the Law,[1857] who is designated[690] to perfect the whole community, is able to bring each person to perfection (in the measure of ability) in accordance with the declaration 'Speak to men in the measure of their intelligences!'[2078]; but it is not possible to increase a man's ability over what he was given at genesis[1956] or has acquired by custom, so the words of the Legislator will sometimes be precise and sometimes ambiguous,[2079] and in respect of unicity he may at one time proclaim absolute removal, at another sheer assimilation.[2080] Likewise concerning Man's end, so that each class attains its due and carries off its share.

In the same way, the philosopher[8] sometimes employs demonstrative syllogisms,[2081] sometimes contents himself with persuasive arguments,[2082] and sometimes holds fast to poetic and imaginative notions[2083]—and all so as to guide aright each person in the measure of his insight. Now, the convictions of each group, blundering[2084] along as they are on the road to perfection, differ in both form and position;[2085] but so long as they follow the First Man of Virtue (who is the Regulator of the City of the Virtuous),[2086] there will be no prejudice or contention[2087] among them, albeit they appear to differ in community and doctrine.[2088] Indeed, the differences in communities and doctrines that have arisen among them from the different imprints of fancies and exemplars[2089] (all seeking the same end),[1416] are comparable to differences in foods and clothes, which vary in kind and colour but all have one type of advantage as end.

Now, the Head of the City followed by these people, who is by right the Mightiest Ruler and Head of Heads,[2090] settles each group in its own place and location, and organizes authority and service[2091] among them. Thus, each body of people relative to another body are subordinates, but relative to a third are superiors, until one reaches a group having no fitness for authority, and these are the Absolute Servants.[2092] The people of the city become like the existent things in the universe in the matter of gradation: each one in a rank corresponding to the ranks occurring among existent things from the First Cause[1994] to the Last Caused.[2093] This is following the Divine Way, which is Absolute Wisdom.[2094] If, however, they deviate from following the Regulator, the Irascible Faculty[90] in them seeks to overcome the Rational Faculty, so that prejudice and contention and opposition of doctrine arise among them. If they find the Head to be missing, moreover, each one starts up with a claim to authority, and every one of the estimative or imaginative forms vouchsafed to them[2095] itself becomes an idol, drawing one group into its following with the resultant appearance of discord and disagreement. It will become evident by induction[2096] that most of the doctrines held by those in error derive from the doctrines of the men of right, for error has in itself no reality or foundation or basis.

The people of the Virtuous City, however, albeit diversified throughout the world, are in reality agreed, for their hearts are upright one towards another and they are adorned with love for each other. In their close-knit affection[2097] they are like one individual; as the Religious Legislator[1859] says (peace be upon him!): 'Muslims are (like) a single hand against all others, and the Believers are as one soul.' Their rulers, who are the regulators of the world,[2098] have control of the enactments of laws and of the most expedient measures in daily life: this, by modes of control that are congenial[1177] and appropriate[550] to time and circumstance, a particular control in the enactments of laws and a universal control in the enactments of expedient measures. This is the reason for the interdependence of faith and kingship, as expressed by the Emperor of the Iranians, the Philosopher[8] of the Persians, Ardashīr Bābak:[2099] 'Religion and kingship are twins, neither being complete without the other.' Religion is the base and kingship the support: just as a foundation without support avails nothing, while a support without foundation falls into ruin, so religion without kingship is profitless, and kingship without faith is easily broken.

However numerous this class may be, i.e. kings and regulators of The Virtuous City, whether at one time or at different times, nevertheless their rule is the rule of one individual, for their regard is to one end,[1416] namely ultimate felicity, and they are directed to one object of desire, namely the true destination.[2100] So the control exercised by a successor on the rulings of his predecessor,[2101] in accordance with best interest, is not in opposition to him but represents a perfection of his law. Thus, if the successor had been present in the former time, he would have instituted that same law;[1070] and if the predecessor were at hand in the later time, he would effect the selfsame control, for the way of the intelligence is one.[2102] A confirmation of this argument is to be found in the words reportedly uttered by Jesus (peace be upon him!): 'I have not come to cancel the Torah, but I have come to perfect it'.[2103] Control[2104] and disagreement and discord, however, are conceived by the community who are Image Worshippers,[2076] not Seers of the Truth.

*The bases*[54] *of the Virtuous City* fall into five categories:

First, the community characterized by regulation of the City, the Men of Virtue, the Perfect Philosophers,[742] who are distinguished from their fellows by the faculty of intellection[2105] and by accurate opinions on momentous affairs. Their craft is to know the realities of existent things, and they are called the Most Virtuous Ones.[2106]

Secondly, the community who bring the common people and the

lower elements to degrees of relative perfection,[2107] calling the generality of the City's inhabitants to (acceptance of) the conviction of the first group, so that whoever is apt for their homilies and counsels may progress above his own degree. Their craft comprises the sciences of Scholastics, Jurisprudence, Elocution, Rhetoric, Poetry and Calligraphy, and they are called the Masters of Tongues.[2108]

Thirdly, the community who preserve the laws of Justice[728] among the City's inhabitants, observing the necessary measurement[2109] in taking and giving, and urging (men) to (practise) equality and compensation.[2110] Their craft comprises the sciences of Reckoning and Accounting, Geometry, Medicine and Astrology, and they are called the Measurers.[2111]

Fourthly, the community characterized by protecting the womenfolk and defending the integrity[2112] of the City's inhabitants, keeping the lords of the Un-Virtuous Cities at a distance from them. In fighting and defending they observe the conditions for Courage and ardour, and they are called the Warriors.[2113]

Fifthly, the community who organize the supplies and foodstuffs for these classes, whether by way of transactions and crafts or by tax-collections or other means, and they are called Men of Substance.[2114]

*Supreme Authority*,[2115] in the case of this City, has four situations:

First, where an Absolute King[1864] is present among them, the mark of such a one being that he strives to unite four things: Wisdom,[6] which is the end[1416] of all ends; complete intellection,[2116] which leads to ends; excellent powers of persuasion and imagination,[2117] which are among the conditions for bringing (others) to perfection; the power to conduct the good fight,[2118] which is one of the conditions of defence and protection. His authority is called the Authority of Wisdom.[2119]

Secondly, where a king is not apparent, and these four qualities are not united in one person but accrue in four (separate) persons; these, however, co-operating together, undertake as one soul the regulation of the City. This is called the Authority of the Most Virtuous Ones.[2106]

Thirdly, where these two kinds of authority are both lacking, albeit a head is present familiar with the traditions[2120] of former heads, who were adorned with the aforesaid attributes. Such a one is able, by the excellence of his discrimination,[1225] to apply each tradition appropriately, and he is furthermore capable of deducing whatever is not explicit[2121] in the traditions of past rulers from that which is explicit. Moreover, he strives to unite excellence of address and persuasion[2122] with ability to conduct the good fight.[2118] His authority is called the Authority of Tradition.

Fourthly, where these (latter) attributes, again, are not united in one person, but accrue in diverse individuals, who nevertheless co-operatively undertake the regulation of the City. This is called the Authority of the Holders of Tradition.[2123]

As for the *other authorities*, subject to the Supreme Authority,[2115] in all one must have regard to craft[562] and to acts; and the culmination of all heads, in authority, is in the Supreme Head. There are three reasons for meriting authority of this kind. First, that the act of one individual should be the end[1416] of the act of another, when the former individual is superior[1881] to the latter. For example, a horseman is superior to a trainer of mounts and to a maker of saddles and bridles.

Secondly, where both acts have one end, but one (individual) is capable of imagining the end from within himself,[2124] and has the (practical) understanding for the discovery of dimensions;[2125] while the other does not have this faculty, but once he has learned the laws of the craft (in question) from the first individual, he becomes able to carry the craft into effect—as with a geometer and a builder respectively. Thus the first individual is superior[1881] to the second. In this type of differentiation there are many degrees, for there is a great discrepancy between the founder of any craft and the person only slightly versed therein; the lowest degree of all is that of the person totally lacking in the capacity for invention, who preserves the directions of the master-craftsman on the matter in hand, carefully following them out so that the task is completed. Such a person is an Absolute Servant,[2126] having no authority in any respect whatsoever.

Thirdly, where both acts are directed towards an end which is itself a third act, albeit one of the two is nobler and more useful to that end. This is the case with the bridle-maker and the tanner relative to horsemanship.

Justice[728] demands that each one should remain in his degree and not overpass it. Nor must one individual be employed in diverse crafts, for three reasons. First, because natures[657] have their particularities, and not every nature is able to engage in every task. Secondly, because the master of a craft, over a long period of time, becomes well versed in the rules of that craft through sharpened scrutiny and mounting aspiration; but when that regard and aspiration are distributed and divided among diverse crafts, all are ruined and fall short of perfection. Thirdly, because some crafts have a (specific) time (for their operation) and cannot be performed after the expiry of this time; thus, where it may happen that two crafts should share the same time, he must in one lag behind the other. Where one individual knows two or three crafts, it is preferable that he be employed in the noblest and the most important and kept from the others. Thus, where each one is engaged in the task for which he is most fitted, co-operation results, goods increase and evils decline.

In the Virtuous City there are individuals remote from Virtue, whose existence may be compared to that of tools and instruments. Since, however, they are subject to the regulation of the Most Virtuous Ones,[2106] they will attain perfection if their perfecting be possible. Otherwise, they may be trained like animals.[2127]

As for the *Un-Virtuous Cities*, we have said that they are either Ignorant, or Impious or Errant.[2128] Ignorant Cities, considered as simples,[2129] fall into six classes: the Necessary Combination; the Servile Combination; the Base Combination; the Combination of Nobility; the Dominant Combination; the Free Combination.[2130]

*The Necessary City* is the combination of a society whose purpose is co-operation to acquire whatever is necessary for the maintenance of (men's) bodies in the way of foodstuffs and wearing apparel. The modes of acquisition thereof are many, some praiseworthy and some reprehensible: agriculture, grazing, hunting, and stealing (whether by guile and deceit or by way of dispute and open hostility). It may also be that one city happens to unite all manner of 'necessary' (means of) acquisitions, or it may be that one city happens to embrace one craft only, such as agriculture or some other craft. The most 'virtuous' of the inhabitants of such cities, occupying the position of Head among them, is the person who can best manage and contrive to acquire necessaries, outdoing the whole community by tricking them and using them in the course of so obtaining these. Alternatively, he is the person who bestows on them most in the way of foodstuffs.

*The Servile City* is the combination of a society who co-operate to obtain wealth and affluence, and who seek to multiply necessaries in the way of treasures and supplies, and gold and silver and the like. Their purpose in amassing what exceeds the measure of need, is simply (the winning of) wealth and affluence, and they reckon it permissible to spend possessions only on the necessities by which the maintenance of (men's) bodies is effected. Their acquisitions are obtained by various modes of livelihood, or in some way that is traditional[2131] in that City. Their Head is that individual whose contriving to obtain and to preserve possessions is the most complete, and who is the best able to direct them aright. The modes of livelihoods in this community may be voluntary (such as commerce and hire)[2132] or involuntary (such as grazing, agriculture, hunting or banditry).

As for the *Base City*, it is the combination of a society which collaborates to enjoy the pleasures of the senses,[2133] such as (are to be found in) foods, drinks, women,[2134] and all manner of folly and sport.

Their purpose therein is the (mere) quest of pleasure, not the maintenance of the body. This City, among the Cities of Ignorance,[2135] is accounted felicitous and to be emulated,[2136] for the purpose of its inhabitants is realized (as something) beyond necessary gain and the winning of affluence. Moreover, the most felicitous and most to be emulated among them is the person with the greatest capacity for the means of play and amusement, and who concentrates most on obtaining the means of pleasure. Their Head is the person who, with these qualities, is best able to assist them to obtain these objects of desire.

As for the *City of Nobility*, it is the combination of a society which collaborates to win ennoblements by word or by deed. Now, such ennoblements are received either from other inhabitants of cities or from each other; and they are taken either on a basis of equivalence or in an attempt to outdo.[2137] Ennobling on a basis of equivalence signifies that they honour one another in the manner of a loan: thus, on one occasion one person will confer some type of ennoblement on another, in order that the latter, on another occasion, may confer on him the like thereof, whether of the same or of a different type. Attempting to outdo means that one person confers an ennoblement on another in order that the latter may return him double therefore. This is in accordance with an entitlement agreed on between them, fitness for such ennoblement[1679] being held by this group to result from four causes: affluence; availability[2138] of the means of play; capacity for more than the (merely) necessary amount without exertion, as in the case of the individual served by a group, whose wants are attended to in all respects; or being of use in regard to these three causes, as when an individual shows kindness to another in one of these respects. There are also two other means by which to merit ennoblement, in the eyes of most inhabitants of Ignorant Cities,[2135] and these are domination and lineage.[2139]

Domination occurs where a person dominates his fellows[660] in one activity or in several, whether in himself or by the intermediacy of helpers and assistants, and through excess of capacity or multiplicity of numbers. To be renowned in this sense is accounted a mighty (cause for) emulation in such a community, to the extent that they recognize as the one most to be emulated that person on whom no unpleasantness can be inflicted, while he himself can so inflict it on anyone he wishes.

Lineage signifies that his forefathers dominated others in affluence, or a sufficiency of necessities, or in benefit to other men, or in toughness and contempt for death.

In the case of ennobling on a basis of equivalence, the transaction[1831] resembles those of dealers in the market-place.

The Head of this City is that person, among all its inhabitants, most fitted for ennoblements. That is to say, if lineage be regarded, his lineage is superior to that of all others; or his affluence will be greater (perhaps), if regard is had to the Head himself. If, again, his usefulness be considered, the best of Heads is the one who is best able to bring men to affluence and wealth, either from his own resources or through good management,[2140] and who is best able to preserve affluence and wealth for them—on condition that his purpose be ennoblement, not wealth; or (it may be the one) who most speedily and in the greatest measure brings them to the attainment of pleasures, yet is himself a seeker after ennoblement, not after pleasure. The seeker after ennoblement is one who desires that his praise, and exaltation and veneration of him shall be published by word and deed, and that other peoples[2141] should remember him thereby both during his own days and after his death.

Such a Head, in most cases, needs to be affluent, for without affluence it is not possible to bring the inhabitants of the City to their gains; and the greater his actions, the greater his need, he conceiving that his expenditure arises from nobility and generosity, not from a solicitation of ennoblement. The property he consumes he obtains, moreover, either by taxation of his own people; or by way of domination, in that he overcomes a community to whom he is opposed in opinions and actions, or against whom he bears some sort of hidden grudge, amassing their property in his own treasury. Then he disburses it in order thereby to win name and fame: by which fame and name he becomes the master of submissive slaves,[2142] while his children after him (to whom he hands down the dominion) are reckoned men of lineage.[2143] It may also happen that he reserves to himself possessions from which no advantage comes to others, so that they reckon those possessions themselves to be a reason for his meriting ennoblement; again, it may be that he confers ennoblement on his peers[660] among the neighbouring rulers, by way of exchange or profit,[2144] thus performing all the varieties of ennoblement.

Such a person will deck himself out with pomp and adornment to produce a fine and splendid and magnificent effect, employing thereto all manner of apparel, furnishings, servants and led horses[2145] so that his impression on others will be the greater; likewise, he will keep people at a distance from himself by the use of a screen, so as to increase thereby the awe which he inspires. Later, when his authority is established, and men become accustomed to their kings and Heads[915] being of this same kind, he will grade men in various ranks, particularizing each one with the type of ennoblement his worthiness demands, e.g. affluence, or praise, or a garment, or a mount, or some other thing; and this, to the end that there may result veneration for his state.

The nearest of mankind to him is the person who most assists him to splendour. Those in quest of ennoblement seek proximity to him by this means so that their ennoblement may grow the greater. The inhabitants of this City reckon other cities, different from themselves, to be Cities of Ignorance,[2135] while relating themselves to Virtue. Indeed, the City of Ignorance most like to the Virtuous City is this one, especially since the ranks of authority are determined, in their view, in accordance with paucity or abundance of usefulness. When ennoblement, in cities like this one, reaches excess,[432] it becomes the City of Despots[2146]—and almost the City of Domination.

As for the *City of Domination*, it is the combination of a society who collaborate together to the end that they may dominate others. Moreover, they collaborate in this way when the whole community participates in love[60] of domination, albeit they diverge in respect to paucity and abundance (of such love) and the end[1416] of domination varies: there are some, for example, who wish to dominate in order to shed blood, while others desire to do so for the sake of carrying off possessions, while yet others have the purpose of prevailing over men's souls so that they may take them into slavery. Thus, differences among the inhabitants of this City are in accordance with the excess and deficiency of this love, but their combining together is for the purpose of domination, in quest of bloodshed or possessions or spouses or souls, which they will wrest from other men. Their pleasure lies in conquest and (the infliction of) humiliation, and for this reason it sometimes befalls that, coming into possession of a desired object without vanquishing anyone (therefor), they will not concern themselves with this object, but pass it over. There are some of them who prefer to overcome by way of fraud and deception, while others have a greater liking for contention and open hostility; still others employ both methods. It often happens that those persons, who desire to dominate over men's blood and possessions by conquest, will come across an individual who sleeps, whereupon they will not busy themselves with laying hands on his blood or property, but first they wake him; for they fancy that it is preferable to kill him in a state where he has the possibility to resist, such conquest coming more pleasurably to their souls. The nature of this group demands conquest absolutely, but they refrain from conquering their own City on account of their need for collaboration in order to survive and to dominate.

Their Head is the person whose management is most successful in employing them for fighting and cunning and treachery, and who is best able to protect them from the domination of their foes. The conduct of this community involves hostility to all mankind, while their customs and practices are such that if they follow them, they will approach domination. Their striving and boasting against one another relate to abundance of domination or to veneration of its state; and they recognize that person as most fitted to boast who has dominated on the greatest number of occasions. The instruments[282] of domination are either psychical (as with regulation)[2147] or physical (as in the case of force),[155] or they lie outside both categories (as with weapons). Among the moral dispositions[1038] of this class are brutality,[2148] hard-heartedness, quickness to rage, arrogance, rancour and eagerness for much eating, drinking and sexual congress; and these latter are sought in a way allied to conquest, killing and humiliation.

As regards the inhabitants of this City, it may be that the whole community participates in this conduct; but it may equally be that those who are dominated are also together with them in one City, with the dominators in equal or diverse gradations. (The divergence between them may lie in the paucity or abundance of the occasions of domination, or in proximity or remoteness with respect to the Head, or in intensity or feebleness of force[155] and opinion.) It may further be that the conqueror in the City is one individual, with the remainder as his instruments[282] in conquest: they may by nature have no will to such an act, but since the conqueror provides for the affairs of their daily life, they lend him their assistance. Such people have a relation to him equivalent to that of predators and dogs in the case of the hunter; the remaining inhabitants of the City, however, stands as slaves towards him, serving him and busying themselves with commercial and agricultural affairs on his behalf; but, so long as he exists, they are not lords of their own souls, the pleasure of their Head lying in the humiliation of others.

Thus, the City of Domination is of three types: first, where all its inhabitants desire domination; secondly, where only some of them do so; and thirdly, where one individual alone so does, he being the Head. Those who desire domination in order to obtain necessities or affluence or pleasures or ennoblements, in reality revert to the inhabitants of the Cities already mentioned. (Indeed, some Philosophers[742] reckon these among the Cities of Domination.) This class also falls into three types on the same analogy. It may also be that the purpose of the inhabitants of this City is compounded of both domination and one of these objects of desire. In this regard, the dominators are of three kinds: first, where their pleasure is in conquest alone; here they dominate over base things, and when they gain power over them it frequently happens that they abandon them, as was the custom with some of the Arabs in the Time of Ignorance.[2149] Second comes the type that employs conquest in the way of pleasure, but refrains from employing it if they may obtain the desired object without it. Thirdly, there are those who desire conquest allied with advantage, but when advantage comes to them by another's free-giving, or in some other way without conquest, they show no regard therefore and refuse to accept it. These people count themselves among men of large aspiration, referring to themselves as 'possessors of manliness'.[2150] The first group, on the other hand, limit themselves to a necessary amount, and there are common people who praise and honour them for this. There are also lovers of ennoblement who commit these acts in the course of acquiring ennoblement: in this regard, they are Despots,[2146] for a Despot is one who loves ennoblement together with conquest and domination.

Now, in the case of the elect in the City of Pleasure and the City of Affluence,[2151] ignorant men consider them fortunate and reckon them more virtuous than (the inhabitants of) other Cities: in just the same way, they reckon the elect in the City of Domination to be men of large aspiration, and they praise them accordingly. It may happen, however, that the inhabitants of these three Cities grow arrogant, showing contempt for others and engaging in prating and boastfulness, conceit and love of praise; they award themselves fine titles; they regard themselves as gracious and elegant, but see other men as stupid and warped in disposition; indeed, relative to themselves, they consider all mankind to be fools. When such haughtiness and arrogance and despotism take hold in their brains, they enter the company of the Despots.[2146]

Again, it often happens that the lover of ennoblement seeks ennoblement for the sake of affluence, and he will show honour to another while soliciting affluence from him, or from yet another; or he may equally desire authority over the inhabitants of the City, and their submission to him, on account of possessions (implicit therein). Yet again, he may desire affluence for the sake of pleasure and sport; but since the greater the dignity, the more readily are possessions won, and as with possessions one may more easily arrive at pleasure; so, for this reason, he is a seeker after pleasure who becomes a seeker after dignity. When superiority and authority accrue to such a man, he acquires great affluence by means of this grandeur so as to win thereby foods and drinks and women[2134] superior in quantity or quality to those available to any other person. In short, there are many ways of compounding these purposes one with another, but once one is aware of the simple manifestations,[173] it becomes an easy matter to know the compounds.

As for the *Free City*, which is also known as the City of the Community,[2152] it is a combination in which each individual stands absolute and at liberty with his own soul,[2153] doing whatever he wishes. The inhabitants of this City are equal and none conceives any augmentation of merit[2154] over another; they are likewise all free, and there is no superiority among them, save for some reason that is an augmentation of freedom. In this City there is great diversity, even the various appetites differing to a point transcending reckoning and computation. The inhabitants of this City form sub-groups,[2155] some similar to each other, some divergent; and all that we have set forth concerning the other Cities, whether noble or base, is to be found in the sub-groups of this City. Each sub-group has a Head, but the body[2156] of the City's inhabitants dominate these Heads, for the latter must do whatever they desire. Reflection will show that there is neither Head among them nor subordinate,[1882] albeit the most praiseworthy person in their eyes is the one who strives for the freedom of the community and leaves them to themselves, protecting them from their enemies and confining himself, in respect of his own appetites, to a necessary amount. The person among them who receives ennoblement, as well as acknowledgement of superiority and obedience, is the one adorned with the likes of these qualities. Again, although they consider the Head equal with themselves, yet when they remark something in him of the order[470] of their own appetites and pleasures, they bestow on him in recognition thereof ennoblements and possessions.

It frequently happens that in such Cities there are Heads from whom the inhabitants derive no advantage; yet they bestow on them ennoblements and possessions in respect of the grandeur they conceive them to possess by virtue of their natural accord with the City's inhabitants, or because of the praiseworthy authority that is theirs by inheritance; and the observance of that due keeps the inhabitants of the City naturally disposed to venerate such men.

Now, all the purposes of Ignorance, as we have enumerated them, may be realized in this City in the completest manner and the fullest measure. This City is the most admired of the Cities of Ignorance, being like a fine garment adorned with variegated designs and colours. Everyone likes to reside therein, as a place where each may arrive at his own fancy and purpose, and for this reason peoples[2141] and sub-groups[2155] make their way towards this City, swelling the number in the shortest time; much propagation and begetting arises, and the offspring are diverse in both innate disposition[1956] and upbringing. Thus, in one City many Cities appear, not to be distinguished one from another, their components interpenetrating and each component in another location (than the proper one). In this City there is no difference between stranger and resident. After a passage of time, there appear virtuous and wise men,[765] poets and orators, and everyone of the many classes of perfect men who, if they be collected together, may be components of the Virtuous City; and likewise men of evil and deficiency.

No City of the Ignorant Cities is greater than this one, the good and evil of which are at an extreme; indeed, the bigger and more flourishing it is, the greater its good and evil.

Authority in the Cities of Ignorance is determined in accordance with the number of Cities themselves; and they are six, as we have said, related to the following six things: necessity, affluence, pleasure, ennoblement, domination or freedom. Now, when a (would-be) Head becomes possessed of these benefits, it sometimes happens that he purchases one of these types of authority by expending possessions. This is particularly the case with authority in the Free City, where no person has any precedence over another, so that they award the Head his authority either as a favour[2157] or in return for some property or advantage obtained from him. A virtuous Head cannot exercise authority in the Free City; if he does, he is speedily deposed or killed, or finds his authority disturbed and much disputed. Likewise, in the other Cities, the virtuous Head is not invested with authority.

It is easier and closer to feasibility to create Virtuous Cities, and the authority of the Most Virtuous Ones,[2106] out of Necessary Cities and Cities of the Community[2152] than out of the other Cities. Domination, again, may be associated with necessity, affluence, pleasure and ennoblement; and in those Cities, i.e. those which are compounded, men's souls are characterized by hardness, coarseness, brutality[2148] and contempt of death, and their bodies by strength and power, violence and (skill in) the arts relating to arms. The inhabitants of the City of Pleasure continually grow more eager and avid, becoming marked by softness of nature and feebleness of opinion; it may even happen, from the dominance of such conduct, that the Irascible Faculty[90] in them grows so corrupt as to have no effect remaining; indeed, in that City the Rational[32] becomes the servant of the Irascible, and the Irascible the servant of the Appetitive—in inversion of the original state of affairs, where Appetite and Irascibility serve the Rational in consort. (An example of this is found in what is told of the desert-dwellers, whether Arabs or Turks, namely that appetites and lust[1902] for women are strong among them, and women exercise dominion over them; yet they shed much blood and indulge in violent prejudice and hostility.)

These, then, are the various types of Ignorant Cities. As for the *Impious Cities*,[2053] the conviction[2158] of the inhabitants of these is in accord with that of the inhabitants of the Virtuous Cities, but their acts are in opposition; they recognize goods, but do not hold fast to them, inclining in fancy and will to acts of Ignorance; since they have Cities to the number of the Cities of Ignorance, there is no need to take up again our discourse on them.

As for the *Errant Cities*,[2056] they are those where a felicity has been conceived similar to Real Felicity, but where a beginning and end[181] have been represented[2159] which conflict with Truth; there, too, acts and opinions have been adopted by which one cannot attain to Absolute Good and Everlasting Felicity. Their number is unlimited. However, anyone conceiving the numbers of the Ignorant Cities and being well grounded in their laws, will find it easier to know the acts, the states and the rules of these.

As for the *Growths*,[2057] which appear in Virtuous Cities (like weeds amid wheat or thorns on cultivated land), they are of five sorts:

First, the Hypocrites,[2160] who are a community from whom proceed the acts of virtuous men, but for purposes other than felicity, such as a pleasure or an ennoblement.

Secondly, the Accommodaters,[2161] who are a community inclining to the ends of the Ignorant Cities, but, thwarted by the laws enacted by the inhabitants of the Virtuous Cities, they in some way bring them into accord with their own fancy (by gloss and interpretation)[2162] so as to attain the object of desire.

Thirdly, the Rebels,[2163] who are a community dissatisfied with the rule of The Virtuous and inclined to the rule of Domination. Accordingly, for some act on the part of a Head not in accord with the nature[663] of the common people, they induce the latter to give up obedience to him.

Fourthly, the Apostates,[2164] and these are a community who do not intend to falsify the laws, but who through misunderstanding are unaware of the purposes of the Virtuous, so that they ascribe them to other ideas and deviate from truth. Such deviation may be allied with a desire to go aright, and devoid of ill-will and hostility; and one should hope that they will find the right path.

Fifthly, the Misleaders:[2165] they are a community whose (power of) conception[2166] is incomplete, and since they are unaware of realities, and cannot (seeking ennoblement, as they do) admit to ignorance, they falsely utter words resembling the truth; these they present to the common people in the form of proofs,[2167] while themselves remaining in perplexity.

The number of Growths may well exceed these, but to produce all that would fit into the area[1570] of possibility would lead to prolixity.

This is what we have to say about the divisions of civic[856] combinations. We shall now proceed to speak of the particularities of the rules of civilized life,[58] and we ask assistance (to this end) of the Creator,[380] glorious and exalted is He! He it is who best prospers and assists!

## FOURTH SECTION

### ON GOVERNMENT[1844] OF THE REALM AND THE MANNERS OF KINGS

Having completed our account of the different types of combinations, and of the authority corresponding to each society,[1945] it is proper that we should concern ourselves with explaining the mode of particular intercourse[2168] subsisting among mankind.

We begin with an account of the conduct of kings. We say: government of the realm, which is the authority of authorities,[2169] is of two kinds, each having a purpose and a necessary consequence.[2170] The divisions of government are: Virtuous Government, also known as the Imamate,[2171] its purpose being the perfection of men, and its consequence the attainment of felicity; Deficient Government, also known as Domination,[886] its purpose being to enslave mankind, and its consequence the attainment of misery. The former Governor[2172] holds fast to Justice,[728] treating his subjects[1535] as friends, filling the City with widespread goods, and regarding himself as the master of appetites. The second Governor[2172] holds fast to tyranny,[985] treating his subjects as servants and slaves,[2173] filling the City with general evils, and regarding himself as the hireling of appetites. Widespread goods are: security, tranquillity, mutual affection, justice,[1034] continence, graciousness and loyalty,[1314] and the like. General evils are: fear, disturbance, strife, tyranny,[985] greed, severity, deceit and treachery, tomfoolery and detraction,[2174] and the like. Moreover, in either state men look to kings and imitate their conduct. As has been said: 'Men have the faith of their kings', and 'Men resemble their own age rather than their ancestors.' And a certain king says: 'We are destiny: whomsoever we raise up, is truly raised; and whomsoever we put down, he is put down'.[2175]

The seeker after kingly rule must strive to unite seven qualities: first, good descent,[2176] for genealogical relationship may easily bring about the inclination of men's hearts and inspire respect and awe in their eyes. Secondly, loftiness of aspiration, and this accrues only after correction[237] of the psychical[302] faculties, the adjustment[1249] of irascibility and the subduing of appetite. Thirdly, firmness of opinion, resulting from accurate insight, excellence of innate disposition,[1956] much study, sound reflection, acceptable experimentations,[2177] and ability to take example from the case of earlier men.

Fourth comes the utmost determination, sometimes called the Manly Resolve or the Royal Resolve.[2178] This is a virtue resulting from the compounding of sound opinion and perfect constancy; and it is impossible to acquire any virtue, or to eschew any vice, if one lacks this virtue (in the first place). Indeed, on this depends the whole process of winning goods, and kings stand of all mankind in greatest need thereof. It is related that an appetite for eating mud manifested itself in the Caliph Ma'mūn,[2179] and the harmful effect of this became apparent in him, so that he consulted physicians to the end that it might be removed. The physicians assembled, employing all manner of medication for the treatment of this disease, but without success. One day, in his presence, they bethought them of a remedy, and the sign was given to produce (medical) books and drugs. One of his boon companions, Thamāma b. al-Ashras, happening to enter and observing how matters stood, said: 'But, Prince of Believers, where is one particle of the Royal Resolve?' Whereupon Ma'mūn told the physicians: 'Leave off treating me, for henceforth it will be impossible[802] for me to fall again into this state!'

Fifthly, endurance of suffering and adversity, and persistence in one's quest without wearying or languishing, for the key to all objects of desire is endurance. As has been said:

'How right that the man of endurance should be granted his wish!
'And that the persistent knocker-on-doors should be admitted!'[2180]

Sixth in the list comes affluence, so that he may not be obliged to desire men's possessions. Seventh, upright assistants. Of these qualities, good descent[2176] is not necessary, great though its effect may be. Affluence and upright assistants may be acquired through the other four qualities, i.e. loftiness of aspiration, (firmness of) opinion, determination and endurance.

It should be known that victory, aside from (any outcome decided by) God's predetermination,[2181] belongs to two sorts of person: the seeker after faith, and the man in quest of revenge.[2182] Any man whose purpose in strife is other than these two, will be overcome in most cases; and of these two, only one is commendable, that of the man in quest of the true faith, the other being blameworthy.

That person truly deserves to rule as king who is capable of treating the world when it falls sick, and of undertaking to maintain its health when it is well. The king is the world's physician, and (its) sickness derives from two things, the Rule of Domination and chaotic experimentations.[2183] The Rule of Domination is abominable in its essence, but appears preferable to corrupt souls; chaotic experimentations are painful in their essence, but appear pleasurable to evil souls. Domination, albeit similar to kingly rule, is in reality its opposite. It should be firmly established, moreover, in the mind of anyone considering the affairs of kingship that the principles underlying states[2184] derive from the agreement of the opinions of a community who, in respect of co-operation and mutal assistance, are like the members belonging to one individual: if such agreement be commendable, we have a true state; otherwise, it is false.

The reason why the principles of states derive from agreement is as follows: each human individual has a limited power, but when many individuals come together, their strengths are inevitably many times the strength of each individual. Now, when those individuals become like one individual in synthesis[1938] and unity, then an individual has emerged in the world whose power is as theirs. However, just as one individual cannot resist many individuals, so also several individuals, diverse of opinions and divergent of fancies, are not able to prevail; for they are as it were separate individuals, who undertake to wrestle with a person whose strength is many times that of each separate individual, and so they are inevitably all overcome. (At least, this is the case) unless they also have an order and a synthesis to equate the strength of the one community with that of the other group. Again when a community does prevail, if its conduct is orderly and it has regard for Justice,[728] its state will endure for long; if not, it speedily vanishes, for a diversity of motives and fancies not only lacks the requirements for unity, but invites dissolution as well.

Most states have continued to grow, so long as their citizens have been steadfast in their determination, and have observed the conditions for agreement. The reason for their stagnation and decline has been the desire of the people for acquisitions, such as possessions and ennoblements, for power and insolence necessarily produce the desire to amass these two commodities. When they become involved in such things, inevitably the men of weak intelligence display a desire for them; then, by intermingling, their conduct spreads to others, so that these too abandon their former conduct, and give themselves up to ease, and to a search for privilege and soft living; they lay down the burdens of warfare and defence, forgetting the habits they have acquired in resistance, and inclining their aspirations to comfort, rest and leisure. Thus, if in this state a conquering enemy should attack them, he may easily wipe out the whole community. Even if this does not happen, the very abundance of possessions and ennoblements leads them to arrogance and haughtiness, so that they display animosity and quarrelsomeness and conquer one another. Accordingly, just as in the state's beginning everyone rising against them in resistance and contention is overcome, so, in decline, they are overcome by the resistance and opposition of anyone rising against them.

To contrive[1843] the preservation of the state implies two things: one, the close accord[1938] of friends; the other, dissension among enemies. In the works[455] of the Philosophers[765] it is recorded that Alexander, having conquered the kingdom of Darius, found the Persians in possession of much gear and equipment, with bold men, many weapons, a numerous horde; and he recognized that, within a short time after he left, men seeking vengeance for Darius would arise, and that the King of Greece[2185] would have a hand in this affair. Yet, to root them out would not be in accordance with the rule of piety and justice. In his concern and perplexity, he took counsel with the Philosopher[8] Aristotle, who said: 'Keep their opinions divided, so that they are occupied one with another, and you will become free of them'. So Alexander installed the local dynasties;[2186]

and from his day to the day of Ardashīr Bābak,[2099] the Persians never succeeded in obtaining sufficient agreement of utterance to enable them to seek their revenge.

The emperor[1137] is obliged to consider the state of his subjects, and to devote himself to maintaining the laws of justice, for in justice lies the order of the realm.

The first condition for justice is that he should keep the different classes of mankind correspondent[2187] with each other, for just as equable mixtures[2188] result from correspondence of the four elements, so equable combinations are formed from the correspondence of the four classes. First come the Men of the Pen, such as the masters of the sciences and the branches of knowledge,[1083] the canon-lawyers, the judges, secretaries, accountants, geometers, astronomers, physicians and poets, on whose existence depends the order of this world and the next; among the natural elements,[1825] these correspond to Water. Secondly, the Men of the Sword: fighters, warriors, volunteers, skirmishers,[2189] frontier-guards, sentries, valiant men, supporters of the realm and guardians of the state, by whose intermediacy the world's organization is effected; among the natural elements,[1825] these correspond to Fire. Thirdly, the Men of Negotiation:[1831] merchants who carry goods from one region to another, tradesmen, masters of crafts, and tax-collectors,[2190] without whose co-operation the daily life of the species would be impossible;[115] among the natural elements, they are like Air. Fourthly, the Men of Husbandry, such as sowers, farmers, ploughmen and agriculturalists, who organize the feeding of all communities, and without whose help the survival of individuals would be out of the question;[802] among the natural elements, they have the same rank as Earth.

Now, just as from the domination of one element over the others there necessarily follow the mixture's deviation from equilibrium[830] and the compound's dissolution, so, from the domination of one of these classes over the other three, there necessarily follow the deviation from equilibrium of the society's affairs and the corruption of the species. Among the words of the Philosophers[765] on this matter are the following: 'The virtue of the cultivators is co-operation in labours; that of the merchants is co-operation in respect of possessions; the virtue of kings is co-operation in opinions and government; and that of metaphysicians[2191] is co-operation in true wisdoms.[2192] Thus they all contribute to the prosperity of Cities with goods and virtues'.

The second condition for justice is that the king should consider the states and acts of the City's inhabitants, determining the rank of each one in the measure of merit and aptitude. Now, men fall into five classes: first, come those who are by nature good, and whose good is communicable.[2193] This class is the best part of creation, having an affinity[1937] in substance with the Supreme Head; thus the closest persons to the emperor[1137] must be this community; there should not be the slightest negligence in venerating them, showing them reverence and honour, esteem and respect, and they must be recognized as Heads over the rest of mankind.

Secondly, those who are by nature good, but whose goodness is not communicable. This community should be held dear, and their needs provided for. Thirdly, those who are by nature neither good nor evil; this class should be made secure and urged to good, so that they may arrive, in the measure of aptitude, at perfection.

Fourthly, those who are evil, but whose evil is not communicable. This community should be treated contemptuously and with disdain, and subjected to preaching and admonition, by means of sermons and prohibitions, encouragements and deterrents; if they abandon their nature and incline to good, so much the better, but if not, they will remain in a contemptuous and abject state.

Fifthly, those who are by nature evil, and whose evil is communicable. This class is the basest of creatures, the residue of existent things; their nature is opposed to that of the Supreme Head, and there is an essential incompatibility[2194] between this class and the one first mentioned. But these people too have gradations, and those whose reform is to be hoped for should be reformed with all manner of discipline and prohibition—or, if this fails, prevented from doing evil. As for the group whose reform cannot be hoped for, if their evil is not general or comprehensive, they should be treated tactfully;[2195] but if their evil is general and comprehensive, it is an obligation[694] to remove it.

There are several gradations in (the process of) removing evil: first, by confinement,[2196] which implies preventing (such people) from mixing with the City's inhabitants; secondly, by restraint,[2197] i.e. depriving them of the control of their own body; thirdly, by banishment,[2198] which involves preventing them from participation in civilized life.[58] In cases where the evil is excessive,[432] leading to the annihilation or corruption of the species, the Philosophers[765] have differed as to whether it is allowable to kill such a person or not. The most plausible[2199] of their opinions is that one should proceed to cut off that one of his members which is the instrument of evil on his part (such as the hand, the foot or the tongue), or to nullify[2200] one of his senses; certainly, one should not make so bold as to kill (in these cases), for to ruin an edifice in which the Truth (mighty and exalted is He!) has manifested so many thousand operations[455] of wisdom,[6] in such a way that its repair and restoration become no longer possible—this is far removed from intelligence.

What we have said about instruments[282] (of evil) is contingent on the evil accruing[86] on his part in act;[361] if, however, such a man's evils are in potency only, no further unpleasantness should be inflicted on him than confinement or restraint. The universal principle in this matter is that one should have regard to the general welfare by primary intention,[397] and to his particular welfare by secondary intention:[400] as with the physician, who treats a given[690] member in accordance with the best interest of the constitution of all members *prima facie*, and then, if he judges that, from the existence of that corrupt member, the corruption of the constitution of the other members will occur, he proceeds to amputate that member, paying it no regard. If, however, no such damage is to be expected, he restricts his utmost aspiration to repairing that member's state. In just the same way, a king should have regard for the reform of each individual.

The third condition for justice is that when the king has completed his regard for the correspondence of the orders and the adjustment[1249] of the ranks, he should preserve equality between them in the division of common goods. In this too, he should have consideration for merit and aptitude. Common goods are the means to well-being:[2201] in the case of possessions and ennoblements, and the like, each individual has an allotment of such goods, for example, any increase or deficiency in which necessarily implies tyranny.[985] Deficiency is tyranny towards the individual himself, while increase is tyranny towards the inhabitants of the City. (It may also be the case, however, that deficiency too represents tyranny towards the inhabitants of the City.)

Next, having dealt with the division of the goods, he must preserve those goods for the people. That is to say, he must not allow any part of these goods to be taken from any person in such a way as may lead to loss for that person or for the inhabitants of the City. If this should happen, however, he must compensate him for the loss that has been inflicted. (The loss of a due by its owners may be either voluntary, as with a sale or a loan or a gift, or involuntary, as with seizure or theft; and each case has its own conditions.) In short, something must come to him by way of exchange, either of the same kind or of another, in order that the goods may remain preserved thereby. Moreover, the compensation must reach him in a way beneficial (or, at least, not harmful) to the City, for whoever recovers his due in such a way that the City loses thereby is a Tyrant[870] himself; and tyranny must be prevented (like all evils) by punishments, to be determined in accordance with the measure of tyranny involved: if the punishment be greater than the tyranny in amount, it becomes tyranny against the tyrant, if less it is a tyranny against the City. (It may also be the case, however, that excess too represents tyranny towards the City.)

The Philosophers[765] have disagreed as to whether every tyranny against an individual is also a tyranny against the City, or not. Those who say that this is in fact so, also say that the forgiveness of the man against whom the tyranny is practised does not remove the (necessity for) punishment from the tyrant; those who say that tyranny against an individual does not involve tyranny against the City, say likewise that by his forgiveness the punishment lapses from the tyrant.

When the king has acquitted himself of the Laws of Justice,[728] he should show kindness to his subjects, for after Justice[1034] no virtue in the affairs of kingship is greater than Kindness.[2202] Basically, kindness means his giving them, in the degree of merit, such goods as may be possible, over and above the measure of obligation.[694] But this should be allied with a sense of awe, for the aura and splendour of kingship arises from this;[2203] and while men's hearts may be inclined by kindness that is employed once a sense of awe is instilled, kindness without awesomeness produces only pride and insolence in subordinates, and increases greed and cupidity. When they become covetous and greedy, the whole realm may be given to one person alone, but he will still not be satisfied therewith. At the same time, the king should compel his subjects to adhere to the Laws of Justice[728] and the Virtue of Wisdom:[6] for just as the ordering of the body lies in the natural temperament,[1797] and the order of the latter in the soul, which itself lies in the intelligence: so the ordering of cities is through the king, whose own ordering lies in government,[1844] the order of which (in turn) lies in Wisdom. When Wisdom is commonly recognized in the City and the Law of Truth[2204] taken as a model, order[1300] results and orientation towards perfection comes into being. But when Wisdom[6] is abandoned, neglect makes inroads on the Law; and then the ornament of kingship is lost, discord breaks out, the vestiges of courtesy[2205] are obliterated, and benevolence is turned to hatred.

The king should not keep petitioners at a distance; nor should he listen to the denunciations of informers without evidence. Let him not barricade the doors of hope and fear against mankind in general. He should consider no shortcoming permissible in respect of (such matters as) warding off aggressors, the security of the highways, the preservation of the frontiers, and the honouring of guards and men of valour. Let him associate and consort with men of virtue and opinion. He should not concern himself with pleasures particular to himself, nor should he seek ennoblements and dominations in accordance with his own merit.[2206] Not for one moment should he empty his thoughts of the management of the realm's affairs, for the power of kings' deliberations to guard the realm is more effective than force of mighty armies. Ignorance as to beginnings necessarily produces unpleasantness in ultimate conclusions.[2207] Where a king does give himself up to enjoyment and pleasure-seeking, neglecting such matters as these, confusion and infirmity overtake the City's business, the enactments[1854] become subject to change,[2208] and the people regard themselves as licensed in (the indulgence of) appetites, the means thereto being available.[2138] At length, felicity turns to misery, close association[1938] becomes mutual hatred and affection is replaced by distance, order [1300] falls into chaos, and the Divine Enactments[1854] are breached. At such a time, it becomes necessary to take up once more (the process of) management[1843] and to seek the Imam of Truth and the Just King.[2209] The people of such an age remain without the possibility of acquiring goods—and all as a consequence of the mismanagement of one person.

In short, he should not think to himself that, having taken control of the reins of the world's loosing and binding, he ought to increase his hours of comfort and leisure (for this is the most ruinous cause of the corruption of royal opinion). Rather should his course be to reduce his hours of play and comfort, and even the hours devoted to necessary affairs, such as eating and drinking and sleeping, or enjoying the society of his wife and children; but his hours of labour and exertion, reflection and administration,[1843] should be increased.

The king should keep his secrets concealed, so as to be able to change his opinion while remaining secure from the misfortune of contradiction. Moreover, if an enemy learns (of his plans), he will take action against them by being on his guard and increasing his vigilance. The following is the way to reconcile the keeping of secrets with the need to consult and to enlist the help of (men's) intelligences: one should consult only men of attainment, aspiration, esteem, intelligence and administrative ability,[1843] who will not publish one's opinion; but one should positively not mention it to those of weak intelligence, such as women and children. When an opinion is settled upon, one should mingle acts requiring the opposite of that opinion with acts which are the first steps towards its execution, refraining from inclination to either of the two extremities, namely in the direction of the opinion or towards its antithesis; for both actions may serve as grounds for suspicion or as a means of deducing and discovering the original idea.[2210]

Informers and spies must continually be employed in seeking out concealed matters, particularly the affairs of enemies, with the ruler ascertaining the opinions of his enemies and opponents from their actions. The greatest weapon in resistance to adversaries is to be aware of what they are contriving.[1843] The way to discover the opinion of great men is as follows. One should study any alteration in outward affairs, having regard to their states and actions in such things as the taking of decisions, and the readying of equipment and supplies; or their bringing together what is dispersed and dispersing what is brought together; or their refraining from that which it has been customary to do, such as summoning the absent and signalling for the departure of those present; or their going to great lengths to seek out information, and showing increased eagerness to discover matters, and to listen to varied and miscellaneous reports, and a greater sense of alertness than usual. One may also make deductions from goings and comings, from matters learned from intimates and familiars (such as the people of the women's quarters), and from what is heard from the mouths of their children, slaves and retainers, who are characterized by want of intelligence and discrimination.

The best method, however, is plentiful conversation with each and every person, for everyone has a friend with whom he is on familiar terms, and to whom he tells his news, great or small; and when there is much discussion and conversation, an indication of what is concealed in men's minds[185] will become apparent. Nevertheless, until all the indications have been studied together and one reaches the end of the succession (of reports), one should make no judgment in any one direction. These, then, are notions of the way to draw forth the thoughts of kings and great men; such knowledge has many uses, both as regards employment in time of need and also for purposes of taking precautions when circumspection is called for.

The utmost efforts should be made to win over enemies and to seek agreement with them, and matters should so be ordered (as far as possible) that the need for fighting and warfare does not arise. If such need does befall, two cases only present themselves: either one begins (hostilities) or one is the defender.[2211] In the former case, the first requirement is that one's purpose shall be only Pure Good[2212] and the quest of the Faith, and that one is on guard against any seeking after superiority or domination; next, one must fulfil the conditions of prudence and misgiving.[2213] Moreover, one should not embark upon warfare without prior confidence in victory; nor should one go to war with a following that is not of one mind in any circumstances whatsoever, for in passing between two enemies lies great peril. So far as possible, the king should not conduct the war in person, for if a defeat befalls, he cannot retrieve matters; while if he gains a victory, he still does not escape the lessening that overtakes the impressiveness, the awe and the glory of kingship (in such circumstances).[2214] To manage[1843] the army's affairs, let him choose a person characterized by three qualities: first, that he be courageous and stout-hearted, having gained full fame and acquired a widespread reputation for that quality; secondly, that he be adorned with accurate opinion and full administrative ability,[1843] being able to employ all manner of stratagems and deceits; thirdly, that he be long-practised and experienced in wars.

So long as it is possible to disperse enemies and to root them out by contriving[1843] and the use of stratagem, it is anything but prudent to employ the instrument of warfare. Ardashīr Bābak[2099] says: 'One should not chastise with a stick where a whip suffices, nor employ a sword where a club will serve'. The last of all contrivings should be (a resort to) warfare: 'The final remedy is cauterization'.[1256] There is nothing reprehensible in creating confusion among one's enemies by resorting to all manner of stratagems, deceptions and false dispatches, but in no circumstances is it permissible to employ treachery.[2215] The most important condition for warfare is to be alert and to make use of spies and scouts.

In war, regard should be had to the profit made by merchants, and one should not proceed to endanger men or equipment so long as there be no expectation of great gain. The site for a battle should be considered, and a place chosen for the men that is easiest to hold and most fitted for that business. Fortifications and trenches should not be employed, save in time of necessity, for the use of these gives the enemy superiority.[2216] Where a person distinguishes himself in battle by a sally or some act of courage, no pains should be spared to confer on him gifts and bounties, praise and commendation. One should show steadfastness and fortitude,[1352] avoiding reckless behaviour and foolhardiness.[2217] To despise a contemptible enemy, not employing all one's equipment and supplies is in no way prudent, for 'how often a small band has overcome a numerous one, by God's permission!'[2218] Once victory is gained, scheming[1843] should not be abandoned, nor should there by any lessening of circumspection and prudence; but, in so far as may be, whoever can be captured alive should not be killed, for there are many advantages in taking prisoners (such as making captives, holding as hostage or to ransom, or placing under an obligation), but in killing there is no profit. After victory, there should be absolutely no killing, and no indulgence of enmity and prejudice, for the position of enemies after victory is the same as that of slaves or subjects. In the works[455] of the Philosophers[765] it is related how Aristotle learned that Alexander, having conquered a town, did not cease to put its inhabitants to the sword. Aristotle wrote him a letter of reproof to the following effect: 'While you had an excuse for killing your enemies before victory, what is your excuse, after victory, for killing your subjects?'

The employment of pardon by kings is a more excellent thing than its use by others, for pardoning when one is able (to do the opposite) is more praiseworthy. Truly, how well on the subject of pardon spoke the one who said:[2219]

'I will take it on myself to forgive every sinner,
'Even though crimes against me increase thereby.
'People come under one of three heads:
'Noble, surpassed in nobility, or equal but adverse.

'As for the one above me, I acknowledge his worth,
'Wherein I follow what is due, that being obligatory;
'As for the one beneath me, if he be disinclined to
'Respond to my suggestion (what then?), though some may criticize;
'As for my like, if he slips or blunders
'I show grace, for grace bids what is due.'

Where a king in war is the defender[2220] and has the power to resist, he must strive in some way to ambush his enemies or to make a surprise attack by night; for in most cases where citizens are subjected to warfare in their own land, they will be overcome. If he have not the power to resist, he should employ the utmost circumspection in devising fortifications and trenches, but applying the expenditure of possessions and all manner of stratagems and ruses in search of peace. So much for the Government of Kings.

## FIFTH SECTION

### ON THE GOVERNMENT OF RETAINERS[62] AND THE MANNERS OF KINGS' FOLLOWERS[63]

As regards converse with kings and leaders,[2221] the generality of men should not fail to counsel them and wish them well with both heart and tongue, putting forth the utmost efforts to publish their praiseworthy qualities and conceal their faults. They must further employ cheerfulness and willingness in discharging the dues directed towards them, such as taxes[2222] and the rest; and they should certainly not allow themselves to feel unwillingness and resentment (in such matters). They should stand ready to obey commands and prohibitions in the measure of ability, sparing no pains to preserve the respect and awe in which they are held. In times of disaster and misfortune, they should freely place at their disposal life and property, house and home, for the protection of the Faith, the community,[2223] wife,[56] children and City.[2224] Persons not designated to the service of kings should not proceed to seek proximity to them, for a ruler's[787] company has been compared to entering the fire or to making free with wild beasts; the person who is tested by living at close quarters with them and knowing them well, suffers the embitterment of all his pleasure in living and enjoyment of life.

The course of the person concerned with the service of kings should be to apply himself to the task he is about, paying close attention to the duty for which he has assumed responsibility. Let him strive to be constantly before the one he serves whenever called for, while at the same time avoiding such unremitting attendance as leads to weariness; for weariness arises from much thronging of people, so that the greater the press of mankind at the court of leaders,[2221] the more liable they are to weariness. Whatever action proceeds from his master, he should praise him, extolling the action in all truth. (If he reflects, it will be evident that there is no action in the world that does not have two aspects, one fair and the other foul, so let him seek the fair aspect of every action and place it to his master's credit, making every effort to mention the latter's commendable acts, whether he be present or absent.)

If the management[1843] of the master be made over to him (e.g. if this individual be his minister, counsellor or teacher), and it be his obligation[694] to make known to the master what is proper for him to do, he should recognize that kings and leaders[2221] are like a torrent coming down from the mountain-top: whoever tries all at once to divert it from one course to another will perish, but if a man first accommodates himself thereto, gently and subtly raising one bank with earth and waste-matter, he will be able to lead it in any other direction he wishes. In just the same way, when diverting a master's opinion from anything comprehending corruption, one must follow the path of subtlety and manipulation,[1843] not instigating him to any action by way of command and prohibition.[2225] Rather should he be shown the way of best interest, being contrary to his own opinion; and he should be aroused to the harmful consequences of his own action; and gradually, in moments of privacy and intimacy, he should be brought (by examples, by tales of past rulers,[2226] and by subtle devices) to see the ill-advised form of his own opinion.

The servant should go to any lengths to keep his master's secrets. The circumspect course in this matter is to keep the master's outward circumstances[2227] hidden as far as he is able, so that when he thus makes concealment his habit (of mind), it becomes easy for him to keep secrets hidden. But the master, on his side, when such a circumstance becomes known about him, should not conceive a suspicion against the servant for divulging secrets; for a concealed secret relating to outward circumstances frequently becomes spread abroad, and leaders[2221] at such times form bad opinions of persons who (in reality) have merited confidence in respect of that secret: the reason why secrets (often) become apparent is that the affairs of the world are continuous one with another, so that it is possible to gain an indication from one to another.

The royal servant must know that kings and leaders[2221] have aspirations by virtue of which they stand apart from other men, namely that they demand service and devotion from all mankind, considering themselves in the right therein as in all that they do. The reason for such conduct is the abundance of praise men lavish on them, and the constant approval of their actions and opinions by high and low that becomes lodged in their ears.

In no way, and in no matter, should he impute a fault to his master, albeit he be on the utmost of easy terms with him. If he sees something in him of which he disapproves, let him not repeat it (to others); but if he should do so inadvertently, let him not confess it, even though a report thereof may have reached the master—for there is a great discrepancy between a report and an admission! When some situation arises between him and his master the disgrace of which reverts to one or other of them, let him so contrive as to turn it against himself, making clear that his master has no fault therein. If he himself be faultless in the matter, let him think of some external cause therefor (the imputation of which deflects from him likewise), so that his being excused in this issue becomes manifest. He should pay heed to whatever is liked or abominated by the master, preferring the former even though he sees it to comprise what he himself dislikes; for let him clearly fix in his mind that nothing is more profitable in servitude than the relinquishment of one's own part. Once this idea is firmly established, in every transaction[1831] or requital befalling between him and his master, in which he sees a part for himself, he will relinquish and shun that part, desiring only the part of the superior;[1881] and at length the fruit of the good (in question) will also accrue to him. But if, at the outset, he concerns himself with demanding his own part, he will not escape upset; and it were preferable to leave affairs alone altogether, rather than to corrupt them in this way.

In attracting benefits from princes,[2221] great subtlety should be employed; and one should on no account proceed to ask for them or importune, giving no play to desire or greed. On the contrary, one should accustom oneself to (a display of) contentment and moderation in demands, for the world itself turns to one who ignores it, while withholding itself from the eager man. What one should strive to do is to seek from leaders[2221] and masters the means of (obtaining) benefits, not the benefits themselves: for example, a free hand in those things that bring about the winning of benefits and the gathering of profits, so that one may both be quit (of the necessity) of asking and have the mastery of many benefits. This may be summarized by saying that one should seek advantage through the master, but not from him; for whenever a man accepts advantage from princes,[2221] they grow tired of him, but whoever derives advantage through them is dearly esteemed by them.[2228]

The servant should, furthermore, so represent himself to his master as being ready to expend all his possessions and acquisitions at the latter's least word, or at the slightest effort he should make. If he does thus he will be safe against the master's desire for his property; but if he keeps a tight reckoning, he will only sharpen the master's cupidity: 'What is withheld is greedily desired, while the freely given is (soon) tired of.'[2229] Let him endeavour, in the position[788] and property he acquires, to seek the master's ornament and elegance, not his own magnificence, for such a course is closer to the full dis-discharge of what is due[2230] and more appropriate to courtesy.[2205] He should be particularly careful not to adopt anything which is the master's unique property, or which would befit other princes[2221] like him: if he does, he exposes that thing to loss and himself to destruction. In no thing should he display independence of the master, however trifling that thing may be. Let him in all circumstances adopt the habit of contentment and satisfaction with whatever comes to him from the master; if he be subject to the master's displeasure and reproof, he must on no account complain of him, or allow hostility and resentment to enter his heart, thus attracting the countenance of retribution[2231] to himself. Thereafter, rather, should he exert himself and employ delicacy, so that, in whatever way may be, there should come about a restoration of some state that removes the master's displeasure.

If he be afflicted at the hand of some governor[2232] who is both unjust and ill-tempered, he should realize that he has fallen between two perils: either he can make his peace with the governor and be at odds with the subject population, which involves the loss of his (standing in matters of) Faith and courtesy;[2205] or he can make his peace with the subjects and be at odds with the governor, in which lies the loss of this world and of his own life. The only escape from these two hazards lies in one of two choices, death or total separation; for even with a governor of displeasing character, there is no course but to observe the necessary loyalty until Almighty God at length bestows separation and release.

In the *Manners*[537] of Ibn al-Muqaffa'[2233] one may read: 'If a ruler[787] treats you as a brother, you must recognize him as your lord; the closer he draws to you, the more you should venerate him. When you take rank in his service, do not employ verbal flattery by continual self-abasements and benedictions at every word, for that is a mark of uncouthness and outlandish behaviour; this, save at a gathering where one may not fall short in this matter. Do not make declaration to him of the claim you have upon him, or the long service you have given him: rather, keep your former claims fresh in his eyes by renewed counsel and continued obedience, in such a way that the last part thereof gives life to the first, for an emperor[1137] forgets a claim of which the end and the beginning are separated, having no ties with any man.'[2234]

No task is harder than to be a ruler's[787] prime-minister,[2235] for there is much competition for his place; those who envy him, moreover, are the ruler's friends, his partners and associates on all occasions, and those desiring his office are constantly seizing the opportunity to set traps and stand ever watchful. No weapon will serve him so well as integrity and rectitude,[2236] whether in secret or in public. Should he become aware of the plotting of an envious man or the calumny of one ill-disposed towards him, let him outwardly behave as though he has no concern therefor; and he should display no anger or hatred of them in his master's presence, for this will only confirm what they say. If matters come to questions and answers, disputation and altercation, let him answer gravely, showing self-control[1199] and adducing proof, for victory is always to the self-controlled man.

In the *Manners* of Ibn al-Muqaffa'[2233] there also occurs: 'The conditions attaching to the service of kings are as follows: the training of the soul to what is distasteful; agreeing with them even in despite of one's own opinion and determining affairs in accordance with their fancies; concealing their secrets, and not enquiring about such matters as they do not inform you of; striving to be apt to please them in all respects; giving credence to their utterances and adorning their opinions; publishing their merits and concealing their faults; bringing close what they wish to have near, and removing what they put at a distance; lightening one's own burden to them and assuming theirs; and adopting as a custom the putting forth of one's whole endeavour in obedience to them.'

Whoever can escape working for a ruler[787] should not choose to involve himself therein, for the ruler is an obstacle between men, on the one hand, and the pleasures of this world and the workings of the next on the other. However, if he should be designated for service, he should not account the ruler's abuse as such, nor so hold his asperity, for pride in power makes him free of tongue against men's good repute without any precedent for displeasure. So, to this extent, one should be tolerant of them, having no fear on that account. But one should avoid the victim of the master's displeasure and the man suspected by him, not coming together with him in any gathering and refraining from praising him or pleading on his behalf, until the master's rage calms and his goodwill may be hoped for; then, in some subtle way, one may make public excuse for him so that he returns to the ruler's pleasure.

Again, from the *Manners* of Ibn al-Muqaffa' one may quote: 'When a governor[2232] addresses you, heed his words with heart and ears, limbs and members, occupying yourself with no thought or action or glance to any other thing or any other person. When seated with the ruler, utter no secret, for whenever two people speak secretely in the presence of another, he feels resentment towards them—and this is all the more so in the case of a ruler. When he asks a question of someone, do not you answer, for that necessarily both lightens your own importance and suggests that you take lightly the questioner and the one asked. Moreover, if the questioner should say "I am not asking you", what answer will you give? Again, if he puts his question to a group of which you are one, do not hasten to answer first, lest the others grow hostile towards you, seeking to find fault with your words and having no mercy on your blunders; rather should you delay till the others speak, and when you recognize the faults and merits of each remark, then offer what you have to say if it be better.

'If the ruler[787] holds you dear, still do not seek precedence over his relatives or his servants of long standing, for this is a characteristic of 'clever' people.[2237] You should know that every man, be he emperor[1137] or subject, may have a natural relationship[2238] to some person, notwithstanding that the latter may be lower than he in rank, and he will prefer his company and society, albeit to all appearances remote from him. The reason for this is the close link of one spirit to another.[2239] How, then, can you be sure, when you seek superiority and precedence over someone, that he does not privately have some favourable access to your master of which the rights cannot fail to be exercised? Thus, both will come forth to dispute with you and to repel you.

'If the emperor[1137] ventures an opinion which you find repugnant, agree with him nevertheless and make a show of humility, for know in truth that he, not you, is the ruler.[787] It is more fitting that you should follow his wishes than that you should seek support and acquiescence from him, while speaking in accordance with your own opinion and fancy.'

This is all that we have to say on this subject, and God best knows what is right!

## SIXTH SECTION

### ON THE VIRTUE OF FRIENDSHIP AND THE MANNER OF INTERCOURSE WITH FRIENDS[64]

Since men are naturally city-dwellers,[2240] with the completion of their felicity lying among their friends and their other associates in the species; and inasmuch as whoever has his completion in something other than himself, cannot become perfect in solitude; so the perfect and felicitous man is the one who spares no pains to win friends; moreover, he includes them in the goods pertaining to him in order that he may acquire with their assistance that which he cannot acquire alone. Throughout his life he finds enjoyment and pleasure in their existence: a real enjoyment and a divine pleasure, as we have said,[2241] not an animal pleasure and a bestial enjoyment. However, such people are most rare, while those engaging in animal pleasure and bestial enjoyment are numerous. Thus, as regards intercourse with friends, it is preferable to limit oneself to a few, for this class (of people) may be compared to salt and seasonings: necessary to food though they are, they still do not take the place of sustenance.

The true friend cannot be found in great numbers, for he is noble and rare, and esteem is one of the concomitants of paucity. Again, since love of him tends to excess[432] (excessive Love, as we have said, occurring in most cases between two people only),[2241] the true friend is not to be found in large numbers. However, the pleasant intercourse and generous encounter which is deservedly employed with him should be employed, undeservedly, with many persons—and this in quest of virtue; for good and virtuous men, in their intercourse with acquaintances, follow the same path as in their intercourse with friends, soliciting true friendship from all. Aristotle has said that men need friends in all circumstances: in prosperity, because they stand in need of their company and assistance, and in adversity, because they have need of their consolation and companionship. Indeed, the need of great emperors[1137] for those worthy of nurture and care is as the need of poor men for those who will show them kindness and favour. The quest for the virtue of Friendship which is the natural disposition of men's souls urges them to associate in transactions,[1953] to converse in fair societies, to sport together, and to combine in exercises, the hunt and meetings for prayer. Thus far the words of the Philosopher.[8]

Isocrates[2242] says: I marvel at people who teach their children the histories of kings and their battles, and accounts of wars and of mankind's hatreds and revenges; yet it never occurs to them that it were better to teach them tales of friendly association,[1297] histories of the winning of Affection[1930] and what is concomitant to that virtue in the way of comprehensive goods, and of Love[60] and companionship, without which living is not possible and in disregard of which life itself is out of the question.[802] For if the whole world and its objects desired were to accrue to a person, albeit he lacked the advantage of this one characteristic, life would be a pestilence to him; indeed, his survival would be an impossibility.[115] If a person counts Affection as a contemptible and insignificant matter, then truly he is so himself; but if he supposes that its acquisition can be easily realized, his supposition is in error, for the winning of friends who emerge from the touchstone of trial with the stamp of confidence can prove extremely difficult.[677]

My conviction is that the measure of Love and the worth of Affection are greater than all the hoards and buried treasures of the universe, more than the stores of kings and the precious things hankered for by the world's inhabitants, the jewels of land and sea, and such things as men delight in—the soil, buildings, furniture and the rest. All these coveted things are not to be weighed against the virtue of Friendship. For none of all these is of any use at the time when there present themselves the pangs of affliction engendered by the beloved; and the world and all it contains cannot take the place of a trusted friend, who assists in a matter of moment or aids in the completion of a felicity proper to this world or the next. Happy the one rejoiced by this grace, even if he be devoid of the rulership of the world! And better yet the state of one who, while involved in kingship, still has this portion of felicity! For one who will apply himself to the affairs of his subjects, undertaking to know their circumstances and looking into the generalities and particularities of kingdoms, in accordance with the usage[1070] of circumspection, will not find adequate to his purpose two ears and two eyes, one heart and one tongue. But when he becomes possessed of numerous ears and eyes and hearts and tongues, identical with[2243] his own, the provinces of his realm seem closer to him and he is able, without arduous exertion, to inform himself of secrets and mysteries and to observe what is absent as though it were present. Yet whence may this virtue be looked for if not from a sincere friend, and how shall it be made desirable save through an affectionate companion? Thus far the words of the Philosopher.[2244]

Having made known what is the state of this momentous blessing and this imposing virtue, we must speak of how one gains and pursues it; after which we must suggest the method for its preservation, so that the seeker after this virtue should not be like the person who desired a fat sheep and was fobbed off with one suffering from a swelling. As the poet has put it:[2245]

'I guard her against sincere glances from you,
'By the fact that you reckon fat in one whose fat is a swelling!'

(One may mention) in particular that Man, alone among the animals, is given to artifice[2246] and guile and the display of virtue for hypocritical[1511] reasons: for example, he will freely expend his possessions, albeit niggardly, so as to be characterized by liberality; or he will embark upon fearful enterprises, despite cowardice, so as to become noted for courage. The other animals, however, do not shrink from a free display of their natural dispositions,[1659] standing remote from feinting and the desire to impress[2247] and from artifice[2246].

The seeker after this virtue who lacks discrimination[1225] may be compared to a person who has no knowledge of the natural properties[657] of herbs. In the eyes of such a one, most plants will appear similar, so that he proceeds to take up something, conceiving it to be sweet, and finds it bitter; or he makes to use a herb which he thinks to be a food when it is in fact a poison; but once he learns how they should be obtained, he runs no risk. Likewise, a man should not come to love fraudulent and deceptive persons, who present themselves in the form of virtuous men and good; for when they have cast someone into the snare of falsification, they will—like wild beasts—make him their prey and repast.

The way to proceed in this matter is as Isocrates[2242] says: When one wishes to profit from a person's friendship, one should first investigate his state—in what manner, in the days of childhood, he guarded his precious substance,[2248] and what were his dealings[1831] with parents, contemporaries and kindred. If these are found to be proper, there is hope of a fitting love on his part; otherwise, one should deem it necessary to have nothing to do with him, for a person who has not preserved his own being,[1971] and has become a byword for filial ingratitude,[1762] will not observe the dues of others. Next, one should examine his conduct towards friends he has had in the past, appending this to the first enquiry. Again, one should pursue his conduct as regards gratitude and ingratitude for graces received. It is not that the point of gratitude is recompense, for it sometimes befalls that paucity of means renders one unable to make recompense. But the grateful man does not consider it permissible to allow the intention of recompense to lapse, nor to leave the tongue idle of goodly mention (where favours have been received); whereas the ingrate is careless of publishing the fair mention that is within everyone's capacity, making the most of every kindness done him and regarding it as his right. In truth, no disaster has so calamitous a power to make away with grace as does ingratitude.

One should consider the reason why, among the attributes of the wretched, none is more ruinous than ingratitude: indeed, in the Arabic language 'blasphemy' itself derives from this.[2249] But among the attributes of the felicitous, no quality reaches the rank of gratitude: indeed, the augmentation of grace and the constancy thereof are based upon gratitude.

It is absolutely necessary to recognize this disposition[1313] in a person for whose fraternity[2250] one conceives a desire, to the end that one should not be afflicted by the ungrateful man, who counts contemptible the favours of brothers and the largesse of princes.[2221] One should consider, moreover, how much he may incline to pleasure and the (gratification of) appetite, for a strong arousement to these necessarily carries a reluctance to observe the rights of brothers. Let a salutary glance be also given to the state of his love for gold and silver, and his eagerness and passion for acquiring and amassing these; for while most intimates are noted for their display of mutual love, and will admit of no negligence in exchanging good counsel, yet when their dealings[1831] with each other touch one of these two ores,[2251] strife erupts and they quarrel like dogs, haranguing and disputing with each other in loud voices, using the arguments of the 'clever,'[2252] and the expressions of the base and storing up material[2040] for enmity.

Next, one should consider where one finds him to stand with regard to love of authority and respect, for someone enamoured of domination and superiority will not employ equity in Affection[1930] or be satisfied with equal giving and taking; on the contrary, haughtiness and arrogance will lead him to despise friends and to behave disdainfully towards them. Affection and unselfish admiration[1502] cannot become complete in alliance with such a characteristic: in the long run, only hostility and resentment can result. Finally, one should consider to what extent one finds him to be taken up with singing and music, different varieties of sport and play, and listening to all manner of impudence and jest, for excessive indulgence[432] in such matters necessarily implies that he will be distracted from assisting and consoling friends;[651] and that he will tend to fly from recompensing them by kindness or by taking the trouble to discharge obligations, or by entering with them into affairs involving hardship.

If he passes these tests, being free from the vices we have enumerated, one should count him a virtuous friend, and lose not a moment in guarding him fast and desiring his friendship: for 'there is no pride save in a virtuous friend', and one of the Philosophers[765] has said: 'Truly, I marvel at one who grieves when he has a virtuous friend!'

Moreover, finding one true friend, it is preferable to limit oneself to him, for perfection is greatly to be prized. At the same time, with a multiplicity of friends arises the obligation to discharge diverse duties, so that one becomes forced to deal with certain matters while overlooking others; for it often happens that opposite states succeed each other: thus, one is obliged to display gladness, while assisting one friend, in his joy, but to be sorrowful in accordance with the sorrow of another; or, because one friend is exerting himself in some matter, one must show alacrity in moving, while another's reluctance becomes a reason for purposing to remain still. Amid such states, only perplexity can result and the neglect of one aspect or the other.

In excess of eagerness in quest of virtues, one must not busy oneself with the pursuit of friends'[651] minor faults, for if a man follows such a course, he will find no person immune; and the result thereof will be loneliness and solitude inasmuch as he will remain deprived of the virtue of Friendship. Rather is it incumbent[694] to overlook those trifling faults from the reproach of which no man can be free, and to reflect upon the faults of one's own soul so as to be able to bear with the like thereof in another. As the Religious Legislator[2253] has said (peace be upon him!): 'Happy the man whose concern is with his own fault rather than the faults of men!' One must also be on guard against the enmity of a person with whom one has formerly enjoyed friendship, or such intercourse as is one of the adjuncts of friendship, heeding the words of the poet:

'Your enemy may be derived from your friend,
'So do not seek many companions;
'For poison, in most cases that one sees,
'Comes from food or drink!'[2254]

It is likewise an obligation,[694] when a friend is secured, to exert oneself in caring for him and making much of him; no single right of his, however small, should be lightly regarded, and matters of moment concerning him should be attended to. In fortune's vicissitudes one should be his support, and in times of prosperity one should greet him with smiles and a pleasant manner; in eye and face, in motion and rest, the marks[455] of gladness and rejoicing must be displayed to his gaze, and one should not content oneself with abundance of warmth in the heart, for hearts[740] are known only to the Custodian of Secrets:[2255] 'If your love is concealed in the innermost recess, then seek a friend knowledgeable in mystery!' If you behave thus, his confidence in affection and his peace of mind will grow daily, nay momentarily ,whether present or absent, for since he observes the joy and gladness of your temper with his own eyes, he becomes sure of your affection: true warmth, when friends meet, stays not concealed, nor is it very difficult to recognize in another's appearance his joy on one's own account.[2256]

One should make free display of the same conduct towards those for whose affairs one has evident concern, such as friends, children, followers and retainers; one should have regard to praising and commending such persons, whether present or absent, but without the extravagance that leads to flattery or the ceremony that invites abhorrence. To protect this concept from the taint[755] of flattery and the turbidity[533] of hypocrisy one must aim at sincerity in words and deeds, for deviation from the road of sincerity is flattery as regards externals and hypocrisy as touches inward sense, and both of these are reprehensible. One must make it one's custom to adhere to this path, in no wise allowing access thereto to procrastination and disregard. Assiduity in such conduct brings with it Pure Love and invites Complete Trust,[2257] and thereby results the love of strangers and of persons with whom no previous acquaintance has befallen. A dove will make his home in a person's dwelling, becoming familiar with him and making the rounds of his women's apartments and the bounds of his house, and he will bring together near that man his own semblances and likes: in just the same way, when men become aware of a person's disposition,[1313] desiring to associate with him and being gladdened by his familiarity,[1946] they will direct towards him their contemporaries and their equals. Indeed, an articulate[32] animal has the better of an inarticulate one when it comes to fair description, the spreading of praise and the publication of good qualities.

It should be recognized that just as it is incumbent[694] to allow friends to share with one in joy, and to eschew private and solitary enjoyment of the world's amenities, so it is even more obligatory[694] to participate with them in loss; the discharge of this latter obligation, moreover, makes a greater impression in the eyes of men, for it has been said: 'Pretensions to brotherhood are many in prosperity, but brothers are recognized in adversity!' Since this is so, in calamities and disasters, and in the vicissitudes of states and times that may befall[1136] one's friends, one should count it more than ordinarily necessary[2258] to console them with one's person and property and to show them all concern and care. In this, one should regard it as unlawful[2259] to await their request, whether it be made openly or by allusion: on the contrary, it is one's duty, sagaciously and with discernment, to discover what is concealed in their minds[740] and locked in their hearts. In accomplishing wants, one must strive one's utmost to bestow before the request is made, and in sorrow and anxiety one must share and divide; in this way one may undertake some part of the friends's burden of suffering, while he will find a lightening and a relief in concord and participation.

If one attains a rank of greatness and lordship, one should absorb[2260] one's companions and friends into that ennoblement[1851] together with oneself, but without giving oneself any preponderance thereby or defiling (the gesture) with the taint[755] of condescension. Again, if at any time one senses in a friend some coolness or deficiency of familiarity,[1946] one should exert oneself all the more to frequent him and to win him over; for if, for one's own part, one delays in this—whether on account of jealousy or arrogance, or unwillingness to humble oneself, or the perpetration of some ill-natured behaviour—the link of affection may be severed and weakness may attack the bonds of friendship. This being so, one cannot be secure against a decline in this state. It may even be that one is later overcome by shame and embarrassment, on account of which one desires to break away and to separate. The commendable custom in this matter, however, is to repair the situation as soon as possible, bringing the point at issue and the reason for the estrangement into the open from a pure heart, without malice or false pretences, for many are the blessings of truth. If the friend be the offender, let a reproof be administered blended with (a measure of) grace, for 'reproof is the life of Affection, and in reproof is life between peoples'.[2261] Thus one will erase the mark thereof totally from oneself and from the friend as well.

However, let no one account constant attention to be the cause of Love's perpetuation alone: rather should it be recognized as ever operative[2262] in all things and causes. That is to say, for example, that if there is neglect in care for mount or clothing or dwelling-place, or any other matter, and close attention to each be not allied to continuity, one cannot be secure from that thing's corruption and diminishment. Accordingly, since the shape of gateway and wall inclines to disturbance and ruin from negligence in care for them, you may well consider the effect of brutality[2148] towards a person from whom all goods are hoped, and of ignoring one in whom lies the expectation of participation in both ease and adversity; for the damage to be expected from disorder in the first category is limited to the loss of one class of benefit, while the varieties of damage to be looked for from brutality[2148] to friends and the severance of their affection are of many kinds. Thus, if they become enemies and their benefits turn to harms, there will be infinite fear from the mischiefs accruing from their hostility, while in addition there results the severance of hope of something for which there can be no substitute. By adherence to constant attention, however, one may be quit of this hurtful outcome and derive enjoyment from this virtue.

Now although contention[2263] with all persons is reprehensible, the use thereof with friends is even more so. For from contention results the eradication of affection, the reason being that contention is the cause of disagreement, and disagreement is the cause of divergence,[2264] which comprehends all evils; while the very quest of intimacy and friendship has itself become necessary in the first place in order to eschew divergence. Nevertheless, it frequently happens that a person engages in contention with his friends, maintaining that contention brings about a whetting of the mind, a sharpening of the wits. Thus, in circles where gather leaders[2221] and men of discernment he begins to contend with his friends, departing from the principles of good manners and uttering expressions proper to the ignorant and the common people, so as to make clear to those present how abandoned and confused his friends are. In private, he does not recall this action, applying it only in situations where the latter have less nicety of insight, less readiness in answer and less recollection of ideas. Indeed, the purpose of showing off his 'cleverness'[1747] before that gathering is to confuse these issues for them by embarrassment. In truth, such a person belongs among the oppressors[2265] and despots[1658] of the age, for despots, when they become insolent with great wealth and favour, stigmatize each other as contemptible and insignificant, attacking each other's manhood[2205] and deeming it commendable to search out each other's faults and defects; eventually, matters between them reach the point of hostility and they endeavour to make away with each other's favours, so that the business terminates in bloodshed and all manner of evils. And all this is among the consequences and concomitants of contention.

Let a man be careful not to act stingily with friends over the science or the accomplishment[2266] by which he is adorned, or in respect of the trade or craft[2267] in which he is skilled. Rather let him so contrive that none can charge him with love of usurpation[2268] or with preferring to stand alone in that matter; for harsh behaviour[2269] towards friends in the matter of worldly goods (which are characterized by restriction of location,[2270] and marked by the deprivation and deficiency necessarily arising as a result of pressure on the part of some)[2271] is abominable: how much more so, then, in the case of acquisitions which grow in the spending and become deficient through stinginess, for competition[2272] for these, and pressure on them, in no way call for deficiency, and a full share for one does not necessitate loss for another!

So much should be known, that stinginess in the matter of sciences arises either from want of wares,[2273] or from a quest for superiority in the eyes of the ignorant, or from fear that some remissness or deficiency should appear in the one who has acquired, or from envy; and all these categories are abominable and reprehensible. But it frequently happens that a person does not content himself with stinginess in his own science, but is also stingy of the science of others, reproving and blaming them for publishing and instructing in the latter. Of this class, there are many persons who have obtained possession of a virtuous man's publication[2274] and have kept it from those wishing to be instructed therein, even obliterating its traces. These people act repugnantly to affection and bring about the severance of the friend's desire.

Any companion or adherent of such a person must be careful of daring to mention any of the affairs or matters of his friend in a disapproved manner,[2275] let alone what may pertain to his soul; or of taking the liberty of relating the fault of anything attaching to him, let alone what may concern the fault of his essence. Indeed, no creature among his connections or dependants[2276] must conceive even the desire to commit such a thing, whether seriously or in jest, explicitly or by allusion. How is it possible, moreover, to support the unseemly mention of a person whose eyes and heart you are, as well as being his deputy and representative[2277] in his absence; nay, rather, you are he in very self. If something of this kind comes to his hearing, moreover, he will make no doubt that the source thereof was your opinion, or that you were (at least) complacent about the matter. Hence, he will become averse to you, and friendship will turn to enmity.

When a fault is perceived in a friend, one should make accord with him, albeit a subtle accord,[2278] in which lie both guidance and admonition of him, for the master-physician treats with alimentary regimen the pain which the non-master attacks by surgery. By 'accord', it is not intended that one should overlook his fault or keep it concealed from him: such a notion is sheer betrayal, involving leniency in a matter of which the harm will revert to both. When admonishing one's friends for their faults, it is preferable that one should first do so by an instance or an anecdote relating to another; if this is of no avail, one should, by way of allusion, include some hidden, disguised reference to him in the midst of one's utterance. If, finally, the need befalls for plain speaking, one should bring the matter up when alone with him, after advancing such preliminaries as exact confidence and recalling such circumstances as invoke peace of mind and increase sympathy and warmth of feeling.

Such a conversation should of course be kept concealed from the ears of other friends and companions, to say nothing of strangers and enemies, for a friend deserves better than that one should expose him to the reproof of his adversaries and the slights of his enemies. Where friendship is concerned, one must be thoroughly on one's guard against the interference of calumniators, giving absolutely no scope for their words to be listened to. Evil men, in the guise of counsellors, penetrate among the good, transmitting a remark from friend to friend in the course of pleasant conversations, but polluting it with the taint[755] of transposition and adulteration and presenting it in the ugliest form; indeed, if they find scope for greater boldness, they will defile its form, in the sight of the person concerned, with fabricated conversations and lies they have themselves concocted, until their friendship passes into enmity.

The ancients have compared the calumniátor to a person who scratches at the foundations of stout walls with his nails, making a place for his finger-tips, until, when by limitless probing and searching he finds a chink, he enlarges it with a pickaxe; in this manner he ruins the bases of the wall and becomes the cause of the building's collapse. Many anecdotes and instances have been cited in this connection, one being the tale of the Lion and the Ox in the book of Ꝩalila and Dimna.[2279] Now, the purpose of producing such stories is as follows: a strong wild beast is exposed to annihilation by a mighty animal through the deceit of a weak fox; or a conquering king, thanks to the interference of a calumniator presenting himself in counsellor's form, corrupts his intent towards his own ministers and counsellors (who are the mainstay of the realm and the axis whereon all activity turns), so that after giving them exceeding power and authority, even preferring them before his own children, he inclines to resentment and hostility and proceeds to assault them, subjecting them to death and torture. In just the same way, it may be that with friends he should be on guard against their slandering, even though he has tested their circumstances by time, has stored up their friendship in days of adversity, and has given them a place equivalent to that of the spirit in the heart. These verses have been well uttered in this connection:

> 'O! the great ones whose love I have known,
> 'While equally all have known mine.
> 'I was the "ransomed one" among them, while they
> 'Made oaths by the life of my head.
> 'But enemies carried tales between us,
> 'Until we parted, each going his own way.'[2280]

Circumspection in preserving Love,[60] the need for which is apparent in virtue of the need for civilized life,[58] is one of the most important of matters of moment; deficiency may not be allowed access thereto, nor may the notion of unity[2281] fail, for most of the virtues of character we have enumerated are confined to preserving the order of sociability,[1938] without which the existence of the species cannot be. For example, the need for Justice is to amend transactions[2282] so that they may remain safeguarded from the vice of Tyranny.[985] The need for Continence is to control bodily appetites, in order that monstrous offences may not befall the individual and the species. The need for Courage is in order to ward off terrifying things so as to embrace safety.

To display some virtues, one has need of external means,[2283] as when one requires the acquisition of properties for Freedom,[769] Liberality[2284] and Justice, so as to be able to perform the act of free men,[768] and to be capable of rewarding what is fair as well as of obligatory[694] requital. The greater the need, the greater the requirement for external materials; but it is virtually impossible[677] to obtain materials[494] without honest helpers and sincere companions. To fall short in winning sociability[1938] leads to falling short in the acquisition of Felicity. This is the reason why it has been ruled that no vice in matters temporal and spiritual is more reprehensible than idleness and sloth, for such states cut men off from all goods and virtues, expelling them from the wearing of human garb.[2285] As we have said, the farthest of men from virtue are those who depart from civilized life[58] and sociability[1938] and incline to solitude and loneliness.[2286] Thus, the virtue of Love and Friendship is the greatest of virtues, and its preservation is the most important of tasks. This is why we have spoken at such length of this matter, for this is the noblest topic in the present Discourse viewed from the standpoint of the foregoing ideas. And God knows best!

## SEVENTH SECTION

### ON THE MANNER OF INTERCOURSE WITH THE CLASSES OF MANKIND[65]

A man must consider the relationship of his own state to the states of all the classes of mankind, his relationship to each class necessarily falling into one of three categories: in rank he is either superior to that class, or comparable[2287] to it, or beneath it. If he be above it in rank, such consideration prompts[754] him to preserve that degree so that it should not incline to deficiency; if he be comparable, he is prompted to rise above that degree on the ascending stairway of perfection; if he be beneath, he strives to attain the degree of that class. The state of association varies, likewise, as the states of the ranks vary: association with the higher class is (to be conducted according to principles) apparent from what we have recorded in the Fifth Section (of the present Discourse). Association with the comparable[2287] class is of three kinds: association with friends, with enemies, and with persons who are neither friends nor enemies. Friends are of two classes, true and not true.[2288] Association with true friends has already been spoken of.

As for association with friends who are not true, but who imitate true friends, being not devoid of some sort of artificiality[2246] and blandishment, the following course should be adopted: as opportunity allows, one should be courteous and kind, not neglecting for a moment to persuade and be tactful, to be patient and to treat openly;[2289] but one's own secrets and faults should be kept concealed from them, likewise private conversations, one's circumstances, one's means of profit and the amount of one's property. Nor should one take them to task for their shortcomings, or reprove them for neglecting their dues, or concern oneself with retribution therefor—(at least) so long as one may hope for reform of the relationship and for their reform. It may be that some of them, in the course of time, will attain the degree of the pure and of sincere friends.[2290] In the measure of capacity, one should console them, considering it necessary to enquire after their relatives and dependents; one should also undertake to fulfil their needs, manifesting cheerfulness in one's dealings with them, whether naturally or by effort. In a case of dire necessity, one should offer them a helping hand. In short, one should employ all manner of generosity, urbanity[2291] and good faith, so that all men have an increased desire for one's friendship; and when a discrepancy befalls in their rank and they attain to a greater place[788] or ennoblement,[1851] one will seek their friendship the more. However, attachment or proximity one should not seek more than ordinarily.

Enemies are of two kinds, near and distant, and each category has two divisions, public or private. Persons with a grudge should be reckoned among open enemies, but envious people belong to the category of secret foes. One should be more on one's guard against the enemy near at hand inasmuch as he is aware of one's secrets and foibles, and one should reckon it incumbent[694] to be circumspect with him when eating or drinking or on other occasions. The general principle for the management[1844] of enemies is that if one can make them friends by forbearance, sympathy and gracious treatment, removing the roots of resentment and hostility from their hearts, it is indeed the best contrivance[1843] to adopt. Even if this be not so, so long as in courtesy[2205] men behold one another's open affectation (of friendship) and politeness,[2292] they must take great pains to preserve such a state of affairs. In no wise should one permit a display of enmity, for the suppression of evil by good is good, but the suppression of evil by evil is evil. No attention should be paid to the 'cleverness'[1747] of one's enemies, and in such situations one should employ indulgence, forbearance and tact. One should consider it absolutely necessary to be on one's guard against prolonged strife and contention, for the display of hostility necessarily does away with benefits, exposes fortunes to (the danger of) disappearance, and calls for constant worries and unbroken anxieties, the wastage of possessions and ennoblements, the endurance of oppression, humiliation and bloodshed, and all manner of other evils; and a life that is spent in contriving[1843] and worrying, and in close attention and application to such acts as these, is both wasted and unhappy in this world and the cause of misery and loss in the next.

The causes of voluntary enmity[2293] are five: contention over property; contention over rank; contention over objects of desire; engaging in (the satisfaction of) appetites so as to cause dishonour to a man's womenfolk; and difference of opinions. The way to avoid each category is to be on guard against its cause.

One should investigate the circumstances of one's enemies, entering deeply into the examination of news concerning them; thus one may become aware of their guile and deception, and by doing likewise succeed in frustrating their endeavours. Complaints regarding enemies should be clearly brought to the ears of princes[2221] and other men, in order that they should not accept their garbled accounts, and that the ruses devised by them should not gain prevalence, but rather that their (every) word and deed should become the object of suspicion. One should ascertain well what are the faults of one's enemies, becoming aware of their very pith and marrow; let them be stored up, with all due circumspection for their concealment, for (constantly) publicizing an enemy's faults leads to his becoming hardened in them and unaffected by it; but if one reveals them in one's own time, his defeat and subjection will result. Again, it is proper to give the enemy warning of some part of them before publication, so that, realizing that men are aware of his faults and defects, he becomes faint-hearted and weak in his opinion.[2294] In this connection, attention to the truth is a most important condition, for falsehood is one of the motives[684] for the adversary's power and ascendancy. One should gain awareness of the tempers and customs[2295] of each category so as to ward off each thing with something corresponding[2287] to it. Likewise, one must ascertain what causes them anxiety and vexation, for triumph lies enclosed in such matters as these. The best policy,[1843] in this connection, is to win for oneself true precedence over one's opponents and competitors, taking the lead in the virtues in which it is feasible for both sides to participate; thus are brought about both the perfection of one's own essence and the enfeeblement of one's antagonists. It is a condition of prudence and sagacity[2296] that one should feign friendship with enemies, as well as being on good terms and mingling freely with their friends, for it is more easily possible in this way to know their failings and the places where they slip and stumble.

Uttering abuse against enemies, cursing them and attacking their personal honour—all such behaviour is extremely reprehensible, and also remote from intelligence; for such acts cause no harm to their souls or possessions, whereas the offender's soul and essence are immediately damaged, inasmuch as he has both imitated the 'clever' ones[2297] and also given his opponents scope for reproach and the assumption of authority. It is said that a certain person soiled his tongue before Abū Muslim[2298] of Marw with (an attack on) the honour of Naṣr-i Saiyār, conceiving that this would please Abū Muslim and that he would think well of him for it. But Abū Muslim pulled a sour face, chiding him roughly for this and saying: 'It is one thing for me to stain my hands with their blood to some purpose, but what purpose or advantage will there be in polluting one's tongue with their honour?' When enemies, moreover, are victims of a calamity from which one is oneself not secure (the like of which, indeed, one expects and looks for),[2299] one should on no account gloat over them, displaying joy and gladness, for this is a sign of reckless exultation,[2300] and one is in a sense gloating over oneself!

If the enemy comes under a man's protection, taking his sanctum[2301] for a refuge, or (otherwise) relies on something demanding loyalty and trust, one may not employ perfidy, guile or treachery, but use instead only courtesy[2205] and generosity. Indeed, a man should so act that blame and reproach attach particularly to the enemy, while his own good faith and fair conduct become known to all.

There are three degrees in the matter of repelling the harm of one's enemies: first, if this be feasible, reforming them in their souls; if not, then the relationship itself must be reformed. Secondly, one may refrain from mingling with them by removing oneself from their neighbourhood, or by choosing to go on a long journey. Thirdly, one may suppress and subjugate them, this being the ultimate policy[1843] of all, which may be proceeded with on six conditions: first, that the enemy be evil in his essence and that there is no feasible way of reforming him; secondly, that one sees no escape for oneself from his attack in any way save by suppression; thirdly, that one recognizes that if the enemy gain the victory he will do more than one will oneself commit; fourthly, that one shall have witnessed an open intention and effort on his part to make away with one's goods; fifthly, that in suppressing him one shall not be characterized by any vice like treachery or perfidy; and finally, that no reprehensible consequence be expected for such action, either in this world or the next. Even so, if his suppression can be effected at the hand of another enemy, it is preferable that it be so; for it is one of the concomitants[1170] of prudence[2302] to seize an opportunity when a respite is available.

As for the envious man, he should be kept sorrowful in heart and consumed in body by a display of graces and a show of virtues and other things, such as to call forth rage and annoyance on his part, but without including any vice. At the same time, one should beware of his ruses, striving to ensure that people are apprised of his inward inclinations.[2303]

As for association with persons who are neither friends nor enemies, this too falls into diverse categories: one should greet each person as he deserves, for this is more nearly in accord with best interest. For example, one should serve counsellors[2304] (i.e. that class which freely gives counsel to all), mingling with them, listening to their words, and displaying cheerfulness and joy at sight of them. But let no man hasten to accept what is said by everyone, nor be deceived by the externals of men's utterances; let him rather reflect until he becomes aware of each man's purpose, distinguishing the true from the false, and then proceeding in accordance with the way that is most accurate. Again, the upright[2305] (i.e. that category concerning itself disinterestedly[2306] with the betterment of relationships) should be praised and extolled, and kept in particular esteem by means of ennoblements and all manner of marks of honour; they should also be imitated, for their ways[2307] are praiseworthy in the eyes of all mankind. With 'clever' people[2308] restraint[2309] should be employed, no heed or attention being paid to their 'cleverness',[1747] so that they may desist from causing annoyance. If one should in fact be afflicted by their abuse and 'clever tricks',[693] let this be accounted contemptible, no grief or pain being shown thereat and no requital being engaged in on their account. On the contrary, one should proceed, calmly and steadily, to reform the situation, or else give up and abandon frequentation of them altogether; not choosing, as far as may be, to associate with this class, but regarding it as forbidden[2259] to dispute with them or to pay them back.[2310] With arrogant people[2311] one should not be humble but act with them as they themselves act, so that they may be hurt and restrained thereby: 'Arrogance towards the arrogant man is an act of charity.'[2312] Humility towards such people only brings on[808] scorn and contempt, for they are assured of their own rightness, imagining that everyone has the obligation[694] to proffer them service and humility; but if they find the opposite to be the case, they will recognize that the fault lies with them, and it may even be that they come to (adopt) a submissive attitude and an agreeable behaviour.

One should mingle with men of virtue, considering it incumbent[694] to draw profit from them; likewise, every opportunity should be taken to aid and assist them, and every effort made to become of their number. With bad neighbours and incompatible kinsmen[2313] one must be forbearing[609] and employ tact and politeness; for one must realize as an assured fact that the base are more patient in body, while the noble are so in soul. In just the same manner and fashion, one should use with every man that which intelligence demands, or which is indicated by prudence and sagacity,[2296] striving to reform both the generality of mankind and one's own particular adherents[2314] in the measure of capacity.

As for subjects,[2315] they fall likewise into several categories. Let those willing to learn[2316] be looked after, and the circumstances of their natural disposition[657] and conduct kept under consideration: if they be apt to the various branches of the sciences and characterized by good conduct, they should not be kept from learning, or asked to assume any obligation or burden on this account, but every effort should be made to fulfil their needs. But in the case of those with depraved natures,[2317] who (would) learn for purposes of greed, let them be ordered to correct their dispositions,[2318] admonished for their faults, and perfected in accordance with capacity; let them, however, be restrained from any science that may be a means of their attaining to corrupt purposes. The stupid[2319] should be urged to do something more suitable to their understanding and more comprehensive of advantage, and thus retrained from wasting their lives. Beggars, if they be insistent, should be deterred from their importunity and accession to their petition delayed, unless they be sincerely in need, for a distinction must be drawn between the needy and the covetous man: the covetous man should be restrained from his desire and not assisted to what he seeks, for this may be the means of his reform, but the needy should be given gifts and comforted, and aided with the wherewithal of daily life. Indeed, so long as it does not lead to an upset in the affairs of his own soul and of those dependent on him, the needy man should be given preferential treatment. The weak should be given a helping hand, and mercy should be shown to them; and the oppressed[2320] should be given aid.

In all that concerns good, one should form the intention of truth and purity, assimilating oneself to the Absolute Good, who is the Source of goods and the Diffuser of ennoblements, exalted and sanctified be He!

## EIGHTH SECTION

### ON THE TESTAMENTS ATTRIBUTED TO PLATO, PROFITABLE IN ALL MATTERS; AND THE CONCLUSION OF THE BOOK[2321]

Having completed our exposition of the problems of Practical Philosophy[2322] in the manner set down at the beginning of the book, and having put forth some effort in treating fully its various categories and reporting the words of the masters of this discipline, we have purposed that the book should conclude with a chapter from the utterances of Plato of profit to the generality of men: namely, the testament that he gave to his pupil Aristotle. He says:

Know Him whom you worship[2323] and observe His due. Be always at teaching and learning, but place worship[2324] before the pursuit of science. Do not test men of science with the abundance of your knowledge, but respect their condition by refraining from evil and mischief.

Ask nothing of Almighty God the benefit of which will be cut off from you, but be assured that all gifts are from His Majesty, and seek from Him lasting graces and advantages that cannot leave you. Be always alert, for evil has many occasions, and harbour no desire for that which may not be done. Know that God's vengeance on man is not in displeasure and reproach, but intended to rectify and to discipline. Do not confine yourself to aspiring after a worthy life so long as a worthy death be not joined therewith; and count not life and death worthy unless they shall have been a means to the acquisition of good.

Do not proceed to rest and sleep before first having called your soul to account on three heads: first, you should reflect whether during that day any fault may have occurred on your part, or not; secondly, you should reflect whether you have acquired any good, or not; thirdly, you should reflect whether you have culpably omitted any matter, or not.

Again, remember what you were originally and what you will become after death. Molest no one, for the workings of the universe are exposed to change and decline: unfortunate the one who is careless to recall the outcome and refrains not from slipping!

Be not arrogant about your stock[2325] of things lying outside your essential being. In doing good to the deserving, do not wait to be asked, but take the initiative before the request. Count not as wise[8] one who rejoices at any of the world's pleasures, or frets and grieves at any of the world's misfortunes. Always be mindful of death, and take example from the dead. Recognize that Man's vileness derives from his speaking much to no purpose, and know him from his declarations on things that do not concern him. You must know that whenever one meditates ill to another, that soul has accepted evil and that man's course[2326] embraces evil.

Reflect often, then put into words, and then into action, for circumstances change. Be loving to every man and slow to rage, for anger (easily) becomes customary to you. When a man has need of you today, do not delay the relief of his necessity until tomorrow, for how shall you know what may happen on the morrow? If a person be caught up in an affair, assist him, save for the one caught up in his own evil actions. Do not hasten to judge your rivals until you understand what they say. Be not wise[8] in words alone, but in words and deeds both; for wisdom[6] in speech remains in this world, but wisdom in deeds reaches the other world and endures there. Moreover, if in well-doing you take trouble, the trouble will not last but the good action does so; if, on the other hand, you derive pleasure from evil, the pleasure will not last but the bad action will. Be mindful of the day when you are called, but are deprived of the organs of hearing and speech: (for then) you will neither hear nor speak nor be able to be mindful.

Know for sure that you are directed to a place where you will recognize neither friends nor enemy: therefore, in this (present) place attribute deficiency to no man. Recognize truly that you will come to a place where master and slave are equal, so be not arrogant here. Have your provisions ever ready for the road, for how shall you know when the journey will begin? Know that of God Almighty's gifts none is better than Wisdom.[6] Wise[8] is the person whose thoughts, words and actions are equal and alike. Reward good and let evil pass. At all times recall, retain and understand your own business. Understand[1776] your state and grow not weary of any one of this world's momentous affairs, and at no time slacken or delay. Count it not permissible to pass beyond goods, making no evil act your means to the acquisition of that which is fair. Turn not aside from a more virtuous thing for the sake of a passing joy, for (in doing so) you have turned from a lasting joy.

Be a lover of Wisdom,[6] and listen to the words of the wise;[765] put the fancy of the world away from you, and do not abstain from commendable manners.[537] Begin no enterprise before its time: and when you are engaged in a task, be so engaged for cause of understanding and insight.[2327] Be not arrogant and conceited in your wealth, and lay not yourself (thus) open to the misfortunes of defeat and abasement. So deal with a friend that you need no arbitrator;[860] but with an enemy in such a way that you may triumph in the arbitration. Use 'cleverness'[1747] with no one, but humility with all. Count no humble man as contemptible. Do not blame your brother for what you excuse in yourself. Rejoice not in sloth, nor rely on fortune, nor regret good deeds. Jest with none.[2328] Be ever attentive to following the course of justice[1034] and rectitude, adhering to good things so that you may become fortunate, if God Almighty will!

These are the testaments of Plato, with which we proposed to conclude the book, and here we cease our utterance. May God Almighty confer on all the success of attaining goods and winning fair ennoblements, making them eager in quest of that which pleases Him! He is gracious, the One who answers, and to Him is the return, and to Him do I come back penitent.[2329]

The book has been completed by the aid of the Most Generous King.[2330]

# *Notes*

1. This doxology contains several quotations from the Koran and elsewhere, not all strictly accurate. In a manner familiar to Islamic scholars, these quotations have been inserted as an integral part of the sentence-structure. Such skilful dovetailing cannot always be reproduced in English, but all such passages are indicated by quotation marks.

2. Ṭūsī, in excusing himself for having served the Ismā'īlīs of Quhistān, uses a typical Shī'ite tradition justifying *taqīya*, i.e. strictly speaking, the concealment of one's faith to save one's life, but—by extension—taking the line of least resistance in any difficult situation. However, he can here almost be regarded as implying that he sees himself merely as an unheroic Sunnī! Of the five versions I have used, only Lahore 1952 and 1955 give *yaqī* ('protects'); the others provide a Sunnī flavour by writing *yūfī* or *yuwaffī* ('fulfils'), which seems to destroy the argument. Strictly speaking, all the readings (in Arabic they differ only by one dot) involve a grammatical looseness unlikely in a genuine, early tradition: the use of the indicative, instead of the jussive, in a quasi-conditional clause. The transition from formality and mannerism to the bald 'there was nothing else I could do', corresponds to the Persian.

3. While this is a Persianized form of a common title of Ibn Miskawaih's treatise, Ṭūsī is clearly only alluding to that fact here, not quoting the title as such. Cf. Notes 39 and 237.

4. Respectively 'Practical Wisdom' (*ḥikmat-i 'amalī*), 'Civic Wisdom' (*ḥikmat-i madanī*) and 'Domestic Wisdom' (*ḥikmat-i manzilī*). Ṭūsī means that Ibn Miskawaih treats only of Ethics. Cf. Note 39.

5. 'Moral Wisdom' (*ḥikmat-i khulqī*). Cf. Note 39.

6. 'Wisdom' (*ḥikmat*).

7. *'ilm* and *'amal* respectively.

8. 'Wise man' (*ḥakīm*).

9. Koran 11:272.

10. *ḥikmat-i naẓarī* and *ḥikmat-i 'amalī* respectively.

11. Respectively: *'ilm-i mā ba'd al-ṭabī'a*, *'ilm-i riyāḍī*, and *'ilm-i ṭabī'ī*.

12. *uṣūl* and *furū'* respectively.

13. 'The Divine Science' (*'ilm-i ilāhī*).

14. *falsafa-i ūlā*.

15. *'ilm-i handasa*.

16. *'ilm-i 'adad*.

17. 'Science of Aspect' (*'ilm-i hai'a*).

18. 'Laws *or* Judgments of the Stars' (*aḥkām-i nujūm*).

19. *'ilm-i ta'līf*.

20. *'ilm-i mūsīqā*.

21. Respectively: 'Science of Spectacles and Mirrors' (*'ilm-i manāẓir u marāyā*); 'Science of Reparation and Equation' (*'ilm-i jabr u muqābala*); 'Science of Drawing Weights' (*'ilm-i jarr-i athqāl*).

22. 'The Commonly Accepted relating to Nature' (*samā'-i ṭabī'ī*). This corresponds to Aristotle's supposed eight books of Physics.

23. *basā'iṭ-i 'ulwā u suflā* (cf. Note 173).

24. *samā' u 'ālam*.

25. *arkān u 'anāṣir*.

26. *'ilm-i kaun u fasād*.

27. 'Sublime impressions' (*āthār-i 'ulwà*).

28. *'ilm-i ma'ādin*.

29. 'Growing' (*nāmī*).

30. 'Science of Plants' (*'ilm-i nabāt*).

31. 'Science of Animals' (*'ilm-i ḥayawān*).

32. 'Speaking' (*nāṭiq*). Cf. Note 135.

33. 'Science of the Soul' (*'ilm-i nafs*).

34. Respectively: *'ilm-i ṭibb*; *'ilm-i aḥkām-i nujūm* (see Note 18); and *'ilm-i falāḥat*.

35. *'ilm-i manṭiq*.

36. The foregoing section may be compared with various other schemes set out in Ch. 11 of *Introduction à la Théologie Musulmane*, by L. Gardet and M. M. Anawati, Paris 1948.

37. 'Acts connected with skills' (*af'āl-i ṣinā'ī*).

38. *jamā'atī bi-mushārakat*.

39. Respectively: 'The Correction of Dispositions' (*tahdhīb-i akhlāq*); 'The Regulation of Households' (*tadbīr-i manāzil*); 'The Government of Cities' (*siyāsat-i mudun*). Cf. Notes 3, 4 and 5.

40. *dar aṣl yā ṭab' bāshad yā waḍ'*.

41. *ādāb u rusūm*; 'agreed opinion' = *ittifāq-i ra'y*.

42. *nawāmīs-i ilāhī*.

43. *'ibādāt u aḥkām*.

44. *ḥudūd u siyāsāt*.

45. *'ilm-i fiqh*.

46. *tafṣīl, pl. tafāṣīl*. Used for the particular application of a general principle.

47. *ijmāl*.

48. *maqāṣid*.

49. *faḍā'il*.

50. *anwā'*.

51. *radhā'il*.

52. *'adālat*.

53. *manāzil*.

54. *arkān*.

55. *amwāl u aqwāt*.

56. *ahl*.

57. *khadam u 'abīd*.

58. *tamaddun*.

59. *māhīyat*.

60. *maḥabbat*.

61. *irtibāṭ-i ijtimā'āt*.

62. *khidmat-i khadam* (cf. Note 57). Some texts omit 'of the service'.

63. *ādāb-i atbā'-i mulūk*.

64. *ṣadāqat . . . mu'āsharat bi-aṣdiqā'*.

65. *aṣnāf-i khalq.*
66. *dar ma'rifat-i mauḍū' u mabādi'-i īn nau'.*
67. *musallam bāyad dāsht.*
68. Koran 91:10.
69. *taṣauwurāt.* Cf. the work of this name, ed. W. Ivanow (1950). p. xxix.
70. *jauhar-i basīṭ.*
71. *idrāk-i ma'qūlāt bi-dhāt-i khwīsh.*
72. *'āqil.*
73. Respectively: *wāsiṭa, mustadill, madlūl.*
74. *ḥāll,* 'that which subsists, settles, comes to rest, in something'. (Cf. Note 81). 'Inhere' is sometimes preferable.
75. *maḥmūl u maqbūl-i. . . .*
76. *ḥāmil u qābil.*
77. *ṣuwar-i ma'qūlāt u ma'ānī-yi mudrakāt.* (Cf. Note 84).
78. *qābil-i tajzi'a.*
79. *salb-i waḥdat.*
80. *qābil-i inqisām.*
81. *maḥall,* 'the place of settling, or subsisting'. (Cf. Note 74).
82. *qābil-i qismat.*
83. *mustamirr u 'āmm.*
84. *ṣuwar-i ma'qūlāt u maḥsūsāt* (cf. Note 77).
85. *tāmm u kāmil mutamaththil.*
86. *ḥāṣil āyad.*
87. *'ulūm u ādāb.*
88. *mutakaiyif u muttaṣif na-shavad.*
89. *qūwat-i shahwī.*
90. *qūwat-i ghaḍabī.*
91. *az idrāk-i murādāt-i khwīsh.*
92. *az ghalaba-i amthāl-i īn ma'ānī va ḥuṣūl-i mudrakāt-i jismānī.*
93. *ra'yhā-yi ṣaḥīḥ u ma'qūlāt-i ṣarīḥ.*
94. *ḥirṣ u sharah.*
95. *az jins-i khwīsh.*
96. *mutanabbih.*
97. *az īn tafāwut-i fāḥish āgāhī na-yābad.*
98. *ḥukm kunad.*
99. *istinbāṭ kunad.*
100. *ba'ḍī-rā taṣdīq kunad va ba'ḍī-rā takdhīb.*
101. *īn 'ulūm.*
102. *istifāda na-tavān kard.*
103. *na-girifta bāshad.*
104. *chih āla miyān-i ū va dhāt-i ū va miyān-i ū va dhāt-i khwīsh mutawassiṭ na-mī-tavānad shud.*
105. *ḥaqīqat-i nafs.*
106. *bāqī mānad.*
107. *bi-ifnā-yi ū.*
108. *bāqi bāshad.*
109. *fanā'.*
110. *bi-'ainihi.*
111. *mulāqī.*

112. *ittifāqī buvad na ḍarūrī.*
113. *dar ṣūrat-i madhkūr.*
114. *ḥulūl* (cf. Note 74).
115. *mumtani'.*
116. *qā'im bi-dhāt-i khwīsh.*
117. *bi-ṭarīq-i istiqrā'.*
118. *bar qarār-i khwīsh.*
119. *jawāhir-i mujarrada ki az danas-i haiyūlī muqaddas. . . .*
120. *maḥall yā makān.*
121. *nafs-i nabātī ki ẓuhūr-i āthār-i ū.*
122. *ashkhāṣ-i insān.*
123. *nafs-i ḥayawānī.*
124. *qūwat-i ghādhiya.*
125. Respectively: *jābhiba, māsika, hāḍima, dāfi'a.*
126. *qūwat i munmiya.*
127. *mughaiyira.*
128. *qūwat i taulīd-i mithl dar nau'.*
129. *muṣauwira.*
130. Respectively. *qūwat-i idrāk-i ālī; qūwat-i taḥrīk-i irādī.*
131. *mashā'ir-i ẓāhir.*
132. Respectively: *bāṣira, sāmi'a, shāmma, dhā'iqa, lāmisa.*
133. *ḥawāss-i bāṭin.*
134. Respectively: *ḥiss-i mushtarak, khayāl, fikr, wahm, dhikr*
135. *qūwat-i nuṭq* ('The Power of Speech', cf. Note 32).
136. *'aql-i naẓarī.*
137. *taṣarruf dar mauḍū'āt.*
138. *'aql-i 'amalī.*
139. *tamyīz-i ū az naẓā'ir-ash.*
140. *yak nafs-i mujarrad-ast yā nufūs u quwā-yi mukhtalifa.*
141. *ru'yat.* Cf. Note 413. Professor Hourani suggests 'mental perception, cogitation' here and throughout.
142. *iktisāb.*
143. *dar aṣl-i fiṭrat.*
144. *ra'y, ru'yat, tamyīz, irādat,* respectively.
145. *ma'ākil u mashārib u manākiḥ* (for last see Dozy II:721:1).
146. *iqdām bar ahwāl.*
147. *maẓhar.*
148. *mauḍi'-i fikr u ru'yat.*
149. *ma'din-i ḥarārat-i gharīzī* (cf. Note 165).
150. *tauzī'-i badal-i mā yataḥallal.*
151. Respectively: *nafs-i malakī, saba'ī, bahīmī.*
152. *yak ḥadd-i ma'nawī.*
153. *yak ṣūrat-i jinsī-yi hayūlā-yi ūlā jumla-rā muqauwim (ast).*
154. *mutanauwi'.*
155. *qūwat.*
156. *qurb-i murakkab bi-i'tidāl-i ḥaqīqī ki ān waḥdat-i ma'nawī-st.*
157. *chand khāṣṣīyat-i buzurg.*
158. *ightidhā'.*
159. *nafḍ-i ghair-i mulā'im.*
160. *isti'dād.*

161. *qūwat-i baqā'-i shakhṣ zamānī-yi dirāz va tabqiya-i nau'.*
162. *faḍīlat bar nisbatī-yi maḥfūẓ* (see Dozy, I:305:1) *afzāyad.*
163. *mabādī-yi ṣuwar-i mawālīd.*
164. *mabādī-yi mawādd.* Lahore 1952 and 1955 alone add *taulīd* ('of generation') after *mawādd.*
165. *ḥarārat-i gharīzī.* (Cf. Note 149).
166. *ulfat u 'ishq.*
167. *qudrat . . . bar ḥarakat-i irādī u iḥsās.*
168. *silāḥ-hā-yi tamām.*
169. *ālāt-i ramy.* The author refers, of course, to quills.
170. *ālāt u asbāb-i farāghat.*
171. Some texts have 'or' (*yā* instead of *bā*).
172. *īthār-i ān bar abnā-yi jins.* Humā'ī clearly takes this to mean '*preference* for them (one's own children) to one's fellows'.
173. *basā'iṭ* (cf. Note 23). Professor Hourani points out that the words 'former' and 'latter' seem to have been misapplied here.
174. *mafṭūr.*
175. *mānand-i sūdān-i maghrib.* The reference is, of course, to Africa generally, albeit to North Africa in particular.
176. *bi-isti'māl-i ālāt u instinbāṭ-i muqaddimāt.*
177. *īn ma'ānī dar-ū kamtar bāshad.*
178. *qūwat-i ḥads.*
178a. *qaul.*
179. *bi-waḥy u ilhām.*
180. *az muqarrabān-i ḥaḍrat-i ilāhīyat* (cf. Note 192).
181. *mabda' u ma'ād.*
182. *juz ḥaqīqat-i ḥaqā'iq u nihāyat-i maṭālib ki ān ḥaqq-i muṭlaq buvad.*
183. Koran 55:27.
184. *khuṣūṣīyat.*
185. *ḍamā'ir.*
186. *zubda-i kā'ināt.*
187. Though this refers to the Shī'ite and mystical beliefs on the position of the *nūr-i muḥammadī* in creation, it is striking to see the rational justification cited as ultimately the significant one.
188. *bar wafq-i maṣlaḥat.*
189. *īshān-rā muzāḥ al-'illa gardānīda* (See Dozy, II:158:1).
190. *bar gharīzat-i ū markūz shuda.*
191. *'ulūm u ma'ārif u ādāb u faḍā'il* (some texts eliminate the third conjunctive particle, and presumably substitute an *iḍāfa*).
192. *mujāwarat-i mala'-i a'lā bi-yābad va az muqarrabān-i ḥaḍrat-i ṣamadī shavad* (cf. Note 180).
193. *paighambarān u ḥakīman u imāmān u hādīyān u mu'addibān u mu'allimān.* So most versions: some substitute 'ruler' (*ḥākim*) for 'philosopher', others omit the last two classes.
194. *nafīs yā khasīs, laṭīf yā kathīf.*
195. *ta'aiyun u taḥaqquq-i māhīyat-i ū mustalzim-i ān khāṣṣīyat ast.*
196. *ān-rā bar bī-hunarī u khasāsat-i ū ḥaml kunand*: a fairly good sample of Ṭūsī's stylistic playfulness, for the appropriateness of *ḥaml* ('carrying') can hardly be coincidental in the context.
197. *ma'nā* (elsewhere rendered as 'idea', 'sense', or 'meaning').

198. *bi-kasal u i'rāḍ.*
199. *bar murād-i khwīsh qādir-tar.*
200. *'āqil*, but all except Lahore 1952 and 1955, have *'aql* ('intelligence').
201. *ṣāḥib-i himmat.*
202. *qūwat-i dhātī.*
203. *af'āl-i khāṣṣ-i khwīsh.*
204. *ṭalab-i 'ulūm-i ḥaqīqī u ma'ārif-i kullī.*
205. *mumārasat-i mushākalāt.*
206. *dar ṭalab-i maqṣūd.*
207. *barkhī bi-sabab-i ḍa'f-i ru'yat az mulābasat-i mawāni'.*
208. *tawajjuh bi-ṭaraf-i naqīḍ.*
209. *az jihat-i tamakkun-i. . . .*
210. Respectively: *salāmat, sa'ādat, ni'mat, raḥmat, mulk-i bāqī, surūr-i ḥaqīqī, qurra-i 'ain.* It will be noticed that Ṭūsī, in the subtlest Shī'ī manner, implies that these terms are just as figurative and inadequate to express the whole as are the more obvious metaphors that follow.
211. Koran 32:17.
212. A famous Tradition. popular among mystics: a Biblical parallel is obvious, I Corinthians ii, 9.
213. Koran 24:39.
213a. Cf. remark in Introduction, Note l.
214. *shauq-i ū bi-sū-yi idrāk-i ma'ārif u nail-i 'ulūm.*
215. *maṭlūb-i ḥaqīqī u gharaḍ-i kullī.*
216. *'ālam-i tauḥīd.*
217. *maqām-i ittiḥād.* It will be noticed how easily Ṭūsī passes from philosophy to theology, and even to mysticism.
218. *chihra-i ḍamīr.*
219. *ā'īna-i khāṭir.*
220. *bi-tasālum-i īshān akhlāq-i ū marḍī gardad.*
221. *aḥwālī-ki bi-i'tibār-i mushārakat uftad.*
222. *'ilm mabda'-st u 'amal timām.*
223. *gharaḍ az wujūd-i insān.*
224. *bar marātib-i kā'ināt bar wajhī-yi kullī wāqif shavad.*
225. *bar wajhī az wujūh.*
226. *juz'īyāt-i nā-mutanāhī ki dar taḥt-i kullīyāt mundarij bāshad.*
227. *quwā u malakāt-i pasandīda.*
228. *bar mathāl-i īn 'ālam-i kabīr.*
229. *'ālam-i ṣaghīr.*
230. *khalīfa-i khudā-yi ta'ālā.*
231. *az auliyā-yi khāṣṣ-i ū gardad.*
232. *insānī-yi tāmm-i muṭlaq.*
233. *dar fanā' u istiḥāla.*
234. *ḥukm kardand bi-buṭlān-i mardum.*
235. *ba'd az talāshī-yi binya.*
236. *ma'ād-i māddīya.* So Lahore 1952 and 1955 and Cambridge; some versions have *ma'ād-i ū.* The former means that they cannot look forward to the prospect of a world-to-come such as they know here below; the latter would imply that they take no stock in Man's (or the body's) future generally after death.
237. *tahdhīb*: a fairly rare extension of the sense of this word, the basic

connotation of which is 'polishing, working hard at a thing (often with a view to improving it)'. Cf. Note 3.

238. *nafs-i nafīs.*

239. *akhass-i mawālī* (the latter word may also, of course, mean 'masters').

240. *bar sabīl-i mutājara u murābaḥa.*

241. Respectively: *bārī . . . khāliq . . . mub-di'.*

242. *az aṣnāf-i īn nau'-i mudāwāt u 'ilāj.*

243. *dar madhāq-i taṣauwur-i īshān.*

244. *dar ḥaqq-i jamā'a-i īn khabīthān.* So the Lahore texts, but others have: *dar ḥaqq-i īn jamā'at: īn khabīthan. . . .*

245. *bi-nuṣrat-i ū va da'wat bā ū.*

246. *talbīs.*

247. *ki faḍā'il milkī-yi ḥaqīqī na-dārad.*

248. *īn sukhan-rā az hawā-yi nafs kharīdār.*

249. *shubahāt-i bī aṣl.*

250. *mustaḥaqq-i karāmāt-i buzurg.* This includes the possibility of being allowed to work miracles.

251. *walī-yi khudā va ṣafī-yi ū-st.*

252. *raushan-tar tanbīhī.*

253. *ḍa'f-i muqāyasa.*

254. *agar-chi nafs-i bahīmī bar nafs-i 'āqila mustaulī shavad.*

255. *bi-qadr-i andak inti'āshī ki. . . .*

256. *waqāḥat ki az lawāzim-i tarākhī buvad bi-nuqṣān.*

257. *wājib.*

258. *chirā kitmān u instinkār-i ān az faḍīlat u murūwat mī-shumārand.*

259. *qadr-i ḥifẓ-i i'tidāl-i mizāj u qiwām-i ḥayāt.*

260. *bi-al-'araḍ ḥāṣil āyad.*

261. *qadr-i ānchi muqtaḍā-yi ḥifẓ-i nau' u ṭalab-i nasl buvad.*

262. *qā'ida-i ḥikmat.*

263. *az ḥibāla-i ū khārij bāshad.*

264. *Koran* 12:53; 75:2; 89:27.

265. *yakī ṣāḥib-i adab u karam ast dar ḥaqīqat u jauhar.*

266. *adīb.*

267. *mauḍū' u markab.*

268. *īn ma'nā nazdīk ast bi-ta'wīl-i ānchi az tanzīl naql uftāda.*

269. *muhaiyij-i ḥamīyat buvad.*

270. *imḍā-yi 'azīmat . . . isti'māl bāyad kard.*

271. *mu'āwadat.*

272. *ḥakīm-i auwal*: literally 'The First Philosopher', a common designation of Aristotle.

273. *qudamā'-i ḥukamā.*

274. *farasī.* Some texts have *firishta* ('angel'), which is accepted by D. M. Donaldson, *Studies in Muslim Ethics*, 175.

275. *bar wajh-i i'tidāl.*

276. Reading *khāristān*, with some versions, rather than *ghāristān* ('group of caves').

277. *ḥākim . . . ḥukūmat.*

278. *āfāt u 'awāriḍ.*

279. *tasālum u imtizāj.*
280. *mu'aththir.*
281. *yā khẉud si nafs.*
282. *ālat.* This doubtless refers to the body as a whole.
283. *ihmāl-i siyāsat-i rabbānī.*
284. *fisq.*
285. *kufr.*
286. *waḍ'-i ashyā' dar ghair-i mawāḍi'.*
287. *ẓulm bi-ḥaqīqat hamān-ast.*
288. *ra'īs-rā mar'ūs . . . gardānīdan.*
289. *intikās-i khalq.*
290. Respectively *ghāyat* and *gharaḍ.*
291. *sa'ādat-i ū-st ki bi-iḍāfat bā ū khair-i ū ān-ast.*
292. *auwal-i fikr ākhir-i 'amal buvad va ākhir-i fikr auwal-i 'amal.* The Tehran text omits the latter half of the aphorism.
293. Though Donaldson takes this as referring to Avicenna (p. 178), Ibn Miskawaih is clearly intended.
294. *'umr-rā dar īn ma'na ta'thīrī nīst.*
295. *agar taufīq musā'adat kunad.*
296 *muqtaḍā-yi 'aql-i ū.* The sense seems clear enough, but one would have expected *khẉīsh* as the pronoun.
297. *ḥukamā-yi mutaqaddim.* In contrast with *muta'akhkhirān* ('moderns') of a few lines before. Cf. Note 328.
298. *yakī muṭlaq va yakī bi-iḍāfat.*
299. *maqṣūd az wujūd-i maujūdāt.*
300. *ghāyat-i nāfi'.*
301. *sa'ādat ham az qabīl-i khair-ast.*
302. *nafsānī.*
303. *yaksān.*
304. *bi-majāz.*
305. *na bi-sabab-i ra'y u ru'yatī buvad ki. . . .*
306. *bi-sabab-i isti'dādī buvad ki. . . .*
307. *bi-bakht u ittifāq ta'alluq dārad.*
308. *az jihat-i rasīdan bi-muqtaḍā'ī buvad.*
309. *chīzī-yi mutaṣauwar.*
310. *agar ān gharaḍ dar nafs-i khẉīsh khair buvad.*
311. *tawajjuh bi-khairāt-i parāganda-i iḍāfī.*
312. *va khairī-ki* (var. *chīzī-ki*) *na-khair buvad bi-khair na-shumarand.* The variation between *chīz* and *khair* occurs more than once in this passage, but with no real effect on the general sense.
313. *farfūziyūs,* a common misreading for *farfūriyūs.* In a sense this undoubtedly refers to Porphyry of Tyre, but it should be borne in mind that, like many another pre-Islamic figure, he had an almost legendary existence for most Muslim thinkers. He is often referred to, for example, as a boon-companion of Alexander, and was accordingly regarded as a contemporary, and not simply a transmitter, of Aristotle.
314. Respectively: *sharīf, mamdūḥ, khair bi-qūwa, nāfi' dar ṭarīq-i khair.*
315. *va dīgar chīz-hā-rā sharaf az-ū 'āriḍ shavad.*
316. *isti'dād-i īn khairāt ast.*

317. *li-dhāti-hi maṭlūb na-buvad balki bi-sabab-i chīzī-yi dīgar maṭlūb buvad.*

318. *yā ghāyāt and yā ghair-i ghāyāt.*

319. *yā tāmm and yā ghair-i tāmm.*

320. *balki bā ān khair-hā-yi dīgar bi-bāyad.*

321. *ta'allum-i 'ilm . . . 'ilāj . . . riyāḍat.*

322. *yā nafsānī buvad yā badanī yā khārij az har du.*

323. *ma'qūl . . . maḥsūs.*

324. *maqūlāt-i 'ashara.* The better texts have the unlikely *ma'qūlāt* ('intelligibles'). For what is still perhaps the neatest and most convenient account of these 'categories', see E. J. W. Gibb's *History of Ottoman Poetry*, Book I, Ch. II, particularly p. 41, Note 2. The words 'have firmly located' render *yāqin karda and*, which one could also translate by 'recognize (for sure)'. Some texts have *ta'yīn k.*, 'to assign', which amounts to much the same thing.

325. *aṣnāf.*

326. *ladhdhāt-i nafsānī u jismānī.*

327. *tanāsub-i ajzā'.*

328. *ḥukamā-yi qudamā'.* Cf. Note 297.

329. *ajnās-i faḍā'il.*

330. Respectively: *ḥikmat, shajā'at, 'iffat, 'adālat.*

331. *badanī u ghair-i badanī.*

332. *khāmil al-dhikr . . . darvīsh . . . nāqiṣ-i a'dā'.*

333. *fi'l-i khāṣṣ.*

334. *fasād-i 'aql va radā'at-i dhihn.*

335. *rawāqīyān.*

336. *ṭabī'īyān.*

337. *qismī-yi nafsānī va qismī-yi jismānī.*

338. *munḍamm.*

339. *muḥaqqiqān-i ḥukamā'.* Probably Fārābī and Avicenna: cf. Ghazālī's First Preface to his *Tahāfut.*

340. *madkhalī u majālī,*

341. *bar ru'yat u 'aql muqarrar.*

342. *ḥarīṣ.*

343. *ghaḍūb.*

344. *bi-iḍāfat bā shakhṣī-yi mu'aiyan sa'ādatī-st juz'ī.*

345. *naẓar-i failasūf.*

346. *taḥqīq-i jumlagī-yi ḥaqā'iq.*

347. *i'tidāl-i mizāj.*

348. *māl u a'wān.*

349. *ahl-i khair.*

350. *muqtaḍā-yi ru'yat bar ḥasb-i amal u irādat.*

351. *jaudat-i ra'y.*

352. *wuqūf bar ṣawāb dar mashwarat.*

353. *salāmat-i 'aqīdat az khaṭa'.*

354. *ma'ārif.*

355. *umūr-i dīnī.*

356. *sa'īd-i kāmil buvad 'alā al-iṭlāq.*

357. *dar ba'ḍi abwāb va ba'ḍī iḍāfāt.*

358. *mādda.*

359. *ṣinā'at-i mulk.*
360. *khāṣṣ ast bi-insān -i tāmm.*
361. *bi-al-fi'l.*
362. *hayūlā.*
363. *mādda.*
364. *faḍīlatī-yi rūḥānī.*
365. *bahā'im u an'ām.*
366. *makānī.*
367. Presumably, the perfection of both the corporeal and the spiritual parts.
368. *'ulwīyāt.*
369. *jismānīyāt.*
370. *asrār.*
371. *rūḥānīyāt.*
372. Koran 7:178; 25:46.
373. Another good example of Ṭūsī's stylistic virtuosity: in both cases the form is *m'rḍ*, which I read (*dar*) *ma'raḍ* and *mu'riḍ* respectively.
374. *izāḥat-i 'ilal.* A favourite term with Ṭūsī (cf. Note 189).
375. *shi'ār sākhta.*
376. Cf. passage quoted from Aristotle between Notes 272 and 273.
377. *mawādd-i fānī.*
378. *binya.*
379. *majāl u ikhtiyār.*
380. *bāri'.*
381. A physician and translator better known as Sa'īd b. Ya'qūb (fl. early tenth century A.D.); see Brockelmann, *Geschichte der Arabischen Litteratur*, S I, 369.
382. *maḥsūs.*
383. *ḥissī.*
384. *umūr-i ū mutawajjih buvad bi-ṣawāb-i tadbīrī-yi mutawassiṭ dar faḍīlat.*
385. *az taqdīr-i fikr khārij na-y-uftad.*
386. *har-chand mashūb buvad bi-taṣarruf dar maḥsūsāt.*
387. *bi-juz'-i 'aqlī.*
388. *'ināyat.*
389. *tashabbuh-i har kasī bi-'illat-i ūlā.*
390. *ilāhī-yi maḥḍ.*
391. *khair-i maḥḍ ghāyatī buvad maṭlūb li-dhāti-hi wa-maqṣūd li-nafsi-hi.*
392. *ṣādir az lubāb u ḥaqīqat-i dhāt-i ū buvad.*
393. *dīgar dawā'ī-yi ṭabī'at-i badanī.*
394. *'awāriḍ-i takhaiyulātī ki. . . .*
395. *mabda'-i auwal ki khāliq-i kull ast.*
396. *hamīn ḥukm dārad.*
397. *bi-qaṣd-i auwal.*
398. An inaccurate quotation (or an adaptation) from Koran 17:45.
399. *khārijīyāt.*
400. *bi-qaṣd-i thānī.*
401. *faḍl.*
402. *chīzhā'ī-ki mufaḍḍal 'alaih ast.*

403. *ghāyat-i quṣwā.*
404. *az barāyi nafs-i fi'l.*
405. *ya'nī nafs-i faḍīlat u nafs-i khair.*
406. *'awāriḍ-i nafsānī.*
407. *khawāṭirī-ki az ān 'awāriḍ ṭārī shavad.*
408. *andarūn.*
409. *shi'ār.*
410. *ma'rifat.*
411. *qaḍāyā-yi ūlā.*
412. *'ulūm-i awā'il-i ūlā.*
413. *ru'yat*, but vocalized by Lahore 1952 and 1955 as *rawīyat*, i.e. 'reflection'. The defective Persian orthography makes this a constant stumbling-block in such passages.
414. i.e. Aristotle, the alleged author of the last few pages.
415. *sa'īd-i muṭlaq.*
416. *dar taḥt-i taṣarruf-i ṭabā'i'.*
417. *ajrām-i falak.*
418. *kawākib-i sa'd u naḥs-i ū.*
419. *musta'idd-i ta'aththur u tamakkun na-buvad mānand-i īshān.*
420. *ḥadd-i sa'ādat-i su'adā'.*
421. *malaka.*
422. *qillat-i mubālāt bi-'awāriḍ-i dunyāwī.*
423. *ki dar ḍamīr-i ū mutamakkin shuda bāshad.*
424. *ḍa'f-i ṭabī'at.*
425. *ghalaba-i jubn bar gharīzat.*
426. *munfa'il-i ān āthār.*
427. *ghmrī* (*sic*).
428. *'adam-i ma'rifat.*
429. *ḥarakāt-i nā-munāsib.*
430. *murtāḍ.*
431. *i'tidāl.*
432. *ifrāṭ.*
433. *tafrīṭ.*
434. *thābit u ghair-i mutaghaiyir.*
435. *chunān-ki dar ḥāl-i brnāms bi-ramz gufta and.* Near the end of Book I, Ch. 10, in the *Nicomachean Ethics*, Aristotle mentions Priam of 'the heroic legends' in just such a connection, and there seems little doubt that it is Priam with whom we have to do here, disguised by phonetic change, by vocalic instability, and by the common confusion of Arabic *n* and *y*. Aristotle's reference was undoubtedly 'cryptic' enough to Ṭūsī, hence the eager identification with the archetypal figure of Job; again, this is a common enough procedure with most mediaeval Muslim writers, who are quite unhistorical where the 'barbarian' non-Islamic cultures are concerned.
436. *dar har ḥāl ki bar-ū 'āriḍ shavad.*
437. *fāḍiltarīn fi'lī ki munāsib-i ān ḥāl buvad.*
438. *ṣabr u mudārā.*
439. *ghāyat-i shahāmat-i dhāt.*
440. *kibr-i nafs.*
441. *qiwām.*

442. *irtikāb-i fi'lī-yi rakīk na-kunad.*
443. *maghbūṭ.*
444. See Note 435 above.
445. As throughout, Aristotle is intended, though there is rarely any word-for-word correspondence with Aristotle's writings as known, and there is at times an obvious case for ruling him out as the author of a particular passage or remark.
446. *qawā'id.*
447. *aqsām-i sairathā.*
448. *bi-ḥasb-i basāṭat.*
449. *sairat-i ladhdhat . . . nafs-i shahwī.*
450. *sairat-i karāmat . . . nafs-i ghaḍabī.*
451. *sairat-i ḥikmat . . . nafs-i 'āqila.*
452. *jumla mukhtār u mamdūḥ.*
453. *ghāyat-i maṭālib.*
454. *az tawātur.* Cf. Note 459 below.
455. *āthār.*
456. *ladhdhatī-yi tāmm u bi-al-fi'l.*
457. *bi-ḥadd-i shīftagī u 'ishq rasad.*
458. *nang dārad ki sulṭān-i 'ālī-rā musakhkhar-i shaiṭān-i baṭn u farj kunad.*
459. *az tawātur u ta'āqub.* Cf. Note 454 above.
460. *ladhdhat-i 'aqlī.*
461. *ri'āsat-i dhātī.*
462. *khair-i muṭlaq u faḍīlat-i tāmm.*
463. *ḥukamā-yi qadīm.* Cf. Note 328.
464. *dar hayākil u masājid.*
465. *firishta ki muwakkal ast bar dunyā.*
466. *bar ma'ānī-yi masā'il-i gudhashta tanbīh yābad.*
467. *fi'lī . . . infi'ālī.*
468. *bi-ḥasb-i naẓar-i auwal.*
469. *az jihat-i imtinā'-i ū az infi'āl.*
470. *qabīl.*
471. *zawāl-ra bi-d-ān rāh ast va inqiḍā' u tabaddul bi-d-ān dar āyad.*
472. *dar ḥālatī.*
473. *ṣaḥīḥ.*
474. *dar badāyat u nihāyat.*
475. *nazdīk-i ṭabī'at-i marghūb buvad.*
476. *mumārasat.*
477. *infi'āl-i ṭab'.*
478. *bi-indirās-i qūwat-i gharīzat.*
479. *nihāyat.*
480. *ān-rā ma'ādī na-buvad.* There is a likely allusion, both here and in the next two Notes, to its not enduring into the after-life.
481. *ham dar mabda' va ham dar ma'ād.*
482. *ma'ād-i ḥaqīqī.*
483. *taqwīm-i ṭarīqat.*
484. *bi-raunaq-i ḥikmat.*
485. *agar luzūm-i ān sairat-rā muqtadā sāzad.*
486. *tarbiyat yāfta bāshad.*

487. *mustalzim-i jūd bāshad.*
488. *ṣāḥib-i alḥān.*
489. *khāṣṣīyat.*
490. *jūd-i majāzī.*
491. *amwāl u a'rāḍ-i dunyāwī.*
492. *bi-badhl nāqiṣ shavad.*
493. *qillat-i dhāt-i yad.*
494. *mawādd.*
495. *taṣarruf-i ṣurūf.* As so often in this text, the passage is full of similar stylistic elegances and allusions.
496. *alami shaqāwa.*
497. *chunīn karāmatī.*
498. *mamdūḥ.*
499. *dar ghāyat-i faḍl.* See *Nicomachean Ethics,* Book I:12.
500. *faiḍ-i dhāt-i muqaddas-i ū-st.*
501. *yā bi-iḍāfat bā ḥaḍrat-i ū.*
502. *yā bi-ittiṣāf bi-khairīyat.*
503. *ū-rā tamjīd kunand na madḥ.*
504. *sa'ādat mufīd-i madḥ ast na ahl-i madḥ.*
505. *khulq malaka-ī buvad nafs-rā.*
506. *tafakkurī u rawīyatī.*
507. *kaifīyāt-i nafsānī.*
508. *ḥāl.*
509. *limaiyat.*
510. *ṭabī'at . . . 'ādat.*
511. *aṣl-i mizāj.*
512. *khabar-i makrūhī-yi ḍa'īf.*
513. *bī takalluf.*
514. *mūjib-i ta'ajjub.*
515. *bi-takalluf dar-ān shurū' namūda.*
516. *bā ān kār ulfat gīrad.*
517. *qudamā'.*
518. *az khawāṣṣ-i nafs-i ḥayawānī.*
519. *yā nafs-i nāṭiqa-rā dar istilzām-i ū mushārakatī ast.*
520. *mumtani' al-zawāl.*
521. *ḥādith shavad.*
522. *intiqāl az-ān nā-mumkin.*
523. *irādatī.*
524. *mulābasat u mulāzamat.*
525. Reading *qūwat-i tamyīz u ru'yat* for *qwt tmyz u rwyt.* Cf. Note 413 above.
526. *ta'dīb u siyāsat.*
527. *sharā'i' u diyānāt.*
528. *ta'līm u tarbiyat.*
529. *qaḍīyah* (*sic*).
530. *dar bad'-i* (*badw-i*) *fiṭrat.* Cf. Note 545 below.
531. *zajr-i fawāḥish.*
532. *ṭīnat-i suflā va wasikh-i* (*wasakh-i*) *ṭabā'i'.*
533. *kadūrāt.*
534. *az ibtidā-yi nushū'.*

535 *kitāb-i akhlāq va kitāb-i maqūlāt*. Cf. Note 445 above.

536 *har-chand ḥukm (-i) 'alā al-iṭlāq na-buvad*. The Tehran modern printed version has a useful *īn* before *ḥukm*; the Cambridge photostat (Lucknow 1891) reads *ḥakīm*, which (if correct) would give a sense 'although such a man does not become wise in the full sense of the word'.

537. *ādāb*.

538. *ḥukamā-yi muta'akhkhir*. Cf. Note 297 above.

539. *ṣaḥīḥ ast bar ṣūrat-i ḍarb-i duvvum az shakl-i auwal*.

540. *muqaddima-i ṣughrā*.

541. *ḥusn-i sharā'i' ki siyāsat-i khudā-yi ta'ālā ast*.

542. *muqaddima-i kubrā*.

543. *dar nafs-i khwīsh baiyin*.

544. *bi-bardagī*.

545. *dar ibtidā-yi fiṭrat*. Cf. Note 530 above.

546. Cf. Note 413 above.

547 *aṣḥāb-i tamyīz u fikr*.

548. *mānanda*.

549. *mushābih*.

550. *munāsib*.

551. *muqtaḍā-yi mizāj-i ū . . . dar aṣl*.

552. *yā ān-chi 'āriḍ shuda bāshad bi-ittifāq*.

553. *ḥirṣ*.

554. *takabbur*.

555. *mu'addib-i auwal*.

556. *namūs-i ilāhī . . . 'alā al-'umūm*.

557. *mu'addib-i thānī*.

558. *ahl-i tamyīz u adhhān-i ṣaḥīḥ-rā az īshān*.

559. *bi-aṣnāf-i siyāsāt u ta'dībāt iṣlāḥ-i 'ādāt-i īshān kunand*.

560. *īn ma'ānī-rā dar bāb-i īshān bi-taqdīm rasānand*.

561. *jabbār-an wa-ikhtiyār-an*.

562. *ṣinā'at*.

563. *tavānad būd*.

564. *dar dhāt-i khwīsh*.

565. *istiṣlāḥ*.

566. *muta'alliq bi-qudrat-i khāliq va ṣan'-i ū-st*.

567. *tajwīd*.

568. *ra'y u ru'yat*. But cf. Note 413 above.

569. *agar maṣdar-i khāṣṣīyat-i khwīsh na-bāshad*. The reference-back here is to the Fifth Section of the First Division of the present Discourse.

570. *ashkhāṣ*.

571. *nāmīyāt*.

572. *dar yak silk na-tavān āvard*.

573. Jalāl Humā'ī, p. 14, Note 5, attributes the line to Buḥturī, in a *dāl qaṣīda* in praise of Abū (sic) al-Fatḥ b Khāqān. He notes minor textual variations. I have not been able to confirm this reference, but Professor Hourani assures me that the sentiment is variously attributed to Galen and others.

574. *bi-i'tibār-i ān qūwat-hā maṣdar-i af'āl u āthār-i mukhtalif mī-shavad*.

575. *mabda'-i fikr u tamyīz u shauq-i naẓar dar ḥaqā'iq-i umūr.*

576. *shauq-i tasalluṭ u taraffu' u mazīd-i jāh.*

577. The references in question are dispersed throughout the First Division, but the Third Section is the most pertinent, especially for the technical terms involved. The Second and Sixth Sections are also largely relevant.

578. *bi-i'tidāl buvad dar dhāt-i khwīsh.*

579. *shauq-i ū bi-iktisāb-i ma'ārif-i yaqīnī buvad.*

580. *ḥādith shavad.*

581. *va bi-taba'īyat faḍīlat-i . . . lāzim āyad* (on the second and third occasions of occurrence the first group of words immeditely precedes the last).

582. *va tahaiyuj-i bī-waqt u tajāwuz-i ḥadd na namāyad dar aḥwāl-i khwīsh.*

583. *ḥilm.* Lucknow 1891, and Lahore 1952 and 1955, all have *'ilm,* obviously in confusion with the preceding subdivision.

584. *dar atbā'-i hawā-yi khwīsh.*

585. *'iffat.*

586. *sakhā'.*

587. *va har si bā yak-dīgar mutamāzij u mutasālim shavand.*

588. *az tarakkub-i har si ḥālatī-yi mutashābih ḥādith gardad.*

589. *ijmā' u ittifāq-i jumlagī-yi ḥukamā-yi muta'akhkhir u mutaqaddim.*

590. *yakī idrāk bi-dhāt u dīgarī taḥrīk bi-ālāt.* See First Division, Second Section; also cf. Note 577 above.

591. *chunān-ki bāyad u chandān-ki shāyad bī ifrāṭ u tafrīṭ.*

592. *bar wajhī bāshad ki bāyad.*

593. See above the sentence containing Notes 587 and 588.

594. The difficulty is partly one of terminology, arising from the fact that Ṭūsī uses only one word (*ḥikmat*) for both 'philosophy' and 'wisdom'. Thus he must harmonize this passage, where Wisdom is one of the four virtues discussed in Ethics, with the introductory passage (cf. between Notes 37 and 39) where Ethics is one of the three divisions of Practical Wisdom.

595. *va īn qismī-yi madkhūl buvad.* The term commonly means 'weak, diseased', of either bodies or arguments (see Dozy, I:427:2).

596. *chunān-ki bāyad.*

597. *mādām ki athar-i ān faḍīlat ham dar dhāt-i ū buvad tanhā.*

598. *minfāq.*

599. *ghayūr.*

600. *mustabṣir.*

601. *'ilm.*

602. *rajā' u haibat.*

603. *sabab-i siyādat u iḥtishām.*

604. *dar rusūm-i īn faḍā'il gufta and ki. . . .*

605. *ma'rifat.*

606. *har-chi samt-i wujūd dārad.*

607. *dānistanī . . . kardanī.*

608. *ra'y.*

609. *ṣabr.*

610. *ḥurrīyat*. The Montreal text (Tehran, n.d.) alone has *khairīyat* ('goodness').

611. *ta'abbud-i hawā-yi nafs*.

612. *ba yak-dīgar ittifāq kunand va qūwat-i mumaiyiza-rā imtithāl namāyand*.

613. *ikhtilāf-i hawā-hā va tajādhub-i qūwat-hā*.

614. *inṣāf u intiṣāf*.

615. Respectively: *dhakā', sur'at-i fahm, ṣafā-yi dhihn, suhūlat-i ta'allum, ḥusn-i ta'aqqul, taḥaffuz*, and *tadhakkur*.

616. *az kathrat-i muzāwalat-i muqaddimāt-i muntija*.

617. *sur'at-i intāj-i qaḍāyā*.

618. *suhūlat-i istikhrāj-i natā'ij*.

619 *ḥarakat az malzūmāt bi-lawāzim*. Cf. Dozy, II:528:1 for *malzūm*.

620. *tā dar-ān bi-faḍl-i makthī muḥtāj na shavad*.

621. *isti'dād-i istikhrāj-i maṭlūb*.

622 *ḥiddatī . . . dar naẓar*. The first word is so marked in some texts; Montreal (Tehran, n.d.) has *waḥdatī*; and *ḥidatī* (both = 'oneness') seems a possibility as far as sense goes.

623. *tā bī mumāna'at-i khawāṭir-i mutafarriqa bi-kullīyat-i khwīsh tawajjuh bi-maṭlūb kunad*.

624. *ṣūrat-hā'ī-rā ki 'aql yā wahm bi-qūwat-i tafakkur yā takhaiyul mulakhkhaṣ va mustakhlaṣ gardānīda bāshad*.

625. *mulāḥaẓa-i ṣuwar-i maḥfūẓah* (*sic*).

626. Respectively: *kibr-i nafs, najda, buland-himmatī, thabāt, ḥilm, sukūn, shahāmat, taḥammul, tawāḍu', ḥamīyat*, and *riqqat*.

627. *ḥarakāt-i nā-muntaẓim*.

628. *'āriḍ shudan-i amthāl-i ān*.

629. *muḥāfaẓat-i ḥurmat yā dhabb az sharī'at*.

630. *'adam-i ṭaish*.

631. *muḥāfaẓat-i millat yā ḥurmat*.

632. Respectively: *ḥayā', rifq, ḥusn-i hudā, musālamat, da'at, ṣabr, qanā'at, waqār, wara', intiẓām, ḥurrīyat*, and *sakhā'*.

633. *inḥiṣār-i nafs buvad dar waqt-i istish'ār. . . .*

634. *inqiyād-i nafs buvad umūrī-rā ki ḥādith shavad az ṭarīq-i tabarru'*.

635. *damātha*.

636. *raghbatī-yi ṣādiq*.

637. *ḥīlat-hā-yi sutūda*.

638. *mujāmalat namāyad*.

639. *az sar-i qudrat u malaka*.

640. *farā-gīrad*.

641. *riḍā dahad bar ān-chi sadd-i khalalī kunad*.

642. *mujāwazat-i ḥadd*.

643. *bar wajh-i wujūb u ḥasb-i maṣāliḥ*.

644. *mutamakkin shavad bar iktisāb i māl*.

645. *infāq-i amwāl*.

646. *bi-maṣabb-i istiḥqāq*.

647. Respectively: *karam, īthār, 'afw, murūwat, nail, mu'āsāt, samāḥat*, and *musāmaḥat*.

648 *az har mā-yaḥtājī-ki bi-khāṣṣa-i ū ta'alluq dāshta bāshad bar-khāstan*.

649. *tamakkun . . . qudrat.*
650. *ifādat.*
651. *yārān.*
652. *qūt u māl.*
653. *. . . . ki wājib na-buvad. . . .*
654. Respectively: *ṣadāqat, ulfat, wafā', shafaqat, ṣila-i raḥim, mukāfāt, ḥusn-i shirkat, ḥusn-i qaḍā', tawaddud, taslīm, tawakkul, 'ibādat.*
655. *asbāb-i farāghat-i ṣadīq.*
656. *tajāwuz (az).*
657. *ṭabā'i'.*
658. *mujāzāt.*
659. *az minnat u nadāmat khālī bāshad.*
660. *akfā'.*
661. *riḍā' dahad u bi-khwush-manishī u tāza-rū'ī ān-rā talaqqī namāyad.*
662. *bar īshān i'tirāḍ jā'iz na-buvad.*
663. *ṭab'.*
664. *bi-khilāf-i ān-chi bāshad mail na-kunad.*
665. *khāliq.*
666. Cf. Notes 180 and 192 above.
667. *ṣāḥib-i sharī'at.*
668. *taqwā-rā . . . shi'ār u dithār-i khwud sāzad.*
669. *dar bādi' al-naẓar.*
670. Respectively: *jahl, jubn, sharah* and *jaur.*
671. *har qaid ki dar taḥdīd-i faḍīlatī mu'tabar buvad chūn ihmāl kunand. . . .*
672. *pas har faḍīlatī bi-mathāba-i wasaṭī ast va radhā'il ki bi-izā-yi ū bāshad bi-manzila-i aṭrāf mānand-i markaz u dā'ira.*
673. *muḥīṭ.*
674. *ḥukamā'.*
675. Given in Persian. This is, in one form or another, one of the most popular Traditions with the moralists. Cf. Wensinck, III; 139; jisr.
676. *wujūd*; a use of the *maṣdar* in a correct but unusual way, which well illustrates Ṭūsī's mastery of Arabic.
677. *muta'adhdhir.*
678. *tamassuk bi-d-ān ba'd az wujūd.*
679. Given in Arabic. This is a rather more developed argument than that in the *Nicomachean Ethics*, Book II:5.
680. *fī nafsi-hi.*
681. *mānand-i i'tidālāt-i nau'ī u shakhṣī nazdīk-i aṭibbā'.*
682. *ham az-īn qabīl bāshad.*
683. *har shakhṣī-yi mu'aiyan.*
684. *dawā'ī.*
685. *i'ṭā-yi uṣūl u qawānīn.*
686. *iḥṣā-yi juz'īyāt.*
687. Lahore 1952 consistently vocalizes *dar* as *dur* ('pearl'), doubtless because of the proximity to 'ring', thus making the carpenter superfluous. Montreal (Tehran, n.d.) and others specifically mention 'two classes' at the end of this sentence.
688. *dar 'amal tavānad āvard.*
689. *dar har mauḍi'ī.*

690. *mu'aiyan.*

691. *taqdīr-i iḥtiyājī ki bāshad.*

692. *a'dād-i fasādī ki. . . .*

693. Respectively: *safah, balah, tahauwur, jubn, sharah, khumūd-i shahwat, ẓulm* and *inẓilām.*

694. *wājib.*

695. *gurbuzī.* The other connotations of this word are, of course, 'deception, flattery, valour'.

696. *ta'ṭīl.*

697. *bi-irādah* (*sic*).

698. *khilqat.*

699. *jamīl.*

700. *az rū-yi ikhtiyār.*

701. *ladhdhāt-i ḍarūrī.*

702. *shar' u 'aql.*

703. *az ghaṣb u nahb.*

704. *amwāl u aqwāt.*

705. *aṣnāf.*

706. *chūn ma'nā dar taṣauwur āyad az 'ibārat farāghatī ḥaṣil āyad.*

707. *tā dīgarān bar-ān qiyās kunand.*

708. *khubth u balādat.*

709. *sū'-i ikhtiyār.*

710. *sur'at-i takhaiyulī ki bar sabīl-i ikhtiṭāf uftad.*

711. *iltihābī-ki bi-sabab-i mujāwazat-i miqdār nafs-rā az maṭlūb bāz dārad.* All my texts except the Avery MS have the rather meaningless *mujāwarat* for *mujāwazat*; the same MS reverses the order of the extremes, but I have not followed this.

712. *dar istinbāṭ-i natā'ij ta'khīr uftad.*

713. *mubādaratī-ki istinbāṭ-i ṣuwar-rā majāl na-dahad.*

714. *ta'aṣṣub ki bi-ta'adhdhur mu'addī buvad.*

715. *fikr.*

716. *idrāk.*

717. *'ināyatī-yi zā'id bi-ḍabṭ.*

718. *bī-fā'idah* (*sic*).

719. *isti'rāḍī ki. . . .*

720. *waqāḥat u kharaq.*

721. *isrāf u bukhl.*

722. *takabbur u tadhallul.*

723. *fisq u taḥarruj.* Only Montreal (Tehran, n.d.) has the last word so, and obviously correctly, written, others of my text basing it on JRḤ and KHRJ. Montreal is also alone in reversing the order of these two vices as given here.

724. *wujūdī.*

725. *sakhāwat u shajā'at.*

726. *'adamī.*

727. *fadīlatī ki bi-faḍl-i rujhānī dar yak-ṭaraf mausūm na-bāshad.*

728. *'adālat.*

729. The reference is doubtless mainly to the Seventh Section of the First Division of the present Discourse.

730. *mūjibāt.*

731. *takmīl-i quwā-yi nāqiṣah* (*sic*).
732. *dhāt-i ū majma'-i* (*mujammi'? mujmi'?*) *īn ṣifāt buvad.*
733. *ta'alluq bi-qūwat-i naẓarī dārad.*
734. *'amal.*
735. *maẓhar-i āthār.*
736. *ḥaqīqat.*
737. *mabda'.*
738. *bi-ṭarīq-i taqlīd u talaqquf farā-girifta bāshand.*
739. *wuthūq-i nafs u bard-i yaqīnī ki. . . .*
740. *ḍamā'ir.*
741. *taqrīr.*
742. *ḥukamā'.*
743. *maṣdar.*
744. *'amal-i a'iffā'.*
745. *ham az ān jins dar māhīyat.*
746. *bī-naṣīb.*
747. *az mumārasat u tajriba ghāfil.*
748. *az shahr-hā dūr-tar uftāda bāshand.*
749. *az tawātur-i tanāwul u idmān.*
750. *'urūq u au'iya.*
751. *ḥāssah* (*sic*) *u ālat.*
752. *nuqṣān-i khilqat.*
753. *dar mabda'-i fiṭrat.*
754. *bā'ith.*
755. *shā'ibah* (*sic*). There is considerable minor textual variation at this point; for once, Lahore 1952 (and 1955) and Montreal (Tehran, n.d.) are in agreement, so I have followed them, albeit aware of some degree of tautology offensive to English-attuned ears.
756. *mushtahayāt.*
757. *bi-jihat-i murād-i riyā'.* Some texts have *mirā' u* in place of the penultimate word, with the sense 'for the sake of rivalry and affectation'.
758. *bi-ṭam'-i mazīd-i jāh.*
759. *nafs u māl u 'irḍ u ḥaram.*
760. *mujūn u maḍāḥik u anwā'-i mulhiyāt.*
761. *ahl-i murābaḥah* (*sic*).
762. *badhl-i amwāl.*
763. *ranj ṭalabīdan.* The Avery MS and Humā'ī's *Muntakhab* both have the plausible *ribḥ* ('profit') in place of *ranj*.
764. *bar sabīl-i tabdhīr buvad.*
765. *ḥukamā'.*
766. *ḍarūrī.*
767. *makāsib-i jamīlah* (*sic*).
768. *aḥrār.*
769. *ḥurrīyat.*
770. *dar māl nāqiṣ-ḥaẓẓ.*
771. *bakht u rūzgār.*
772. *farākh-dast u khwush-'aish u maghbūṭ u maḥsūd-i 'awāmm.*
773. *barā'at-i sāḥat az madhammat.* The first part of this expression is more or less a cliché, less striking in Persian than in English.
774. *aghmār.*

775. *qiyādat-i fujjār.*

776. *aghniyā' u mulūk.*

777. *tuḥfah* (*sic*) *burdan-i ghamz u si'āyat u nammāmī u ghībat.*

778. *li-dhāti-hā.*

779. *bi-al-'araḍ u bi-qaṣd-i thānī.*

780. *'illat-i ūlā ki jawād-i maḥḍ ast.*

781. *ṭabī'at-i sharah bāshad na ṭabī'at-i faḍīlat.*

782. *ḥirṣ u nahmat.*

783. *chīzī-ki jārī-yi majrā-yi māl buvad.*

784. *'aiyār-pīshagān.*

785 *'adhāb u nakāl u muthlah* (*sic*) *u ṣalb u qatl.*

786. *qaum u 'ashīrah* (*sic*).

787. *sulṭān.*

788. *jāh.*

789. *aqrān.*

790. *takhaiyul.*

791. *bi-mawāqi'-i ittifāqāt.*

792. *fujūr.*

793. *bar ẓafar mushrif ast.*

794. *maqṣūd.*

795. The different texts each have hereabouts several small but crucial omissions or misreadings of a fairly obvious nature (e.g. *izāla* and even *az izāla* for *az ālat,* 'of any instrument'). I have translated a synoptic version.

796. *dar mabādi'.*

797. *dar 'awāqib-i umūr.*

798. *dar rāh-i bāri'.* A Persian paraphrase of *fī sabīl allāh,* i.e. in martyrdom.

799. *maṣlaḥat-i du-jahānī-yi khwud u ahl-i dīn.*

800. *dīn u millat.*

801. *kūtāh gardānīdan-i dast-i mutaghallib az yārān u 'ashīrah* (*sic*) *va az ahl-i dīn u jihād dar rāh-i khudā-yi ta'ālā.*

802. *muḥāl.*

803. *shujā'-i bi-al-ittifāq.*

804. In Arabic. A common Shī'ite tradition in one form or another. There is some variation between the texts as to the exact wording introducing the tradition, as also about the form of the invocation after 'Alī's name: *'alai-hi al-salām* or *raḍiya allāh 'an-hu.*

805. *mafhūm.*

806. *bi-ṭarīq-i āzmāyish.*

807. *khafa* or *khaba kunand,* literally 'strangle, suffocate'.

808. *mūjib.*

809 *ṣabūr.*

810. *har ḥāl ki ḥādith shavad.*

811. *kasī-ki qaiyim-i umūr-i dīn u mulk buvad.*

812. *bi-chunān kas munāfasat u muḍāyaqat kunad.* There is considerable textual variation here: some substitute *munāqashat* ('dispute') for *munāfasat,* but not all make the then inevitable change to a negative verb (it being, in such case, impossible to take *muḍāyaqat* in the figurative, ironical sense of 'giving a rival a hard time'); some omit *muḍāyaqat*

altogether. I have felt that a positive sense was more appropriate here than a negative, albeit the net result is not in doubt.

813. *'azīz al-wujūd.*

814. *dar ma'raḍ-i intiqāmī uftad.*

815. Reading *dhubūlī . . . ki* rather than the variant *zabūnī* ('weakness').

816. *wabāl.*

817. An almost classic case of the problem presented in a mediaeval Persian text by the easy and inadvertent omission (or insertion) of a negative, combined with lack of the precision and emphasis one would expect in modern English. What Ṭūsī clearly means is that wisdom implies *true* courage and *true* continence, whereas *apparent* courage and continence may be mere shams and hence no necessary indicators of wisdom. (Wisdom itself is, in the nature of the case, always true.) However, the various Persian texts ring every possible change on the insertion and omission of the negative particle in these two clauses, virtually all of which make good sense if one adds qualifying words like the above 'true' and 'apparent'.

818. *riyā' u sum'ah (sic).*

819. *ta'dīl-i qūwat-hā-yi nafsānī.*

820. *taqwīm.*

821. *mu'āmalāt u karāmāt u ghair-i ān.* 'Miracles' can hardly be involved here.

822. *hai'atī-yi nafsānī ki muqtaḍā-yi adab-i kullī buvad.* Probably *muqtaḍī* is also acceptable, giving 'that psychical form which inevitably produces total propriety'.

823. *az rū-yi dalālat.*

824. *musāwāt.*

825. *waḥdat.* It is obvious that true equivalence must reduce multiples to one.

826. *mabda'-i auwal ki wāḥid-i ḥaqīqī ū-st.*

827. *ma'dūdāt.* The Lahore texts have a bad lacuna here.

828. *'illat-i ūlā ki maujūd-i muṭlaq ū-st.*

829. *ṣinā'at-i akhlāq.*

830. *i'tidāl.*

831. *ẓill.*

832. *samt . . . bar-gīrad.*

833. *ḥīlah (sic).* The Lahore texts and the Cambridge photostat (Lucknow 1891) have *ḥilyah* (*sic* = 'ornament'), but this introduces an anomalous factor into the general astronomical imagery.

834. *tawallud-i mawālīd-i thalātha,* the animal, vegetable and mineral kingdoms.

835. *'anāṣir-i arba'a.*

836. *imtizājāt-i mu'tadil.*

837. *muqtaḍī-yi niẓām-i mukhtalifāt-and.* Cf. Note 822 above.

838. *tanāsub.* Thus I have combined the two English terms used more or less interchangeably hereabouts to render *nisbat,* Aristotle's *analogon.*

839. *mumāthalat.*

840. *ki 'ibārat-ast az waḥdat.* Cf. Note 825 above.

841. *muttaṣil* and *munfaṣil* respectively. Cf. hereabouts *Nicomachean Ethics*, Book V, ch. 6.

842. *muntasibāt.*

843. *'adadī, handasī* and *ta'līfī*, respectively; the last is a musical category.

844. *ki muqtaḍā-yi niẓām-i ma'īshat buvad.* The remark in Note 822 above is appropriate here.

845. *mu'āmalāt u mu'āwaḍāt.* A serious lacuna here in the Lahore texts.

846. *ta'addī.*

847. *ta'dībāt u siyāsāt.*

848. *qisṭ.* Montreal (Tehran, n.d.) has an irrelevant interpolation of some length here, the material found below between Notes 884 and 886.

849. *ḥaif.* Another serious lacuna here in the Lahore texts.

850. *munāsabat u musāwāt.*

851. *tasāwī.* cf. *Nicomachean Ethics*, Book V, Ch. 7.

852. *inḥirāfāt.*

853. *nāmūs-i ilāhī.*

854. *wāḍi'-i tasāwī u 'adālat.*

855. *chi manba'-i waḥdat ū-st tā'ālā dhikru-hu.* For the argument here and throughout this paragraph, cf. the opening paragraph of this Discourse (together with its Notes).

856. *madanī.*

857. *tā mukāfāt u musāwāt u munāsabat murtafi' na-shavad.*

858. *pas bi-ḍarūrat bi-mutawassiṭī u muqauwimī iḥtiyāj uftād va ān dīnār ast.*

859. *'ādil-i ṣāmit.*

860. *ḥākim.*

861. *tadbīr u siyāsat buvad va ān-chi bi-d-ān mānad.*

862. *dar kitāb-i nīqūmākhiyā.* Though Book V, Ch. 8, is undoubtedly relevant here, the connection is by no means literal.

863. *az qabīl-i nāmūs-i akbar.* A variant is *az qibal-i*, 'on behalf of. . . .'

864. *muqtadā-yi nawāmīs.*

865. 57:25.

866. *musāwāt-dahanda-i mukhtalifāt.*

867. *'adl-i madanī.*

868. *jaur-i madanī.*

869. *naẓar-i muhandis.*

870. *jā'ir.*

871. *qawā'id-i gudhashta.*

872. *jā'ir-i a'ẓam.*

873. *jā'ir-i ausaṭ.* A bad lacuna here in the Lahore texts.

874. *jā'ir-i aṣghar.*

875. *bar ḥukm-i dīnār na-ravad.*

876. *kasī-ki bi-nāmūs-i ilāhī mutamassik bāshad 'amal bi-ṭabī'at-i musāwāt kunad.*

877. *fasād-hā-yi madanī.*

878. *jihād.* All except Humā'ī and the Avery MS have *maṣāff-i jihād*, without a copula, giving a sense something like 'when fighting the good fight (for Islam)'. This seemed to me too narrow an application here.

879. *ḥifẓ-i furūj az-nā-shāyista-hā*, with a definitely sexual connotation. Only Humā'ī, possibly as a suitable gloss for schools, replaces the first two words by *khwīshtan-dārī* ('self-restraint').

880. *dar dhāt-i khwīsh.*

881. *shurakā-yi khwīsh az ahl-i madīnah* (*sic*).

882. Clearly a reference to Aristotle; cf. *Nicomachean Ethics*, Book V, Ch. 3.

883. *bai' u shary u kafālāt u 'āriyat-hā.*

884. *duzdī-hā u fujūr u qiyādat u mukhāda'at-i mamālīk u guvāhī dādan-i durūgh.*

885. *jafā'.*

886. *taghallub.*

887. *pādishāh-i 'ādil ḥākim*(*-i*) *bi-sawīyat bāshad.*

888. *khalīfa-i nāmūs-i ilāhī.*

889. *al-khilāfa taṭahhur.* I am unable to identify the exact reference, but the general idea is of course the fundamental notion that the highest spiritual office confers its own sanctification.

890. *martaba-i ḥukūmat-i kasī.*

891. *sharaf-i ḥasab u nasab.*

892. *sabab-i ri'āsat u siyādat-i ḥaqīqī.*

893. (*sabab-i. . . .*) *murattab dāshtan-i martaba-i har yakī dar daraja-i khwīsh.*

894. Respectively: *shahwat . . . radā'at.*

895. Respectively: *sharārat . . . jaur.*

896. Respectively: *khaṭa' . . . ḥuzn.*

897. *shaqā' u ḥairatī-yi muqārin-i madhallat u andūh tābi'-i ān uftad. ḥairat* is the clear reading of Montreal (Tehran, n.d.), Humā'ī, and the Avery MS. Other texts appear to have *ḥasrat*, 'regret'.

898. *sharīr.*

899. *ẓalamah* (*sic*).

900. *muqtaḍī-yi iltidhādh.* Cf. Notes 822 and 844.

901. *mabda'-i fi'lī-st ki dar-ū sababī-yi khārij bāshad az dhāt-i ṣāḥib-ash.* So most texts, but the Avery MS and Humā'ī shorten the first group of words to *mabda'-i fi'l dar-ū*, which might yield a translation: 'the principle of action therein is a cause external to the essence of the one associated with it'.

902. *chunīn shakhṣī-yi shaqīy.*

903. *ḥakīm-i auwal*, i.e. Aristotle, but cf. Note 908 below.

904. *wāhib-i khairāt u mufḍī-yi karāmāt.* Cf. Note 821 above. In place of *mufḍī*, the Avery MS and Humā'ī have the equally appropriate *mufīḍ*, 'lavisher'.

905. *wujūb.*

906. *ḥuqūq-i abnā-yi jins u ta'ẓīm-i ru'asā' u adā-yi amānāt u inṣāf dar mu'āmalāt.*

907. *aslāf.*

908. So all except Humā'ī and Montreal (Tehran, n.d.), which leave out the word 'sense', thus suggesting that this is a verbatim quotation from Aristotle. As usual, it is not, though it echoes Book V of the *Nicomachean Ethics* in places.

909. *chi agar mithl-i pādishāhī-yi 'ādil fāḍil bāshad.* This would seem

to be an 'unanswered' condition, which I have rendered as a rhetorical question. The text hereabouts leaves much to be desired syntactically, but all versions are in virtually exact agreement, and the sense is nowhere obscure. The argument here would seem to owe as much to Plato as to Aristotle; at the same time, if not truly Islamic, it is certainly in the spirit of much Persian retrospection on a golden age of good kings, models for all men in subsequent ages.

910. *baiḍa-i mulk.*

911. *ṣanā'i'*. 'Fabrications' might be a suitable rendering.

912. *ẓulm u jaur-i ḥaqīqī.*

913. *sunan-i 'adālat.*

914. *qānūn-i inṣāf.*

915. *mulūk u ru'asā'.*

916. *sa'y-i ṣāliḥ.*

917. *mālik al-mulk(-i) bi-ḥaqīqat.*

918. *tarkīb-i binya(h) u tahdhīb-i ṣuwar.*

919. *kitāb-i tashrīḥ*. Probably Avicenna's *kitāb tashrīḥ al-a'ḍā'* (Brockelmann, S I, 827, 95w).

920. *kitāb-i manāfi'-i a'ḍā'*. Probably a Persianized version of the title of a work by a writer of the late ninth century A.D. (Brockelmann, S I, 417, 8, 2).

921. *kunh-i ḥaqīqat.*

922. Reading *sanā* rather than the equally possible *sanā'*, 'eminence'.

923. An Arabic quotation, the origin of which I have been unable to discover.

924. *'ibādatī-ki bandagān-rā bi-d-ān qiyām bāyad namūd.*

925. Respectively *makhlūq* and *khāliq*.

926. *khidmat-i hayākil u muṣallayāt.*

927. *taqarrub bi-qurbānīhā.*

928. *iḥsān.*

929. *tazkiya(h) u ḥusn-i siyāsat.*

930. *mu'āsāt u ḥikmat u mau'iẓat.*

931. *ilāhīyāt*. 'Metaphysics' can hardly be the better rendering here.

932. *taṣarruf dar muḥāwalātī-ki. . . .*

933. *yak chīz-i mu'aiyan.*

934. *bar yak nau' u mithāl nīst.*

935. *ḥikāyat-i alfāẓ-i ū-st ki naql karda āmad.*

936. *tarjīḥ.*

937. *ṭabaqa-i muta'akhkhir az ḥukamā'.*

938. *wuqūf bi-mawāqif-i sharīfa(h) az jihat-i du'ā' u munājāt.*

939. *i'tiqādāt-i ṣaḥīḥ.*

940. So Humā'ī and the Avery MS (*jūd*): others have *wujūd*, 'existence', which must surely be wrong.

941. *dar mushārakāt-i khalq mānand-i inṣāf dar mu'āmalāt u muḍāra'āt u munākaḥāt. Muḍāra'āt* is the reading of the Montreal text (Tehran, n.d.): the others have *muzāra'āt*, which might be made to mean something similar, but is not a technical term.

942. *jihād bi-a'dā-yi dīn.*

943. *ahl-i taḥqīq*. It is more than usually difficult to be certain what is meant by the use of this term, on the part of a man like Ṭūsī, in this

particular context. He may be referring to the group Ghazālī calls *al-muḥaqqiqūn* (see *Tahāfut*, Bouyges ed., Index p. 421; this term is translated by S. Van den Bergh, *Tahāfut al-Tahāfut*, *passim*, as 'the acknowledged philosophers', which suggests little except a misreading of the Arabic); he may simply mean 'good Muslims'; or he may be hinting at something esoteric.

944. *i'tiqād-i ḥaqq . . . qaul-i ṣawāb . . . 'amal-i ṣāliḥ*.
945. *tafṣīl*.
946. *'ulamā-yi mujtahid*.
947. *'umūm-i khalā'iq*.
948. *ahl-i yaqīn . . . mūqinān*.
949. *ḥukamā-yi buzurg u 'ulamā-yi kibār*.
950. *ahl-i iḥsān . . . muḥsinān*.
951. *bā kamāl-i 'ilm*.
952. *abrār*.
953. *bi-iṣlāḥ-i bilād u 'ibād mashghūl bāshand*.
954. *takmīl-i khalq*.
955. *ahl-i fauz . . . fā'izān . . . mukhliṣān*.
956. *ittiḥād*.
957. *khaṣlat*.
958. *'ulūm-i ḥaqīqī u ma'ārif-i yaqīnī*.
959. *nuqṣān-i qarīḥat*.
960. *la'nat*.
961. *suqūṭ*.
962. *i'rāḍ*.
963. *istihānat*.
964. *ḥijāb*.
965. *istikhfāf*.
966. *ṭard*.
967. *maqt*.
968. Reading *khisā'at* or *khasā'at*, with Humā'ī, the Avery MS and the Cambridge photostat (Lucknow, 1891), against other readings as *khasārat* ('loss') and *khasāsat* ('baseness'), neither of which gives much useful sense here. (Lahore omits the fourth category of fall altogether, obviously without intent). It is true that the *maṣdar* in question is rare, to say the least, but its sense is secured to some extent by the following reference to 'removal' (*dūrī*), assuming this is not an interpolated gloss.
969. *bughḍ*.
970. *shaqāwat-i abadī*.
971. *kasal*.
972. *jahl u ghabāwat*.
973. *tark-i naẓar*.
974. (*tark-i*) *riyāḍat-i nafs bi-ta'līm*.
975. *waqāḥat*.
976. Reading *khalā'at-i 'idhār*, with the Avery MS and Humā'ī only. Other versions read the second word as *ghaddār* ('perfidious') and add *khidā'at* ('deceit', if it be a real form) before the first, doubtless by association of both sense and appearance. The expression, though well attested in Arabic (see Lane, 780, 3), may well have puzzled a Persian scribe.

977. *az khwud rāḍī shudan.*

978. *tark-i inābat.*

979. *tanzīl,* i.e. specifically the Koran.

980. The references are presumably to 3:5 (*zaigh,* though other forms of the same root occur elsewhere); 83:14 (*rāna,* though the text speaks in terms of a hypothetical *maṣdar* of the form *rain*); 2:6 and 45:22 (*ghishāwa,* though several other forms of the same root occur elsewhere); and the several instances of the verb *khatama.*

981. *'ilājī.*

982. *aflāṭūn-i ilāhī,* 'the one concerned with divine things', a not uncommon mode of allusion to Plato in Islamic texts. It is not necessarily, or even probably, an echo of the exaggerated reverence in which Plato was held by his followers.

983. *fi'l-i khāṣṣ-i khwud.*

984. *tawassuṭ.*

985. *jaur.*

986. *'āmm u shāmil ast . . . rā.*

987. *hai'atī-yi nafsānī.*

988. *muqaddir-i maqādīr u mu'aiyin-i auḍā' u ausāṭ.* See earlier in this Section.

989. *ṣāḥib.*

990. *dar ṭabī'at.* This is a fundamental doctrine of Islamic political theory, that natural justice and the divine ordinance must necessarily be in agreement.

991. *muwāfaqat . . . mu'āwanat . . . mutāba'at.*

992. *ṭab'.* A sentence omitted here in the Lahore texts.

993. *mushtarak.*

994. See the end of the previous Section.

995. *qābil-i ḍiddī.*

996. *īn ma'nā . . . taṣauwur bāyad kard.*

997. *'adālat-rā bā ḥurrīyat ishtirāk ast.*

998. i.e. by 'fair means', a notion frequently invoked, but not closely defined, throughout the ethical part of the book. See a few lines farther down in text.

999. *infi'āl.*

1000. *khāṣṣīyat.*

1001. *badhl-i ma'rūf.*

1002. *darvīsh namāyad.* So Montreal (Tehran, n.d.): other texts have a rare *bi-* prefixed to the verb, and in some there seems to be a plausible confusion with the verb *māndan,* 'to remain' and also 'to seem (like)'.

1003. *kasūb.*

1004. In accordance with common practice, I translate two third-person plurals as passives, rather than making them refer to any specific people, though Ṭūsī doubtless had individuals in mind.

1005. *amrī-yi ikhtiyārī.*

1006. *ba'īd tavānad būd.*

1007. There is considerable minor textual variation here, though the general sense, as usual, is not in doubt. I have translated on the basis of the Avery MS and the Montreal text (Tehran, n.d.).

1008. Cf. Note 293 above.

1009. Reading *isti'māl* with the Avery MS, in place of the doubtful *isti'māsh* ('blinding'?) of the other texts.

1010. *tafaḍḍul.* To some extent this problem is a verbal one, for the word connotes as well 'superiority' and 'superfluity', and it derives from the same root as the word I render by 'virtue' (*faḍīla*). See also Notes 1018, 1029, 1030, and 1031 below.

1011. *mustajmi'*: possibly *mustajma'*, 'meeting-place'.

1012. *khulf.*

1013. *iḥtiyāṭ.*

1014. A serious lacuna here in the Lahore texts.

1015. See Note 693 above.

1016. *ān-chi istiḥqāq wājib kunad.*

1017. *ḍā'i'.*

1018. *mutafaḍḍil na-buvad bal-ki mutabadhdhir buvad.* Cf. Note 1010 above.

1019. *sharīf-tar.*

1020. *mubālagha(h) ast dar 'adālat.*

1021. *ṣāḥib-i nāmūs.* Presumably an anticipatory allusion to the Prophet's words covered by Note 1033 below. See also Note 1034.

1022. Respectively: *kullī . . . juz'ī.*

1023. Respectively: *jauhar . . . kam . . . kaif.*

1024. Cf. Note 324 above.

1025. *mutakāfi'.*

1026. Respectively: *kaifīyat . . . kammīyat.*

1027. *misāḥat.*

1028. *mutasāwī.*

1029. *tafāḍul.* Cf. Note 1010 above.

1030. Respectively: *fāḍil . . . mafḍūl.* Cf. Note 1010 above.

1031. *bi-faḍl u 'ināyat-i khwīsh.* Cf. Note 1010 above.

1032. *bar ṭaraf uftad.*

1033. *ṣāḥib-i sharī'at.* The Prophet Muḥammad, considered here less as the immediate transmitter of God's word than as an inspired speaker and legislator. See Note 1021 above.

1034. *'adl* here, as against the longer form *'adālat* elsewhere, but the choice signifies probably nothing more than accurate reporting of the original Arabic; the longer form is used in the passage covered by Note 1021 above.

1035. *nāmūs*, unqualified.

1036. *'āmm u shāmil.*

1037. *dar 'adālat ham qaul-i 'āmm nīst.*

1038. *akhlāq.*

1039. *ṭālib-i aṣnāf-i shahawāt va anwā'-i karāmāt gardad.* Cf. Note 821 above.

1040. *rā'īsī-yi qāhir.*

1041. *qūwat-i tamyīz.*

1042. *khalīfa(h)-i khudā-yi 'azza wa-jalla.*

1043. *dar dhāt-i insānī.*

1044. A bad lacuna here in the Lahore texts.

1045. *sharaf.*

1046. *walī-yi khudā-yi ta'ālā.*

1047. *bi-ihmāl-i siyāsāt.*
1048. *qiwām-i maujūdāt u niẓām-i kā'ināt bi-maḥabbat ast.*
1049. *ḥikmat-i madanī u manzilī.*
1050. *'ulūm-i ḥikmat.*
1051. *tawajjuh.*
1052. *ṭabī'at yā ṣinā'at.*
1053. *muqaddam ast ham dar wujūd va ham dar rutbat.*
1054. *ḥikmat-i ilāhī-yi maḥḍ.*
1055. *tashabbuh.*
1056. *qudrat-i ilāhī.*
1057. *bi-ṭarīq-i taskhīr.*
1058. *bar wajh-i tadbīr.*
1059. *bā ān kamāl muqārin uftad.*
1060. *mā bi ṣadad-i ma'rifat-i ān āmada-īm.*
1061. *bī taqdīm-i ta'allum.*
1062. *qūwat-i takhaiyul.*
1063. *maṭālibī ki mithālhā-yi ān az ḥawāss iqtibās karda bāshad.*
1064. *athar-i khāṣṣ-tarīn nafs va ān qūwat-i tamyīz buvad.* The penultimate word is spelt, as throughout, *tamaiyuz.*
1065. *qūwat-i ḥayā'.*
1066. *shahwat-ī nikāḥ u shauq bi-tanāsul.*
1067. *shauq bi-karāmāt va aṣnāf-i tafauwuq u riyāsāt.* Cf. Notes 821 and 1039 above.
1068. *mabda'-i nuṭq u tamyīz.* Cf. Note 1064 above.
1069. *idrāk-i ashkhāṣ u juz'īyāt . . . ta'aqqul-i anwā' u kullīyāt.*
1070. *qānūn.*
1071. *bar qā'ida-i ḥikmat.*
1072. *akthar-i muhimmāt-i ū makfī buvad.*
1073. *ta'adhdhur.*
1074. *imtinā'.*
1075. *bar faḍīlat maftūr na-bāshad.*
1076. *az umūr-i ṣinā'ī-st.* Cf. the text following Note 1060 above.
1077. *az rū-yi khilqat.*
1078. All the texts except the Cambridge photostat (Lucknow, 1891) have the obviously erroneous *tijārat*, 'commerce', for *nijārat.*
1079. *munāsib-tarīn-i ṣinā'āt bi-d-īn ṣinā'at.*
1080. e.g. al-Rāzī (Rhazes), d. 925 A.D. Cf. Brockelmann S I, 420, and general index; also a translation by A. J. Arberry, *The Spiritual Physick of Rhazes*, London 1950.
1081. *tā ḥāl-i har yakī dar fiṭrat bar qānūn-i i'tidāl ast yā munḥarif az ān.*
1082. *qūwat-i naẓarī.*
1083. *ma'ārif.*
1084. *wahm.* Cf. Note 134 above.
1085. *taḥaiyur u khabṭ.*
1086. *ma'rifat-i a'yān-i maujūdāt.*
1087. *kashf-i haqā'iq u aḥwāl-i ān.*
1088. *mabādi'-i maḥsūsāt.*
1089. *qawā'id-i 'adālat.*
1090. *muhimmāt.*

1091. *fuḍūl*. This may, of course, also be a singular, meaning 'irrelevance, impertinence, interference'.

1092. *sa'ādat-i nafsānī . . . badanī . . . madanī*, respectively.

1093. *ijtimā' u tamaddun*.

1094. *'ilm-i zīnat*, i.e. the care of the hair, the nails and the skin. Cf. Dozy, I:620:1.

1095. *va chūn* (= such as) *'ilm-i nujūm ki muqaddama-i ma'rifat fā'ida dahad*. Cf. Note 18 above. It would seem that the implication is that astrological foreknowledge aids diagnosis.

1096. *millat u daulat*.

1097. *ma'āsh u jam'īyat*.

1098. *'ulūm-i sharī'at az fiqh u kalām u akhbār u tanzīl u ta'wīl*.

1099. *'ulūm-i ẓāhir*.

1100 *adab u balāghat u naḥw u kitābat u ḥisāb u misāḥat u istīfā'* This juxtaposition of arts and technical skills will seem strange to modern eyes. For the last cf. Dozy, II:827:1.

1101. *khaiyir*. So Humā'ī, Montreal (Tehran, n.d.) and the Avery MS. The rest have *ḥurr*, 'free, liberal, noble'.

1102. *mash'ūf* or *mashghūf*.

1103. *'ulūm-i ḥaqīqī u ma'ārif-i yaqīnī*.

1104. *maskharagī u mujūn*.

1105. *waqtī-ki bi-istiṭābat-i nafs u mail-i ṭabī'at mashūb khwāhad būd*.

1106. *fāḍilān-i mubarraz*.

1107. *'ālimān-i mustabṣir*.

1108. *javānān-i musta'idd u muta'allimān-i mustarshid*.

1109. *nuqṣānātī-ki bi-ḥasab-i jibillat-i auwal dar-ū mafṭūr shuda ast*.

1110. *zimām-i 'aql u qaid-i ḥikmat*.

1111. *mubāḥ u murakhkhaṣ*.

1112. *muqaddir*.

1113. *inbisāṭ*.

1114. *mujūn u khalā'at u fisq*.

1115. *fadāmat u 'ubūsat u tund-khū'ī*.

1116. *bashāshat u ṭalāqat u ḥusn-i 'ishrat*.

1117. *ẓarāfat*.

1118. *chi az qabīl-i naẓarīyāt u chi az qabīl-i 'amalīyāt*.

1119. *riyāḍat-i badanī . . . dar ṭibb-i jismānī*. Cf. Note 1080 above.

1120. *naẓar*.

1121. *balah u balādat*.

1122. *mawādd-i khairāt-i 'ālam-i quds*.

1123. *bā kasal ulfat gīrad*.

1124. *intikās* .

1125. *ṭālib-i nau-āmūz*.

1126. i.e. Wisdom, Justice, Continence and Courage. See above the Third Section of the Second Division of the First Discourse.

1127. *bā ṣidq ulfat gīrad*.

1128. *rawīyat*, as against *fikr* (similarly rendered hereabouts). Cf. also Notes 141, 413, 525, etc. above.

1129. *dar 'ilm u barā'at*.

1130. Koran 12:76.

1131. This famous early Islamic ascetic (d. A.D. 728) is the reputed author of words similar to these, according to al-Mubarrad (*Kāmil*, ed. W. Wright, p. 120) and E. W. Lane (*Lexicon*, p. 528, col. 1, *ḥādatha*); but others, e.g. Jāḥiẓ, attribute something like them to 'Umar, the second Caliph (*Bayān*, ed. Cairo, 1947/1366, III, 124). Such situations make much research on early Islam a veritable will-o'-the-wisp.

1132. *bā qillat-i ḥurūf u ghāyat-i faṣāḥat u istīfā'-i sharā'iṭ-i balāghat.*

1133. *ṭālibān-i ni'mat-hā-yi 'araḍī u khāṭibān-i fawā'id-i majāzī.*

1134. *chi mawādd-i ān az umūr-i khārijī u asbāb-i 'araḍī farāham āmada ast.*

1135. *khārijīyāt az ḥawādith salāmat na-yābad va ṭawāriq-i zamāna-rā bi-d-ū taṭarruq buvad.*

1136. *ṭāri'.*

1137. *bādshāh:* cf. Note 1145 below. The passages following, though substantially identical in all texts and reasonably clear in purport, contain several (doubtless original) syntactical infelicities and some scribal errors.

1138. *yakī az khawāṣṣ u muqarrabān-i ḥaḍrat-i ū.*

1139. *ri'āyat-i jawānib-i. . . .* The sense would seem to be that a king is bound to care for all his subjects, whether they are well disposed towards him or not.

1140. *akhaṣṣ al-khawāṣṣ.*

1141. *bi-naqd*, though Montreal (Tehran, n.d.) has *bi-qaṣd* ('intentionally'), which seems inappropriate.

1142. *tavāngar u bī-niyāz.*

1143. *iḥtiyāj bi-andāza-i muḥtāj ilaih.*

1144. *aghnà al-aghniyā'*. The Arabic root here involved connotes both wealth and independence, an idea difficult to turn into English. In the latter sense, it is commonly applied to God in philosophical and mystical writings.

1145. *mulūk*. Cf. Note 1137 above. Kings are normally thought of in classical Islamic theory as temporal rulers, lacking religious sanction and hence often considered to be usurpers.

1146. The first of the Orthodox Caliphs, who ruled from the Prophet's death in A.D. 632 to 634. Montreal (Tehran, n.d.) and the Avery MS have simply 'one of the Caliphs', and the ascription does in fact vary. Cf. Note 1153 below.

1147. *az salāmat sha'mat namāyad: sha'mat* appears in most cases as *sāmit*, which would be meaningless here.

1148. *bahā' u salwat*. The first word may, of course, be read in several different ways, but they would all give some such meaning.

1149. *diram-i rūy-kashīda*. A silver coin made to look like gold will have a short-lived, false and superficial brilliance.

1150. *mādda-i 'umr*: a common use of the first word in Persian.

1151. *dar ḥisāb munāqasha kunad.*

1152. *dar 'afw muḍāyaqa (kunad).*

1153. Cf. Note 1146 above.

1154. Cf. Note 293 above.

1155. The Buwayhid ruler (A.D. 936–983), who effectively became master of much of the Eastern Caliphate. Ibn Miskawaih was one of his officers of state, but survived him by nearly 50 years, to reminisce in the way here suggested.

1156. *kaukaba u dabdaba*. Both words may be translated in a variety of ways.

1157. Literally: 'No! By God's life!'

1158. *bi-tajriba u qiyās*. Lahore has some confusion in the text just previous to this, or it may be a simple omission.

1159. *chūn chashm-ash bar mushāhada-i ān asbāb bi-nishīnad.*

1160. *ni'mat-hā-yi majāzī.*

1161. *ni'mat-hā-yi ḥaqīqī ki dar dhawāt-i afāḍil u nufūs-i arbāb-i faḍā'il maujūd buvad.*

1162. 'The wise Sanā'ī' or 'the Philosopher Sanā'ī' (the word *ḥakīm* has broad connotations) was a mystical and didactic poet of the Ghaznavid court (present-day Afghanistan), who died in about 1150 A.D. The word rendered 'design' may also mean 'inscription', i.e. referring to the Koran.

1163. *istithmār.*

1164. *na'īm-i abadī.*

1165. *nafīs-i bāqī-yi dhātī*: Cf. next Note. The word-play on 'calling forward, presenting, making ready' and 'absenting oneself, being missing' is more effective in Persian than in English.

1166. *khasīs-i fānī-yi 'araḍī*: cf. previous Note.

1167. *kafāf.*

1168. *bi-iqtiṣād.*

1169. *faḍla.*

1170. *lawāzim.*

1171. *bar qadr-i sadd-i ramaq-i ḍarūrat qādir na-bāshad.*

1172. *istīlā-yi ḥirṣ u ta'arruḍ-i makāsib-i danīya.*

1173. *dar mu'āmala ṭarīq-i mujāmala nigāh-dārad.*

1174. *bāyad ki dar aqwāt u aghdhiya ham bi-d-īn naẓar nigarad.* All texts except the Avery MS have the plausible *ṭarīq* ('way, manner') for *naẓar* ('view'); even that text seems to have something looking more like the quite impossible *qṭr*. Only Avery and Montreal (Tehran, n.d.) have the last word as *nikarad*: the rest have the (on all counts unlikely) *na-gardad* ('should not become, walk'), possibly by association with 'way'. The general sense, in any case, is surely that men should at least not be more animal than the beasts in this respect.

1175. *tafaḍḍul-i mādda-i dakhl bar mādda-i kharj.*

1176. *badal-i mā yataḥallal.*

1177. *mulā'im.*

1178. *ṣalāḥīyat-i īn ma'nā.*

1179. *bi-sabab-i istifrāgh-i mauḍi' u khālī kardan-i jāygah-i badal.*

1180. Ṭūsī is suggesting that this is repugnant, as involving an inversion of the proper order of things: nature may concern itself with food, but the intelligence has higher purposes.

1181. *qūwat-i shahwat u qūwat-i ghaḍab.*

1182. *taḥrīk.*

1183. *rawīyat.* Cf. Note 413 above.

1184. *dar taḥṣīl-i īn ma'nā ki maṭlūb-i shauq buvad.*

1185. *qūwat-i nuṭq.*

1186. *dar izāḥat-i 'illat-i nafs-i ḥayawānī.* Cf. Note 189 above.

1187. *mizāj.*

1188. *dawā'ī-yi ṭabī'at(-i) khwud bi-kifāyat-i īn muhimm qiyām kunand.*

1189. *fikr u dhikr.* The word 'careful' in the next sentence renders the Vth Form of these roots: *tafakkur u tadhakkur.*

1190. *tadābīr u taṣarrufāt.*

1191. *bar ḥasab-i ijrā-yi 'ādatī.*

1192. *mukhālif-i 'azm.*

1193. *bi-ta'arruḍ-i safīhī.*

1194. *nadhr u ṣadaqa.*

1195. *dar kutub(-i) ḥukamā' āvarda-and.* Though the issue is not an important one, there is obviously some ambiguity here, resting partly on the indistinguishability of the subjective and objective genitives, and partly on that of the third person plural as used personally or impersonally. Despite the explicit ascription of the incident to the geometrician, it more likely concerns Euclid of Megara, the disciple of Socrates.

1196. *kasalī-yi na-bi-mauḍi'.*

1197. *ū-rā bi-mashaqqat-i mazīd-i a'māl-i ṣāliḥa u muqāsāt-i ta'abī-yi zā'id bar ma'hūd taklīf kunad.*

1198. *ṣaghā'ir-i saiyi'āt,* though its opposite (immediately following) is given simply as *kabā'ir.*

1199. *ḥilm.*

1200. *taḥammul az aqrān.*

1201. *mulāzamat-i īn ādāb.*

1202. *parastārānī-ki bi-khidmat-i sufahā' mubtalā shavand.*

1203. *khanda-hā-yi bī-takalluf.*

1204. *istiẓhār u 'uddat.*

1205. *jālīnūs-i ḥakīm mī-gūyad dar kitābī-ki dar ta'rīf-i mardum 'uyūb-i khwīsh-rā sākhta-ast.* This is conceivably a reference to a lost ethical work by Galen, particularly appropriate here because of the constant parallel Ṭūsī draws between the case of the body and that of the soul. As always, the word rendered 'wise' (*ḥakīm*) may connote 'philosopher' (cf. Note 6 above, and elsewhere). See also Note 1209 below. Professor Hourani reminds me of R. Walzer's 'New Light on Galen's Moral Philosophy', *Greek into Arabic,* 142–63.

1206. *dūstī-yi kāmil-i fāḍil.*

1207. *'ahdī-yi ustuwār bar-ū gīrad.*

1208. *tā bi-chīzī az ān-chi muqtaḍā-yi ta'yīr dānad i'tirāf kunad.* The Lahore texts read *ta'bīr,* clearly in error.

1209. Cf. Note 1205 above It should be emphasized that Ṭūsī is here being unusually explicit about the actual and accessible character of his sources.

1210. Usually known as the Philosopher of the Arabs (*failasūf al-'arab*), he wrote in the first half of the ninth century A.D., and practically all his writings are lost. The appellation given him by Ṭūsī (*az ḥukamā-yi islām*) raises all sorts of problems turning on: (a) the ambiguity of the Arabic term for 'wise man, philosopher' (cf. Note 1205 above), and, (b) the question whether 'of Islam' means 'writing within the Islamic era, as opposed to ancient times' or 'as a Muslim, concerned to harmonize philosophy with the Islamic faith'.

1211. *ṣūrat-hā*. It is possible that, even at this early date, the word may connote 'countenance' in one sense or another.

1212. *infāq-i ān ittifāq uftāda bāshad.*

1213. *ān-chi az dhawāt-i mā infāq mī-y-uftad.*

1214. *bar . . . muqaddar.*

1215. *ifāḍa kardan.*

1216. *īn ma'nà az sukhan-i dīgarān bi-mubālagha nazdīktar-ast dar-īn bāb.*

1217. *'ilm-i ṭibb-i abdān.*

1218. *ṭibb-i nufūs.*

1219. Ṭūsī is alluding principally to the Third, Fourth and Fifth Sections of the present Discourse and Division.

1220. *illā bi-majāz.*

1221. *az yak bāb.*

1222. *qānūn-i ṣinā'ī.*

1223. *inḥirāfāt-i amzija. . . az i'tidāl.*

1224. Principally in the present Discourse, First Division, Third Section.

1225. *tamyīz, daf'* and *jadhb* respectively, the first spelt (as generally in this text) *tamaiyuz.*

1226. Respectively *ziyādat* and *nuqṣān.*

1227. Respectively *ifrāṭ, tafrīṭ* and *radā'at.*

1228. Respectively *khubth, gurbuzi* (cf. Notes 708 and 695 above) and *dahā'.*

1229. *tajāwuz-i ḥadd-i naẓar u ḥukm bar mujarradāt bi-qūwat-i auhām u ḥawāss hamchunān-ki bar maḥsūsāt.*

1230. *balāhat u balādat.* Cf. Notes 693 and 708 above.

1231. *mānand-i ijrā-yi aḥkām-i maḥsūsāt bar mujarradāt.*

1232. *'ilm-i jadal u khilāf u safsaṭa.*

1233. *yaqīnīyāt.* A term of very broad and varied significance as used by Avicenna, and hence, probably, by Ṭūsī.

1234. *'ilm-i kahānat u fa'l giriftan u shu'bada u kīmiyā.*

1235. *bī-ḥamīyatī u ḥawar-i ṭab' u bad-dilī,* (the best reading, with Humā'ī and the Avery MS).

1236. *'ishq u shīftagī bi-kasānī-ki maḥall-i shahwat na-bāshand.*

1237. *shahwat-i muqārabat-i dhukūr.*

1238. *qānūn-i wājib.*

1239. *muhlika.*

1240. *muzmina.*

1241. *ḥairat u jahl . . . dar qūwat-i naẓarī.*

1242. *ghaḍab u bad-dilī u khauf u ḥuzn u ḥasad* (Montreal, Tehran n.d., alone adds *ḥiqd*, 'rancour', here) *u amal* (the same adds *ḥirṣ*, 'greed') *u 'ishq u biṭālat.*

1243. *'ināyat-i yazdānī.* It is as though Ṭūsī stresses his position as a Muslim, above and beyond being a philosopher, by his use of a Persian word for 'divine' which, unlike its Arabic counterpart (*ilāhī*), has no purely metaphysical connotations.

1244. *az ṭarayān-i sababī yā 'illatī.* See Dozy, II:43:1 for form of second word.

1245. *'uḍwī-yi sharīf.*

1246. *nuqṣān-i tamyīz u fasād-i takhaiyul u taqṣīr dar isti'māl-i quwā u malakāt.*

1247. *mu'ālajāt-i kullī.*

1248. *ghidhā' u dawā' u samm u kaiy yā qaṭ'.*

1249. *ta'dīl.*

1250. *taskīn.*

1251. *dar aṣl-i fiṭrat.*

1252. *mutakāfi'.*

1253. *irtikāb-i asbāb-i radhīlatī ki. . . .*

1254. *'uqūbat u ta'dhīb.*

1255. *bā taqdīm-i īfā-yi marāsim-i ān.* The elliptical, un-Persian style here gave me long pause. What Ṭūsī is apparently suggesting is a sort of indirect approach to the problem: one commits oneself by solemn vows to some course of action which cannot easily be followed if one first indulges the bad habit. The process turns presumably on the deterrent effect of the reluctance to break an oath.

1256. This aphorism, given in Arabic, is clearly expected to have an evocative effect (neither Humā'ī nor Lucknow 1891 offers, as according to custom, a Persian rendering), but I am unable to ascribe it.

1257. Respectively: *ḥairat . . . jahl-i basīṭ . . . jahl-i murakkab.*

1258. *ta'āruḍ-i adilla.*

1259. *īn qaḍīya az qaḍāyā-yi ūlà.* The reference is, of course, to Aristotle's self-evident truths.

1260. *jam' u raf'-i nafy u ithbāt.* All except the Avery MS and Montreal (Tehran, n.d.) replace the *iḍāfa* between the first and second pairs of nouns by a simple copula, but this seems to make no sense. The argument is rather that one cannot have, at one and the same time, both affirmation and negation, but equally one cannot have neither: i.e. one must have one or the other.

1261. *ḥukm-i jazm kunad bi-fasād-i yak ṭaraf az du ṭaraf-i muta'āriḍ.*

1262. *taṣaffuḥ-i muqaddimāt u tafaḥḥuṣ az ṣūrat-i qiyās.*

1263. *kitāb-i qiyāsāt-i sūfisṭā'ī.* The reference is undoubtedly to Aristotle's *De Sophisticis Elenchis.*

1264. *mughālaṭāt.*

1265. *nuṭq u tamyīz.* The first word also means 'speech', as well as 'reason', and much of the force of the next few lines is lost in English by the necessity to differentiate the term according to context. The second word (which may also be appropriately rendered 'discrimination' in most cases) is in this case correctly spelt in the Lahore texts and in Lucknow 1891 (cf. Note 1064 above).

1266. *nuṭq.* See previous Note.

1267. *sukhan guftan.*

1268. *muḥāwara.*

1269. *bar wajh-i majāz.*

1270. *bi-ṭarīq-i tashabbuh.*

1271. *asfal al-sāfilīn.*

1272. *nuqṣān-i rutba u khasāsat-i jauhar u rakākat-i ṭab'-i khwīsh ki akhass-i kā'ināt ān-ast.*

1273. A well-known Tradition, quoted in Arabic. Cf. Lane 2978, col. 2.

1274. *i'tiqādī-yi bāṭil.*

1275. *bā wujūd-i ān ṣūrat-i kazh.* As usual, especially at this period, there is always the possibility that the initial phrase means not 'despite' but 'given, assuming'. However, this seemed less appropriate here. The elliptical text here seemed to call for three parenthetical elaborations.

1276. A half-line in a poem attributed to Sanā'ī, one of Ṭūsī's favourite poets. Cf. Note 1162 above.

1277. Reading *bard-i nafs*, with Avery MS, Montreal (Tehran, n.d.) and Humā'ī. The rest have something looking like *barā'at-i nafs* ('innocence of soul'), which seems quite impossible here.

1278. *qūwat-i daf'.*

1279. Respectively: *ghaḍab . . . jubn . . . khauf.*

1280. *shahwat-i intiqām.*

1281. *chunān-ki ḥukamā' gufta and.* This seems to be a somewhat unusual application of Plato's allegory of the Cave (*Republic*, Book 7). Ibn Miskawaih uses it similarly.

1282. Reading *mashghala* (with Humā'ī and Tehran n.d.) for the plausible, but here redundant, *mash'ala* ('torch, link') of other texts.

1283. *dar ghāyat-i ta'adhdhur.*

1284. *bi-ḥasab-i ikhtilāf-i amzija.*

1285. *tarkīb.*

1286. *dar 'unfuwān-i mabda'-i ḥarakat.*

1287. We face here once more the constant (and usually unrewarding) problem of identifying the source of what purport to be Greek references. Most of the texts have the name as *ansuqrāṭīs*, with the initial vowel uncertain as to quality or length: a natural reaction (to which Humā'ī succumbs) is to read the latter as *ā*, yielding (if one allows this to be an example of a Persian habit of assimilating the demonstrative adjective to its noun) 'That (i.e. the well-known) Socrates'. Against this is the fact that the usual Arabo-Persian form of this name is the apocopated *suqrāṭ*. The Montreal text (Tehran, n.d.) has a different name: *buqrāṭīs* (without the *an-* prefix), which is, again, an uncommon long form of the Arabo-Persian name for Hippocrates. My version obtains the form *īsuqrāṭīs* by the simple addition of a dot under the second letter. If the epithet 'Philosopher' should seem to militate against this identification, it should be remembered that the Mediaeval Islamic attitude towards these non-Islamic figures was somewhat casual (cf. Note 435 above and elsewhere), and also that the original term *ḥakīm* is fairly elastic (cf. Note 8 above). Ṭūsī is close to Ibn Miskawaih here (cf. Note 1281 above). I am unable to find a classical scholar familiar with anything approaching this reference. (Since the original writing of this Note, 'Xenocrates' occurs to me as another possibility. Cf. also '*Picatrix*'; *das Ziel des Weisen von Pseudo-Mağrīṭī*, tr. and ed. by H. Ritter and M. Plessner, Warburg Institute, London 1962).

1288. 1. *'ujb*, 2. *iftikhār*, 3. *mirā'*, 4. *lajāj*, 5. *muzāḥ*, 6. *takabbur*, 7. *istihzā'*, 8. *ghadr*, 9. *ḍaim*, 10. *ṭalab-i nafā'isī ki. . . .*

1289. *bar sabīl-i ishtirāk.*

1290. 1. *nadāmat*, 2. *tawaqqu'-i mujāzāt-i 'ājil u ājil*, 3. *maqt-i dūstān* 4. *istihzā-yi arādhil*, 5. *shamātat-i a'dā'*, 6. *taghaiyur (taghyīr)-i mizāj*. 7. *ta'allum-i abdān.*

1291. The fourth and last of the so-called Orthodox Caliphs, who held office from 656 to 661 A.D. For Shīʿites (and to some extent for Sunnites also) he is a paragon of all the virtues, and he is credited with a vast body of moral pronouncements of this kind. See material at Note 1302 below.

1292. *qaṭʿ-i mawādd.* This does not seem to be a technical term, signifying merely those things that feed a disease. Cf. Note 1340 below.

1293. *bi-tadbīr-i ʿaql.*

1294. *ẓannī-yi kādhib.*

1295. *ṣādiq-tarīn-i īn nauʿ.*

1296. *bar sabīl-i istibdād.*

1297. *ulfat.*

1298. *tabāyun u tabāghuḍ u mukhāṣamat.*

1299. *maḥabbat.* This notion is common in Ṭūsī and in most of his predecessors: in its most commonplace formulation, it simply suggests the cohesion of the material universe, but this principle is seldom differentiated from the idea of the pervasiveness of God's love binding all together.

1300. *niẓām.*

1301. *kāna rasūl-allāh . . . yamzaḥu wa-lā yahzilu.* The general idea is common enough, but I cannot trace this particular version.

1302. *lau-lā du'ābatu-hu fī-hi.* The apodosis, as often in these early (or allegedly early) sayings, is left unexpressed, but can easily be conjectured.

1303. A well-known early convert outside the Arabian generality. For the point of the remark, see Note 1291 above.

1304. *chūn shurūʿ namāyand bi-mujāwazat-i ḥadd taʿaddī kunand tā sabab-i waḥshat shavad.*

1305. *kāmin.*

1306. *ḥiqd.*

1307. *iqtiṣād.*

1308. Respectively: *rubba jiddin jarra-hu al-laʿibu; ḥadīthī buvad māya-i kārzār.* Both sayings, Arabic and Persian, are well known in many versions.

1309. *ahl-i mujūn u maskharagī.* Lahore and Lucknow substitute *junūn* for the second word, but 'insanity' is not appropriate here (cf. Note 1104 above).

1310. *ḥurrīyat u faḍl.*

1311. *yak safāhat-i safīhī.* Cf. first term in Note 693 above.

1312. Respectively: *māl . . . jāh . . . mawaddat . . . ḥaram.*

1313. *khulq.*

1314. *wafā'.*

1315. See Note 693 above, and the general area of text to which it relates.

1316. *mushāwarat-i ʿaql u tadbīr-i ra'y.*

1317. *mushtamil bāshad bar khaṭā-yi ʿaẓīm az kasānī-ki bi-saʿat-i qudrat mausūm bāshand tā bi-ausāṭ al-nās chi rasad.*

1318. *ṭabīʿat-i ʿālam-i kaun u fasād ki muqaddar bar taghyīr u iḥālat u ifsād ast.*

1319. *taṭarruq-i āfāt bi-aṣnāf-i murakkabāt.*

1320. *qubba-ī az bulūr.*

1321. *asāṭīr u tamāthīl.* In place of the first word, *asāṭīn* ('columns, pillars') is well attested according to Humā'ī, going back to Ibn Miskawaih himself.

1322. *rūzgār natīja-i ṭab'-i khwīsh dar itlāf-i ān bi taqdīm rasānīd.*

1323. *har ā'īna mutaghallibān u mutamarridān bi-ṭam' u ṭalab bar-khīzand.* I take the verb as a literal Persian rendering of the Arabic *qāma bi. . . .* This gives some idea of the peculiarity of Ṭūsī's style in many places in this work.

1324. *musāmaḥat.* Cf. Note 647 above.

1325. *dar maqām-i ḍarūrat.*

1326. *mulūk-i maghrūr-i bisyār-māl-i fārigh-bāl.* For the first word, Humā'ī alone has *mardumān* ('people').

1327. *jaur.* Cf. Note 670 above, and also (for the general context of the argument) the Fifth and Seventh Sections of the present Division of the First Discourse.

1328. *farṭ-i rujūlīyat.* A less common term than would be expected.

1329. *bi-takhaiyul-i kādhib.*

1330. *jauhar-i ghaḍab.*

1331. *radā'atī.* Cf. Note 1227 above.

1332. *bahā'im-i zabān-basta u jamādāt.*

1333. *farṭ-i tahauwurī.* Cf. Note 693 above. At this point there is some omission and confusion in the Lahore text.

1334. This seems to be no longer true, unfortunately!

1335. *na't-i rujūlīyat.* Cf. Note 1328 above.

1336. *sharah.* Cf. Note 693 above.

1337. *kasānī-ki bi-tartīb-i ān 'amal mausūm bāshand.*

1338. *simat-i shaqāwat.*

1339. *'afw u ighḍā'.*

1340. *chūn ḥasm-i mawādd-i īn maraḍ karda bāshand raf'-i a'rāḍ u lawāḥiq-i ū sahl buvad.* Cf. Notes 1292 above and 1346 below.

1341. *rawīyat.* Cf. Note 413 above.

1342. *mukāfāt yā taghāful.*

1343. *majāl-i naẓarī-yi shāfī u fikrī-yi kāfī.*

1344. *bad-dilī.* Cf. Note 1242 above.

1345. For the particular argument see the text between Notes 1278 and 1280 above; the general argument belongs to the Fifth and Seventh Sections of the present Division of the First Discourse, albeit permeating the thought of the whole book.

1346. *lawāḥiq u a'rāḍ.* Cf. Note 1340 above.

1347. *mahānat-i nafs.*

1348. *sū'-i 'aish.*

1349. *riḍā' bi-faḍā'iḥ.*

1350. *mūjib-i nang.*

1351. *dawā'ī-yi ghaḍabī.* The Persian here uses only one set of terms to cover the faculty of Irascibility (which is neutral in itself) and the vice of Anger (which is to be avoided). I have attempted a distinction.

1352. *thabāt u ṣabr.*

1353. Cf. Note 1351 above.

1354. Cf. the Fifth and Seventh Sections of the present Division of the First Discourse.

1355. *tawaqqu'-i makrūhī yā intiẓār-i maḥdhūrī.*

1356. Respectively: *umūr-i 'iẓām . . . umūr-i sahl.*

1357. *bar har du taqdīr yā ḍarūrī buvad yā mumkin.*

1358. *mumkināt-rā musabbib.* So with Lahore and Lucknow: *sabab* seems less good for the second word.

1359. *muqtaḍā-yi 'aql.*

1360. *istish'ār.*

1361. *pīsh az waqt-i ḥudūth-i ān maḥdhūr.*

1362. *dil bar būdanī-hā nihāda.*

1363. *ḥaqīqat-i mumkin ān-ast ki ham wujūd-ash jā'iz buvad va ham 'adam.*

1364. *jazm kardan bi-wuqū'-i īn maḥdhūr.*

1365. *ham-ān lāzim āyad ki az qism-i gudhashta.*

1366. *agar 'aish bi-ẓann-i jamīl u amal-i qawī u tark-i fikr dar ān-chi ḍarūrī al-wuqū' na-buvad khwush dārad.*

1367. *sū'-i ikhtiyār.*

1368. *bi-ṭabī'at-i mumkin jāhil bāshad.*

1369. *har-chi mumkin buvad wuqū'-ash nā-mustabda'.*

1370. Respectively: *bar mumkin bi-wujūb ḥukm kunad . . . bar mumkin bi-imtinā' ḥukm namāyad.* That is to say: he believes that what he fears through the action of another is bound to happen, while acting as though what is to be feared from his own action cannot possibly happen.

1371. *buṭlān-i tarkīb-i binya.*

1372. *'adam-i dhāt-i ū lāzim āyad.*

1373. *bāṭil u bī-ḥaqīqat.*

1374. *jahl-i maḥḍ.*

1375. *isti'māl nā-kardan-i nafs buvad ālāt-i badanī-rā.*

1376. *jauharī-yi bāqī . . . ki . . . fānī u mun'adim na-gardad.*

1377. *qadr-i ḍarūrī.*

1378. *fuḍūl-i 'aish.* The common singular meaning of the first word ('importunity, busybodying') seems less likely here.

1379. Respectively: *irādī . . . ṭabī'ī.*

1380. *imātat-i shahawāt . . . u tark-i ta'arruḍ-i ān.*

1381. *ḥukamā-yi mutaṣauwifa.* Early Islamic ascetic literature (and it is to this rather than to the later sophisticated writings of the Ṣūfīs that the author is doubtless referring) is very rich in aphorisms of this kind. Both sayings are in the pithiest of Arabic.

1382. *lāzim-i dhāt.*

1383. *mā'it.*

1384. *ḥayāt*, used (as typically by Ṭūsī) as a *maṣdar*, rather than simply as the abstract noun 'life'. I take the sense to be: what could be more ignorant than to suppose that the apparent annihilation of death is real annihilation, when it is in fact a transition to real life? Similarly, with the phrase quoted in Note 1385.

1385. *nuqṣān-i ū bi-tamām-i ū.*

1386. *tammām u sharīf u bāqī.*

1387. *az qaid u asr-i ṭabī'at.* There is perhaps more than a hint here of some esoteric doctrine, innocent on the surface, but accessible only to the elect. Cf. also following Notes.

1388. *jauhar-i sharīf-i ilāhī az jauhar-i kathīf-i ẓulmānī.* The 'when', which is obviously needed to complete the structure, is not in all texts.

1389. *khalāṣ-i ṣafā' u naqā' na khalāṣ-i mizāj u kudūrat.*

1390. *malakūt-i 'ālam u jiwār-i khudāvand-i khwīsh u mukhālaṭat-i arwāḥ-i pākān.*

1391. *az aḍdād u āfat najāt yāfta.* Cf. Note 1387 above and Note 1412 below.

1392. *bi-ālāt-i jismānī u malādhdh-i nafsānī mā'il u mushtāq buvad.*

1393. *qarār-gāh-i khwīsh.*

1394. *ān ẓann kādhib ast.* Cf. Note 1294 above.

1395. *zinda qābil-i athar-i nafs tavānad būd.*

1396. *chīzī-yi bāqī.*

1397. *mūjib-i iqdām bar dhunūb malaka-hā-yi tabāh buvad nafs-rā.*

1398. *baqā'.*

1399. *chūn wāthiq shavad.*

1400. *kā'ināt.*

1401. *falsafa.*

1402. *fāsid.*

1403. *har-ki kaun-i khwud khwāhad fasād-i dhāt-i khwud khwāsta bāshad.* It will be noted that '*kaun*' is rendered by 'existence', though 'coming into being' is perhaps more appropriate, if unwieldy, in this context. It was thought inadvisable here to give *dhāt* the sense of 'essence', but in general I have done so in places where others might well prefer 'self'.

1404. *'āqil-rā bi-muḥāl iltifāt na-y-uftad.*

1405. It should be remembered that it is Ibn Miskawaih who is speaking here, not Ṭūsī, so that the period involved runs from about 620 A.D. ('Alī's young manhood) to 1020 A.D. (some years before Ibn Miskawaih reputedly died).

1406. Ṭūsī speaks here as a sensitive Shī'ite!

1407. *kaudakān ki az shikam-i mādar bi-y-uftāda bāshand.*

1408. *muḍā'af.*

1409. *az ḥadd-i ḍabṭ u ḥaiyiz-i iḥṣā' mutajāwiz shavad.*

1410. *ikhtilāf kardan.* The foregoing few lines exhibit several minor discrepancies among the different texts, but the general line of argument is the same.

1411. *taṣauwur-i ān-ki ṭam'-rā khwud bi-d-īn ārzū ta'alluqī tavānad būd.*

1412. *'uqalā' u arbāb-i kiyāsat.* A suggestion, again, of the esoteric: Cf. Notes 1387–91 above.

1413. *khawāṭir u ḍamā'ir.*

1414. *ḥikmat-i kāmil u 'adl-i shāmil-i ilāhī.*

1415. *bar īn waḍ' u hai'at.*

1416. *ghāyat.*

1417. *buṭlān-i ruṭūbat-i aṣlī.*

1418. *ḍa'f-i a'ḍā-yi ra'īsīya.* The heart, brain, liver, etc. are meant.

1419. *nashāṭ.*

1420. *ālāt-i ṭaḥn.* The teeth are of course what is meant, but the term commonly refers to the grinding of flour.

1421. Cf. the passage referrred to by Notes 124 and 125 above.

1422. *mufāraqat-i dhāt u lubb u khulāṣa-i insān-ast az badan-i majāzī-yi 'āriyatī ki az ṭabā'i'-i arba'a bi-ṭarīq-i tauzī' farāham āvurda and.*

1423. *dar ḥibāla-i taṣarruf-i ū.*

1424. *ḥaḍrat-i ilāhīyat.*

1425. *ẓulamāt-i barzakh.* The sense of this word varies from one writer to another, but it commonly suggests a state between death and resurrection in which the wicked are made particularly uncomfortable. One might describe it as a 'purgatory' for the evil and a 'limbo' for the good. Ṭūsī's use of it here may be esoteric: cf. *EI, barzakh,* and W. Ivanow's edition of Ṭūsī's *Taṣauwurāt* (1950), p. 60 and Note 2.

1426. *darakāt-i dūzakh.*

1427. *sakhaṭ-i bāri'.*

1428. An echo of Koran XII:18 and XXI:112.

1429. *maḥabbat-i biṭālat u ḥuzn u ḥasad.* There is considerable confusion in the various readings as between copula and *iḍāfa.* My version agrees exactly with Humā'ī, Montreal (Tehran, n.d.) and the Avery MS.

1430. *radā'at-i kaifīyat.* Cf. Note 1227 above.

1431. *danā'at-i himmat u khasāsat-i ṭabī'at.*

1432. *shikam-parastī u madhallat-i taṭafful u zawāl-i ḥishmat.*

1433. *isrāf u mujāwazat-i ḥadd.*

1434. *shahwat-i nikāḥ.* Cf. Note 145 above

1435. *irāqat-i ābrūy.*

1436. The most attractive, if not the greatest, figure in the history of Islamic faith and thought, d. A.D. 1111 He was known to the mediaeval West as Algazel. Of his many writings, the allusion here is probably to the great ethical treatise *Iḥyā' 'Ulūm al-Dīn* ('Vivification of the Sciences of the Faith') or its Persian summary *Kīmiyā-yi Sa'ādat* ('Alchemy of Felicity'). At the end of this reference from Ghazalī, Humā'ī leaves a large lacuna (doubtless on grounds of unsuitability in a school-text: it is clear, however, that Ghazālī is already discussing sexual excesses and not merely excesses of appetite in general).

1437. *hameh amwāl-i ra'īyat bi-sitānad.*

1438. *bi-tahdhīb-i qūwat-i tamyīz u kasr-i qūwat-i ghaḍab u ḥuṣūl-i faḍīlat-i 'iffat taskīn-i ū ittifāq na-y-uftad.* Once again, the central ethical technique is to play the faculties off one against the other and so to give rise to virtues.

1439. *mawādd-i ghadhā' u kaimūsāt-i ṣāliḥa.* The frame of reference is Galenian medicine: chyme is food in the primary stage of digestion.

1440. *ahl-i ḥurmat u juft-i ḥalāl.*

1441. *hawā-yi nafs dar bāṭin-i ū.*

1442. *mubāsharat u mu'āsharat-i ū.*

1443. *ẓuhūr-i tazwīr u iḥtiyāl.*

1444. *ḥirṣ u ḥīla.*

1445. *ghāyat-i ḥamāqat u nihāyat-i ḍalālat.*

1446. *tatabbu'-i hawā.*

1447. *qadr-i mubāḥ.*

1448. *'ishq.*

1449. *az jihat-i sulṭān-i shawat.*

1450. *'awāriḍ.*

1451. *'ulām-i daqīqa u ṣinā'āt-i laṭīfa ki bi-faḍl-i rawīyatī makhṣūṣ bāshad.* Cf. Note 413 above and elsewhere.

1452. *nudamā-yi fāḍil u julasā-yi ṣāḥib-i ṭab'.*
1453. *mūjib-i tadhakkur-i khayālāt-i fāsida na-shavad.*
1454. *chi bi-mujāma'at u chi bi-isti'māl-i muṭfi'āt.*
1455. *suqūṭ u ḍarar-i mufriṭ.*
1456. See Note 1429 above.
1457. *mu'addī buvad bi-ibṭāl-i ghāyat-i ījād.*
1458. *mustad'ā-yi ifāḍa-i jūd-i wājib al-wujūd.* God's nature is such that He brings into being. For the first word cf. Note 822 above.
1459. *alamī-yi nafsānī.*
1460. *ki baqā-yi maḥsūsāt u thabāt-i ladhdhāt-rā mumkin shināsad.*
1461. *nā-mumtani'.*
1462. *muḥāl.* The 'conditions of equity' (*sharṭ-i inṣāf*) here probably means only something like 'playing fair' in argument.
1463. *'ālam-i kaun u fasād.*
1464. *az taṣarruf-i mutaḍāddāt khālī.* This is to say that they are not bound by the material facts of wet-or-dry, hot or-cold, etc.
1465. *ṣāfī.* Again, the idea is that of being unalloyed with matter.
1466. *mulābis . . . shavad.* Cf. last two Notes.
1467. Or, in the Lahore-Lucknow versions: 'he cannot be without corruption'. Whatever the exact wording, the argument is one from definition: if, by definition the universe is thus one of dual process, it is impossible to escape one aspect thereof.
1468. The original is in Arabic. I have not discovered any attributed author, but it is typical of much early didactic verse.
1469. Respectively: *maujūd* and *mafqūd.*
1470. The exact terms for 'facility' and 'difficulty' vary between the texts, but the general sense is clear: 'If anyone doubts the feasibility of following this counsel of perfection, let him consider the relative and subjective nature of men's attachments to worldly things'.
1471. *ikhtilāf-i maṭālib u ma'ā'ish-i īshān.*
1472. *ṣinā'at u ḥirfatī-ki bi-d-ān makhṣūṣ buvad.*
1473. Koran XXIII:55 and XXX:31.
1474. *khābiṭ.* An excellent indication of Ṭūsī's knowledge of the finer points of Arabic: the comparative rareness of the word, especially in this sense and particularly in Persian, has put some copyists at fault. Cf. Lahore-Lucknow's *khā'iṭ.*
1475. Koran X:63.
1476. Cf. Note 1210 above. The work in question is probably that in Brockelmann, S I, 373, III 3; this was published by H. Ritter and R. Walzer, *Accademia dei Lincei*, 6th ser., 8:1 (Rome 1938).
1477. *na ḍarūrī buvad na ṭabī'ī.*
1478. See Note 1291 above. The text reads: *iṣbir ṣabra al-akārimi wa-illā tasalla sulūwa al-bahā'imi.*
1479. *ki jārī-yi majrā-yi dīgar aṣnāf-i radā'at ast.*
1480. *bi hīch wajh maraḍī-yi waḍ'ī nazdīk-i ū marḍī na-shavad.* Cf. Note 373 above.
1481. *shammāma.* This may be a nosegay, a *potpourri* or even a highly scented melon. The delight in perfume for its own sake was allowed by the Prophet and is still fashionable in Islamic lands.
1482. *aṣnāf-i muqtanayāt wadā'i'-i khudāy-i ta'ālà-st.*

1483. *bi-ikhtiyār.*

1484. *bi-khwush-dilī.*

1485. *faḍā'ilī ki dast-i muta'arriḍān bi-d-ān na-rasad va mutaghallibān-rā dar-ān ṭam'-i shirkat na-y-uftad.*

1486. *ri'āyat-i jānib bi-ū.* All except Lahore-Lucknow substitute a meaningless *mā* ('our, us') for the final compound. The sense is surely that the return of our lives and possessions to God at any time is a manifest token of *our* dependent relationship.

1487. The argument here rests partly on the earlier discussion of the equity of the successive passing away of one generation after another, partly on the view that God is constantly active towards the juster distribution of material benefits.

1488. *al-mu'minu qalīlu al-mu'nati.* This is not Koranic: it may be offered as either a Prophetic Tradition or emanating from an early ascetic.

1489. *'āriyatī.* It may be observed that the word also commonly signifies (by extension) 'figurative, fictitious, false'.

1490. *tarakkub.*

1491. *khairāt-i dunyawī ki bi-nusqṣān u ḥirmān-i dhātī mausūm ast.*

1492. *jahl bi ma'rifat-i īn ḥāl.*

1493. *mumtani' al-wujūd.*

1494. These are introduced early on in the present Section. Cf. between Notes 1238 and 1242 in the text.

1495. Cf. Notes 1210 and 1476 above.

1496. *'ulamā'*. The word is obviously here used in the most general sense.

1497. *az tangī-yi 'arṣa u qillat-i majāl u ḍīqī ki lazim-i mādda ast.*

1498. *rāghib-rā bi-al-'araḍ ta'alluq-i irāda bi-zawāl-i marghūb-i ū az ghair 'āriḍ shavad.*

1499. *īn ma'nā bi-nazdīk-i ū bi-al-dhāt marḍī na-shavad.*

1500. *muqtaḍī-yi . . . buvad.*

1501. *az ṭabī'at-i sharr-i muṭlaq khīzad.*

1502. *ghibṭa.*

1503. *az ghairī iḥsās karda bāshad dar dhāt-i mughabbaṭ.*

1504. *ḥukm-i ān ḥukm-i sharah buvad.*

1505. *a'rāḍī ki ḥādith shavad.*

1506. *kidhb mubṭil-i khaṣṣīyat-i nau' buvad.*

1507. *ighrā-yi ẓalama.*

1508. *ṣalaf.*

1509. *az lawāḥiq-i ān jahl bi-marātib u taqṣīr dar ri'āyat-i ḥuqūq u ghalaẓ-i ṭab' u lu'm.* The last seems preferable to the *laum* ('blame') of some texts, which may in any case be a mere economy in writing. *Ghalaṭ* ('mistake') for 'coarseness' must be an omission.

1510. *dar ma'nà ṣalaf murakkab buvad az 'ujb u kidhb.*

1511. *riyā'.*

1512. *kidhb buvad ham dar qaul u ham dar fi'l.*

1513. Cf. Note 39 above for the literal rendering of the term.

1514. *tadbīr-i ṣinā'ī.* Cf. Note 1517 below.

1515. *bi-ḥasab-i ṭabī'at.*

1516. *ẓālimān u ghāṣibān.* Some texts (including Lahore-Lucknow) have the equally plausible *ṭālibān* ('seekers', i.e. without any particular right, but not necessarily by violence) for the first word.

1517. *tartīb-i ṣinā'atī*. Cf. Note 1514 above.

1518. *bi-niyābat*.

1519. *juft*.

1520. *sharṭ-i khiffat-i mu'nat*. The problem of all these ancient economies was, of course, basically one of production.

1521. *taqallud-i yak shakhṣ du muhimm-rā*.

1522. *tarbiyat*. See Dozy, 1:506:1, for this less usual sense.

1523. *niẓām-i ḥāl-i ma'āsh*.

1524. *har kathratī*.

1525. *wajhī az ta'līf*.

1526. *nau'ī az tawaḥḥud*.

1527. *ri'āsat-i qaum*.

1528. *si'āsat-i jamā'at*.

1529. *mudabbir-i manzil*.

1530. *zajr u taklīf*. i.e. preventing some people doing some things and compelling others to do others. The other pairs of contrasts seem not to call for comment either as regards sense or in respect of the Arabo-Persian originals.

1531. *manzil*. In the original Arabo-Persian the word means 'stage, stopping-place, dwelling, house, home', according to context. As so often, the point of Ṭūsī's remark is somewhat lost in the English rendering by the fact that the translator is virtually unable to avoid committing himself to one shade of meaning in advance.

1532. *ta'līfī-yi makhṣūṣ*.

1533. *ḥikmat-i manzilī*.

1534. *chi fāḍil u chi mafḍūl*. The varying senses of the root FḌL make it difficult to be absolutely certain that this is the correct rendering, but it is the most likely. In any case, such pairs of contrasts are simply a common stylistic device for making a proposition all-inclusive.

1535. The word for 'pastor' (*rā'ī*) and more particularly that for 'flock' (*ra'īyat*) carry all sorts of connotations from one of the basic senses of the root R'Y ('to keep under watch'). A common meaning of the second word is in fact 'subjects, peasantry'. It is virtually impossible, once more, to keep all these shades of meaning alive in the English. See next Note.

1536. A very well-known Tradition of the Prophet. See previous Note for the difficulty of giving the full flavour of the Arabic original: e.g. compare my version with that of Lane 1110:1.

1537. There is little doubt that, as far as Ṭūsī clearly meant anyone at all, he is referring to the Neo-Pythagorean author of the *Oikonomikos*, a figure of somewhat shadowy dimensions as seen by both modern scholars and the Islamic thinkers (cf. Martin Plessner, *Der Oikonomikos des Neupythagoräers Bryson und sein Einfluss auf die islamische Wissenschaft*, Heidelberg 1928). The name is well masked by typical Arabo-Persian scriptorial defects and by Islamic indifference to the identity of these pagans (cf. Notes 313 and 435 above): there is an initial prosthetic *alif* (i.e. some furtive vowel) to render the *br-* cluster easier to pronounce; the *b* is sometimes mispointed as *y*, or disappears altogether; and the final *n* either disappears into the *s* or interchanges with it. Thus, the Lahore-Lucknow texts have something like *Abrūs*;

Montreal (Tehran, n.d.) has *Airūs* (Eros?); only the Avery MS has *Abrūsun*, carefully vowelled in what is probably a later hand. It is of interest that Avicenna's well-known reference in his treatise on the Divisions of the Sciences (*Tis' Rasā'il*, No. 5, Section 4, On the Divisions of Practical Philosophy) has, in both common editions (Constantinople 1881 and Cairo 1908), a form something like *Arūnis* (a possible form for Valerian). Humā'ī omits the whole of this crucial introductory Section from his *Muntakhab*.

1538. *muta'akhkhirān*. The whole succession of Islamic thinkers, as opposed to the classical philosophers of pagan antiquity. Cf. Note 297 above.

1539. *bi ārā-yi ṣā'ib u adhhān-i ṣāfī*.

1540. *istinbāṭ-i qawānīn u uṣūl-i ān*.

1541. *bar ḥasab-i iqtiḍā-yi 'uqūl*. The unqualified use of words like *'aql* in the plural in this way is particularly common in Ghazālī, but it is a general usage in Arabic.

1542. *al-ra'īs*. This is the unique title accorded to Avicenna (d. 1037 A.D.). It has long been commonly accepted that this part of Ṭūsī's work owes much to Avicenna and hence to Bryson (see Note 1537 above), but there are difficulties in the way of tracing indebtedness to a precise work. According to A. K. S. Lambton (*EI*, article *al-Dawānī*), the work in question is *Tadābīr al-Manāzil*, presumably to be equated with the still unpublished work with the additional title . . . *'an al-siyāsat al-ilāhīya* (Brockelmann, S I, 820, 68q); according to E. I. J. Rosenthal (*Political Thought in Medieval Islam*, Cambridge 1958), the work in question is the *Kitāb al-Siyāsa*, published by L. Cheikho in *Al-Mashriq* (1906), which is presumably to be identified with Brockelmann's (G I, 456, 40) *risāla fī al-siyāsa* (see Rosenthal *passim* and particularly 152 and 285, n.25). In view of Ṭūsī's claim to take only the *khulāṣa* ('essence, gist') of Avicenna, mixed with much other material, identification may seem a somewhat artificial exercise (as well as betraying a misunderstanding of how these writers usually went to work) unless one can point to any sustained and literal borrowing from one particular text in the sense that a modern reader might expect: too often, as here, it is quite impossible for the writer to have verified such assertions in detail. It at least seems likely that the four titles mentioned above all refer to one work.

1543. *aṣl-i kullī*.

1544. See Note 1418 above.

1545. *bar wajh-i ṣawāb maqdūr*. Only Montreal (Tehran, n.d.) has the obviously correct 'or' (*yā*) in this sentence; the others have a misleading *bi* ('by'?).

1546. *ghāyat-i hameh af'āl*.

1547. *ṭabī'atī u khāṣṣīyatī buvad bi-infirād*.

1548. *maqṣadī-yi khāṣṣ*.

1549. Cf. Note 822 above for the dilemma facing one, in carelessly written Persian, over *muqtaḍī* and *muqtaḍà*: is the sense 'requiring' or 'required by', 'producing' or 'produced by'?

1550. *az waḍ'-i ṣinā'at khārij ast*. That is to say: we are not talking about the craft of housebuilding here, but the constitution of a household.

1551. *afḍal-i aḥwāl-i manzil ki maskan buvad.*

1552. *dukkān-hā-yi afrāshta.* See Dozy I:454:2 for this unusual use of the word in the sense of a retaining-pillar.

1553. *sharā'iṭ-i tanāsub-i auḍā'.* Propriety, good taste and proportion are doubtless what is meant.

1554. For 'goldsmiths' (*zargarān*) Lahore-Lucknow have *rūgarān*, which might be emended to *rūygarān* ('coppersmiths, braziers'). The louder noises made by these would seem more appropriate, but there is something unsatisfactory about the emendation. Plato is usually called the Metaphysician rather than the Philosopher (cf. Note 982 above).

1555. The Second Division, Seventh Section. Cf. the material lying between Notes 856 and 875 above.

1556. *ḥāfiẓ-i 'adālat u muqauwim-i kullī u nāmūs-i aṣghar.*

1557. *bi-'izzat-i wujūd-i ū.*

1558. *razānat-i jauhar u istiḥkām-i mizāj u kamāl-i tarkīb.*

1559. *thabāt u qawām-i fawā'id-i muktasab ṣūrat bast.*

1560. *bi-d-īn daqā'iq ḥikmat-i kamālī ki dar umūr-i ma'īshat ta'alluq bi ṭabī'at dāsht luṭf-i ilāhī u 'ināyat-i yazdānī az ḥadd-i qūwa bi-ḥaiyiz-i fi'l rasānīd.* It will be recalled that there are a number of such quasi-mystical, almost neo-Platonist passages in the previous Discourse: God made the universe for Man to adapt to his best use.

1561. *dīgar umūr-i ṣinā'ī.* Cf. Note 1514 above. It will be noted that, whatever the substance of the argument here, much of its form depends on the varied shades of meaning of the Arabic root ṢN': 'art, technique, discipline, craft' must usually be differentiated in English.

1562. *ḥāl-i māl.*

1563. Respectively: *dakl . . . ḥifẓ . . . kharj.*

1564. *kifāyat u tadbīr.*

1565. *māya.*

1566. *'ār.*

1567. *danā'at.*

1568. See Notes 1104 and 1309 above, and the material to which they relate.

1569. Respectively: *sharīf . . . khasīs . . . mutawassiṭ.*

1570. *ḥaiyiz*, against the meaningless *khair* (apparently), 'good', of most texts—an easy scriptorial error.

1571. *aḥrār u arbāb-i murūwat.*

1572. *ṣiḥḥat-i ra'y u ṣawāb-i mashwara u ḥusn-i tadbīr . . . wuzarā'.*

1573. *adab u faḍl.*

1574. Cf. Note 1100 above, also Notes 17 and 18 respectively for the terms usually employed to distinguish Astronomy and Astrology. The category designated is *udabā' u fuḍalā'.*

1575. *suvārī u sipāhgarī u ḍabṭ-i thughūr u daf'-i a'dā' . . . furūsīyat.*

1576. *iḥtikār u siḥr . . . mufsidān.*

1577. *maskharagī u muṭribī u muqāmirī . . . sufahā'.* For the first word cf. Notes 1104 and 1309 above, for the last word cf. Note 693 and the general area of text relating to it.

1578. *nafrat-i ṭab'.*

1579. *furūmāyagān.*

1580. *rūzī-yi farākh.*

1581. *ba'd az ishtimāl bar 'adālat bi-'iffat u murūwat nazdīk bāshad va az sharah u ṭama' u irtikāb-i fawāḥish u ta'ṭīl afgandan dar muhimmāt dūr.* Ṭūsī is saying that to earn one's bread by a respectable craft in itself tends to endow one with many of the virtues, and to protect one from many of the vices, as set out particularly in the Third, Fourth and Fifth Sections, Second Division, First Discourse.

1582. *tabi'a.* Again, a fairly rare use of a word, at least in Persian.

1583. *bī-murūwatī.* 'Politeness' is here used, of course, to cover most of the attributes that go to make a man in the full, humane and civilized sense.

1584. *tathmīr.* The usual implication of this form (cf. Lane, 352:3) is that God confers great wealth on a man. In some texts it seems possible to read *tashmīr,* which would denote something like 'bestirring oneself vigorously'. However, the important consideration here is merely that more wealth should accrue, without regard to how or whence.

1585. The Arabist will recognize here some very sophisticated word-playing on the root 'RḌ: we have *'irḍ* = 'good name'; *muta'arriḍ* = 'petitioner' (cf. Lane, 2005:3); *'araḍ* = 'thing hoped for' (Lane, 2009:1); and *i'rāḍ kardan* = 'turn aside'. Cf. Note 373 above for a similar play.

1586. *bar wajh-i ittifāq.*

1587. *nuqūd u athmān-i biḍā'āt.* While *athmān* may be used as the plural of *thamīn* ('precious'), I take it to be the plural of *thaman,* understanding 'cash values of goods sold'. There is at least some difficulty here: the first alternative represents a somewhat unexpected use of the preposited adjective, the second leaves *biḍā'āt* unqualified as against its similar use in the following category. Some copyists have apparently read *biḍā'āt* as *bi-ṣinā'āt,* but 'crafts' are no longer under discussion.

1588. *ajnās u amti'a u aqwāt u biḍā'āt.*

1589. *amlāk u ḍiyā' u mawāshī.*

1590. *lu'm u taqtīr.*

1591. *az badhl-i ma'rūf imtinā' namāyand.*

1592. *isrāf u tabdhīr.*

1593. *ziyāda az ḥadd dar wajh-i wājib kharj kunad.*

1594. *riyā' u mubāhāt.* The first word also denotes 'hypocrisy', i.e. another shade of the same idea of 'making things seem other than they are'.

1595. *ṣadaqāt u zakāt,* the second being usually considered more of a statutory obligation than the first.

1596. *sakhāwat u īthār u badhl-i ma'rūf.*

1597. *mabarrāt,* probably suggesting substantial endowments.

1598. *sufahā'.* Cf. Note 1577 above.

1599. *bi-ṭīb-i nafs u inshirāḥ-i ṣadr.*

1600. *khāliṣ.*

1601. *ma'būd-i khwīsh.*

1602. *darvīshān-i nihufta-niyāz.*

1603. *ta'jīl.*

1604. *muwāṣalat.*

1605. *isrāf-i maḥḍ.*

1606. *tawassuṭ.*

1607. *inṣāf u 'adālat.*

1608. The contrast is between *'awāmm* and *khawāṣṣ*, but with an unusual application.

1609. *īn-ast qawānīn-i kullī ki dar bāb-i tamauwul bi-d-ān ḥājat uftad.*

1610. *juz'īyāt-i ān.*

1611. *ta'ahhul.*

1612. *qasīm-i ū dar kad-khudā'ī.*

1613. *nā'ib.* Cf. Note 1518 above.

1614. *fiṭnat.*

1615. *waqār u haibat nazdīk-i ahl-i khwīsh.*

1616. *taqdīr nigāh dāshtan dar infāq.*

1617. *bi-mujāmala u mudārāt u khwush-khū'ī.*

1618. *ishtimāl-i ān bar ta'alluf-i bīgānagān u ṣila-i arḥām . . . bīshtar.*

1619. *iḥtirāz(-i ū) az danā'at dar mushārakat u dar nasl u 'aqab bīshtar..*

1620. *bikr.*

1621. *bi-qabūl-i adab . . . nazdīktar.*

1622. *mushākalat-i shauhar dar khulq u 'ādat.*

1623. *nasab.*

1624. *rāghib u ṭālib..*

1625. *bar faḍā'iḥ iqdām kunand.*

1626. *bī-ḥamīyatī.*

1627. *daqīqa-i iqtiṣād,* i.e. even here one should not let the consideration weigh too heavily!

1628. *mustad'ī-yi istīlā' u tasalluṭ u istikhdām u tafauwuq-i īshān bāshad.*

1629. *bi-manzila-i khidmatgārī u mu'āwinī.*

1630. *intikās-i muṭlaq lāzim āyad.*

1631. *'aqd-i muwāṣalat.*

1632. Respectively: *haibat . . . karāmat . . . shughl-i khāṭir.*

1633. *muhīb.*

1634. *hawā u murād-i khwīsh.*

1635. *maḥabbat u shafaqat.*

1636. *dar hai'at-i jamīl dārad.* This refers, presumably, to sparing her from heavy work and providing ample allowance for clothes and cosmetics!

1637. *satr u ḥijāb-i ū az ghair-i maḥārim.*

1638. *āthār u shamā'il u āvāz.*

1639. *ṣila-i raḥim kunad,* implying that he should regard the relationship as quasi-germane.

1640. *daqā'iq-i ta'āwun u taẓāhur.*

1641. *ṣalāḥīyat u shāyistagī.*

1642. *rukhṣat.*

1643. *zanān dar khidmat-i īshān bi-mathāba-i bandagān bāshad.*

1644. *nafs-i insānī bar ta'ṭīl ṣabr na-kunad.*

1645. *farāghat az ḍarūrīyāt iqtiḍā-yi naẓar kunad dar ghair -i ḍarūrīyāt.*

1646. *khurūj.* The exact sense is guaranteed by what follows.

1647. *farṭ-i maḥabbat.*

1648. See the final Section of the previous Discourse, particularly the passage between Notes 1448 and 1455.

1649. *maṣāliḥ-i kullī.*

1650. *malāhī*. The common connotation is that of music and singing and other pastimes forbidden or frowned upon by orthodoxy.

1651. Koran XII: though the Potiphar's wife incident is a triumph of virtue for Joseph, it is feared that women may miss the point and be affected adversely. I have not located the Tradition, and it is conceivable that *dar aḥādīth āmada ast* means merely 'it is said'. Dawānī speaks only of the danger of hearing the Joseph story, thus avoiding the implication that the Koran can ever lead to evil.

1652. *sharāb*, usually implying wine.

1653. *waqāḥat u hayajān-i shahwat*.

1654. *iẓhār-i kifāyat*.

1655. *ḥusn-i taba''ul u iḥtirāz az nushūz*.

1656. *tashabbuh*.

1657. *kanīzak*. This is really a servant-girl, whose only function is to please her lord and master in every respect.

1658. *jabbār*.

1659. *akhlāq*.

1660. *tadbīr*. The word usually has in the present text the technical sense of 'regulation, management, control'.

1661. *khalāṣ*. A general term, without precise legal significance. Cf. Notes 1665 and 1666 below.

1662. *muta'adhdhir*.

1663. *va (bāyad) khwīshtan-rā az-ū bāz kharīd*.

1664. *musāmaḥat u mumāna'at u targhīb u tarhīb*.

1665. *furqat*. Cf. Note 1661 above.

1666. *mufāraqat*. Cf. Note 1661 above.

1667. *ḥukamā-yi 'arab*. It is here hardly likely that this means 'Arab(ian) Philosophers', especially since the remark in point turns on Arabic linguistic niceties of the sort much favoured by early moralists and composers of aphorisms.

1668. Respectively: *ḥannāna . . . mannāna . . . annāna . . . kaiyat al-qafā' . . . khaḍrā' al-diman*. Much of the point of these pithy Arabic terms is lost in English translation, especially since the degree of commentary involved in the latter renders the subsequent Persian observations of Ṭūsī somewhat superfluous.

1669. *ghair-i 'afīfa*. The comparison suggests, of course, that her lack of virtue is so public that her husband's shame is visible to all.

1670. *aṣlī-yi bad*. This rests on the hard-dying belief that bad stock will eventually reveal itself: an important point with the originally race-conscious Arab.

1671. *sū'-i intiẓām*. The argument would seem to be: nothing but a general upset can result from having to do with women at any time, but two particular disasters among many possible may be one's own destruction, body and soul, and one's dishonour through a wife's adultery. Some texts have *intiqām* ('vengeance') for the second word, but I can find no meaning in this.

1672. This fragment of poetry (in Persian) is not ascribed, and is unknown to me.

1673. *binya-i kaudak*.

1674. *qūwat-i tamyīz*. Cf. Note 1064 above and elsewhere.

1675. *najābat.* The term has overtones of both racial excellence and innate goodness.

1676. *isti'dād-i ta'addub.*

1677. *aḍdād.* Since virtues require cultivation, it is folly to expose them at the outset to hostile influences.

1678. *sāda.* The term more exactly signifies 'smooth, simple, naïve'.

1679. *karāmat.*

1680. *'aql u tamyīz u diyānat.* On second word cf. Note 1225 above and elsewhere.

1681. *sunan u waẓā'if-i dīn.*

1682. *īthār-i ān bar ghair.*

1683. *ahl-i sharaf u nabālat.*

1684. *ādāb-i bad.*

1685. *fuḍūlī kunad.*

1686. *maḥāsin-i akhbār u ash'ār.*

1687. The first of these two categories is in fact a metre, but it is one commonly felt to be appropriate to the utterance of brief, emotional poetry; the second category, while later put to many uses, might classically be thought of as pagan and erotic. Of the two poets, the former is the typical figure of swashbuckling paganism (d. *c.* A.D. 540), while the latter is the singer *par excellence* of love, wine and general high living, at a time (some 150 years after the Prophet's death) and in a place (the 'Abbāsid Court) justifying the expectation of more serious concern. He died *c.* A.D. 810

1688. *mukāshafa.*

1689. A quotation in Arabic of unspecified derivation. It is not Koranic, and may well be from some pre-Islamic sapiential source.

1690. *az rū-yi tajāsur.*

1691. *istiḥāla-padhīr na-buvad*, i.e. they are difficult to digest. Most texts confound the issue by omitting the negative.

1692. These terms are the standard translations adopted as far as possible throughout the text. However, they may be given here *en bloc* for reference: *ghaḍab . . . tahauwur . . . sur'at-i iqdām . . . waqāḥat . . . ṭaish.*

1693. *afāḍil u udabā'.*

1694. *waẓā'if-i adab.* In view of the words immediately following, I have rendered thus rather than by something like 'the obligations of courteous behaviour'.

1695. *durushtī.* My 'properly' (= *durust*) has also been equated with this word by some copyists, but the repetition is unusual.

1696. *ta'aṣṣub u ṭama'.*

1697. *mu'allim.*

1698. *buzurg-zāda.*

1699. *andak buvad u nīk mu'lim.*

1700. The laxness of Persian as to subjects of sentences makes it occasionally uncertain, over the last two paragraphs, as to whether the constant 'he' relates to the tutor or the child. I have adopted what seemed at least a plausible division of functions!

1701. *jamīl.*

1702. *tā bi-ma'ālī-yi umūr taraqqī namāyad.*

1703. *aghrāḍ.*

1704. *tharwat u ḍiyā' u 'abīd u khawal u khail u ṭarh-i farsh.* While the general sense of this is simply that of 'all material comforts and services', there are ambiguities in some of the terms: *'abīd* means both 'slaves' and 'servants'; *khawal* means both 'retainers' and 'livestock', as well as 'property' and 'slaves'; *khail* means both 'horsemen' (i.e. mounted escorts) and 'horses'. The last term connotes the whole furnishing of a household by reference to its staple feature, in Islamic lands, the carpet.

1705. *mu'tadil al-mizāj.*

1706. *maqṣūd-i ladhdhāt-i badanī.* Some texts omit the first word, but without affecting the implied sense. The general idea would seem to be that bodily pleasures are not something positive to be striven for, but a neutral absence of pain, which one is under no obligation to avoid.

1707. *'ilm-i akhlāq . . . 'ulūm-i ḥikmat-i naẓarī.* Cf. Notes 5, 10 and 39 above, and the introductory sections of the work generally.

1708. *bi-taqlīd.* It is essential to Ṭūsī's conception, as to all traditional views of education, that practical considerations demand the authoritative inculcation of right thinking and doing before the relatively late stage at which reason is able to scrutinize the principles involved.

1709. *bī-ikhtiyār.*

1710. *firāsat u kiyāsat.*

1711. *tā ahlīyat u isti'dād-i chi ṣinā'at u 'ilm dar-ū mafṭūr ast.*

1712. See the Second Section of the present Discourse, para. beginning with Note 1569.

1713. *dar ṭabā'i' mustauda' ast.*

1714. Koran 6:96; 36:38; 41:11.

1715. *hunarī.* The word also connotes 'excellence, virtue'.

1716. *jawāmi'-i 'ulūm u ādāb.*

1717. *ḥisāb-i dīwān u dīgar 'ulūm-i adabī.* Not merely the general reader will be moved to think twice about my rendering of the former expression in this context, but there seems little doubt that *dīwān* here has nothing to do with poetical collections: the dual function of secretary-treasurer is, after all, an ancient one. The 'other literary sciences' are such things as grammar, syntax and prosody.

1718. *adawāt u ālāt-i ū musā'id na-buvad.* It seems clear that natural abilities are under discussion here, not the tools and implements used in any particular craft.

1719. *hunarī-yi nā-āmūkhta.*

1720. The last two items are: *ḥiddat-i dhakā' u ba'th-i nashāṭ.* The others are obvious and uncontroversial.

1721. *dar ḍabṭ-i daqā'iq-i ān faḍl-i naẓarī isti'māl kunad.* The 'speculative virtue' is the ability to theorize.

1722. *sinā'āt u ādāb.*

1723. *shamātat.* The original links both effects jointly to both categories of person, but this is doubtless merely usage.

1724. *raḥl-i ū judā sāzqnd.*

1725. This is the rugged terrain at the S.W. corner of the Caspian Sea, famed for its hardy warriors.

1726. *ḥijāb.* This may or may not include wearing the veil.

1727. It is possible to substitute 'sing' or 'recite' for 'read', but this seems an improbable rendering here. There is nothing specifically Islamic about this prohibition, and such accomplishments were not uncommon in the first centuries of Islam.

1728. *bā kafu'-ī muwāṣalat* (*bāyad*) *sākht*.

1729. *mutaqaddim*. Stress the second syllable of 'precedent'.

1730. *mihtarān*.

1731. *kināya*.

1732. *alfāẓ-i gharīb u kināyāt-i nā-musta'mal*.

1733. *bar sabīl-i ta'rīḍ kināya kunad az ān*.

1734. *muzāh-i munkar*.

1735. *safīhān*. Cf. Note 1577 above.

1736. *'awāmm*.

1737. *bi-qubḥ*. Omitted in some texts.

1738. *mūḥish*.

1739. See last item in Note 1692 above.

1740. *mukhannath*.

1741. *ahwajān*.

1742. *bi-zānū nishastan*, lit. 'sit on the knees'.

1743. It is perhaps not without significance that Dawānī elaborates the fingers as the 'finger-joints', but omits the second puzzling item entirely.

1744. *girānī na-namāyad*.

1745. *bi-sabab-i ihmāl-i adabī*. The general sense is clearly that it is ultimately less trouble to acquire good new habits than to keep bad old ones; but the original is, it should be said, unduly prolix in one place and misleadingly elliptical in another.

1746. *sufra*. Some lines earlier, the words used are *khwān* and *mā'ida* respectively. None of these, of course, really denotes here anything approaching a European table set for dinner, especially a modern one.

1747. *safāhat*. Cf. Note 1577 above: the common rendering of 'folly' will not suffice in the present text, since Ṭūsī uses the word in the sense of a foolishness which thinks itself clever and makes itself a nuisance to others.

1748. *tursh-rū'ī u qabḍ*.

1749. *nadīm*.

1750. *khiradmandī u hūshyārī*.

1751. *agar ḍa'īf-sharāb buvad*.

1752. *maqām-i iḥtiyāṭ*.

1753. *ghathayān*.

1754. *ṣāḥib-i jamālī*. The in some degree homosexual implication of this is beyond doubt.

1755. *sufahā'*. For the full implications of this word, compare Notes 1577 and 1747 above.

1756. *'āqil-i fāḍil ki qawānīn u uṣūl-i af'āl-i jamīla ḍabṭ karda bāshad*.

1757. *sharā'iṭ u daqā'iq*.

1758. i.e. in A.D. 1264–65, when Ṭūsī was about 63 years of age, and some ten years before his death. The title and the introductory sentences of this Section vary slightly from recension to recension. The Avery MS omits it altogether. The style seems to have been harmonized with the main part of the work.

1759. This is the formula Ṭūsī commonly employs in reference to Hulagu (see my article *Nasir ad-Din Tusi on the Fall of Baghdad*, in the Journal of Semitic Studies, vol. VII, No. 1, p. 27, Note 1); however, since the period to which he here assigns the incident could well take in that ruler's death, the reference may equally be to his son Abaqa. Perhaps this was the first visit of inspection under the new reign?

1760. *malik al-umarā' fī al-'ālam*. This has the ring of a formal title, something like Supreme Commander-in-Chief; and Ṭūsī's heavy use of honorifics and benedictions leaves little doubt that this was an official of first-rate importance, doubtless one of several outstanding Persians (like himself) who had passed into Mongol service. It is all the stranger, therefore, that I have been unable to find any other references to him: at the same time, I have probably been handicapped by Ṭūsī's sparing use of names, itself assuredly justified by the man's accepted fame and importance. His criticism seems somewhat to have nettled Ṭūsī, who in the passages immediately following is once or twice barely polite in acceding to what he regards as a superfluous request from a man of true discernment. One cannot help wondering, either, why this man was only 'outstanding in *most* virtues'!

1761. *tālī*. The quotation is from the Koran 17:24.

1762. *'uqūq*.

1763. Passages similar to that referred to in Note 1761 above occur at 2:77, 4:40, 6:152, to mention only three. Cf. Note 979 above.

1764. *asbāb-i mulāṣiq*. A somewhat unusual term to express the idea of the intermediate links in chains of causality.

1765. *farhang u hunar u ṣinā'āt u 'ulūm u ṭarīq-i ta 'aiyush*.

1766. *mushārik u musāhim-i pidar ast dar sababīyat*.

1767. *atharī-ra ki pidar mu'addī-yi ān-ast mādar qābil shuda ast*.

1768. *sabab-i aqrab*.

1769. *mubāshir-i tarbiyat-i jismānī*.

1770. The passages of the Koran referred to in Notes 1761 and 1763 above associate the first obligation with either or both of the other two.

1771. *aṣḥāb-i sharā'i'*, i.e. those to whom a revelation has been made, which for practical purposes here means the accepted prophets.

1772. *bar sabīl-i mujāmala kardan na bar sabīl-i mukāshafa u munāza'a*. If I understand this aright, this passage is remarkable for its tolerant humanity: one may not disobey God out of hate and self-will, but some indulgence will be shown to one displeasing Him in an effort to be kind to parents!

1773. *minnat u ṭalab-i 'iwaḍ*.

1774. Cf. Note 1771 above.

1775. *rūḥānī-tar*.

1776. *ta'aqqul*, a term technically rendered as 'intellection'.

1777. *jismānī-tar*.

1778. Cf. Note 1773 above.

1779. *bi-mathāba-i*.

1780. One or more pairs of opposites of this kind will commonly serve as a way of expressing totality of action; i.e. the meaning here is: 'by all the various and never-ending tasks they perform', their masters are enabled to preserve their vigour and their awe-inspiring and dignified appearance.

1781. *ḥājāt u irādāt.*

1782. *daqīqa-i inṣāf u 'adālat.*

1783. *firāsat u ḥads u tawahhum.* For the last, Lahore and Lucknow texts have *tafahhum* or *tafhīm,* of which the former is perhaps barely acceptable ('trying to understand').

1784. *khulq tābi'-i khalq uftad.* This could of course be read (and translated) in the opposite order without really affecting the sense.

1785. *ṣāḥib-i kiyāsat u dahā'.* For the last word cf. Note 1228 above, especially since it is there allied with the word here rendered as 'deception' (cf. also Note 695).

1786. *shahāmat-i bisyār.* For this somewhat imprecise term see Note 626 above.

1787. *ālāt.* Cf. Note 1718 above.

1788. *na-shāyad ki inkār-i ū 'ain-i ṣarf bāshad az ān kār.* The Persian scholar will note the pun involved.

1789. *murūwat.* Cf. Note 1583. above.

1790. *'azl u ṣarf.*

1791. *nāṣiḥān.*

1792. *iṣlāḥ.*

1793. *ta'dīb u taqwīm.*

1794. *iṣrār.*

1795. *ta'dīb u tahdhīb.* Cf. Note 237 above, and also Note 39, for the last word—a key one in Ṭūsī.

1796. *khidmat-i nafs-rā.*

1797. *ṭabī'at.* Cf. next Note below.

1798. Respectively *ḥurr bi-ṭab' . . . 'abd bi-ṭab' . . . 'abd bi-shahwat.* It is, of course, possible to treat each combination as noun plus adjectival phrase linked by *iḍāfa,* the sense being much the same in either case.

1799. *ta'allum-i adab-i ṣāliḥ.*

1800. (*bāyad*) *murtāḍ gardānīd.*

1801. *faṣāḥat u dahā'.* Cf. Note 1785 above for last word, albeit here used wholly favourably.

1802. *jafā-yi ṭab' u qūwat-i shahwat.*

1803. *kiyāsat.* Cf. Note 1785 above.

1804. *zīrakī.*

1805. *kifāyat.*

1806. *qūwat-i ḥiss u ḥads u fahm.* So Lahore and Lucknow. Montreal (Tehran, n.d.) has an omission, giving 'strength and intuition and understanding', while the Avery MS, again, gives 'strength of intuition and conjecture' (*wahm*).

1807. The last two terms are: *qasāwat u bī-ḥifāẓī.*

1808. *fiṭrat.* The 'earlier' reference is doubtless to the early Sections of the book, particularly Discourse One, First Division, Fifth Section.

1809. *muta'akhkhir.*

1810. Respectively: *mukammilāt . . . mu'iddāt.*

1811. *ṣūrat-hā'ī-ki az wāhib al-ṣuwar fā'iḍ shavad bi-ṭarīq-i ta'āqub.* Cf. Ṭūsī's *Taṣauwurāt* (ed. W. Ivanow), pp 11 and 147.

1812. *nuṭfagī*. A remarkable instance of the flexibility of Persian!
1813. *bi-iḍāfat*.
1814. *mu'īn-i juz'ī*.
1815. *bi-sar-i khẉud*.
1816. *nisbat bi*. . . .
1817. *khidmat*.
1818. *āb*.
1819. Respectively: *khidmat-i bi-al-dhāt* and *bi-al-'araḍ*.
1820. Died *c*. A.D. 950. One of the 'founding fathers' of Islamic Philosophy, and reckoned (as his title implies) second only to Aristotle by subsequent Muslim writers. While much of his writing has not survived (including no doubt materials known to Ṭūsī), we are fairly well served in the present connection of political thought: see *The Fusul al-Madani of al-Farabi*, edited with an English translation, introduction and notes, by D. M. Dunlop (Cambridge 1961), both for its own relevance and its references to parallel material in Fārābī and others. See also N. Rescher, *Al-Fārābī: An Annotated Bibliography*, University of Pittsburgh 1962.
1821. *aqwāl u nukat*.
1822. *'anāṣir*, i.e. earth, air, fire and water. Cf. Note 1825 below.
1823. *az rū-yi insānī*.
1824. *jauharī-yi mujarrad*.
1825. *ṭabā'i'*. Cf. Note 1822 above. Dozy (II:22:2) says this is an alchemical usage.
1826. *ḥayawānāt-i tawalludī*. Cf. next Note below.
1827. *ḥayawānāt-i tawāludī*. Cf. previous Note.
1828. *ma'danīyāt*.
1829. See the text between Notes 164 and 167.
1830. See the text immediately following Note 1820.
1831. *mu'āmala*. A favourite term with Ṭūsī for relationship between man and man, and one of general Islamic usage.
1832. *madār*.
1833. *bi-takāfī u tasāwī*.
1834. i.e. an infinite number of individuals trying to accomplish separately one of the tasks of life is no improvement on one person trying to do so with all.
1835. *ḥikmat-i ilāhī*. An alternative rendering would be 'Providence'.
1836. *qūwat-i tamyīz*. Cf. Note 1225 above.
1837. *lau tasāwà al-nās la-halakū jamī'an*. I have not been able to identify.
1838. *ijtimā'*. Clearly, the term is used here in a general sense.
1839. *bar wajhī-yi khāṣṣ*. Cf. Note 1531 above.
1840. *jam'īyatī-yi makhṣūṣ*.
1841. The passage from 'Man' to 'life' is all in Arabic, and doubtless represents an echo of Aristotle's famous dictum (*Politics* I:2). Cf. Text at Note 856 above.
1842. *mutaghallib*. Cf. Notes 886 above and 1848 below.
1843. *tadbīr*.
1844. *siyāsat*.
1845. See text between Notes 850 and 870, and particularly at the sentence following Note 860. We have here an excellent demonstration

of the relative unity of the work and of the centrality of I:2:7 to that unity.

1846. *siyāsat-i ilāhī*. This has always been the basic preoccupation of all political thinkers in Islam: the ideal state informed and sustained by Revelation.

1847. *siyāsāt-i basīṭa*, i.e. the four elementary, uncompounded types, which would not normally be found in their simplicity.

1848. Respectively, the terms employed are: *siyāsat-i mulk* (or *malik*); *siyāsat-i ghalaba* (the latter could be regarded either as an abstract noun, as here, or as a plural of the persons so characterized, the 'domineering ones', cf. Note 1842 above); *siyāsat-i karāmat*; *siyāsat-i jamā'at*. It will be realized, particularly in view of what Ṭūsī immediately goes on to say in clarification, that these terms only have a very indirect relationship to the classes of government (both good and bad) elaborated by Aristotle (or Plato, who is shortly drawn into the argument). For some attempted equations, and some very valuable discussions and references, cf. Dunlop, *op.cit.* in Note 1820 above (particularly his Notes 25–29), and Rosenthal, *op. cit.* in Note 1542 above (particularly his Chapter X and the Notes thereto). See also the immediately following Notes below.

1849. *siyāsat-i fuḍalā'*. Even Plato's commendation of Monarchy in *The Republic* IV makes any straightforward identification none too easy at this point. More obvious is the relationship to Fārābī's 'Ideal City' or 'Virtuous City' (*al madīnat al-fāḍila*).

1850. *siyāsat-i khasāsat*. This seems to involve something like the equating of tyranny with democracy (the latter in the pejorative Platonic sense, *Republic* VIII).

1851. *karāmat*. The term has a number of fairly well established senses in Arabo-Persian. It was doubtless felt appropriate, by the early translators, to render the Greek *timē* ('honour, worth'), though one may doubt to what extent it is proper to equate here with Plato's timocracy (cf. Dunlop, *op. cit.* Note 28).

1852. *firaq-i mukhtalifa*: probably all that is meant here is 'people with varying purposes'. We seem to have in this category of government a distant descendant of Aristotle's 'polity' or 'constitution' (*Politics* III:7), but Ṭūsī almost immediately proceeds to link it with 'monarchy', giving the new amalgam a specifically Islamic tinge. All this crucial discussion is lacking in Dawānī.

1853. *muwazza' gardānad*. Cf. Plato, *Statesman*, towards end.

1854. *auḍā'*. The term is used here to denote non-rational ordinances, whether those of a human and arbitrary nature or those instituted by divine inspiration. Cf. Note 1862 below.

1855. *aḥkām-i 'aqlī*.

1856. *rūjḥān-i tamyīzī u faḍl-i ma'rifatī*.

1857. *ṣāḥib-i nāmūs*.

1858. *muḥdathān*. Rosenthal, *op. cit.* 215–16 is almost certainly wrong in his reading and interpretation of this word, though his argument may have merit.

1859. Respectively: *shāri'* . . . *sharī'at*. This Islamization of the Greek prototypes (see Note 1852 above) has already been foreshadowed more than once, most notably in the text at the sentence following Note 861.

1860. ***hum aṣḥāb al-quwā al-'aẓīmat al-fā-iqa***. There are several passages in *The Republic* V which might be regarded as the original of this remark.

1861. ***hum alladhīn 'ināyat allah bi-him akthar***. I am unable to find any close correspondence to this reference, though several passages in both Aristotle and Plato echo this general idea.

1862. ***dar taqdīr-i aḥkām***. Cf. Note 1854 above.

1863. ***ta'yīd-i ilāhī***. Cf. Note 1869 below.

1864. ***malik 'alà al-iṭlāq***, i.e without qualification.

1865. ***ṣinā'at-i mulk***. As elsewhere, the last word could be read ***malik***, i.e. 'of a king', with the same sense.

1866. ***imām . . . imāmat***. Ṭūsī here speaks, of course, as a Shī'ite. Cf. Note 1869 below.

1867. ***mudabbir-i 'ālam***. For a discussion of this term (which would normally be used in Islamic thought only in reference to God) cf. Rosenthal, *op. cit.*, p. 301, Note 25. Cf. also Note 1883 below.

1868. ***insān-i madanī***. See previous Note, and compare Ṭūsī's very general view of this man's role with that of Dawānī: 'the man who watches over the affairs of the city in a fitting manner'.

1869. Respectively *nāṭiq . . . asās*. This is pure Ismā'īlī doctrine. The terms are well attested, as may be seen in any standard article or work on Ismā'īlism, but see particularly Ṭūsī's own *Taṣauwurāt*, W. Ivanow ed., p. xlii (*asās*) and Chs. XXIV and XXV (*nāṭiq*, or more usually the pure Persian word *gūyā*). It is to be observed that this passage is omitted in the Avery MS and in Humā'ī, while the Montreal text (Tehran, n.d.) adds 'Philosophers' after 'some' (*qaumī az ḥukamā'*). Dawānī does not not have it either, but his divergence is especially great hereabouts.

1870. ***mustaḥiqq-i mulk ū buvad dar ḥaqīqat***. See following Note.

1871. ***agar-chi bi-ṣūrat hīch-kas bi-d-ū iltifāt na-kunad***. This, again, is pure Ismā'īlism, though it has at different times been the position of Shī'ism generally and, indeed, of most Muslims: God's chosen ruler on earth is not necessarily the *de facto* authority, and may not even be known to the mass of mankind. Indeed, that is why the world is usually in such dire straits!

1872. ***marāsim***.

1873. ***wilāyat-i taṣarruf***.

1874. ***ḥikmat-i madanī***, 'civic wisdom' (cf. Note 4 above). The English rendering 'Politics' covers both this theoretical aspect and the practical process of government (see the term used in Note 39 above).

1875. ***qawānīn-i kullī***.

1876. ***mauḍū'-i īn 'ilm hai'atī buvad jamā'at-rā***.

1877. ***ra'īs-i hameh ṣinā'āt***. See *Nicomachean Ethics* I:2.

1878. See the text at Note 1876..

1879. ***maḥalla***. This may be anything from a street to a district.

1880. ***umam-i kibār***. The modern equivalent might be nations. Cf. Note 1886 below.

1881. ***ra'īs***.

1882. ***mar'ūs***.

1883. Respectively: ***ra'īs-i 'ālam . . . ra'īs-i ru'asā'***. Cf. Note 1867 above.

1884. *muṭā'-i muṭlaq u muqtadā-yi nau'* . . . *bi-istiḥqāq*.

1885. *dar ḥukm-i ān yak shakhṣ*.

1886. *ummat*. Cf. Note 1880 above.

1887. See the second paragraph and subsequently in the present Section.

1887a. *ta'līf*.

1888. *maḥḍ-i jaur u ẓulm*. Ṭūsī has already argued (between Notes 1877 and 1878) that human association is the only just state.

1889. *mu'āmalāt* . . . *bar qā'ida-i inṣāf*. Cf. Notes 614, 914 and 1831 above.

1890. See Note 725 above.

1891. *ahl-i faḍl u tamyīz*. *Faḍīlat* is the word usually rendered as 'virtue', *faḍl* being less precise: 'merit, excellence, superiority, accomplishment, learning.' For the second term cf. Note 1225 above and elsewhere. Generally, cf. also Note 1856 above.

1892. *muqaddir-i auwal*.

1893. In the previous Section *passim*.

1894. In particular in the Seventh Section of the Second Division of the First Discourse, final paragraph. Cf. also Note 1299 above.

1895. Respectively: *ittiḥād-i ṣinā'ī* . . . *ittiḥād-i ṭabī'ī*, or *ṭab'ī*.

1896. Reading *qishr*, but some texts have *qasr* (omitting three dots). In the first case, the idea would seem to be that one takes the shape of the other as closely as does a rind; in the second, where the meaning is that of 'force', we have the less satisfactory idea that the artificial is a forced imitation of the natural.

1897. *naṣafa*. The Avery MS and Humā'ī have the more plausible reading *niṣf* (the ordinary word for 'half'). The point of this argument is, of course, lost in English.

1898. *munṣif mutanāza'-fīhi-rā bā ṣāḥib-i khwud munāṣafa kunad*.

1899. *tanṣīf az lawāḥiq-i takaththur bāshad*.

1900. *qudamā'-i ḥukamā'*. In as far as this means a coherent school, rather than a continuing philosophical tendency, the probable intention is Empedocles. The title *aṣḥāb-i maḥabbat u ghalaba* may be an echo of the Empedoclean 'Love and Strife', but cf. Notes 886 and 1848 above, and 1916 below.

1901. I have used 'some' and 'some measure of' to convey the force of the unity-suffix in the original Persian.

1902. *'ishq*. The use of this word here rather than the constant *maḥabbat* is clearly deliberate. The former is commonly felt to connote violent (often sexual) passion, the latter disinterested affection, but any such marked contrast might be out of place here; rather, perhaps, is the former the external and physical expression of the latter.

1903. *sarayān* . . . *dar jumlagī-yi kā'ināt*.

1904. *bar-ū fā'iḍ shuda ast*. At the act of creation.

1905. *dar 'urf-i muta'akhkhirān*. i.e. the Islamic philosophers, as opposed to the Greeks. Cf. Note 297 above.

1906. *qūwat-i nuṭqī* (cf. Note 135 above): i.e. that love is an act of the intelligence (and the will), an act proper to human beings only.

1907. *marākiz*. It should be observed that the grammatical construction, and hence that of the argument, from here to the end of the paragraph is extremely loose. As usual, however, the intention of Ṭūsī is clear enough for practical purposes.

1908. *gurīkhtan-i īshān az dīgar jihāt*. Cf. Note 1917 below.

1909. *mushākalāt*. See Note 1937 below.

1910. *bar nisbat-hā-yi mu'aiyan u maḥdūd*.

1911. For the first and the last, see Note 843 above. The second is *massāḥī* (or *misāḥī*) and refers to surface-measurement.

1912. *mabda'-i af'ālī-yi gharīb*.

1913. *khawāṣṣ u asrār-i ṭabā'i'*.

1914. *tanaffurāt-i mizājī*. The opposite of the 'affinities that have arisen in their mixing' (see Note 1909 above).

1915. *nafrat-i sang-i bāghiḍ al-khall az sirka*. I am unable to discover any very obvious and striking opposite of magnetic attraction, though this has every appearance of being a well-known technical term. Pliny, XXIII:27, has several examples of vinegar's alleged power to split stone, cure gout-stone, etc.

1916. *az qabīl maḥabbat u mabghaḍat*. Cf. Note 1900 above.

1917. *mail u harab*. Cf. Note 1908 above.

1918. *ḥayawānāt-i ghair-i nāṭiqa*.

1919. *ulfat u nafrat*..

1920. *sarī' al-'aqd wa-al-inḥilāl*. The word for 'slow' is *baṭī'*. Cf. Note 1925 below.

1921. *maṭālib*.

1922. *bi-ḥasab-i basāṭa*.

1923. Respectively: *ladhdhat . . . naf' . . . khair*.

1924. *asbāb*, so rendered to avoid confusion with the almost immediately following *'illat*.

1925. *zūd bandad u zūd gushāyad*. The word for slow is *'dīr'*. Cf. Note 1920 above.

1926. *bā shumūl-i wujūd*. Cf. next Note.

1927. *bā 'izzat-i wujūd*. Cf. preceding Note.

1928. *iqtiḍā'-i imtinā'-i infikāk kunad*.

1929. *az ṣadāqat 'āmm-tar*.

1930. *mawaddat*.

1931. *'ishq*. Cf. Note 1902 above.

1932. *jauhar-i basīṭ-i ilāhī*.

1933. *walah*..

1934. *'ishq-i tāmm u maḥabbat-i ilāhī*.

1935. *muta'allihān*. It should be stressed that this word often has a prejorative connotation for Muslims, since God's very transcendence makes any meaningful assimilation an almost blasphemous conception. In the present case, it is clear that Ṭūsī is at least sceptical of their claims.

1936. Despite the varying distortions of this name in the several recensions, it is clear that Heraclitus is intended.

1937. The terms 'affinity', 'concordant' etc. are varying parts of speech from the same root and forms: SHKL III and VI.

1938. 'Synthesis' is used to translate various formations based on 'LF II and V. It should be stressed, however, that alongside its basic sense of 'putting together, composing', it has clear connotations of 'sociability, affection, familiarity'. Cf. Notes 843 and 1887a above.

1939. *dhawāt u ḥaqā'iq*.

1940. Respectively: *ittiṣāl . . . infiṣāl*.

1941. *shahawāt u karāmāt*. Ṭūsī often makes the point that the quest for honour and admiration can be as powerful (and as unworthy) a motive as mere satisfaction of animal appetites. Cf. Notes 821 and 1851 above regarding the second term.

1942. There is a harking back here to much of the esoteric teaching of the First Discourse, and the length and frequency of this type of argument should not be ignored in favour of what are felt by some scholars to be Ṭūsī's essential political ideas in the purely practical sense. See remark in Note 1845 above about the work's unity. 'Majesty' is 'Beauty' in some texts (*jamāl* for *jalāl*); for the term 'effuse' see Note 1904 above.

1943. *ṣafā-yi tāmm*.

1944. Cf. Notes 1920 and 1925 above and the argument in those places.

1945. *jam'īyat*.

1946. *mu'ānasat*.

1947. As so often, the philological point of this argument is lost in English: the term rendered by 'fellowship' and that for 'Man' are usually regarded as derived from the same root 'NS. It is possible, however, for a poor Arabic scholar (or a wit) to try to relate the second to the root for 'forgetfulness' NSY. The general thought is nevertheless clear: man is by his very nature sociable, a fact having implications wider than the purely philological or literary, but supported by considerations from those areas.

1948. *uns-i ṭabī'ī*.

1949. *ḥikmat-i ḥaqīqī*. Cf. Note 1835 above. The argument is that God has made man to be thus by nature and then reinforced the inclination by religious ordinances (*sharā'i'*) and the commonly accepted behaviour of polite society (*ādāb-i maḥmūd*).

1950. *'ibādāt*.

1951. *sharī'at-i islām*.

1952. *namāz-i jamā'at-rā bar namāz-i tanhā . . . tafḍīl nihāda bāshad*.

1953. *mu'āmalāt*. Cf. Note 1831 above.

1954. *waḍ' kard*.

1955. The two occasions are those of the great Feasts: the Feast of Sacrifices (on the 10th of the Pilgrimage Month) and the Feast of Fast-breaking at the end of Ramaḍān.

1956. *fiṭrat*.

1957. *ṣāḥib-i sharī'at*, i.e. specifically the Prophet Muḥammad.

1958. *shar'*.

1959. *az taṣauwur-i īn 'ibādāt u talfīq-i ān bā yak-dīgar*.

1960. These two clauses (desirable to complete the sense) are found only in Montreal (Tehran, n.d.) and Humā'ī. The text hereabouts has several minor infelicities in the different recensions.

1961. *'āshiq u ma'shūq*. There is no question that the reference here is to sexual love: cf. Note 1902 above.

1962. *maḥabbat-i lauwāma*.

1963. *fasād-i nīyat*.

1964. *istibṭā'*.

1965. *ṣu'ūbat-i shumūl-i ān.*

1966. *munāsabat-i jauhar,* i.e. such men are already substantially identical. Cf. next Note below.

1967. i.e. it is individuation alone that keeps such substantially identical beings apart. Cf. previous Note.

1968. *mutafaḍḍil u mun'im.*

1969. *maḥabbatī-yi dhātī.*

1970. *ham-nafs* (or *ham nafas*)*-i khwud.* The first expression denotes 'sharing the same soul', the second refers to one 'sharing the same breath'. The sense is obvious.

1971. *wujūd.* In Persian the term commonly means 'body', hence my addition of the world 'physical' to the normal meaning of 'existence'.

1972. Cf. text at Note 1764.

1973. *mustakhlaṣ.*

1974. *khayālī dar pas-i ḥijābī.*

1975. *ma'lūl u musabbab.*

1976. Cf. text between Notes 1774 and 1775 above.

1977. Respectively: *abawī . . . banawī . . . akhawī.*

1978. *riyāsatī-yi taghallubī.* Cf. Note 1848 above.

1979. Cf. Note 1916 above.

1980. *infi'ālāt u kudūrāt-i āfāt.* i.e. such love is ever active and pure.

1981. *'ālim-i rabbānī.* Another probable Ismā'īlī term (cf. Notes 1869 and 1871 above). W. Ivanow, in his translation of Ṭūsī's *Taṣauwurāt* (p. 33), renders it 'blessed with Divine knowledge'.

1982. *'ārif na-bāshad.* Another pregnant term: it may be pointed out that there is no contrast here between the roots 'LM and 'RF, as is so often supposed to be the case.

1983. *tawahhum,* sometimes rendered elsewhere as 'conjecture, estimation'.

1984. *khāliq u ma'būd-i khwud.*

1985. *maḥḍ-i tauḥīd u mujarrad-i īmān.* Though such ideas are not limited to Islam, these particular terms are of key importance in the Islamic faith.

1986. Koran 12:106.

1987. *mudda'ī-y-ān . . . muḥaqqiqān-i īshān,* respectively.

1988. Koran 34:12.

1989. *maḥbūb.*

1990. *sabab-i maḥsūs u 'illat-i qarīb.* Cf. Notes 1764 and 1768 above, and the argument of the text thereabouts.

1991. *mutammim-i wujūd u mubqī-yi dhawāt.* It is teachers, in other words, who bring a human being to his full development and lead the essential part of him to eternal life.

1992. *sabab-i auwal.* Cf. Note 1994 below.

1993. *rabbī-yi jismānī u rabbī-yi rūḥānī.* One suspects that the old propagandist and indoctrinator speaks here! Some texts have *abī* ('a father') in second place, and Dawānī follows this: the sense would be the ostensibly more innocent 'master of the body and father of the spirit', but it is difficult to avoid the impression that Ṭūsī really sees the teacher as the disciple's master in a very full sense of the word.

1994. *'illat-i ūlà.* Cf. Note 1992 above.

1995. After first two words of my rendering, this quotation is in Arabic, suggesting that it is taken bodily from an Arabic source. Dawānī Persianizes it somewhat, though he does not hesitate to quote Arabic immediately afterwards.

1996. Respectively: *faḍīlat-i tāmm . . . ḥikmat-i khāliṣ*.

1997. *shirk-i ṣirf*.

1998. *jahl-i maḥḍ u sakhf-i muṭlaq*.

1999. *mu'āsharat-i bi-wājib*.

2000. *nīyat-i khair*.

2001. *ma'ārif u āshnāyān-rā bi-manzila-i dast u pā dārad*. i.e. they are mere instruments and appendages of his essential self, as against friends, who are like his very soul. Most texts replace 'hands and feet' by 'friends' (*dūstān*): what precedes, as well as what follows, seems to me to rule this out as anything more than a scriptorial confusion.

2002. *ahl u 'ashīra*. As in the Third Section of the Second Discourse, the first term doubtless connotes primarily the wife or wives.

2003. *radā'at-i hai'atī ki dar dhāt-i ū mutamakkin buvad*.

2004. *radā'at mahrūb 'an-hā buvad ṭab'an*.

2005. *ū-rā bī-khwud gardānad*. The term is sometimes used in describing mystical ecstasy, but it often has (as here) connotations of foolish unconcern with reality. 'Accidental pleasures' are those having no essential reality, as explained *passim* in the First Discourse.

2006. The whole argument here harks back markedly to the First Discourse, particularly the Tenth (and final) Section of its Second Division. There is a distinct divergence here in Dawānī.

2007. *mulāzim-i iḥsān*.

2008. *ladhīdh u maḥbūb mukhtār buvad*.

2009. *murīd u muqtadī*. There may be esoteric implications here: the first term is well known in mystical usage.

2010. *ḥālatī-yi ghair-i mu'tād*. The reference is, of course, to impulsive acts of kindness prompted by unusual circumstances.

2011. An Arabic proverb, involving an unusual employment of the word *rabb* as the *maṣdar* of *rabba* ('to order, regulate'—the sense I have given to *tartīb* a few words previously).

2012. Respectively: *muḥsin . . . muḥsan ilai-hi*.

2013. *ma'rūf-kunanda*. The kindness here must be gratuitous.

2014. *chūn maṣnū'i ū mustaqīm buvad maḥabbat-i ū bi-ghāyat bi-rasad*. Since in this case the praiseworthy act is done to someone in particular, the doer's pleasure in the act passes into love for the object thereof.

2015. *ākhidh munfa'il ast u mu'ṭī fā'il*.

2016. *ḥurrīyat*. There is a temptation to render this by 'liberality', but compare the list of terms in Note 632 above.

2017. See Note 1923 above and the passage to which it refers.

2018. *juz'-i ilāhī*. The 'divine part' in Man referred to again a few lines later.

2019. *samāḥat u badhl u mu'āsāt*. For these terms in their proper context cf. Note 647 above.

2020. *shahāmat u kibr-i nafs*. For these terms in their proper context see Note 626 above.

2021. *inṣirāf bi-umūr-i 'aqlī u isti'māl-i ra'y-hā-yi ilāhī*.

2022. *akhlāq u faḍā'il-i insānī.*

2023. *arwāḥ-i pākān u firishtagān-i muqarrab.* This passage is strongly reminiscent, in its rhapsodic and possibly esoteric character, of several in the First Discourse, particularly in the First Division.

2024. *muqarrabān-i ḥaḍrat-i ilāhī,* i.e. the angels as above.

2025. *usṭuqusāt-i arba'a.* A more common term is that used in 1822.

2026. *abrār-i muṭahhar.*

2027. *chīzī-yi basīṭ ki umūr-i 'aqlī u aṣnāf-i khairāt bi-d-ū mutashabbih bāshand.*

2028. *istiḥqāq-i ism-i maḥabbat-i ū.*

2029. *lafẓī iṭlāq karda ast ki dar lughat-i mā iṭlāq na-kunand.*

2030. *ta'ahhud-i ū kunad.*

2031. *az ḥayāt-i ṭab'ī u quwā-yi nafsānī munazzah u mubarra' bāshad.*

2032. Whatever the general applications of this statement, it may be pointed out that for Muslims the Prophet Muḥammad is *par excellence* the Chosen One of all mankind, and sometimes of all Creation.

2033. *bāzī bā rāḥat mānad.*

2034. *ṭabī'ī al-shakl bahīmī al-aṣl.*

2035. *insī.* While this could theoretically be read otherwise (e.g. *unsī*), this sense is virtually guaranteed by what follows.

2036. *himmat-hā-yi ḥayawānāt-i murda,* i.e. 'dead' in their lack of both soul and intelligence.

2037. *'āqibat.*

2038. *bi-juththa khurd.* This term, again, usually connotes a *dead* body. Cf. Note 2036 above.

2039. *az kāffa-i khalā'iq buzurgvār-tar . . . jauharī-yi ra'īs.*

2040. *māya.*

2041. *gharīzat-i pāk u ṭab'-i nīk.*

2042. *bi-shar'.* Again, there is more than a suggestion here of an unorthodox point of view, one shared from different sides by Ṣūfī mystics and Ismā'īlī theorists: the Law is for the masses.

2043. *sharī'at,* i.e. pre-eminently of Islam.

2044. *najābat.* Nobility of character and race is again implicit here.

2045. *bi-tarbiyat-i muwāfiq makhṣūṣ gardad,* i.e. one strengthening his innate qualities.

2046. *ḥaqq.*

2047. *tafalsuf u iṭrāḥ-i 'asabīyat.* Both terms may be either favourable or pejorative: the alternatives (which can hardly apply here) would be 'dabbling in philosophy and rejecting zeal (or solidarity)'.

2048. *ta'dīb-i shar'ī va yā ta'līm-i ḥikamī.* The element of pressure involved tempts one to read the last word as *ḥukmī* ('legal, authoritative, related to judgment'), but this is probably both irrelevant and anachronistic. Cf. Dozy II: 310: 2.

2049. *ḥukmī u khāṣṣīyatī u hai'atī.* The first word is probably used here in the vague general sense of 'situation, how a thing stands both in itself and in relation to other things'. This meaning, though common in philosophical writings and in popular usage, is poorly attested in lexicons.

2050. *az rū-yi ta'alluf u tarakkub.* Cf. Note 1938 above.

2051. *madīna-i fāḍila . . . madīna-i ghair-i fāḍila.* Cf. particularly Notes 1848–52 above and the related text.

2052. *madīna-i jāhila*. See reference in Note 2051 above.
2053. *madīna-i fāsiqa*. See reference in Note 2051 above.
2054. *qūwat-i fikrī*.
2055. *ba khwud qānūnī dar takhaiyul āvurda bāshand.*
2056. *madīna-i ḍālla*. See reference in Note 2051 above.
2057. *nawābit*, i.e. like vegetation or weeds.
2058. *bar yak wajh*.
2059. *muqauwam bi-tahdhīb u tasdīd-i 'aqlī*.
2060. *muqaddar bi-qawānīn-i 'adālat u sharā'iṭ-i siyāsat*.
2061. *fiṭrat-hā-yi salīm u 'ādāt-i mustaqīm*. The justification of diversity as a principle of order will be found in the First Section of the present Discourse (text, between Notes 1834 and 1838). We pass here to the relation of such a principle to the theory of Prophethood, once again viewed in a context that may be Ismā'īlī, and certainly has esoteric overtones. Cf. next Note following.
2062. *ta'yīd-i ilāhī u irshād-i rabbānī*. Cf. Note 1863 above.
2063. *qūwat-hā-yi darrāka*.
2064. See Note 134 above.
2065. *ma'rūf-i nafs*, i.e. God.
2066. *muthul u khayālāt u ṣuwar*. Subsequently, the first word occurs in its Persian form as *mithāl-hā* or as *amthila*. Cf. Note 2089 below.
2067. *afāḍil-i ḥukamā'*.
2068. *ma'rifat-i 'aqlī-yi ṣirf*.
2069. *ghāyat-i idrāk-i īshān taṣauwurī buvad*. The first word is ambiguous and may be rendered 'object' rather than 'utmost', but this would not seem to affect the sense.
2070. *tanzīh az ān wājib dānand*. There are probably strong Islamic overtones here, the object of 'removal' (i.e. exaltation above all else) being God Himself. Cf. Note 2080 below.
2071. *aḥkām-i ṣūratī ki dar khayāl-i īshān mutamaththil buvad*.
2072. *ahl-i īmān*.
2073. *auḍā' u lawāḥiq*.
2074. *ahl-i taslīm*, i.e. those who concur in the ideas of others. Cf. Dozy I: 679:1.
2075. *mustaḍ'afān*. Cf. Dozy II: 10:1.
2076. *ṣūrat-parastān*.
2077. *qibla*, i.e. the point by which Muslims orientate themselves in worship. A touch of this kind gives the argument a reassuring Islamic context. See also Note 2094 below.
2078. *kallimū al-nās 'alà qadri 'uqūli-him*. In several similar forms (Dawānī varies somewhat, for example) this *ḥadīth* is particularly popular with Shī'ites. Its possible esoteric implications are obvious.
2079. Respectively *muḥakkam . . . mutashābih*. Cf. Dozy I: 311: 1 and 726: 2. Cf. also Koran 3:5.
2080. Respectively *tanzīh-i ṣirf . . . tashbīh-i maḥḍ*. Cf. Note 2070 above. Few statements justifying the esoteric attitude could be put more bluntly, and shockingly, to orthodox Muslims.
2081. *qiyāsāt-i burhānī*.
2082. *iqnā'īyāt*. Cf. Dozy II:413: 1.
2083. *shi'rīyāt u mukhaiyalāt*.

2084. *munkharit.*

2085. *ṣūrat u waḍ'.*

2086. *fāḍil-i auwal ki mudabbir-i madīna-i fuḍalā' bāshad.*

2087. *ta'aṣṣub u ta'ānud.*

2088. *millat u madhhab.* These words have varying connotations in different contexts, but it may be suggested that while the second is usually a religious division within Islam, the first may take in other religions as well.

2089. *ikhtilāf-i rusūm-i khayālāt u amthila.* Cf. Note 2066 above.

2090. *malik-i a'ẓam u ra'īs-i ru'asā' bi-ḥaqq.* Cf. Notes 1871 and 1883 above.

2091. *riyāsat u khidmat.*

2092. *khadam-i muṭlaq.* Cf. Note 2126 below.

2093. *ma'lūl-i akhīr.*

2094. *sunnat-i ilāhī ki ḥikmat-i muṭlaq ast.* Once again (cf. Note 2077 above) reassuring Islamic terms are juxtaposed with references to philosophical ideas.

2095. Cf. argument above in text between Notes 2067 and 2074.

2096. *istiqrā'*, i.e. there is a sufficient number of obvious and actual cases to justify the drawing of this conclusion: the wrong (*bāṭil*) is a perversion of the right (*ḥaqq*).

2097. *ta'alluf u tawaddud.* Cf. Note 1938 above.

2098. Cf. Note 1867 above. The phrase following reads: *dar auḍā'-i nawāmīs u maṣāliḥ-i ma'āsh taṣarruf kunand.*

2099. The Sasanian, ruled A.D. 226–241. He became a stock originator of wisdom in mediaeval Muslim literature, particularly that written (as here) in a Persian and Shī'ite atmosphere. The original is in Arabic and may have come from several sources, but cf. Ardashīr's last testament as given in the *Shāhnāma* of Firdausī (e.g. Turner-Macan ed. p. 1412) for an impressively full and repetitive statement of this theme. The idea has served many causes in Islam and been attributed to other authorities.

2100. *yak maṭlūb . . . ma'ād-i ḥaqīqī.*

2101. Respectively: *lāḥiq . . . sābiq.*

2102. Quoted in Arabic: *ṭariq al-'aql wāḥid.*

2103. A version of Matthew 5:17, quoted in Arabic from one of the Arabic recensions known in the mediaeval Islamic world.

2104. It is clear that *taṣarruf* is here used in the unfavourable sense of 'arbitrary judgment and action', but it is doubtless those exercising it who are here at fault, since it belongs rightfully only to kings.

2105. *qūwat-i ta'aqqul.* Cf. Dunlop, *Fuṣūl*, p. 84, Note 30. He is doubtless right in seeing this as *in effect* 'practical wisdom', but the dichotomy he introduces by *translating* so seems to me unjustified and foreign to the spirit of mediaeval thought. Cf. Note 2116 below.

2106. *afāḍil.* Cf. Note 2067 above and its context.

2107. *jamā'atī ki 'awāmm u furūtarān-rā bi-marātib-i kamāl-i iḍāfī mī-rasānand.*

2108. *dhū* (doubtless for *dhawū*) *al-alsina.* All the sciences given here will be found in Notes 1098 and 1100 above, save the third (*khaṭābat*) and the fifth (*shi'r*).

2109. *taqdīr-i wājib.*

2110. *tasāwī u takāfī.* The essential point of reference here is the Seventh Section of the Second Division, First Discourse.

2111. *muqaddirān.* The first two sciences will be found in Note 1100 above; the others are *handasa u ṭibb u nujūm* (for the last cf. Note 18 above and context).

2112. *baiḍa.* Cf. Note 910 above and context.

2113. *mujāhidān.* 'Ardour' represents *ḥamīyat,* for the *jam'īyat* of Lahore and Lucknow.

2114. *mālīyān.* Both Dunlop (*Fuṣūl,* p. 50, para. 53) and Rosenthal (*Political Thought,* p. 218) emphasize the connotation of 'wealth' in this title: this seems to me only incidental to the fact that they are the class responsible for commodities rather than services. The term for 'tax' (*kharāj*) has important Islamic associations, but too much should not be made of this.

2115. *riyāsat-i 'uẓmā.*

2116. *ta'aqqul-i tāmm.* Cf. Note 2105 above.

2117. *jaudat-i iqnā' u takhaiyul,* cf. Note 2082 above.

2118. *qūwat-i jihād.* It is questionable whether one should, with both Rosenthal and Dunlop *passim,* render this simply 'holy war' in the narrowly Islamic sense. It seems to me rather that once again (cf. Note 2094 above) Islamic-sounding terminology is skilfully interwoven with the purely philosophical. See again Note 2120 below.

2119. *riyāsat-i ḥikmat.*

2120. *sunan* (with, subsequently, the singular *sunnat*). Once again, it seems to me, the remarks in Notes 2094 and 2118 above apply.

2121. *istinbāṭ-i ān-chi muṣarraḥ na-y-āyad.* More important than the bare principle of legal precedent here is the implication for the organic development of a society based on necessarily finite revelation. The word 'rulers' is not in the original, which simply has 'past ones' (*gudhashtagān*).

2122. *khiṭāb u iqnā'.* Cf. Note 2117 above.

2123. *riyāsat-i aṣḥāb-i sunnat.*

2124. *takhaiyul-i ghāyat az tilqā-yi nafs-i khwud.*

2125. *ta'aqqul-i istinbāṭ-i maqādīr.* Cf. Note 2105 above: the distinction drawn by Dunlop is clearly applicable here.

2126. *khādim-i muṭlaq.* Cf. Note 2092 above. The 'invention' they lack is *istinbāṭ,* elsewhere rendered 'deduction' (Notes 99 and 2121) and 'discovery' (Note 2125).

2127. The argument of these two paragraphs relates to the text between Notes 1835 and 1838.

2128. For the original terms and their importance, see Notes 2051, 2052, 2053 and 2056 above.

2129. *bi-ḥasab-i basāṭat,* i.e. in an uncompounded state.

2130. These terms, which may in some cases be compared with those listed in Notes 1848–51 above (as well as with Dunlop, *Fuṣūl,* particularly Notes 25 and 28; and Rosenthal, *Political Thought,* particularly pp. 135–37 and Notes thereto), are as follows: (1) *ijtimā'-i ḍarūrī*; (2) *i. nadhālat*; (3) *i. khissat*; (4) *i. karāmat*; (5) *i. taghallubī*; (6) *ijtimā'-i ḥurrīyat.* It may be briefly noted here that in the earlier passage (3) and (5) would appear to be identical, while the present (1) and (2) do not appear in any obvious guise. The exact form of (2), moreover, as will be seen from the arguments in Dunlop and Rosenthal, is open to dispute: some texts even have the curious and unlikely form (with doubtless the same intended meaning as I have given) of *madhāllat*. Most of what follows is missing in Dawānī.

2131. *ma'hūd*, i.e. 'of long standing', 'accepted as familiar'.

2132. The Arabic term is as ambiguous as the English: *ijārat*.

2133. Literally 'the pleasures of sensible things', *ladhdhāt-i maḥsūsāt*.

2134. *mankūḥāt*. Cf. Note 145 above.

2135. *mudun-i jāhilīya*. The use of a variant on the term previously employed, and one redolent with Islamic overtones of disapproval for pre-Islamic society, may be intentional. Cf. Note 2149 below.

2136. *maghbūṭ*.

2137. Respectively: *bar tasāwī . . . bar tafāḍul*. Cf. Note 2144 below.

2138. *musā'adat*: used of propitious or favouring situations.

2139. *ghalaba u ḥasab*.

2140. *yā az qibal-i khwud yā az ḥusn-i tadbīr*, i.e. either by contributions from his own purse or by leading them in the paths of gain and and economy. The third word, a somewhat unusual use in Persian, is given in some texts as *qabīl*, which would offer no useful sense here ('of his own kind'?).

2141. *umam*. A term which would normally imply other communities than his own, and this may be intended here.

2142. *mālik-i riqāb*.

2143. *ḥasīb*.

2144. *mu'āwaḍa yā murābaḥa*. Cf. Note 2137 above.

2145. Cf. Note 1704 above.

2146. *madīna-i jabbārān*. I use this term to preserve a distinction from *jā'ir* (rendered 'tyrant'), cf. Notes 872–4 above and elsewhere. Cf. also Notes 2148 below and 1658 above.

2147. *tadbīr*. i.e. administrative ability.

2148. *jafā'*. Cf. Note 2146 above.

2149. *jāhilīyat*. Cf. Note 2135 above. The pagan Arabs were notorious for capturing spoils and then frittering the proceeds away in wasteful entertainments.

2150. Respectively: *buzurg-himmatān . . . aṣḥāb-i rujūlīyat*.

2151. These are respectively the Base City and the Servile City: see Note 2130 above and text following. 'Elect' = *khawāṣṣ*.

2152. See Notes 1848 and 2130 above.

2153. *muṭlaq u mukhallà bāshad bā nafs-i khwud*.

2154. *mazīd-i faḍlī*. This sentence and the next one or two show divergences in the different texts: some have omissions, some differences in order, and all certain minor corruptions and grammatical infelicities.

2155. *ṭawā'if*. A term of wide application in Islamic usage, but always suggesting some fragmentation from a whole.

2156. *jumhūr*.

2157. *bi-tafḍīl*. Some texts seem to have *bi-tafaḍḍul*.

2158. *i'tiqād*.

2159. *tawahhum namūda*.

2160. *murā'īyān.*

2161. *muḥarrifān,* literally the 'inverters, twisters, falsifiers'.

2162. *tafsīr u ta'bīr.* The second of these terms often suggests, in an Islamic context, a twisting of meaning for tendentious ends.

2163. *bāghīyān.*

2164. *māriqān.*

2165. *mughāliṭān.*

2166. *taṣauwur.*

2167. *dar ṣūrat-i adilla.*

2168. *kaif īyat-i mu'āsharat-i juz'ī.* It should be noted that Dawānī is far ampler in this Section than Ṭūsī, using many lavish examples.

2169. *ri'āsat-i ri'āsāt.*

2170. *lāzim.*

2171. Cf. Note 1866 above.

2172. *sā'is,* i.e. the one responsible for government.

2173. *khawal u 'abīd.* For the first term cf. Note 1704 above.

2174. *ghībat.* For 'tomfoolery' in its proper context, see Notes 1104 and 1309 above.

2175. All these are well-known Arabic proverbs. The connection between the first two and the third seems somewhat forced, depending primarily on the double sense of *zamān*: 'age' or 'destiny'.

2176. *ubūwat,* literally 'paternity'.

2177. *tajārib-i marḍī,* i.e. drawing on things one knows from experience to be proper. Cf. Note 2183 below.

2178. *'azm al-rijāl . . . 'azm al-mulūk.*

2179. The 'Abbāsid Caliph, son of Hārūn al-Rashīd, who died in 218/833. His reign is often considered the most brilliant in Islamic history in terms of intellectual activity, but it was marred by much intolerance on the part of the 'enlightened'.

2180. In Arabic, badly corrupt in most texts. There are Traditions to this effect also.

2181. *ba'd az taqdīr,* i.e. God may ordain otherwise, but this is normally the case.

2182. *ṭālib-i dīn . . . ṭālib-i tha'r.* Ṭūsī, as a true Muslim, goes on to condemn the second with its pagan, pre-Islamic associations.

2183. *mulk-i taghallubī . . . tajārib-i harjī.* For the sense of the first term, cf. the long passage on the City of Domination in the preceding Section; for the second term, cf. Note 2177 above.

2184. *daulat-hā*; elsewhere *duwal.* The exact nature of these political entities is irrelevant to the argument here.

2185. *malik-i rūm.* A common term in mediaeval Islam for the Byzantine Emperor, who (particularly in Sasanian and early Islamic times) might be considered the prime inciter of disturbance in Persia. Its use here, however, points to little more, in all probability, than the usual lack of historical sense (cf. Notes 313 and 435 above).

2186. *mulūk-i ṭawā'if,* i.e. petty kings, subordinate rulers (cf. Note 2155 above).

2187. *mutakāfi'.* The argument here parallels certain passages in I:2:7. Cf. Note 1025 above.

2188. *amzija-i mu'tadila.* Cf. Note 836 above.

2189. Three terms here (*mujāhidān . . . muṭauwi'a . . . ghāziyān*) have more or less distinct Islamic overtones of meritorious fighting for the Faith. Cf. Note 2118 above.

2190. *jubāt-i kharāj*. Cf. Note 2114 above.

2191. *ilāhīyīn*, Arabic genitive plural, the original quotation being in Arabic.

2192. *al-ḥikam al-ḥaqīqa* (or more probably *al-ḥaqīqīya*). The plural often denotes 'aphorisms' (which may, of course, be wise and philosophical), but is probably to be explained here as an attempt to conform to all the other necessary plurals in this quotation. Cf. Note 1949 above.

2193. *muta'addī*, i.e. passes from him to others.

2194. *munāfāt . . . dhātī*.

2195. *bi-īshān mudārātī ri'āyat bāyad farmūd*.

2196. *ḥabs*, i.e. putting them in prison.

2197. *qaid*, which I take to mean 'fettering', but not necessarily in prison. Hence my reading of the following phrase as *man' buvad az taṣarrufāt-i badanī*, whereas some texts have the last word as *madanī*: this latter would give a sense something like 'depriving them of civic jurisdictions', which seems to be covered by the category immediately following.

2198. *nafy*.

2199. *aẓhar*.

2200. *ibṭāl*, e.g. putting out the eyes.

2201. *salāmat*.

2202. *iḥsān*. Something like charity and supererogatory acts are what Ṭūsī seems to have in mind. Cf. the long section around Note 2000 above, in the Section on Love (III:2). Another rendering might be 'beneficence'.

2203. *farr u bahā-yi mulk az haibat bāshad*. The first word, which I have rendered 'aura', is a well-known Persian term suggesting the *mystique* of true kingship. The *Shāhnāma*, the great national epic composed some 200 years earlier by Ṭūsī's fellow-townsman Firdausī, employs the word countless times.

2204. *nāmūs-i ḥaqq*. The implication of this term is doubtless religious (cf. Note 853 above and elsewhere, and the text between Notes 1856 and 1859); it may be remarked, with some degree of significance, that the term for 'law(s)' in the immediately preceding passages is *qānūn* (*qawānīn*), which is more scientific in character.

2205. *murūwat*, for the connotations of which cf. Note 1583 above ('vestiges', *rusūm*, also signifies 'customs, usages', but no suitably ambiguous term offers in English, and the one I have chosen is more or less dictated by the presence of 'obliterated'). What Ṭūsī does here is to make Wisdom or Philosophy the *sine qua non* of all good order, whether religious, political or private.

2206. Some texts have '*not* in accordance with merit', i.e. inappropriate or unworthy. This is possible, but the emphasis here seems to be on the king's duty to forget himself and his desires whether as regards pleasure or in matters like dignity and a sense of power.

2207. i.e. it is the king's duty to be informed of affairs from their inception and long before they become unmanageable.

2208. *dar badal uftad*. It should be remembered that Ṭūsī conceives ideally of a static society based on absolutes.

2209. *imām-i ḥaqq u malik-i 'ādil*. For the reference of this argument to its proper context, see the text between Notes 1853 and 1874 and also the relevant Notes to that passage. It is difficult not to suspect here that Ṭūsī is thrusting at the luxury-loving and ineffectual Caliphs of the time, the last of whom he was eventually to help bring down himself: it may be remarked that the phrase 'such an age', immediately following, is literally, 'this age'.

2210. That is to say, one should create diversions and smokescreens.

2211. *yā bādi' buvad yā dāfi'*.

2212. *khair-i maḥḍ*.

2213. *ḥazm u sū'-i ẓann*.

2214. Cf. Note 2203 above: once the king is seen at close quarters on the battlefield, something of his atmosphere is lost.

2215. *ghadr*.

2216. *isti'māl-i īn mūjib-i tasalluṭ-i dushman gardad*. Probably, what is meant is that this gives the enemy the initiative.

2217. *ṭaish u tahauwur*. Ṭūsī uses both terms many times as aberrations of basic virtues: for the latter in such a context, see Note 693.

2218. Koran 2:250. The reference is to Saul v. the Philistines and, more particularly, to the combat of David and Goliath; but the text is commonly given Islamic relevance.

2219. In Arabic: fairly corrupt in all versions, but not difficult to restore. I am unable to discover the probable author: it is typical of much mannered moralistic verse, particularly of the first few centuries of Islam. There are one or two word-plays not easy to reproduce.

2220. See Note 2211 above and text at that point.

2221. *ru'asā'*, the term commonly rendered 'Heads' in the earlier parts of this Discourse; it corresponds here to the vague use of 'princes' in English.

2222. *kharāj*. Cf. Note 2114 above.

2223. *millat*. Cf. Note 2088 above.

2224. Ṭūsī here uses the Persian *shahr*, but still with the sense of 'city-state, polity' with which he invests *madīna* throughout.

2225. Once again, we have a term with Islamic connotations: all Muslims have the duty, in their daily lives, to exhort their fellows to do good and to deter them from evil. What Ṭūsī says here, however, is simply that prudence forbids any attempt to influence a ruler by the sort of direct methods often justified with one's ordinary companions.

2226. See Note 2121 above.

2227. i.e. the sort of irrelevant and insignificant details about the great on which modern journalism thrives!

2228. The sense is that the courtier or state-official should endeavour to assure himself comfort and a regular income from being invested with profitable offices, rather than continually begging for sporadic favours!

2229. A most pithy Arabic proverb: *al-mamnū' maḥrūṣ 'alaih wa-al-mabdhūl mamlūl minhu*.

2230. *istīfā'*.

2231. A rare use of the word *gunāh* ,which usually means 'sin'.

2232. *wulāt*, and later its singular *wālī*. As usual throughout this Section, the term does not seem to be used with any precision, and certainly not in distinction from the other exalted personages mentioned. The advice generally is on how to deal with the very highest levels of society.

2233. A celebrated Persian convert to Islam and suspected apostate, executed in 142/759. He is credited with the translation into Arabic of much early Persian writing, some of Indian provenance, e.g. the fables of Kalila and Dimna. The work here referred to is doubtless *Al-Adab al-Kabīr*, which was of major significance in introducing into Islamic literature the present type of writing on manners and royal virtues. I have not always been sure where the alleged quotation was supposed to end, relying on style.

2234. *va raḥim bā hameh kas maqṭū' darad.*

2235. *wizārat*, the office of *wazīr*. The scope of this post varied at different times, but its holder was virtually the chief executive of state in most cases.

2236. *ṣiḥḥat u istiqāmat.*

2237. *īn khulq az akhlāq-i sufahā' buvad.* For the penultimate word, as here rendered, cf. Note 1747 above and its own reference.

2238. *munāsabatī-yi ṭab'ī*, i.e. an affinity of natural disposition.

2239. *ittiṣāl-i rūḥ . . . bi-rūḥ.*

2240. *mardum madanī bi-al-ṭab' ast.* Cf. Note 1841 above.

2241. In the Second Section of the present Discourse, where Love, as the principle of human association, is most fully discussed.

2242. See Note 1287 above for this identification, and 2244 below.

2243. *bi-ma'nà-yi. . . .*

2244. *ḥakīm*. The reference is to the person I am identifying as Isocrates: cf. Note 2242 above for the beginning of the alleged quotation, and also 1287 for a discussion of the use of the present term.

2245. In Arabic, with some degree of corruption. My colleague Professor M. E. Marmura points out that the poet is Mutanabbī, and the relevance is clear: 'I do not need to protect my she-camel (or whatever it may be) against the unlucky consequences of your looking favourably upon her since you cannot tell good fat from the swelling of disease'; when dealing with Friendship it is equally important to know the true from the spurious. The verse is also linked to the argument by the use of the root ṢDQ ('friendship, sincerity').

2246. *taṣannu'.*

2247. *isti'māl u isti'māsh.* Lane (2157:1 and 2158: 3 respectively) would support such senses, but cf. Note 1009 above and the passage to which it refers.

2248. *gauhar-i nafīs.*

2249. And this is why the 'wretched' are in Hell. Philologically, it might be better to say that the same root KFR underlies the Arabic words for 'ingratitude' and 'blasphemy, unbelief'.

2250. *mu'ākhāt*: hence the mention of 'brothers' lower down.

2251. *sang-pāra*: doubtless a deliberately depreciatory term.

2252. See Note 2237 above.

2253. *shāri'*: i.e. the Prophet Muḥammad, cf. Notes 1859 and 1957.

2254. In Arabic: the sense here is not that a former friend may poison one, but that just as poisonous materials derive from familiar things that one may be inclined to eat or drink, so enemies will arise among a host of indiscriminately-won friends. My colleague Professor Marmura informs me that the lines are by the 'Abbāsid poet Ibn al-Rūmī.

2255. *mutawallī-yi sarā'ir*, i.e. God.

2256. Once again (cf. e.g. Note 373 above) there are word-plays I cannot reproduce on the root SHKL: *shakl* ('appearance') and *mushkil* ('difficult, obscure').

2257. Respectively: *maḥabbat-i khāliṣ . . . thiqat-i tāmm*. There may be mystical overtones here, and accordingly I have capitalized these terms.

2258. *ziyāda az ma'hūd lāzim.*

2259. *maḥẓūr*: a term of semi-legal severity.

2260. *mustaghraq . . . gardānad*, i.e. to immerse, even to drown, somebody in a delight: a term often having mystical overtones.

2261. *al-'itāb ḥayāt al-mawadda wa-fī al-'itāb ḥayāt baina aqwām.* The idea is not uncommon: cf. Lane 1943:1.

2262. *muṭṭarid.*

2263. *mirā'.*

2264. *tabāyun.*

2265. *ahl-i baghy.*

2266. *'ilm u adab.* While the former term is wholly technical and specialized, the latter connotes something like our humanities, 'polite learning' accompanied by the appropriate state of mind and conduct. Cf. Note 2274 below.

2267. *ḥirfat u ṣinā'at.*

2268. *istibdād*: 'monopolization' would be an alternative, albeit somewhat modern-sounding.

2269. *muḍāyaqa.*

2270. *ḍīq-i maḥāll*: i.e. only a limited space is available for material goods, which in turn limits their volume.

2271. *muzāḥamat dar jānib-i ba'ḍī*: some will get more than their share, leaving less for others.

2272. *mumāna'at*: see Lane 3024:3.

2273. *qillat-i biḍā'at.*

2274. *taṣnīf-i fāḍilī.* While this could be rendered 'a learned man's work' (cf. Note 2266 above), I think the emphasis is here more on the virtue, i.e. the lack of stinginess, of the original author than on his learning.

2275. *wajhī-yi nā-pasandīda.* The Avery MS alone omits the negative (= 'dis-'), which also would give sense of a kind. Much seems to turn on the question of 'such a person's' identity. Is it the stingy man or friends in general? Is there some hiatus here?

2276. *muttaṣilān u muta'alliqān.*

2277. *khalīfa u qā'im(-i) maqām.* There would not seem to be any significant overtones in the use of these words here.

2278. *muwāfaqatī-yi laṭīf.*

2279. See Note 2233 above.

2280. In Arabic. I have not located the author, and this type of poetry, regretting the passing of great days and of social acceptance, is very common. The middle lines refer to a manner of speech indicative of great affection and intimacy.

2281. *ma'nā-yi ittiḥād*. There are probable mystical overtones here (cf. Text around Notes 956 and 1904 above). The importance of Love as the essential principle of civilized life has been demonstrated in the Second Section of the present Discourse. The 'virtues of character' *faḍā'il-i khulqī*) have been treated at length in Discourse One, Second Division, 3 and 4.

2282. *taṣḥīḥ-i mu'āmalāt*: cf. Note 1831 above. For the terms used for the virtues here, see the specific Note-references given and also the two Sections indicated in the foregoing Note.

2283. *asbābī-yi khārij*. This point too is touched on in the aforementioned places.

2284. *sakhāwat*. Cf. Notes 632 and 725 above, and also the definitions of 'freedom' and 'liberality' respectively given between Notes 643 and 646 in the text.

2285. *mardum-rā az libās-i mardī bi-dar barand*.

2286. See the end of the First Section of the present Discourse, following Note 1887.

2287. *muqābil*: probably, though not explicitly, equal to the other rank; it is, as it were, its 'opposite number'.

2288. *ḥaqīqī u ghair-i ḥaqīqī*. The second term would not seem to be used in any seriously pejorative sense: they are not friends in the true sense of the term.

2289. *mu'āmala bi-ḥasab-i ẓāhir*. Cf. Note 1831 above. What is probably intended is that they should be treated as though they were 'true' friends.

2290. *aṣfiyā' u auliyā-yi mukhliṣ*.

2291. *khalq*. So, at least, I read this and take it to mean: cf. Lane 800:1, for this combination of notions touching on 'fabrication' and 'smoothness'. This does not necessarily conflict with the terms preceding and following: *all* these lines of approach are to be employed.

2292. *riyā'ī u mujāmalatī-yi ẓāhir*.

2293. *'adāwat-i irādī*. The five categories are: *tanāzu' dar milk*; *t. dar martaba*; *t. dar raghā'ib; iqdām bar shahawātī ki mūjib-i inhitāk-i ḥaram buvad; ikhtilāf-i ārā'*.

2294. *dil-shikasta u ḍa'īf-ra'y*.

2295. *shiyam u 'ādāt*.

2296. *ḥazm u kiyāsat*. Cf. Notes 1785 and 2213 above.

2297. *sufahā'*. Cf. Note 1577 above.

2298. The leader of the 'Abbāsid rebellion against the Umaiyads in Khorasan, which heralded the downfall of the Umaiyads (A.D. 749) and their replacement, until the extinction of the Caliphate 500 years later, by the House of 'Abbās. The name following is that of the Umaiyad governor of the area.

2299. e.g. death and bereavement.

2300. *baṭar*.

2301. *ḥarīm*, i.e. taking refuge in the innermost part of his house.

2302. *ḥazm*. See Note 2296 above.

2303. *sarīrat*.

2304. *nuṣaḥā'*. Ṭūsī's own elucidation makes clear the special, but non-technical, sense in which the term is to be understood.

2305. *ṣulaḥā'*. Once more (cf. foregoing Note), Ṭūsī defines his usage: the word has connotations of 'reform', 'good life' and 'peace(-making)'.

2306. *az rū-yi tabarru'*: rendered a few lines earlier as 'freely gives. . . .'

2307. *madhāhib*: a word here having apparently purely secular significance, albeit with a moral colouring: cf. Note 2088 above.

2308. *sufahā'*: cf. Note 2237 above.

2309. *ḥilm*.

2310. Reading *mujāzāt* with Lahore and Lucknow: the omission of one dot gives the alternative reading *mujārrāt* ('hostilities'), preferred by other texts, and this certainly accords with the preceding phrase.

2311. *ahl-i takabbur*.

2312. *al-takabbur ma'a al-mutakabbir ṣadaqa*. Presumably intended as a Prophetic Tradition.

2313. *'ashīra-i nā-sāz-kār*.

2314. *khuṣūṣ*: a term used to contrast with the preceding 'generality' (*'umūm*).

2315. *zīr-dastān*: probably, though not necessarily, subjects of a ruling sovereign.

2316. *muta'allimān*: i.e. 'students, scholars'. Cf. Note 2319 below.

2317. *khudāvandān-i ṭabā'i'-i radī'*.

2318. *tahdhīb-i akhlāq*: cf. Note 3 above.

2319. *balīdān*: i.e. the unteachable, the contrast being with the natural learners of Note 2316 above.

2320. *maẓlūmān*.

2321. The aphorisms in this Section are of course not necessarily regarded as coming from one Platonic corpus: even Ṭūsī uses the term *mansūb*, with its suggestion of doubt. They will be recognized to have many parallels and resemblances over a wide area of time and space, but their Muslim clothing is worn with an air of comfortable familiarity. Dawānī has most of this Section (in paraphrase to a great extent), but then goes his own way for several pages.

2322. See Note 10 above for the term, and also the Preamble in general.

2323. *ma'būd-i khwīsh*. In theory, at least, this could mean an idol. Cf. Note 1601 above.

2324. *'ibādat*. So the Avery MS: the other versions have *'ināyat*, 'care, solicitude, God's care (= Providence)'.

2325. *māya*, there being here a contrast with the 'essential being' (*dhāt*) which follows.

2326. *madhhab*. Cf. Note 2307 above.

2327. *az rū-yi fahm u baṣīrat*.

2328. Cf. the text earlier, particularly between Notes 1300 and 1308.

2329. A free synopsis of Koranic themes.

2330. *al-malik al-wahhāb*, i.e. God. Not all versions have the same ending.

# INDEX

Plain Arabic numerals refer to pages in the text. Arabic numerals preceded by N refer to the main body of Notes. The figures 21 and 22 followed by lower-case letters from a to x refer to the Notes to the Introduction. Capital Roman numerals denote the three main Discourses, the Sections usually following these as Arabic numerals (e.g. III:4 refers to the Third Discourse, Fourth Section, beginning on p. 226); however, since the First Discourse is further subdivided into two Divisions, I:2:5 refers to First Discourse, Second Division, Fifth Section, beginning on p. 85. Only the most important Notes have been indexed apart from the page references in the text, but it can usually be assumed that any English-language or Latin-alphabet entry involving a technicality will have a Note reference wherever it occurs.


Abaqa, N 1759

'Abd al-'Azīz al-Nīshāpūrī, 178, N 1760

*abrār*: *see* Dutiful ones

Absolutely obeyed one, the, 194

Abū 'Alī (*see also* Miskawaih): on youth and felicity, 59–60; quoting Aristotle on ranks of virtues and felicity, 66–68; on injustice, 105–6; on the plight of kings, 116; on perverse anger, 134; on death and over-population, 140–41; identification of, N 293

Abū Bakr: on the plight of princes, 116

Abū Muslim: on abuse of enemies, 255

Abū Nuwās, 168

Abyssinians: loyalty of, 132

Accommodaters, the: a growth in virtuous cities, 226, N 2161

Accountants (*see also* Reckoning), 230

Acts: relationship of, in virtuous cities, 217; criterion of punishment based on, 231–32

*adab*, N 2266; *al-Adab al-Kabīr*, *see Manners* of Ibn al-Muqaffa'

'Aḍud al-Daula, 116

Affection: (*ulfat* q.v.) an animal inclination, 197; (*mawaddat*) close to friendship, 197, 198, 204; in virtuous cities, 215; 243, 246, 248

Affluence (*see also* wealth): city of, 223, N 2151; domination with, 225; in kings, 228

After-life: sensual view of, 53–55

Agriculture: Science of, 28; craft of, 158, 218, 222; class engaged in, 230

Aid: of three kinds, 187; varying needs for, 188–89, 194, 195

*akhlāq* (*see also* disposition, ethic, *tahdhīb*): definition of, 21–a; *Akhlāq-i Jalālī*, otherwise called *Lawāmi' al-Ishrāq* . . . (*see also* Dawānī and *Practical Philosophy of the Muhammadan People*), 9, 17, 20; *Akhlāq Muḥsinī*, 17; *Akhlāq-i Nāṣirī* (*see also Nasirean Ethics* and Ṭūsī): significance of, 9–12, 17–19; setting in genres, ditto; 'original' recension of, 14, 21–b; style of, 15–16, 22–n; circumstances of writing of, 25–26; unity of, N 1845, N 1942 and *passim*

Alamūt, 12

Alchemy: a depravity, 123

Alexander the Great: acting against anger, 135; on teachers, 204–5; and the conquered Persians, 229–30; reproved by Aristotle, 236; N 313

Algebra, science of, 28

'Alī b. Abī Ṭālib: on courage, 93; on anger, 129, N 1291; overly given to jesting, 131; his descendants computed, 141; on grief, 146

*'ālim*, N 1981, N 1982

*Anatomy, Book of*: *see Kitāb-i Tashrīḥ*

Angels: above human virtues, 208–9

Anger: treatment of, 128–35; vengeance its principle, 128; compared to natural phenomena, 128–29; causes of, 129; consequences of, 129; treatment of its causes, 129–35; is a tyranny, 133–34; confused with courage, ditto; arising from greed, 134–35; a property of the weak, 134; Alexander and, 135; gravest sickness of soul, 135; induced by wine, 169, 206; in city of domination, 222; an easy habit, 259
Animals (*see also* bodies): trained animals and lower grades of men, 46, 218; above ignorant men, 127; varying needs of, for own species and for aid, 188–89; inclined to ease, 209; display true dispositions, 244
Apostates, the: a growth in virtuous cities, 226
Appetite: treatment of excess, 142–44; gluttony and its consequences, 142; dangers and disappointments of sexual appetite, 142–43; Ghazālī on latter, ditto; passionate love (*'ishq*), 143–44; 148, 160; excited by drink in women, 164; to be controlled in young, 168–69; powerful in Arabs, 184; 199; conflict of, 206; not in angels, 209; in city of domination, 222; diverse, in free city, 223–4; of Arabs and Turks, 225; in kings and tyrants, 227; in friends, 245; 252, 254
Aptitude tests, 171, 172
Arabs: characteristics of, 184; pagan, as example of city of domination, 222, N 2149; appetites of, 225
*'araḍ*, 15 and *passim*
Arberry, A. J. 21–i, 21–j, 22–l, 22–n, 22–r
Arbitrator: second requisite of Justice, 97–99, 191; 260
Ardashīr Bābak: on faith and kingship, 215, N 2099; 230; on war, 236
*'ārif*, N 1982
Aristotle (see also First (ancient) philosopher), 18; as logician, 28; on ethics, 59; on goods, 61; some followers of, on felicity, 62; analyses felicity, 62–63; says virtue needs material for outward expression, 63, 71; on ascending degrees of felicity, 63–64; quoted in adaptation on ranks of felicity, 66–68; on truly felicitous man and others, 68–69; on constancy of true felicity, 69–70; on rightful praise and glorification, 73; on teachability of evil men, 76; on money, 97; on tyrants, 98; says justice whole of virtue, 98–99; says fitness for rule only in justice and wisdom, 99; divides recipients of justice into three, 100; on service of God, 102; on unregulated faculties, 108; on moderation, 118; on four types of simple government, 191, N 1847–48; on lawgivers, 191; on civic man, 192, N 1868; on complete felicity, 208–10; says virtues must be practised, 210; says only a few good by nature, 210; advises Alexander, 229–30, 236; on friends, 243; testaments received by, from Plato, III: 8, N 2321; N 313; identification of, N 414, N 445; N 908, N 1263; *De Sophisticis Elenchis* of, N 1263; N 1820, N 1841, N 1861; *see also Nicomachean ethics*
Arithmetic: *see* Reckoning
Arrogance: a cause of anger, 129; close to conceit, 131; children to be restrained from, 169; in city of domination, 222; in decaying polity, 229; not for friends, 246, 248; how to treat, 257; over lineage, 259; over wealth, 260
*asās* (foundation) 192, N 1869
Assent, the people of, 213
Assured ones, the, 103
Astrology, 27, N 18; 28, 112 (science of the stars), 158, 216
Astronomy: defined, 27, N 17; practitioners of, 230
Attainers, the (the sincere ones), 103
*Auṣāf al-Ashrāf*, 13
Authority: *de facto v. de jure*, 192, N 1871, 234, N 2209; 214; supreme, in virtuous cities, has four situations, 216–17; of wisdom in virtuous cities, 216; of most virtuous ones, 216; of tradition, 216; of holders of tradition, 217; other authorities in virtuous cities, 217–18; true authority

Authority—continued
lacking in cities of ignorance, 224–25
Aversion: an animal reaction, 197
Avicenna (Ibn Sīnā), 10, 12, 13, 16, 17, 22–o; as source of second discourse, 155, N 1542; N 293, N 339, N 919, N 1233, N 1537

Baghdad, capture of, 9, 21–d, N 2209
Barnāmis, 69, N 435; *see also* Priam of Troy
*barzakh*, N 1425
Baseness (*see also* government): the base city, 218—19; the base man patient in body, 257
Beggars: how to deal with, 257–58
Blacksmith, craft of, 158, 189
blasphemy: linked with ingratitude, 245, N 2249
Bodies: as such, undifferentiated, 43–44; gradation of mineral (solid) bodies, 44; of vegetable bodies, 44–45; of animal bodies, 45–46; body as organ of soul, 62; close relation of body and soul, 124
Botany: defined, 28; as model for choice of friends, 244–45
Brain, 43, 124
Bryson, 17; as source of second discourse, 155, N 1537, N 1542
Byzantines: loyalty of, 132; characteristics of, 184

Calligraphy, craft of, 112, 158, 171, 216
Calumny: a danger to all relationships, 251–52
Canon-lawyers, 230; *see also* Jurisprudence
Carpentry, craft of, 158, 189
Categories: the Ten, 61, N 324; *Book of*, 76
Cause, the first (primary), 67, 91, 95, 204, 214
Cave, Plato's Allegory of the, 128, N 1281
Centre: *see* middle
Charitable donations: rules governing, 160–61
Children (*see also* parents): discipline of, II:4, 72; early growth and training of, 109–10, 166–67; one of domestic bases, 154; elementary religious, moral and social training, 167–70; control of appetitive faculty in, 168–69; wine forbidden to, 169; plain living, exercise and good company recommended for, 169, 172; modesty and graciousness to be instilled in, 169–70; training of, by a tutor, 170–71; choice of 'craft' for, 171–72; training of daughters, 173; parents' respective roles towards, 179; love between parents and children, 180, 202–3; respect of, for parents, extends to certain others, 181; inclined to ease, 209; secrets not for, 234, 235; defence of, 237; display of concern for, 247
Chivalry, craft of, 158
Cities (*see also* civilization, combination, community, government): various conditions of, III:3; definition of, 190; administration of 191; 193, 194; virtuous (or ideal), N 1849, 211, 212–18, and *passim* till 226; virtuous and un-virtuous, 211–12, 224, 225; ignorant, 211, 218–25 (allegedly ignorant, 221, 226); impious, 211, 218, 225; Errant, 211, 218, 225–26; ranks of virtuous, 213–14; adaptation of revelation to these, 214; regulator of virtuous, 214, 215; citizens of virtuous, really all united, 215; legislators of all virtuous, in fundamental agreeement, 215; five bases to virtuous, 215–16; authority in virtuous, 216–18; necessary cities, 218, 225; servile cities, 218; base cities, 218–19; cities of nobility, 219–21; cities of despots, 221; cities of domination (variously understood), 221–23; cities of pleasure, 223, N 2151, 225; cities of affluence, 223, N 2151; free cities (cities of the community), 223–25; latter encompass all others, and are most popular and diversified, 224; compounded ignorant cities, 225; growths in virtuous cities, 212, 226, defence of cities, 237
Civilization (civilized life): the reason for, III:1; a special combination, 190; called forth by love, 199; as adopted by the un-virtuous, 211

'Cleverness' (ingenuity), 87, 123, 158, 174, 176, N 1747, 177; towards parents, 180, 182; towards kings, 242; among friends, 246, 249; among enemies, 254, 255; how to deal with, 256–7; 260
Combination, 190, 192; hierarchy of, 193–94; modes of attachment in, 194, 200, 211, 212; six combinations of ignorant cities, 218–25
Commerce: less reliable than craft, 158; not among angels, 208; in servile cities, 218; in cities of domination, 222; class engaged in, 230; this class and war, 236
Community (*see also* cities, civilization, combination, government), 192; great communities, 193, 194, 200, 212, 214, 215; cities of the, 223; unity of, essential to survival, 228–30; defence of, 237
Composition, science of, 27
Conceit: a cause of anger, 130; close to arrogance, 131; enters into pretentiousness, 149; among Indians, 184
Conjuring: a depravity, 123
Contention (quarrelsomeness. strife): a cause of anger, 131; in a good cause, 136; in children, 168; where head of city lacking, 214–15; in cities of domination, 221; in decaying polity, 229; unworthy of friends, 249–50; to be avoided, even with enemies, 254; three sorts of, a cause of voluntary enmity, 254
Continence (*see also* Virtue), 62, 80, 81; comprises twelve species of virtue, 83; pseudo-continence, 89–90, 142, 159, 195; desirable in wives, 161, 162, 164; in daughters, 173; not found in angels, 209, 227; social reason for, 252
Co-operation: Man's essential need of, 189; requires combination and management (both q.v.), 190–91; avoidance of, condemned, 194–95; essential to growth and survival of polity, 228–30
Courage (*see also* Virtue), 62, 79–81 *passim*; comprises eleven species of virtue, 82–83; confused with foolhardiness, 88; pseudo-courage, 91–94, 195, 244; confused with anger, 133-34; is the virtue of the irascible faculty, 136, 158; among Turks, 184; not found in angels, 208–9, 216; social reason for, 252
Courses: courses of pleasure, generosity and wisdom, 70–71
Cowardice (faintheartedness), 85, 87, 94; treatment of, 135–36; how overcome by certain philosophers, 136
Crafts, 15; more reliable than commerce, 158, or inherited wealth, 172; three grades of, 158, 189; pre-eminence in, achieved by perseverance, 158–59, 172, 217; conducive to virtue, 159, N 1581; a sound basis for marriage, 172; one suited to every nature, 182, 217; why diverse and in need of order, 189–90; craft of kingship, 192; supreme craft is politics, 192; all require hierarchy of authority, 194; consideration of, in virtuous cities, 217; masters of, 230; skill in, to be freely shared, 250
Cupping, craft of, 158
Cutler, craft of, 158

*Daf' al-aḥzān: see Greifs, Warding Off*
Dailam, 172
Darius (Codomannus), 229
Date-palm: noblest of vegetable kingdom, 44–45; special need of, for aid, 188
Daughters, training of, 173
Dawānī, Jalāl al-Dīn Muḥammad b. Asad (*see also Akhlāq-i Jalālī* and *Practical Philosophy of the Muhammadan People*), 9, 10, 11, 12, 20, 21–e, 21–f, N 1542, N 1651, N 1852, N 1868, N 1993, N 1995, N 2006, N 2078, N 2130, N 2168, N 2321
Death: fear of, *see* fear; ultimate goal of knowledge, 138; is true perfection, 138–39, 141–42; nature of, 137–39; 'voluntary' and 'natural', 138; no pain in, 138; and over-population, 140–41; preferable to longevity, 141–42
Depravity (perversity), 123, 126, 128, 134, 142, 144, 146, 205
Despots, city of, 221; definition of,

Despots—*continued*
223, N 2146; friends who behave like, 249
Detestation: opposite of love (q.v.), 196–97
*dhāt*, 15, N 1403
*dhikr*, N 134, 42
Dimashqī, Abū 'Uthmān, 66, N 381
Discipline, 15; why needed, 72; as against nature, 109; essential to virtue, 110; 157; of children, 167–71; of appetitive faculty in children, 168–69; administered by a tutor, 170–71; of man must be begun young, 172; of servants, 183
Discrimination (distinction): see *tamyīz*; excess, neglect and depravity of, 123
'Disposers', 187
Disposition (*see also akhlāq* etc.): limit and nature of, I:2:1; correction of, is noblest discipline, I:2:2; excellence of (*see also* virtue), I:2:3; need for correcting, 72, 257; definition of, 74; whether associated with animal or rational soul, 74; whether natural, 74–77; formed first by religion, secondly by philosophy, 77; raises man from lowest to highest station, 79; correction of, 109, 112, 133, 161, 162, 167; of slave, 183; in virtuous cities, 212; in cities of domination, 222; in animals, 244
Distinction: *see* Discrimination
Divine ordinances (Commandments, Edicts, Laws etc.): definition of, 29, N 42; 77, N 556; positor of equality and justice, 97–99; and justice in harmony, 104–5, 191; broken by self-indulgent ruler, 234; *see also* Law etc., *shāri'*, *sharī'at*
Divine Science: *see* Metaphysics, Theology
Divination: a depravity, 123
Domination (*see also* government, Love): brings corruption and deficiency, 196, 204; as entitlement to honour, 219–20; cities of, 221–3 (variously classified, 222); in association with necessity, affluence, pleasure and ennoblement, 225; preferred by rebels, 226; is deficient government, 227; causes world's sickness, 228; sometimes confused with royal rule, 228; not for kings, 233; not for friends, 246
Drinking: *see* Manners; eating and drinking
Dutiful ones, the, 103
Dyeing, craft of, 158

Eating and drinking, 168–69, 175-78
Economic(s) (*see* also Philosophy, Domestic; households): forms subject of second discourse; definition of, 21–a; 25, N 4; second definition of, 28, N 39
Elocution, 216
Empedocles, N 1900
Emulation: how different from envy, 148; 219
Enemies (*see also* war): dissension should be sown among, 229–30, 236; misleading of, and spying on, 234–36, 254–55; treatment of, 236–37, 254–56, 260; making, from friends, 246–47, 249, 250, 251, 254; categories of, 253–54; five causes of enmity, 254; not to be abused or gloated over, 255; deal justly with submissive, 255; protection against, 255–56; conditions for hostility, 256
Ennoblement: *see* nobility
Envy: treatment of, 147–48; compound of ignorance and avidity, 147–48; connected with grief, 148; Kindī on, 148; a great evil, not becoming to men of knowledge, 148; and emulation, 148; 161; in children, 168; in enemies, 254, 256
Equality: why impossible among men, 190, 216; in free cities, 223; in division of common goods, 232
Equilibrium, 44, N 156; the umbra of unicity, 95; justice comprehends all equilibria, 104, 108, 111, 114, 123, 125, 131, 133, 135, 155, 156; in walking and riding, 174; in medicine, 192; true equilibrium, 193, 230
Equity, 81, 196, 246
Equivalence: implies unicity, 95; noblest relationship, 95; implies ordering of diversities, 96, 97; in ennoblements, 219

Espionage (*see also* enemies), 234–36, 254–55
Ethic (ethical, ethics): forms subject of first discourse; principles of, I:1; ends of, I:2; definition of, 21–a, 26, N 5; further definition of, 28, N 39; subject-matter and axioms of, 35–36; *Book of*, 76; spiritual medicine, modelled on physic, 111, 114, 122–26; as stage in education, 171, N 1707; *see also* ***akhlāq*** etc.
Euclid (the geometer, or of Megara), and chastening of soul, 120, N 1195
Evil: and error have infinite possibilities, 211; general evils, as found in deficient government, 227; dealing with evil men, 231–32; all evil lies in divergence, 249; to be met with good, not evil, 254; to be avoided, 258; may not be wished to another, 259
Excess (*see also* Neglect; Appetite), 69, 86–88 *passim*, N 432, 114, 122, 123, 126, 128, 133, 134, 142, 143, 195, 221, 243
Exegesis, science of, 112
Expenditure(*see also* Wealth):household, under control of wife, 161; used to get rid of a wife, 165
Experimentations: acceptable, 227, N 2177; chaotic, cause of the world's sickness, 228, N 2183

Faculties: appetitive (concupiscible), 39, 42, 43, 49, 50, 57, 79, 80, 81, 90, 110, 111, 119, 125; Ghazālī on, 142–43; to be controlled in young, 168–69; 225, 227
- attractive, 42, 80, 110, 123; excess, neglect and depravity of, 123–24; diseases of, 142–49
- augmentative, 42, 43
- conversive, 42
- digestive, 42
- of generation, 42, 110
- imaginative, 42, 82, 109
- of intellection, 215, N 2105
- intuitive, 46
- irascible, 39, 42, 43, 45, 49, 50, 57, 79, 80, 110, 111, 119, 125, 136, 142, 149, 214, 225, 227
- nutritive, 42, 43, 109, 110, 142, 187
- of organic perception, 42
- practical, 51, 52
- of rationality, 42, 43, 79, 119, N 1185, 125; and love, 196, 211, 214, 225
- repulsive, 42, 80, 110; excess, neglect and depravity of, 123; main diseases of, 128–142
- retentive, 42
- speculative, 112; main diseases of, 126–28
- theoretical, 51
- of voluntary motion, 42
- failure of faculties, 124; playing faculties off against each other as a technique of ethics, 125, 142, N 1438; *see also* Soul

Faintheartedness: *see* cowardice
Faith, the: people of faith, 213; the faith and kingship, 215, 227; quest of, a condition of victory, 228, N 2182, 235; defence of, 237
Falsehood: its nature and consequences, 149; enters into pretentiousness, 149; identical with hypocrisy, 149; in children, 168; to be avoided in speech, 174; among Indians, 184; to be avoided, even against enemies, 254
Fārābī, Abū Naṣr al-, 10, 18–19; as source of third discourse, 187; on role of snakes and wild beasts, 187–88, N 1820; N 339; N 1849; ***Al-Fārābī: an Annotated Bibliography***, N 1820
***farr***, N 2203, N 2214
***fauz: ahl-i fauz, fā'izān*** (***mukhliṣān***): *see* Attainers
Favour: is justice in augmentation, 106–7
Fear: treatment of, 136–42; of the necessary and the possible, 136–37; fear of death, 137–42; 206; unknown to angels, 209; 227
Feast days: *see* Prayer
Felicity: a principal topic of I:1:7; degrees of, I:2:8; 46, 47, 48, 52; how differs from good, 60; only applicable to man 60; subdivision of, 61–68; lies in virtues, 62; as seen by stoics, some naturalists and some Aristotelians, 62; analysed by Aristotle, 62–63; a gift of God, 63, 209; belongs to complete man, 63; early philosophers find only

Felicity—*continued*
after death, 63; Aristotle and others recognise ascending degrees of, even in life, 63–64; viewed by 'moderns', 64; first rank of, and its subdivisions, 64–65; second rank of, 65–66; Aristotle on ranks of, (in adaptation), 66–68; Aristotle on true and sham, 68–69, 208–9; Aristotle says true felicity constant, 69–70; divine felicity, 71, 208; pleasure of, 71–73, 209; implies liberality, virtue, wisdom, 72, 89; produced by justice, 73, 89; whether deserving of praise or glorification, 73; of three kinds, 112; eternal, 136; latter impossible in errant cities, 225; true, in death, 139; ultimate felicity, 144, 145, 146, 215; 148; false felicity, 205–6, 209; latter in errant cities, 225; Aristotle on complete felicity, 208–10; lies in moderation, 210; three classes of felicitous person, 210–11; attained through virtuous government, 227; found among friends, 242–43; dependent on sociability, 252

Fellowship: enjoined by reason, religion and good manners, 199–201

Fight, the good: *see jihād*; *also* War

*fikr*, N 134, 42, N 148, N 385, N 547, N 575, N 1128, N 1189, 212

First determinant, 195

First (ancient) philosopher, the (*see also* Aristotle), 57–58, 100; on Heraclitus, 198; on false friends, 205; on kindness and love, 207; on true felicity, 210

first principle, 67, 95, 212

Flight from: an inorganic reaction, 197

Food: basic reason for social organisation, 153–54; as a 'disposer' towards perfection, 187

Foolhardiness (*see also* Courage), 87; confused with courage, 88, 134; brought on by wine, 169; in war, 236

Foolishness, 87, 123

Forms: as 'perfecters', 187; bestower of, 187; of compounds and combinations, 211; perceived by soul, 213, 214

Fortitude, 81, 136

Foundation, the: *see asās*

Friends (friendship) (*see also* Love): forms subject of III:6; use of, for self-improvement, 120–21; less general than love, 197; based in young on pleasure, 198; based in old on profit, 198; based in good men on good, 198, 243; latter class of friendship rare, 202; philosophers on, 202; friendship in rulers a deviation from justice, 202; treachery in, 205; gradations of, 205; worthless friends, 206; true friends few, 242–43; good men seek, in all, 243; Isocrates on value of, 243–44; caution in choice of, 244–46; often part over money, 245–46; inconveniences of having many, 246; tolerance of faults in, 246; enemies made from, 246–47, 249, 250, 251, 254; to be cherished in all circumstances, 247–49, 260; extension of friendship, 247–48, 253; contention unworthy of, 249–50; parsimony in intellectual goods ill becomes, 250; correcting faults of friends, 250–51; calumniators a danger to, 251–52; love and friendship the greatest virtue, 252; noblest topic in third discourse, 252; true friends and others, 253

*Fuṣul al-Madanī* (*see also* Fārābī), N 1820, N 1848, N 1851, N 2105, N 2114, N 2118, N 2125, N 2130

Galen: refutes sensualists, 54; on man's nature, 75–76; on need for self-criticism, 120–21, N 1205; N 1439

Gambling, 'craft' of, 158

Generation and corruption, science of: defined, 28, 41

Generosity (*see also* Course), 182, 220, 253

Geometry: defined, 27, 35, 128, 216; geometers as a class, 230; *see also* Reckoning

Ghazālī, al-, (*see also Iḥyā' 'Ulum al-Dīn, Tahāfut al-Falāsifa*), 10, 17, 18; on appetite, 142–43, N 1436, N 339, N 943

Gibb, Sir Hamilton A. R., 17, 22-k, 22-t

Gluttony (*see also* Appetite), 123; to be checked in children, 168–69
God (*see also* Divine, Love, Truth, Providence, Wisdom, etc.): service of, according to philosophers and others, 100–104, 160; needs requital less than parents, 179; a simple, to which intellectual things and goods assimilate in some measure, 209; the supreme philosopher, 209; Plato says, to be given prime due, 258
Good: absolute and relative, 60–61; how different from Felicity, 60; subdivision of, 61; pure good, 67, 68, 73, 198, 199, 202, 208; latter as a purpose in war, 235; absolute good, 71, 258; latter unattainable in Errant Cities, 225; general, superior to individual, 194, 232; one of man's ends, 197; a motive of love, 197, 208; a motive of passion, 198; a motive of friendship in men of good, 198; love of, 208–10; only one road to, 211; recognized, but not realized, by impious cities, 225; widespread goods in virtuous government, 227; five grades of men in relation to, 230–31; distribution and preservation of goods, 232–33; supererogatory goods, 233; lost by self-indulgent king, 233–34; lasting good, 258
Government (*see also* Cities; Kings, Manners of, etc.): of realm, forms subject of III:4; a special form of management, 191; divine, 191, N 1846; four types of simple government according to Aristotle, 191, N 1848; government of governments, 191; connection between government of a king and that of community, 191; virtuous, is the Imamate, 227; deficient, is domination, 227; qualities required in aspirant to kingly, 227–8; requisites for growth and survival of states, 228–30; king's duties of, in justice, 230–33; of four distinct classes in polity, 230; and control of evil, 231–32; and distribution and preservation of goods, 232–33; role of kindness in, 233; efficient, demands dedication, 233–34; and espionage, 234–36; and war, 235–37
Grammar, science of, 112
Greed: a cause of anger, 134–35; 159; to be discouraged in children, 168–69; found in Persians, 184; 227; in subordinates, 233, 239, 257–58; as motive for learning, 257
Grief: useless against inevitability and naturalness of death, 139–40; nature and treatment of, 144–47; **Griefs, Warding Off,** 146; naturally evaporates in time, 146; based on undue attachment to 'loans', 146–47; a result of envy, 148, 206
Growths, in virtuous cities, 212; five, out of many, 226
*gurbuzī*, N 695
*gūyā*: *see nāṭiq*

Habits: as against states, 74; as related to disposition (q.v.), 74; failure of, 124, 133; *see also* use
*Ḥall Mushkilāt al-Ishārāt*, 13
Harm: all reducible to four causes, 99–100
Ḥasan of Baṣra, on lower souls, 115
Head: necessary to each combination, 193–94; head of heads, 194, 214; head of world, 194; duty of, towards general good rather than individual, 194, 232; of city, 214; supreme head, 217, 231: of necessary cities, 218; of servile cities, 218; of base cities, 219; of cities of nobility, 219–221; of cities of domination, 221–23; in free cities, 224–25; faced by the rebels (q.v.), 226
Heart, the, 43
Heavens, the, and the world: defined, 28
Heraclitus, on love, 198
Hippocrates, N 1287
*ḥiss-i mushtarak*, N 134, 42
House: advice on siting and building of, 156–57
Households (*see also* Economic(s), Wives, Servants, Co-operation): general discussion of, II:1; reason for emergence of, 153–54; five bases of, 154; regulation of, 154–56, 161–84; definition of, 154, 190; sources of second discourse on, 155; management of, by wife,

Households—*continued*
161, 163; often ruined by wealthy wife, 162, 166; or by jealous wife, 163; or by idle wife, 164, 165; man is 'heart' of, 163; in hierarchy of combinations, 193, 194
*ḥukm*, N 2049
Hulagu, 9, 12, 13, N 1759
Humā'ī, Jalāl ad-Dīn, 14 and *passim* in Notes
Husbandry, men of, 230; *see also* Agriculture
Hypocrisy: a dual falsehood, 149, 204; the hypocrites, a growth in vituous cities, 226; peculiar to man, 244, 247

Ibn al-Muqaffa': on dealings with rulers, 240, 241, 242; N 2233
Ibn al-Rūmī, N 2254
Ibn Sīnā: *see* Avicenna
Ideal: *see* Cities
Idleness and sloth: deadly diseases of faculty of attraction, 144; a danger in wives, 163–64, 165; 205; the greatest vice, 252, 260
Ignorance: simple, 126–27; compound, 127–28; compound reverts to simple, 128; leads to fear of death, 137, 138, 139, 141; leads to grief, 146; involved in envy, 147; cities of, 211, 218–25
*iḥsān* (*see also* Kindness) N 2202; *ahl-i iḥsān* (*muḥsinān*): *see* Well-doers
*Iḥyā' 'Ulūm al-Dīn* (*see also* Ghazālī), 22–u
Image worshippers, the, 213, 215
*Imām* (the Imamate), 29, 192, 227; of truth, 234, N 2209
Imru' al-Qais, 168, N 1687
Inclination to: an inorganic reaction, 197
Income: *see* Wealth
Indians, characteristics of, 184
Infidelity (*see also* Ingratitude), 59
Ingenuity (*see also* 'Cleverness'), 87, 158, 174, 182
Ingratitude (*see also* infidelity): most ruinous attribute of the wretched, 245, N 2249
Injustice, 59, 87; differs from tyranny (q.v.), 99; why injustice is possible, 105–6, 132; the, of solitaries, 194–95
Inscription, alleged, in ancient temples, 71
Inspiration (*see also* Revelation): divine, 191
Instrument: as aid, 187, 188, 194; instruments of domination, 222
Intelligence: one with intelligent and intelligible, 40; speculative, 42; practical, 42, 81; complete, 63; divine, 67, 68; pure, 68, 110, 132, 144; desirable in a wife, 161, 162; naturally weak in women, 162, 163, 167, 178; characteristic of Persians, 184, 190; most illustrious part of creation, 210, 212, 215
Interpretation, science of, 112
*'ishq* (love, passion, q.v. both), N 166, N 1448, N 1902; as related to *maḥabbat* (q.v.), 197–98
Ismā 'īlism: *see* Ṭūsī
Isocrates: on anger, 129, N 1287; on value of love and friendship, 243–44; on choice of friends, 245
Ivanow, W., 13, 20, 21–i, 22–l, 22–r, N 1425; and *passim* in Notes

*Jauhar*, 15
Jesting: a cause of anger, 131; improper, condemned, 174; not desirable in friends, 246; condemned by pseudo-Plato, 260
Jesus: on the law, 215
*Jihad* (the good fight), 216, N 2118, 235; N 2189; *see also* War
Job, 69, 70; *see also* Priam of Troy, with whom confused!
Joseph *sūra*: reading of, harmful to women, 164, N 1651
Judges, 230; *see also* Jurisprudence
Jurisprudence, science of: defined, 29, 112, 216; *see also* Judges, canon-lawyers
Justice (*see also* Virtue): as the supreme virtue, analysed, I:2:7; one of four virtues, 62, N 330; as a pleasure, 70–71; produces felicity, 73; blends other three virtues, 80; derived from wisdom and *vice-versa*, 81; defined, 81; comprises twelve species of virtue, 84–85; pseudo-justice, 94–95, 195; meaning of, 95; true mid-point of all virtues, 95; implies ordering of diversities, 96; threefold application of, to daily life, 96–97; positor of equality and, is divine commandment,

Justice—*continued*
97; depends on divine commandment, human arbitrator and money, 97; civic justice, 98; is all virtue, 98; with wisdom is true mark of ruler, 99; Aristotle's threefold division of, 100; why is due to God, 100–4; differs from other virtues in centrality, 104; in harmony with divine ordinance, 104–5; often associated with liberality, but really distinct, 105; justice in augmentation is favour, 106–7; universal reference to, 106–7; a psychical affection, 104, 107; universal justice first applies to one's own soul, 107–8; Aristotle on unadjusted faculties, 108; a substitute for love, 108, 196, 112, 133, 135; divine encompassing justice, 141, 147, 157, 159, 161, 178, 179; towards servants, 181, 189, 191; dependent on understanding of politics, 193, 202, 204, 205; not in angels, 208, 212, 216, 217, 227; essential to life of polity, 229; first concern of king, 230; conditions for, 230–33; next virtue after, is kindness, 233; social reason for, 252; property needed for display of, 252, 260

Kalila and Dimna, fables of, 251, N 2233
*karāmat* (nobility q.v.; ennoblement), 199, N 1941, 219–21, N 2130; N 1848, N 1851
*khalīfa* (*see also* vice-gerent), N 2277
*kharāj* (tax), N 2114, N 2190, N 2222
*khayāl*, N 134, 42, N 2064, 212; N 2071, 213
*Kīmiyā-yi Sa'ādat*: *see* Ghazālī
Kindī, Ya'qūb al-, on profiting from others' bad examples, 121; on self-examination and self-chastisement, 121–22; on need to practise virtue, 122; on grief, 146, N 1476; on envy, 148; N 1210
Kindness: and love, 206–8, N 2012, N 2013, 219; a duty of kings, 233, N 2202, 246
Kings (*see also* Cities, Government, Kingdom, Kingship): manners of, III:4; manners of followers of, III:5; plight of, 116, N 1145; special need for polygamy of, 163; absolute kings, 192, N 1864, 194, 216; definition of, 192; as models for the people, 227; seven qualities required in, 227–28; as the world's physicians, 228; first concern of, with justice, 230; conditions for observance of justice by, 230–33; and ordering of society, 230–31; and punishment, 231–32; must both distribute and preserve goods, 232–33; and kindness, 233; must be accessible and dedicated, 233–34; renewal of search for just king, 234; secrets of, 234, 238, 241; and espionage and deception, 234, 235, 236; and war, 235–37; ordinary man's duty to, 237; retainer's duty to, 237–39; persuasion of, 238; placating of, 238–39, 241, 242; how to profit through, 239; avoiding displeasure and cupidity of, 239–40, 241, 242; a dilemma in service of, 240; Ibn al-Muqaffa' on relations with, 240, 241, 242; shun service of, if possible, 241; shun one in displeasure of, 241; have need of subjects and the poor, 243; value of friends to, 244; should not listen to calumny, 251
Kingdom (*see also* government, kings): management of, 191
Kingship (*see also* Government, Kings): craft of, 192; and the faith, 215; greatest virtue in, is kindness, 233; aura of, 233, N 2203, N 2214; demands dedication, 233–34; endangered by war, 235
*Kitāb-i Manāfi'-i A'ḍā'*, N 920, 101
*Kitāb al-Siyāsa* (of Avicenna?), N 1542
*Kitāb-i Siyāsat* (of Plato?), 191, N 1860
*Kitāb al-Ṭahāra*, 20; *see also Purity, book of, Tahdhīb al-Akhlāq* and Miskawaih
*Kitāb-i Tashrīḥ*, N 919, 101
*Koran, The*, 18; 26, N 9; 36, N 68; 46, N 183; 50, N 211, 213; 57, N 264; 65, N 372; 67, N 398; 98, N 865; 104, N 980; 115, N 1130; 142, N 1428; 145, N 1473; 146, N 1475; 164, N 1651; 171,

*Koran—continued*
N 1714; 178, N 1761, N 1763; 204, N 1986, N 1988; 236, N 2218; 260, N 2329; N 1; N 2079

Labour: *passim* in second and third discourses; division of, 153, 182, 189–90, 217–18
Lambton, A. K. S., 21–e, 22–k, N 1542
Law: (religious) law, 112, 191, N 1859, 199, 200, N 1958, 210; custodian (possessor) of (religious) law (lawgiver, legislator), 106, N 1021, 107, N 1033, 179, N 1771, 191, N 1859, 200, 201, 214, 215, 246; custodian not needed in every age, 192; *see also* Divine ordinances, *shāri'*, *sharī'at* lesser law, 157; law of justice, 189, 233; law, prime need in government, 191; upheld and interpreted by regulator, 192; perfection of, in virtuous cities, 215; law of truth, 233, N 2204
*Lawāmi' al-Ishrāq fī Makārim al-Akhlāq*, 20; *see also Akhlāq-i Jalālī* and Dawānī
Lawgiver, (*Religious*): *see* Law, *shāri'*
Learning: not to be paraded, 258; man of divine learning, 204, N 1981; *see also* Scholars
Legislator, (religious): see Law, *shāri'*
Liberality (*see also* Virtue): implied in felicity, 72; true and metaphorical, 73, 80, 81; distinguished from freedom, 83; comprises many species of virtue, 83–84; confused with prodigality, 88; pseudo-liberality, 90–91, 244; associated with justice, but distinct, 105; inhibited by solitude, 195; not found in angels, 209; property needed for display of, 252
Lies: *see* Falsehood
Life, 'voluntary' and 'natural', 138
Limbo: *see barzakh*
Literature, science of, 112; uses of, in education, 168–71
Liver, the, 43
Locality, the: in hierarchy of combinations, 193, 200
Logic, science of: defined, 28, 35, 112, 126
Longevity, disadvantages of, 141–42
Love (*see also* Friendship, *'ishq*, *maḥabbat*, passion): forms subject of III:2; effects ordering of generables, 108, 196; superior to justice, 108, 196; preserves order of world, 131, N 1299; dangers and treatment of passionate love (*'ishq*), 143–44; excessive love (*maḥabbat*) a danger to husbands, 164; parents' and children's, 180, 202–3, 204, 207; natural and voluntary, 180, 197; between masters and servants, 183, 202; is a yearning for social synthesis, 195, 199; a cause of union, 196; a quest for perfection, 196, 199; and the rational faculty, 196; contrasted with magnetic attraction and animal affinity, 196–97; voluntary, of four kinds, 197, 208; more general than friendship, 197; contrasted with passion, 197–98; divine love, 198–99, 201, 204, 205, 209; endures between good men, 199, 202; often produced by natural sociability, 199; mutual or unilateral, 201; reproachful love, 201–2, 207; fraternal, 203; between ruler and subject, and among subjects, 203–4; false love of God, 204; uniqueness of love of teachers, 204–5; confusion in grades of, 205; false and true, 205–7; and kindness, 206–8; of wisdom and of good, 208–10, 243; central to civilised life, 252; greatest virtue and noblest topic in third discourse, 252
Love and domination, school of, 196, N 1900
Loyalty: common among Byzantines and Abyssinians, 132, 184, 182, 227, 255
Lust, 123

*Maḥabbat* (*see also 'Ishq*, Love, Passion): N 1635, N 1647; as related to *'ishq*, 197–98
*Mala'-i a'là* (sublime assembly), 47, 53, 64
*Ma'mūn*: and the royal resolve, 227–28
Man (*see also* Mankind; Soul, Human or Rational): the noblest

Man—*continued*
of existent beings, I:1:4, 78, 189; primitive, 46; noblest men approach angels, 46; culminates in prophets and saints, 47, nobility of, dependent on will and reason, 46–47; degrees of nobility in, 46–47; needs guides and prophets, 48; degraded by nature, 47–48; has unique perfection, 51; purpose of his existence, 52; as microcosm, 52; complete and absolute, 52; reality of, lies in rational soul, 62; complete man, 63; nature of, as seen by stoics and others, 75; nature of, according to Galen, 75–76; nature of, according to Aristotle, 76; by nature a citizen, 97, 190, N 1841, 242; stages of proximity to divine, 103; stages of exclusion from divine, 103–4; natural growth of, 109–10; disciplined growth of, 110–12; true humanity, 110, 112; name of man metaphorically applied to the ignorant, 127; aided by all creation, 188–89; needs aid and society of own kind in special way, 188–89, 193, 252; equality impossible to, 190; civic man, 192, N 1868; may not live alone, 194–95, 252; different ends of, 197; compounded of opposite natures, 198; may enjoy a unique pleasure, 198–99, 209; natural sociability of, often produces love, 199; his rightful aspiration, according to Aristotle, is divine life, 209–10; rarely good by nature, 210; four distinct classes of, in polity, 230; five grades of, in relation to goodness, 230–31; punishment of evil in, 231–32, 258; duties of, towards rulers, 237; is only animal given to artifice and hypocrisy, 244
Management: needed in a combination (q.v.), 190–91; special type known as 'government' (q.v.), 191; of kingdoms, 191; resumption of, after chaos, 234
Mankind (*see also* Man): association with classes of, III:7; discrepancies among, 78–79, 189–90; three categories of, relative to oneself, 253; category of, less than friends, 253; category of, who are hostile, 236–37, 253–56; general run of, 256–57; reform of, a first duty, 257; relations with subordinates among, 257–58; relations with poor and unfortunate among, 257–58
Manners: and customs, defined, 29; of social behaviour, 173–78; of speech, 173–74; of movement and rest, 174–75; of eating, 175–76; of drinking, 176–78; *Manners*, of Ibn al-Muqaffa', 240, 241, 242, N 2233
*manzil*: ambiguity of term in Arabo-Persian, N 1531
Marāgha, 12
Maskūya, 20, 21–dd; *see* Miskawaih
Mathematics: analysed, 27–28; 112; as remedy for compound ignorance, 128
Matter: indestructible, 41; in relationship, 187; as aid, 187, 188, 194; incapable of true synthesis, 198–99
Measurers, the, in virtuous cities, 216
Mechanics, science of, 28, N 21
Medicine, 28, 35; a model for ethical training and treatment, 111, 112, 114, 122–25 *passim*, 251; a model for domestic regulation, 155–56; as a craft, 158; a model for political craft, 193, 194, 216
Metaphysics (*see also* Theology): defined, 27, N 11, 35
Meteorology: defined, 28, N 27
Middle: used in two senses, 86; centrality of justice, 104, 122, 125, 136
Minerals (*see also* Bodies): ignorant man falls below, 127; role of, in aid, 188–89
Mineralogy: defined, 28
Ministers, craft of, 158; perils of prime-ministers, 240–41, 251
Minstrelsy, craft of, 158
Miskawaih, Abū 'Alī Ahmad ibn (*see also Purity, Book of*; *Tahdhīb al-Akhlāq*; and Abū 'Alī), 9, 12, 21–dd, 15, 16, 19, 20, 25, 26; N 293, N 1281, N 1287, N 1321, N 1405
Misleaders, the: a growth in virtuous cities, 226
Moderation: in material and sensual things, 56; not always

Moderation—*continued*
advisable, 161; in requiring beauty in a wife, 162
Money: value of, not always understood, 90–91; as 'silent' mediator and adjuster, 97–98, 157, 191; Aristotle on, 97; convenience of, 157; often destroys friendship, 245–46
Monopoly: as a 'craft', 158
movement and rest: *see* Manners
*muḥaqqiqān, muḥaqqiqūn* (*see also taḥqīq, ahl-i*), N 339, 62, N 943
*mukhliṣān*, N 955; *see* Attainers
Multiplicity: necessitates inferiority, 95; causes disorder, 108; equity involves, 196; right is removed from, 211
Music, science of: defined, 27, 95
*muta'allihān*, 198, N 1935
Mutanabbī, N 2245

Name, importance of, 166
Nāṣir al-Dīn 'Abd al-Rahīm b. Abī Manṣūr, Governor of Quhistān, Ṭūsī's patron, 25
*Nasirean Ethics, The*, 26; *see Akhlāq-i Nāṣirī* and Ṭūsī
*nāṭiq* (Speaker), 192, N 1869; *see also nuṭq*
Natural Science, 27; analysed, 28; 35, 36, 40, 42, 112
Naturalists: veiw of felicity held by some of, 62
Nature: as against use, 74; as against discipline, 109
Neglect (*see also* Excess), 69, N 433, 86–88 *passim*, 114, 122, 123, 126, 128, 142, 195
Negligible ones, the, 213, N 2075
Negotiation, men of, 230; *see also* Commerce, Tax-collectors, etc.
Neighbours: choice of, 156; bad neighbours, 257
Neo Platonism, N 1560
*Nicomachean Ethics* (*see also* Aristotle, first (ancient) philosopher), 97, N 862; N 435, N 499, N 679, N 841, N 851, N 882, N 908, N 1877; probably also 76, N 535
Nobility (ennoblement): government of, 191; love is quest for, 196; cities of, 219–21; in cities of domination, 222, 223; in free cities, 224; with domination, 225; in hypocrites, 226; in decadent polity, 229; apportionment of, 232; not for kings, 233; should be conferred on upright, 256; the noble are patient in soul, 257; diffused by God, 258; *see also karāmat*
Number, science of: defined, 27
*nūr-i muḥammadī*, N 187
*nuṭq* (*see also Nāṭiq*), N 135; ambiguity of, in Arabo-Persian, N 1265, N 1266; *nuṭqī*, N 1906

Oaths: to be discouraged in children, 169–70
*Oikonomikos, the*, of Bryson: N 1537
Optics: *see* Perspective
Over-population, regulated by death, 140–41

Pain: has no part in death, 139
Parents (*see also* Children): rights of, II:4a; disobedience to, 178, 180–81; rights of, mentioned *passim* throughout work, 178; Koranic sanction and rational support for observing rights of, 178; observance of their rights a part of justice, 178–79; father's role, 179, 180, 207; mother's role, ditto; their rights compared to those of God, 179, 204–5; how to discharge rights of, 179–80; love between parents and children, 180, 202–3, 204
Parsimony: its causes, 149, 159, 160, 161; towards parents, 180; among Byzantines, 184, 207; in intellectual goods, 250
Passion (*see 'Ishq*, Love): ambivalence of, 197–98; utter, 198
Pederasty, 124
Pen, men of the, 230
Perception, image-wise, 213
'perfecters', 187
Perfection: of the human soul, I:1:6; meaning of, I:1:7; 50; of man is dual, 51; of theoretical faculty, 51; of practical faculty, 51–52; of both these faculties together, 52; almost identical with purpose, 52; defined, 78; highest, lies in unicity, 95, 196; 138, 154, 155, 156; all existent beings have, in one or two categories, 187; 191, 192; man's, dependent on others, 193, 195;

Perfection—*continued*
194; effected by love, 196; 197, 203, 212, 214; relative perfection, 216; 217, 218, 227, 231, 233, 255
Perplexity: treatment of, 126; of the misleaders, 226; arising from a plethora of friends, 246
Persians: characteristics of, 184
Perspective and optics, science of, 28, N 21
Perversity: *see* Depravity
Philosopher, 26, N 8; the 'critical philosophers', 62, N 339 (*also* 103, N 943); enjoys unique pleasures, 209; supreme, is God, 209; most virtuous philosophers, 213; perfect philosophers in virtuous cities, 215; in cities of ignorance, 224
Philosophy (*see also* Practical philosophy, Primary philosophy, Speculative philosophy, Wisdom): definition of, 26, N 6; analysis of, 26–29; second to revelation (q.v.) in forming dispositions (q.v.), 77; only for the highest minds, 77; ambiguity of term in Arabo-Persian, 80–81, N 594; domestic philosophy (*see also* Economic(s), Households), 155, N 1533; responsibility to acquire latter is general, 155; 212; basis of all order, 233, N 2205
Physicians, 230; *see also* Medicine
Physics, accepted: Defined, 28, N 22
'*Picatrix*', N 1287
Pilgrimage, the: *see* Prayer
Plato, 18; testaments attributed to, III:8, N 2321; on the savage and the bestial soul, 57; on felicity, 61; on justice, 104, N 982; cave allegory of, 128, N 1281; on death, 138; on choice of residence, 157; on lawgivers, 191, N 1860; on kings, 192, N 1867; on primacy of worship over science, 258; says learning not to be vaunted, 258; says to seek only lasting good, 258; counsels nightly self-examination, 258; advises remembrance of death, 258–59; says to speak little, but to act, 259; says not to do evil, 259; counsels to help others freely, 259; says arrogance to be avoided, 260; advocates humility and charity, 260; N 1848, N 1849, N 1850, N 1851, N 1853, N 1861; *see also* Politics, **Republic, Statesman.**
Pleasure (*see also* Course): intellectual is essential, but sensory accidental, 71; these contrasted in operation, 72; active and passive, 71–72; of felicity, 71–73; psychical, 139, 148, 160; true sense of bodily pleasure, 171; one of man's ends, 197; a motive of love, 197, 208; a motive of passion, 197–98; a motive of youthful friendship, 198; all pleasures in conflict, 198; one pleasure unique to man, 198–99; love for, fades, 199; connubial, as source of love, 201; associated with profit as source of love, 201–2; vain pleasures, 206, 218–19; true pleasures, 208; of wisdom is supreme, 209; and the base cities, 218–19; in cities of nobility, 220; in cities of domination, 222–23; city of pleasure, 223, N 2151; with domination, 225; among the hypocrites, 226; not for kings, 233–34; yearning for, in friends, 245; derived from evil does not last, 259
Plessner, M., N 1287, N 1537
Pliny, N 1915
Poets, 230
Poetry: moral use of, in instruction, 168; studied by secretaries, 171; best loved by its own author, 207, 216
Politics (*see also* Cities, etc.): forms subject of third discourse; nature and virtue of, III:1; 25, N 4; defined, 28, N 39; defined again, 192, N 1874; the supreme craft, 192; study of, incumbent on all, 193; fruits of such study, 193; *Book of*, by Plato, 191, N 1860; Aristotle's *Politics*, N 1841, N 1852
Polygamy: undesirable, but necessary to kings, 163
Porphyry of Tyre, 18, 61, N 313
Practical philosophy (*see also* Philosophy): forms subject of whole work; 25, N 4, 26, 27; defined and analysed, 28–29; 42, 52,

Practical philosophy—*continued*
80–81; completion of exposition of, 258
*Practical philosophy of the Muhammadan people*, 21–g; *see also Akhlāq-i Jalālī*, Dawānī
Prayer: communal, better than solitary, 200, 243; reason for institution of Friday prayer, 200; reason for institution of feast days, 200; reason for institution of Pilgrimage, 200–1
Precious things, quest of: a cause of anger, 132–33
Pretentiousness: its nature and consequences, 149; compounded of conceit and falsehood, 149
Priam of Troy, 18; as 'Barnāmis', 69, N 435; confused with Job, 69–70
Pride: a cause of anger, 130–31; in subordinates, 233
Primary philosophy (*see also* Philosophy): defined, 27, N 14
Primary propositions (Primary intellectual knowings), 68
Prodigality: some confuse with liberality (q.v.), 88; 90–91
Profit: one of man's ends, 187; a motive of love, 197, 208; has no part in passion, 198; motive of mature friendship, 198; love for sake of, fades, 199; connubial, as source of love, 201; associated with pleasure as source of love, 201–2, 208; in cities of domination, 222; through, but not from, kings, 239; from association with the virtuous, 257
Property and provisions: regulation of, II:1; limited control of, by wife, 161, 163, 164
Proportion (*see also* Relationship), 96 f., N 838
Prophets and saints: the noblest of beings, 47
Providence, divine (*see also* God), 124, N 1243, N 1835
Psychology: defined, 28, N 33, 79
Psycho-somatic relationships, 124
Punishment, 231–33; corporal, 231–32; only for acts, 231–32; whether always necessary, 232–33
Purgatory: *see barzakh*
*Purity, Book of*, 25, 66; *see also Kitāb al-Ṭahāra, Tahdhīb al-Akhlāq* and Miskawaih
Pythagoras, on felicity, 61

*Qābūsnāma*, 17
*qaṣīda, the*, 168, N 1687
*Qawā'id al-'Aqā'id*, 13
Quhistān, 12, 24, 25

*Rajaz*, the, 168, N 1687
Rationality (*see also* Soul, human or rational): unique human property, 49, N 135
*Rauḍat al-Taslīm*, 13; *see also Taṣauwurāt*
*Rawīyat* (*see also ru'yat*), N 1128 (and references there to earlier Notes), N 1183, N 1341
*ra'y* (opinion), 43, N 144, 60, N 305, 78, N 568, 81, 132, N 1316
Rāzī, al-: Fakhr al-Dīn, 13; Muḥammad b. Zakarīyā' (Rhazes), 13, N 1080
Reading and writing: forbidden to women, 173, N 1727; *see also* Calligraphy
Rebels, the: a growth in virtuous cities, 226
Reckoning (arithmetic; geometry; surveying; accounting), 112, 128, 158, 171, 216, 230
Regulator: of world, 192, N 1867; needed in every age, 192; of virtuous cities, 214
Relationship (*see also* Proportion): continuous, 96 f.; discrete, 96 f.; numerical, 96 f., 196; geometrical, 96 f.; synthetic, 96 f., 196; superficial, 196; N 838
*Republic, The*, N 1281, N 1849, N 1850, N 1860; *see also* Plato
Resolve, manly or royal, 227–28
Retainers, royal: regulation of, III:5
Revelation and inspiration (*see also* Divine ordinances etc.), 46, N 179; priority of, over philosophy in initial formation of disposition, 77; adaptation of, to suit various grades of men, 214
Revenge: *see* vengeance
Rhetoric, science of, 112, 158, 171, 216
*Al-Risālat al-Mu'īnīya*, 13
*Risāla fī al-Siyāsa*, N 1542
Ritter, H., N 1287
Rosenthal, E. I. J., 22-k, N 1542, N 1848, N 1867, N 2114, N 2118, N 2130
*ru'yat* (*see also rawīyat*), N 141, 43, 46, 49, 50; N 148, 47; N 305, 60;

*ru'yat—continued*
N 341, 62; N 350, 63; N 525, 75; N 568, 78

*Ṣadaqāt u zakāt* (charitable donations, q.v.), N 1595, 160
Sa'īd b. Ya'qūb, N 381; *see also* Dimashqī
Salmān the Persian, on 'Alī's playfulness, 131, N 1303
Sanā'ī, 117, N 1162, N 1276
Savings: *see* Wealth
Scale-making, craft of, 158
Scholars and scientists, 230
Scholastic: *see* Theology
Scorn: a cause of anger, 131; towards parents, 180; in the arrogant, 257
Secrets: royal, 234, 238; 241; Custodian of, 247; to be kept from casual acquaintances, 253
Secretaries, 230; *see also* next item
Secretaryship, training for, 171–72
Senses, the: five external and five internal, 42; 123
Sensualists, the, 53–56
Servants and slaves: regulation of, II:5; form one of domestic bases, 154; controlled by wife, 163; comparable to limbs and organs, 181; should be prized, 181; how to choose, 181–82; should be fittingly employed, 182; should be given security, 182; devoted servants, 183; should be scrupulously treated, 183; control and discipline of, 183; advantage of employing slaves over freemen, 183; categories of, and their merits, 183–84; and masters often at odds, 202; inclined to ease, 209; absolute servants, 214, 217; in cities of domination, 222; as sources of information, 235; of kings, III:5; friendship towards, 247
Service: as aid, of two kinds, 187, 188, 189, 194
*Shāhnāma*, the, 17, N 2099, N 2203
Shame, 83, 88, 110; importance of, in child, 167
*shāri'* (*sharī'at*) (*see also* Divine ordinances; Law; Revelation etc.), 24, 97; N 1951, N 1957, N 2043, N 2253
Similitude: synonymous with unicity, 96
Simples, 45, 51
*ṣinā'at*, 15, N 1561
Sincere ones, the: *see* Attainers
*siyāsat: see* Government; *Kitāb* (two items); *Risāla; Siyāsatnāma*, 17
Slaves: *see* Servant and,
Sleep and rest, 169; *see also* Manners
Sloth: *see* Idleness and,
Sluggishness of appetite, 87, 123
Sociability: virtues all tend towards, 252; existence depends on, 252; lack of, deprives of felicity, 252; N 1938; *see also* *Ulfat*
Societies (*see also* cities etc.): divisions of, III:3, 211
Socrates: on felicity, 61; on grief, 147; on need to train when young, 172; N 1287
Solitaries: selfishness of, 194–95; lack of virtue in, 252
*Sophisticis Elenchis, de* (*Book of Sophistical Syllogisms*), 126, N 1263
Sophistry: a depravity, 123
Sorcery, craft of, 158
Soul, the: several senses of, 41–42
- angelic, 43, 56, 57–58, 79, 81
- animal, 42, 74, 81, 119; two faculties of, 42, 80
- bestial, 43, 53, 55, 56, 57–58, 67, 79, 80
- concupiscible, 70
- imperative, 57
- intelligent, 55, 56, 70, 79, 80
- irascible, 57, 70, 81
- peaceful, 57
- reproachful, 57
- savage, 43, 56, 57–58, 67, 79
- sensory, 67
- vegetative, 41–42, 44; three faculties of, 42
- human or rational (*see also* Man), I:1:2; faculties (q.v.) of, I:1:3, 212; perfection and defect of, I:1:5, 6; preserving health of (retention of virtues), I:2:9; treating sickness of (removing vices), I:2:10; existence of, self-evident, 36; is a substance, 36–37, 212; is simple, 37; not a body, 37–39; perceives by essence, controls by organs, 39–40; not sensed, 40; immortal, 40–41 (but some do not accept this, 52–53); like a craftsman, 41, 42–43; one

Soul—*continued*
particular faculty of, 42; ultimate end of, 49, 50; degradation of, 49–51; and dispositions (q.v.), 74, 81; health of, preserved by good associations, 113–14; should be strenuously exercised, 114–15; its gains against worldly gains, 115–19; health of, demands control and mortification of appetites (q.v.), 119–20; health of, benefits from criticism, 120–21; scrutiny, punishment and practical exercise of, 121–22, 258; preliminaries to treatment of, 122–24; general remedies for, 124–26; simple diseases of, 123–24; compound diseases of, 124; psycho-somatic interaction, 124; playing faculties of, off against each other, 125; ditto, for vices, 125; mortification of, 125; treatment of diseases of speculative faculty of, 126–28; ditto, for repulsive faculty, 128–42; ditto, for attractive faculty, 142–49; some men shun own, 205–6; love of own and of others', 206–8

Speaker, the: *see nāṭiq*

Specialisation, in crafts: ***passim*** in II and III; 182, 189–90, 217–18

Speculative philosophy (*see also* Philosophy): definition and analysis of, 27–28, N 10; 42, 51, 80–81, 128; as stage in education, 171, N 1707

Speech: *see* Manners; and rationality, N 135, N 1265

Spirits, the pure, 139, 208

Stars, science of: *see* Astrology

States: as against habits, 74

*Statesman, The,* N 1853; *see also* Plato

Stoics, the: view of felicity held by, 62; their view of man, 75

Street-sweeping, 'craft' of, 158

Sublime company (assembly): *see mala'-i a'la*

Substance, men of, in virtuous cities, 216, N 2114

Suffering of wrong, 87, 132

Ṣūfīs, the, 138, N 1381

Surveying: *see* Reckoning

Sword, men of the, 230; *see also* Warriors

Syllogisms, 214; *Book of Sophistical, see Sophisticis Elenchis, de*

Synthesis, 194, 195, 198, 199, 206, 228, 229, N 1938; *see also* combination, sociability, love etc.

*Tadābīr al-Manāzil* (*'an al-Siyāsat al-Ilāhīya*), N 1542

*tadbīr*, N 1660

*Tahāfut al-Falāsifa* (*see also* Ghazālī), 22–w, N 339, N 943

*tahdhīb-i akhlāq* (*see also akhlāq*; disposition, correction of), 25, N 3; *Tahdhīb al-Akhlāq* (*wa-Taṭhīr al-A'rāq*), 9, 20; *see also Kitāb al-Ṭahāra, Purity, Book of* and Miskawaih

*taγqlq* (*see also Muγaqqiqgn*), *ahl-i*, N 943, 103

*Tajrīd al-'Aqā'id*, 13

*tamyīz* (distinction, discrimination), 43, N 144, 75, N 525, 77, N 547, N 558, 79, N 575, 108, N 1041, 110, N 1064, N 1068, 123, N 1225, 124, N 1246, 126, N 1265, 142, N 1438, 167, N 1674, N 1680, 190, N 1836, 191, N 1856, 195, N 1891, 212, 216, 244

Tanning, craft of, 158

*taqīya*, N 2

*Taṣauwurāt*, 13, 21–i, N 69, N 1425, N 1811, N 1869, N 1981

Tax-collectors, 216, 230; *see also kharāj*

Teachers: love for, has special rank, 204–5

Thamāma b. al-Ashras, 228

Theology (*see also* Metaphysics): defined 27, N 13; 112; scholastic theology, 112, N 1098, 216; the supreme science, 192

Thompson, W. F., 21–g; *see also Akhlāq-i Jalālī*

Tongues, masters of: in virtuous cities, 216

Tradition, authority of, 216; authority of the holders of tradition, 217; traditions of the prophet, 44–45, 112, 127, N 1273; on pride, 130; on jesting, 131, N 1301; 155, N 1536; 164, N 1651, 182, 189, 214, N 2078, 257, N 2312

Treachery: a cause of anger, 131; common among Turks, 131, 184;

Treachery—*continued*
in friendship, 205; in cities of domination, 221, 227; not lawful in war, 236; or with enemies, 255, 256
Truth: Absolute, 46; seers of, 215; not found in errant cities, 225; as God, 231; law of, 233, N 2204; Imām of, 234, N 2209; as an intention, 258
Turks, the: given to treachery, 131; characteristics of, 184; appetites of, 225
Ṭūsī, Naṣīr al-Dīn (*see also Akhlāq-i Nāṣirī*): birth and death, 12; his Ismā'īlī period, 12, 24–26; defects to Mongols, 12, 24; in service of state, 12; retirement and research, 12; references for life of, 22–1; some works of, 13; references for works of, 22–m; character, 9, 12–13, 21–c, 22–1; and a critic of the *Akhlāq*, 178, N 1760; as an Avicennan, 12, 13, 19, 155, N 1233, N 1542; as a Shī'ite, 22–1, N 1406, N 1866, N 1871, N 2078, N 2099, N 2209; and Ismā'īlism, 11, 12, 13, 19, 21–b, 21–i, N 1869, N 1871, N 1981, N 1993, N 2023, N 2042, N 2061, N 2062, N 2080, and *passim* in text; and Ṣūfism, 13, 21–j, N 1299, N 2042, N 2257, N 2260, N 2281; and the Koran (q.v.), 18, N 1; virtuosity of style of, 15–16, N 373, N 495, N 676, N 1165, N 1323, N 1384, N 1474, N 1582, N 1585, N 1788, N 1812, N 2140, N 2256
Tyranny (*see also* Tyrant, Injustice), 85; civic, 98; comprises all vice, 98–99; differs from injustice, 99; on both peripheries of justice, 104; anger as tyranny, 133–34; a consequence of pretentiousness, 149; avoidance of, 158, 181; under a ruler lacking *de jure* authority, 192; if politics ignored, 193; of solitaries, 194–95, 227, 232–33, 252
Tyrant (*see also* tyranny): a nullifier of equality, 98; the most monstrous, the average, and the petty, 98; 104, 232–33

*Ulfat* (familiarity; *see also* Affection, sociability), N 166, N 1297, N 1919, N 1938
'Umar, N 1131
Unfairness, a cause of anger, 132
Unicity: is highest perfection, 95; God is source of, 97; variously proclaimed, 214; *see also* Equivalence and similitude
Unrighteousness, 59
Upset of creation, 59
Use (*see also* Habit): as against nature, 74; *Uses of the Members, Book on the, see Kitāb-i Manāfi'-i A'ḍā'*

Van den Bergh, S., N 943
Vegetables (*see also* Bodies): role in aid, 188–89
Veil, wearing of, 173, N 1726
Vengeance: licit and illicit, 94; perverse, 123; relation of, to anger, 128, 129; 132, 135; a condition for victory, 228, N 2182; God's, is a rectification, 258
Vice (*see also* Virtue): classes of, I:2:5; removal of (treating sickness of soul, q.v.), I:2:10; infinite number of, opposed to each virtue, 85–86; pairs of, at opposite extremes, 86–87; species of (not all having names), 87–88; all, comprised by tyranny (q.v.), 98–99; even minor vices dangerous, 120; only figuratively the opposite of virtue, 122; playing off vices against each other to win virtues, 125; worst, is idleness and sloth (q.v.), 252
Vice-gerent (*see also khalīfa*), 99, 108
Victory: conditions for, 228; does not justify complacency, 233
Village, the: a defective combination, 194
Virtue (*see also* Vice, Disposition): classes of, I:2:3; species of, I:2:4; and pseudo-virtue, I:2:6; acquisition of, I:2:8; retention of (preserving health of soul, q.v.), I:2:9; justice (q.v.) is the supreme virtue, I:2:7, and blends other three, 80; virtues comprise felicity, 62; pure virtue, 68; complete virtue, 71; ranks of, according to aristotle, 66–68; of

Virtue—*continued*
knowledge, 79; of wisdom, 79–80, 233; of mildness, 79; of courage, 79–80; of continence, 80; of liberality, 80; material needed for expression of, 63–71, 252; expression of, entitles to praise, 81; unlimited possibilities of compounding, 85; each opposed by an infinite number of vices, 85–86, but two at extremes, 86–87; all virtue lies in justice, 98; no one created in a state of, 111; must be practised and diffused, 122, 148; speculative virtue, 172, N 1721; pseudo-virtues, 195; love is a quest for, 196; the divine virtue is ultimate, 208; human virtues irrelevant to angels, 208–9; not produced by wealth, 210; must be practised, 210; needs to be imposed on most, 210–11; first man of, 214; men of, in virtuous cities, 215; all virtues tend to sociability, 252; greatest is love and friendship, 252; excellence in, is best defence, 255; men of, to be frequented, 257

virtuous (*see* Cities, Government), 191, N 1849; the most virtuous ones, in virtuous cities, 215, 218, 225; authority of later, 216; non-virtuous men in virtuous cities, 216; cities of nobility like virtuous cities, 221; virtuous men in cities of ignorance, 224; the virtuous hated by rebels and misunderstood by apostates, 226; the virtuous in quest of friendship, 243, 257

Viziers: *see* Ministers

Vows, use of, 125, N 1255

*Wahm*, N 134, 42, N 1084, 112, N 1229, 123, N 2064, 212; *tawahhum*, N 1983, 204

Walzer, R., 20, N 1205

War (*see also* Enemies, *jihād*, Warriors), 235–37; to be avoided if possible, 235, 236, 237; lawful conditions for, 235, 256; conduct of, 235–36, 237; treatment of enemies in, 236–37, 254–56; defensive, 237

Warriors, in virtuous cities, 216; *see also* Sword, men of the

Wealth (*see also* Affluence, Expenditure), 157–61; income, 157–59; custody of, 159; expenditure of, 159–61; not essential in wife, 162; purpose of, 171; inherited, less sure than craft, 172; inequality in, 190, 207, 210; as against substance, N 2114; and affluence in servile cities, 218–20; and affluence in cities of domination, 222, 223

Well-doers 103, N 950; well-doing 259; N 2202; *see also* Kindness

Wet-nurse, importance of, 166–67

Wine: not for women, 164; not for children, 169; manners of drinking, 176–78

Wisdom (*see also* Philosophy, Virtue, Course), N 6, 62, N 330; pure, 67, 205; as pleasure, 71; virtue of, 79–81; ambiguity of, in Arabo-Persian, 80–81, N 594; derives from justice and *vice versa*, 81; comprises seven species of virtue, 82, opposed by fourteen species of vice, 87–88; pseudo-wisdom, 89; true Wisdom implies other virtues, 94, N 817; with Justice, is true mark of ruler, 99; divine, 109, 153, 189, N 1835, 195; perfect, 141, 191; True, 199, 230, N 2192; love of, 208–10, 212; absolute, 214; authority of, in virtuous cities, 216, 231; is basis of all order, N 2205, 233; in word and deed, 259

Wives (*see also* Households); regulation of, II:3; dual function of, 153–54, 161; choice of, 161–62; control of, 162–64; of kings virtually slaves, 163; three cautions concerning, 164; easy social life and drink bad for, 164; and a husband's favour, 164–65; types of bad wife, 165, 166; how to deal with bad wife, 165–66; lack of, better than bad marriage, 166; defence of, 237

Xenocrates, N 1287

*Yaqīn: ahl-i yaqīn* (*mūqinān*), *see* Assured ones; *yaqīnīyāt*, N 1233

*Zīj-i Īl-Khānī*, 13

Zoology: defined, 28